Silent Eloquence

D1453322

Classical Literature and Society

Series Editors: Michael Gunningham & David Taylor

CLASSICAL LITERATURE AND SOCIETY

Silent Eloquence
Lucian and Pantomime Dancing

Ismene Lada-Richards

Duckworth

First published in 2007 by
Gerald Duckworth & Co. Ltd.
90-93 Cowcross Street, London EC1M 6BF
Tel: 020 7490 7300
Fax: 020 7490 0080
inquiries@duckworth-publishers.co.uk
www.ducknet.co.uk

A catalogue record for this book is available
from the British Library

ISBN 978 07156 3491 2

Typeset by Ray Davies
Printed and bound in Great Britain by
CPI Bath

Contents

For Juliette

Editors' Foreword

The aim of this series is to consider Greek and Roman literature primarily in relation to genre and theme. Its authors hope to break new ground in doing so but with no intention of dismissing current interpretation where this is sound; they will be more concerned to engage closely with text, subtext and context. The series therefore adopts a homologous approach in looking at classical writers, one of whose major achievements was the fashioning of distinct modes of thought and utterance in poetry and prose. This led them to create a number of literary genres evolving their own particular forms, conventions and rules – genres which live on today in contemporary culture.

Although studied within a literary tradition, these writers are also considered within their social and historical context, and the themes they explore are often both highly specific to that context and yet universal and everlasting. The ideas they conceive and formulate and the issues they debate find expression in a particular language, Latin or Greek, and belong to their particular era in the classical past. But they are also fully translatable into a form that is accessible as well as intelligible to those living in later centuries, in their own vernacular. Hence all quoted passages are rendered into clear, modern English.

These are books, then, which are equally for readers with or without knowledge of the Greek and Latin languages and with or without an acquaintance with the civilization of the ancient world. They have plenty to offer the classical scholar, and are ideally suited to students reading for a degree in classical subjects. Yet they will interest too those studying European and contemporary literature, history and culture who wish to discover the roots and springs of our classical inheritance.

We wish to express our especial indebtedness and thanks to Pat Easterling, who has from the start (1999) been a constant source of advice and encouragement without which the series would probably never have got going at all. From Cambridge too there is Robin Osborne who, if ever we were at a loss to think of an author for a particular topic, almost always came up with a suitable name or two and was never stinting of his time or opinion. More recently, we have been lucky too to receive much advice and assistance, chiefly with regard to Latin scholars in the United States, from Tony Woodman, now at Virginia. And we cannot fail to mention one person whose help and criticism has been throughout invaluable and that is the late John W. Roberts, editor of the recently published *Oxford Dictionary of the Classical World.* We owe him no small debt of gratitude. Finally, we should like to thank Deborah Blake, Duckworth's Editorial Director, for her continued support and enthusiasm.

Michael Gunningham
David Taylor

Acknowledgements

The seeds of this book lie in my article ' "A Worthless Feminine Thing"? Lucian and the "Optic Intoxication" of Pantomime Dancing', published in *Helios* (Lada-Richards, 2003a). Material originally included in that article has been reworked in parts of Chapters 4, 5 and 6, but the reader familiar with the article piece will recognise the echo of its arguments at several junctures in *Silent Eloquence*. Many thanks to the Editor of *Helios*, Professor Steven Oberhelman, for his kind permission to re-use material in this way.

Richard Hunter and Edith Hall have given the project wholehearted support from its inception, while Jaś Elsner has offered shrewd comments on some of my pantomime-related writings and much needed encouragement at a critical time. I could not be more grateful to them. My greatest debt is to Pat Easterling, who, as always, could not have been more generous with her time, encouragement, enthusiasm, ideas, and so much more. I can only hope that this volume goes some way towards repaying her intellectual investment in the story of ancient pantomime; for her friendship and personal interest in my affairs no repayment will ever be even remotely adequate.

Completion of this book was made possible by financial support provided by the AHRC in the form of a Research Leave Award, for which I am profoundly grateful.

It is also a pleasure to thank Michael Gunningham, who first approached me on behalf of Duckworth and enthusiastically supported a proposal on pantomime dancing, even though the book he was initially after was one on Aristophanes! David Taylor's cheerful editing rescued me from many a blunder and Deborah Blake saw the book to the press with exemplary skill and patience: heartfelt thanks to both.

For debts of a personal kind, I can never thank enough my husband David, for his loving support of my totally non-scientific interests, and especially Mary Richards, without whose generous help with childcare and much else the project would have taken considerably longer in the making. Finally, this book is dedicated, with love, to our little Juliette, already talented *prima ballerina*. May she always love to dance!

Abbreviations

AJA = American Journal of Archaeology

AJP = American Journal of Philology

ANRW = Aufstieg und Niedergang der römischen Welt (ed. H. Temporini and W. Haase; Berlin 1972-)

ARV² = Attic Red-Figure Vase-Painters, 2nd edn. (ed. J.D. Beazley; Oxford 1963)

BCH = Bulletin de Correspondance Hellénique

BICS = Bulletin of the Institute of Classical Studies

CIL = Corpus Inscriptionum Latinarum (Berlin 1863-)

CPh = Classical Philology

CQ = Classical Quarterly

F.Delphes = Fouilles de Delphes (Paris 1906-)

G&R = Greece and Rome

GRBS = Greek, Roman, and Byzantine Studies

IC = Inscriptiones Creticae, 4 vols (ed. M. Guarducci, F. Halbherr; Rome 1935-)

I.Ephesus = Die Inschriften von Ephesos (ed. H. Wankel, R. Merkelbach et al.; Bonn 1979-81)

IG = Inscriptiones Graecae (Berlin 1873-)

IGR = Inscriptiones Graecae ad res Romanas pertinentes, 4 vols (ed. R. Cagnat et al.; Paris 1901-27)

IJCT = International Journal of the Classical Tradition

ILS = Inscriptiones Latinae Selectae, 3 vols (ed. H. Dessau; Berlin 1892-1916)

I.Magnesia = Die Inschriften von Magnesia am Maeander (ed. O. Kern; Berlin 1900)

I.Priene = Inschriften von Priene (ed. F. Hiller von Gaertringen; Berlin 1906)

I.Stratonicea = Die Inschriften von Stratonikeia, 2 vols (ed. M. Çetin Sahin; Bonn 1981-90)

JRS = Journal of Roman Studies

K-A = *Poetae Comici Graeci* (ed. R. Kassel and C. Austin; Berlin and New York; 1983-)

PCPS = Proceedings of the Cambridge Philological Society

PG = Patrologiae Cursus Completus. Series Graeca, 161 vols (ed. J.-P. Migne; Paris 1857-66)

P Hib. = *Hibeh Papyri* (ed. B.P. Grenfell and A.S. Hunt; London 1906)

PL = *Patrologiae Cursus Completus. Series Latina*, 221 vols (ed. J.-P. Migne; Paris 1844-64)

P&P = *Past and Present*

RE = *Real-Encyclopädie der classischen Altertumswissenschaft* (ed. A. Pauly, G. Wissowa, W. Kroll; Stuttgart 1893-1980)

RÉG = *Revue des Études Grecques*

RG = *Rhetores Graeci* (ed. L. Spengel; Leipzig 1853-6)

SEG = *Supplementum Epigraphicum Graecum* (ed. J.J.E. Hondius et al.; Leiden 1923-)

*SIG*³ = *Sylloge Inscriptionum Graecarum*, 3rd edn (ed. W. Dittenberger et al.; Leipzig 1915-24)

TAPA = *Transactions and Proceedings of the American Philological Association*

YCS = *Yale Classical Studies*

ZPE = *Zeitschrift für Papyrologie und Epigraphik*

The following abbreviations are used for frequently cited ancient works:

Lucian, *Dance* = *On the Dance* (*De Saltatione*)

Lucian, *Professor* = *Professor of Rhetoric* (*Rhetorum Praeceptor*)

Flavius Philostratus, *Lives* = *Lives of the Sophists* (*Vitae Sophistarum*)

Quintilian, *Training* = *Training of the Orator* (*Institutio Oratoria*)

Tacitus, *Dialogue* = *Dialogue on Orators* (*Dialogus de Oratoribus*)

Introduction: Setting the Scene

A sultry afternoon in Syrian Antioch, some time in the summer of 163 AD. Lucius Verus, Marcus Aurelius' co-emperor, has just arrived in the city, ostensibly to take control of operations against Rome's enemy, the Parthians, in reality eager to immerse himself in the full range of theatrical delights abundantly on offer in the Hellenised East. Once seated in the theatre, he joins the entire city, the rich and the poor, the masters and their servants, men and women, illiterate and educated alike, in cheering his most beloved artist, a dancer he will style in later years 'Apolaustus', that is, 'pleasing', 'delectable'. Some among the viewers are busy trying out for themselves the gestures so skilfully delineated on the stage. Others leap up and down in a frenzy, their senses fully intoxicated with an array of images and sounds: the sinuous, supple, deliciously unfolding lines of a voluptuous body, whose sensual movement wafts it gently across the stage; the haunting voices of a singing chorus, as well as a full orchestra of string, wind and loud percussion instruments. The vast majority, however, are simply mesmerised, eyes fixed on the performer's limbs and torso moving to the rhythm, minds entranced by hands and fingers which display harmonious drawings in space. The dancer's mask is beautiful, his clothes are splendid, and his allure is such that women in the audience swoon and men become inflamed with desire.

It is precisely this most intriguing and flamboyant mode of entertainment that forms the subject of this book, namely, pantomime dancing and its virtuoso artist, the 'pantomime' (*pantomimos*) or simply 'dancer' (*saltator, orchêstês*).[1] Our most crucial aid and compass in our attempt to navigate the vast expanse of cultural discourses on both sides of the Mediterranean basin at the time pantomime reigned (roughly between the end of the first century BC and the end of the sixth century AD) will be Lucian's little dialogue *De Saltatione* (*On the Dance*), probably composed around the middle of the second century AD in Antioch, at the time Lucius Verus was stationed there (see Chapter 12§2). An undervalued gem in the Greek literature of the empire,[2] Lucian's treatise is a boldly imaginative document, the first attempt in Western theatrical history to map the somatic and mental qualities required of a successful stage-performer. Moreover, as it was composed against a background of suspicion of the theatre or even full-blown anti-theatricality, the treatise should also be seen as the first extensive rehabilitation of the professional stage-artist in

Western culture. Despite its formidable appeal for many centuries, however, Graeco-Roman pantomime remains to date one of the least explored and least understood performance genres of antiquity, long due for reappraisal.[3] For this reason, some preliminary clarifications are in order.

Ancient pantomime was an expression-filled dance form, predicated on the mute delineation of character and passion. Impersonating in close succession a series of characters (drawn predominantly from Greek myth and classical tragedy), to the accompaniment of instrumental music and verbal narrative (partly recited and partly sung), a male masked dancer celebrated the spectacle of form 'in flux', the human body's marvellous capacity to mould and re-mould itself in a fascinating array of sensational configurations. With every nerve and muscle under perfect rhythmical control, the dancing soloist reached out to his audience by means of an affective vocabulary of steps and gestures: 'speaking through the entrancing quiver of the palm' (*Greek Anthology* 9.505, 17), he was master of a 'wonderful art' (Anonymous, *Latin Anthology*, I.1 [Shackleton Bailey] 100, 9), which intrinsically downplayed verbal language as a mode of communication in favour of conversing 'through gesture, nod, leg, knee, hand and spin' (Sidonius Apollinaris, *Poem* 23.269-70). Yet to insist too much on pantomime's pure corporeal narrative runs the risk of obfuscating its character as a fully integrated spectacle, a 'hybrid' mode of performance. Very much like opera today, pantomime was 'a spectacle of excess', a lavish multi-media extravaganza. Emotionally absorbing as well as technically staggering and hauntingly beautiful in the eyes of its admirers, the spectacle seduced its fans by bombarding them with auditory as well as visual delights. As Lycinus, the genre's advocate in Lucian's *On the Dance*, says of pantomime's visual and aural saturation,

> If it is the richness of the human voice that you seek, where might you find it elsewhere [than in pantomime], or which auditory pleasure could be more brimming with vocal tones or more melodious? If it is the more high-pitched sound of the double pipe and Pan's pipes that you like, in pantomime you may enjoy even this in abundance (*Dance* 72; cf. *Dance* 68).

If we are dealing with such an electrifying art form, 'diversified, wholly harmonious and richly musical', as Lucian's Lycinus puts it (*Dance* 7), what hope do we have of ever reconstructing this lost experience today?

First, although there are several, shorter or longer, clumsy or supremely eloquent, verbalisations of various aspects of the dancer's silent art, no immediate record of the narratives which accompanied the dancer's gestural discourse survives: we have none of the countless pantomime libretti, the so-called *fabulae salticae*, that were in circulation in antiquity, and not a trace of the exceedingly popular, albeit unceasingly maligned, songs which punctuated the performance.[4] Moreover, we know lamentably little about the ancient pantomime's bodily presence. Lacking every single type of modern evidence that could have been of use to a historian of the dance (choreographic notations, photographs and video recordings, performance programmes, press reviews, or even dancing manuals), we can at best detect the faded traces of his movements through the performative arenas of the ancient world or hear the distant echoes of his eloquent gesticulations. His material, historical body has vanished for ever, or has left precious little in its wake to help us reconstruct its physicality. Our best chances of glimpsing it in action, along with the entire genre of Graeco-Roman pantomime, are provided by inscriptions, historiography, literature (including two lengthy defences of the genre and its dancer, namely Lucian's *On the Dance* and Libanius' *On Behalf of the Dancers*) and art. With the exception of those inscriptions that offer a factual record of individual performers' honours, achievements and career, however, none of the above categories of sources offers an unmediated and uncoloured description of the genre and its artist.[5] They merely 'refract' the pantomime body's presence, allowing us to see how it was gazed at by other bodies – in admiration or disgust, adulation or vituperation. And although we owe even this partial view to all those who focused on pantomime while holding their pen or brush or chisel, we are also painfully conscious that they have adulterated their object irrevocably, appropriated it and made it part of their own textual or artistic discourse. We can now only 'read' *their* 'reading' of the pantomime's real body.[6]

Predictably, the problem is much exacerbated when we turn to textual sources (for the greatest part literary and historiographical), for it is they in particular that prove treacherous, heavily embroiled as they are in the broader debates on pantomime's social and political substance or its aesthetic, moral and educational value. All the while our gaze travels through such texts, the dancer's body which we seek to reconstruct mutates just as much as it mutates *in* performance. With the slightest change of focus, what seems to be an empowered body in an emperor's court, desired and desiring, sometimes even positioned on the apex of social hierarchies, gives way to a marginalised body, the site of cultural defilement and moral dissolution. Under the formidable eye of a Christian bishop, a body hailed as 'the canon of Polyclitus' (Lucian, *Dance* 75) in terms of symmetry and beauty (cf. Lucian, *Dance* 30, 63, 81) becomes twisted, disjointed and 'fragmented',[7] the inverse image of the body owned by a well-trained élite youth (cf. Chapter 9§2). Similarly, a body praised by its fans for its exactitude, precision and perfect self-control emerges from the pen of its detractors as body-matter explosive, unbridled and incontinent – in Arnobius' view, dissolved into 'disorderly motions' (*Against the Gentiles*, 2.42). All contemporary or near-contemporary evaluations are mediated by each writer's own cultural positioning, including his own pre-determined assumptions as to what constitutes the perfect masculine body and what deviates from ideal male deportment, or even his outright contempt for bodily matters.[8]

14

Introduction: Setting the Scene

It is a central tenet of this book that our forays into the experience of Graeco-Roman pantomime are methodologically sound only insofar as we accept that neither the documents of praise nor those of denigration are objective accounts, reproducing in descriptive terms the spectacle's artistic and cultural parameters. They are merely documents engaged in their own discursive struggles, pulling pantomime into their own orbit and projecting onto it their own culturally conditioned anxieties and fears. Consequently, the quest for pantomime's real essence in any *single* ancient text is a dangerously misleading exercise, for what might seem at first glance an objective snapshot of the dancer's body is usually no more than the distillation of a socially constructed *attitude* towards that same body. Trying to read *against* a text's 'dominant' voice, on the other hand; being sensitive to the idioms, undertones, cadences and modulations of both verse and prose; looking at the interstices of *several* discourses, and paying particular attention to the notional encounters and divergences between a multiplicity of texts, each with its own rhetorical agenda, are infinitely safer ways of arriving at a fuller grasp of pantomime's physical dramaturgy, as well as entering the broader matrix of its many cultural reverberations.

Most importantly, as we shall have ample opportunity to witness in this book, pantomime's cultural affiliations were also 'on the move'. Anchored now in the 'higher' registers of culture, now in the 'lower', and now in the murky, indeterminable ground 'in-between', they followed the ebb and flow of the narrative which domiciled the genre – enveloped it, that is, within its own textual fold. The single ultimate certainty on ancient pantomime can be summed up thus: the genre's fabulous impact on large popular audiences in all corners of Rome's vast empire can never be recaptured in its pure, 'raw', unmediated form. We can glimpse it only 'through a glass darkly', in the ways it was refracted in or calibrated by the accounts of the literate few who had reason to comment on some aspect of the genre or its artist. Yet, frustrating though it is to realise that pantomime can never be dissociated securely from the verbal discourses which have preserved its vestiges for us today, the very awareness of its elusiveness alerts us to important truths.

In the first place, our inability to reconstruct 'the' authentic experience of pantomime dancing facilitates the realisation that a uniform way of perceiving the genre and the dancer was a mirage even during the long centuries of its triumph on the Greek and Roman stages. As this book will demonstrate, in a world of ever-shifting cultural priorities, fundamentally diverse in terms of values, orientations, educational discourses and rival ideologies, pantomime existed, flourished, and left a mark on its cultural universe as an irreducibly kaleidoscopic spectacle, protean in itself as well as exciting protean responses in its addressees. As was the case with many other cultural 'texts' in the ancient world, pantomime meaning could be seen to take shape invariably at the point of pantomime's reception, becoming infinitely re-jigged, re-written, re-appropriated, defined and re-defined or debated by hundreds of thousands of fans and countless opponents. Even above and beyond the evanescent nature of all dance, pantomime stood for markedly different things within the context of the different interpretive communities that made up the vast conglomerate of imperial culture. Thus the image of the dancer fashioned by the intellectual sympathetically disposed to the kind of entertainment the spectacle provided[9] was probably worlds apart from the dancer haunting the dreams of the man in the street, illiterate and with at best a tenuous grasp of myth and legend. The intellectual would have been able to admire in the dancing star the embodiment of literary qualities, such as 'vividness' (*enargeia*) and 'clarity' (*saphêneia*), or even the revival of a glorious Hellenic past, effected by means of a virtuosic incarnation of the manifold figures drawn from the Greek mythical repertoire (see Chapter 7). Luxuriating in the delirium of erotic stimuli emanating from the dancing body, on the other hand, the man in the street would have allowed himself to yield to successive waves of feeling or enjoy fantasies unthinkable within the narrow possibilities of a patriarchal society, with its strictly regimented structures. And then again, the pantomime of the simple man was radically different from the image of the dancer constructed by the supercilious man of letters or, even more so, the Christian priest responsible for the spiritual health of his flock: where the former saw harmless pleasure, the latter, a community's self-appointed intellectual or moral guardian, detected the onset of cultural or ethical disintegration – worse, incurable disease.

Even beyond these gross distinctions, however, which appear so obvious to us today, a pantomime auditorium must have been criss-crossed and subdivided innumerable times by the 'discrepant experiences'[10] of the many different sectors of a city's or province's multi-lingual, multi-cultural community. It cannot be stressed too strongly that no theatre audience can be considered a monolith, a completely uniform spectating body made up of individuals who, sharing *exactly* the same socio-political background, educational and intellectual panoply, aesthetic and cultural codes, are likely to mobilise *exactly* the same 'interpretive strategies' (Fish 1976: 476) in their ways of decoding the constituent elements of a particular spectacle. Yet a pantomime performance in a buzzing cosmopolitan city, such as, say, second-century AD Antioch or Alexandria or Ephesus, constituted an even greater melting-pot, the auditorium being segmented along irreconcilable cultural faultlines and incommensurable 'horizons' of literary or aesthetic 'expectations'.[11]

Considered against such variegated cultural landscapes, pantomime seems to have functioned as the great blank canvas upon which very diverse groups of viewers chose to project their fantasies and dreams or inscribe their desires. The very fact that this type of entertainment, unique as it was in the ancient world, did succeed in carrying thousands of different bodies on the wings of a single dancer's electrifying narrative of fleshly sensuality speaks volumes with respect to the genre's real nature, namely its subliminal function as a cultural adhesive or a kind of common psychic coinage, cutting across socio-political and educational divides, as well as any other form of audience stratification. Although we shall never be able to reconstruct with exactitude what pantomime really meant, either in the luminous centre or the many hazy corners of the imperial cultural mainstream (in itself a spectacularly unhomogeneous intellectual terrain), we can at least be fairly sure that, for its fans as well as its detractors, for the élites and simple folk alike, pantomime shifted the boundaries and challenged the notions of emotional expressiveness more boldly than any other performative genre in the ancient world.

Secondly, the awareness of how much of pantomime's 'realia' and surrounding aura is irrevocably lost to us today demands the more judicious appreciation of what we hold securely in hand – a corpus of material by no means small in either size or significance. With all their manifold shortcomings, either on account of elliptical information or in terms of lack of objectivity, the majority of our sources testify to pantomime's centrality in the workings of imperial culture. Even when they are unequivocally biased and distorting, perceptions of the genre enshrined in Greek and Roman narratives are neither less relevant nor less valuable to our inquiry. Take, for example, the venomous Christian tirades against the dancer's gender-bending and eroticism, which will be discussed at length in Chapter 5§1-2. All the while bishop and patriarch alike lash out against the body which, in their view, has shamelessly forfeited or danced away its own virility, they bear eloquent testimony to pantomime's active role in shaping public configurations of gender and desire. It is only in view of pantomime's total social 'embeddedness' that the extent of Christian anxiety becomes fully intelligible: neither pantomime as a genre nor the responses to it were marginal discourses, dissociated from the social, political and cultural core of imperial and late antique communities. Fretting over the loss of cultural snapshots that we are never likely to obtain deflects our attention from the whole range of meanings which pantomime generated in its own cultural context. It is time we realised that setting out to uncover what people thought *about* pantomime is just as important as trying to establish what pantomime really *was*.

Above all, however, our sources offer ample reason to believe that pantomime's contemporary impact was so forceful that the genre and its artist did no less than 'colonise' the cultural subconscious of imperial subjects, seeping into the deepest crevasses of the empire's symbolic order. As we shall see frequently in what follows, pantomime was no mindless entertainment, detaining the eye and titillating the ear with a transient, skin-deep pleasure. Just as philosophers thought with big ideas or apprentice orators thought (and fought) with declamatory scenarios, the simple folk in the empire thought for centuries *with* and *through* the countless stories that pantomime made so readily and regularly available to them. As for the lettered upper classes, they too, whether they deigned to occupy themselves with pantomime or not, could not avoid being affected by its presence. As Chapter 9 in particular will argue, the educated imperial subjects, all the while denigrating pantomime, turned the genre into a crucial instrument in their own exercises of cultural self-definition. When thinking of themselves and their preferred occupations as 'different from' or even 'superior to' pantomime and its dancer, they were not merely expressing their disdain towards the lower social orders, absorbed in their boorish, crude, illiberal pursuits: they were constantly re-mapping their own intellectual and cultural world and, with pantomime's aid, repositioning themselves in it, defining their own domain of cultural legitimacy. Quite simply, pantomime was extremely 'good to think with' in the 'symbolic economy' of the empire.

If there is a single pantomime-related myth, then, that this book is particularly anxious to dispel, it is that pantomime was a minor player (if a player at all!) in the cultural debates that shaped the imperial world. Rather than being a self-contained aesthetic realm, whose meaning should be sought within its own borders, pantomime provided a dynamic site for a multiplicity of social, cultural, and political ferments. A melting-pot of social identity construction, the pantomime auditorium was a wonderful terrain where cultural configurations could be fashioned or contested, competing models of individuality or subjectivity explored, and important negotiations between élite and popular culture played out. The pantomime's body was not a neutral space, but an important tool for society's many and tangled ways of drafting and re-drafting the ever-shifting boundaries between the 'self' and the 'other', the high and the low, the cultivated and the boorish, the intellectual and the corporeal. Unless the cultural historian stops to listen to the genre's echoes, resonating through artefacts and texts, the intellectual no less than the socio-political history of imperial and later antiquity is bound to remain incomplete. To follow the genre's and the dancer's intricate meanderings from text to text today may well seem like embarking on an inconsequential tour of the outskirts of imperial culture; in reality, however, it means travelling to that same culture's very centre. And although the scope of the series to which this book belongs makes an exhaustive, all-embracing 'cultural poetics' of pantomime dancing out of place, I hope this study will nevertheless become a catalyst for a better understanding of the ways in which the genre permeated, coloured and defined the fabric of imperial life in the Roman West as much as in the Hellenised East.

Pantomime Dancing Through the Centuries

§1. Greek and Roman ancestry

Pantomime entered the consciousness of modern scholarship inextricably interwoven with a myth: that of its 'introduction' into Rome at the end of the third decade BC or even its 'invention' in that same city by two Eastern performers, Pylades from Cilicia and Bathyllus from Alexandria.[1] Although there is every reason to believe that it acquired its definitive form at the time of Augustus, thanks to the catalytic contribution of Pylades and Bathyllus, it is very misleading to imagine that pantomime dancing appeared in Rome out of the blue towards the end of the first century BC. Lucian's Lycinus, who considers the pantomime of his own time as an aesthetic form that 'has reached the very peak of its accomplishment', highlights the period of Augustus as that of a decisive turn in the genre's quest for 'beauty' (*Dance* 34) and understands its development as a gradual process. Early forms of dancing (of which we hear almost without interruption in *Dance* 8-24) provide its 'roots and foundations' (*Dance* 34), while smaller incremental steps (*Dance* 7) lead to the 'flowering and consummate fruition' of the genre that a second-century AD fan would have been able to experience (*Dance* 34). To be sure, Lucian's *On the Dance* follows its own rhetorical agenda. Yet its portrayal of the genre as an aesthetic form with a long period of evolution is entirely plausible and can indeed be corroborated with the aid of our scanty historical markers.

To take the Greek tradition first, a significant remote ancestor of imperial pantomime can be found in the writings of the fourth-century historian Xenophon and concerns the mimetic interpretation of a given mythological theme by means of dancing. At the end of Xenophon's *Symposion* (9.2-7) the wealthy Callias' dinner-guests are entertained by two dancers belonging to a Syracusan dancing-master (*orchêstodidaskalos*). Dancing to the accompaniment of *aulos* (double pipes), the young artists enact the nuptials of Ariadne and Dionysus, impersonating the god of wine and his bride and signalling the divine couple's mutual love with gestures, postures and words. Although this episode is isolated and cannot be placed in the direct genealogy of pantomime dancing, it brings sharply into relief both the rudiments of pantomimic art as the corporeal, mimetic presentation of a mythological plot and the overall impression of verisimilitude and the effusion of *pathos* that are also part and parcel of pantomime aesthetics (cf. Chapter 3§4).[2]

Around the middle of the third century BC, however, an epigram of

Dioscorides (*Greek Anthology* 11.195) offers invaluable insights into the genre's early life, as it foregrounds two dancers of ritual and mythological subjects engaged in some sort of competition. A certain Aristagoras 'danced (*ôrchêsato*) the role of a *gallus*'[3] to much applause, while the speaker himself, who 'laboured a lot' with 'the story of the warlike Temenidae', ended his performance disappointed. Tragedies entitled *Temenidae* and *Temenos* are attributed to Euripides and if, as Weinreich and others believed,[4] the speaker was a dancer rather than a singer or reciter of tragic/epic poetry, we are faced, as early as the high Hellenistic period, with some of the characteristics of the fully-fledged pantomime genre. I mean here the affinity of dance material to tragic myth and tragedy itself (see Chapter 2§2) and the complex choreography demanded by the pantomime libretti, which required the performer to interpret in succession all the characters featuring in a mythical plot, including those involving gender-change (in this case the female Hyrnetho). Even if the speaker were a different kind of performer, Aristagoras' dance contains in itself the kernel of the pantomime genre. Not only is Dioscorides' syntax[5] typical in literary references to pantomime dancing, but Attis and the entire circle of the Magna Mater (Cybele) remained throughout antiquity among the most popular (and most lambasted) pantomime topics.[6]

The next scraps of evidence date from almost two centuries down the line, around the 80s BC. The title 'pantomimos', designating a specific, identifiable kind of performer, can be read on an inscription from a city in Asia Minor, thus bringing the genre's history some 60 years back from the alleged time of its Roman 'birth' (Robert 1930: 117). It appears that a local benefactor named Zosimus hired the 'pantomime' Ploutogenes, an artist 'able to beguile men's souls with his art',[7] in order to spice up with some real 'entertainment' the public dinner he offered to his fellow-citizens. As Jones (1991: 195) notes, we should imagine Ploutogenes performing in the theatre of Priene, while the diners/spectators were eating. 'Pantomimos' as a professional qualification was restored by Robert (1938: 11-13) on an inscription from Delphi dating from the years 84-60 BC, while an inscription dating from the end of the first century BC or the beginning of the first century AD commemorates the victorious performance of Furius Celsus, a Roman citizen, 'dancer of myths' (*mythôn orchêstês*), in the theatre of Gortyn in Crete.[8] Given the date of the inscription, the mythological nature of the dance and the styling of the performer in a way so closely reminiscent of the pantomime artist's later titles (see Chapter 2§2), the dance in Gortyn must have been some early form of pantomime performance. Against the fallacy of pantomime's Augustan 'birth', then, the genre's Greek antecedents are impeccable or, as Jory (1981: 147) writes, 'there existed in Greece both in nature and in name forerunners of those entertainers who dominated the stage in the Roman Empire'.

Even in Rome, where, as we shall see in Chapter 5, attitudes to dancing ranged from ambivalence to open hostility, the ground was ready to nurture the seed sown by Bathyllus and Pylades. As scholars have shown, the influential form of dancing that took flesh in Rome through the intervention of the two Eastern virtuosi found a 'firm Italian base' (cf. Jory 1995: 151) for the flights of their ingenuity. In the first place, there was the so-called *ludus talarius*, a much loved sub-literary, lascivious form of stage-entertainment, comprising dancing (Cicero, *On Moral Duties* 1.150) in an ankle-length robe (the so-called *tunica talaris*), singing and instrumental music provided by lyres, flutes, castanets and cymbals (see primarily Jory 1995). More importantly, dancing was already an integral part of the mime, a largely improvisational and often sub-literary theatrical genre which enjoyed extremely high popularity in Republican and imperial Rome. As both men and women performed in mimes, *mimi* as well as *mimae* danced,[9] the latter, of course, more voluptuously than the former, and Garton (1972: 232) rightly saw in such mimetic dancers 'the forerunners' of Augustan pantomime. In addition, spectators at the great public games could enjoy the so-called *embolia*, 'balletic interludes, performed between the acts or while the next play was being prepared' (Wiseman 1985a: 27, with n. 43), and inscriptions preserve the names of several *emboliariae*, female performers of such entr'actes.[10] In Lucretius' poetic fantasy, the delicious image of 'dancers swaying their supple limbs' haunts the memory and dreams of theatre-goers for days after the games are over (*On the Nature of Things* 4.978-83). In private as well as public venues, from the *symposia* of the great and powerful,[11] often adorned by dancing girls of tender age,[12] to magnificent public extravaganzas,[13] dancing was a very common feature well before the Pyladean revolution. Crucially, the kind of performance involved could sometimes comprise the key attribute of pantomimc dancing, i.e. the danced impersonation of a mythical character. As Velleius Paterculus (*History of Rome* 2.83.2) records, the powerful L. Munatius Plancus danced the sea-god Glaucus at a banquet, naked, with a body painted blue, reeds around his head and a fish tail to boot (see Wiseman 1985a: 47).

In any case, such mythical impersonations carried out in the midst of dancing were by no means a novelty in the Roman cultural tradition. As Wiseman (2000) has demonstrated, a corpus of engraved bronze *cistae* and mirrors, dating from the late fourth and early third centuries BC and relating broadly to the world of Latium, offers unparalleled insights into a burgeoning theatrical/ritual culture associated with the Dionysiac tradition of ritual and theatrical *mimesis*. Most interesting for us here is Wiseman's conclusion that a vital element of such a culture was the nude erotic dancing of female mime performers in mythological burlesques inspired by Greek tragedy. Besides, from as early as the sixth century BC onwards, dancing in satyr-costume is attested in Etruscan art (Wiseman 1988: 3-4), while Livy's famous digression (*From the Foundation of Rome* 7.2.3-13) into the origins of drama and the *ludi scaenici* in Rome in 364 BC 'clearly presupposes a long-standing Etruscan tradition of mimetic dance' (Wiseman 1988: 5).[14]

The richest mine of information comes from the end of book 7 of Dionysius of Halicarnassus' *Roman Antiquities* (7.70-3), where dancing (both in armour and satyric) as part of processions at festivals, triumphs and funerals of eminent men features as one of the countless proofs adduced by the author in corroboration of his main thesis that the founders of Rome were in reality Greeks (7.70.1-2 and 7.72.18). On the evidence of the first Roman historian, the third-century BC Fabius Picus,[15] Dionysius talks of 'choruses of men impersonating satyrs' during the procession of the original *Ludi Romani*, complete with the characteristic loincloth of such mythical creatures, as well as goatskins and manes with hair that stood upright. Other performers, dressed in shaggy tunics, impersonated the Sileni and all danced 'the Greek dance called *sikinnis*' (7.72.10).[16] Moreover, Dionysius adds his personal testimony that the *sikinnis* was also danced in his own day (first century BC) by performers dressed up as satyrs in the funeral processions in honour of deceased noblemen (7.72.12).

How much the Roman satyrs' dancing had to do with the beginnings of imperial pantomime we cannot tell. According to Aristonicus, a grammarian from Alexandria who may have taught in Rome and was a contemporary of both Dionysius of Halicarnassus and the first exponents of the Roman pantomime (hence a possible eyewitness to their innovations), the satyric *sikinnis* was one of the elements that fed into the new genre (see Athenaeus, *Sophists at Dinner* 20e). Diogenianus, for his part, one of the interlocutors in Plutarch's *Table Talk*, refers to Bathyllus' pantomime as a danced imitation of 'Echo or some Pan or Satyr revelling with Eros' (Plutarch, *Moral Essays* 711e-f).[17] The Etruscan and Roman tradition of dancing satyrs may then, after all, have contributed something to the lightheartedness and almost burlesque nature of the genre in the way it was shaped by one of its great Augustan innovators, Bathyllus (Athenaeus, *Sophists at Dinner* 20e). In any case, it is a reasonable certainty that, long before the 'registered' birth of pantomime as a separate genre, dancing, including dancing in mythical costume, was a major element of private and public entertainment in Roman life.

§2. Chronological span

What exactly happened in 23 or 22 BC Rome, when Pylades (I) and Bathyllus (I)[18] are credited with the introduction of a new form of entertainment into the capital, will remain forever obscure. Yet, as Jory (1981) argued persuasively, the contribution of the two Eastern performers must have been significant enough to signal a second beginning for the genre, the radical transformation and enrichment of dance entertainment as previously known in the city. As far as can be gauged from our scanty sources,[19] the innovations may have revolved around the areas of musical and vocal accompaniment for the dancing soloist. A chorus was probably substituted for a single vocalist and 'an increased musical component' (Jory 1981: 157), including flutes and pipes, given a central part in the performance.[20] As Rome was the launching pad for the revamped genre, it comes as no surprise that Greeks could refer to pantomime as 'the Italian dance' (Athenaeus, *Sophists at Dinner* 20e), while at the same time being fully conscious of pantomime's Anatolian roots, especially its Egyptian origins.[21] In the voice of the pantomime detractor embedded in Libanius' defence of the genre, Egypt was 'the first to bring into the world the pantomime evil' (Aelius Aristides in Libanius, *Oration* 64.80). Of infinitely greater consequence, however, is the fact that throughout its long life pantomime existed as a cultural amphibian.

A quintessentially Greek genre refashioned at the seat of the empire, with the blessing of the first Roman emperor and his closest entourage, it was rapidly exported to the East, taking its own alma mater by storm, while constantly retaining, as it were, a double subject 'consciousness': having 'become Roman', it also 'stayed Greek', to borrow Greg Woolf's (1994) now classic formulation on individual and collective cultural experiences in the imperial East. Most importantly, in their vigorous attempts to negotiate their own standing vis-à-vis the Roman superpower, provincial élites were quick to realise pantomime's supreme 'symbolic capital' as a mediator between two cultures which rubbed shoulders rather awkwardly with one another. The imperial festivals of the Greek East, where pantomime for the first time took its place amid the competitive arts in the second half of the second century AD (see Chapter 4§2), or monuments such as the intriguing Sebasteion in the city of Aphrodisias in Caria, are examples of élite manipulation of pantomime's ability to bridge the 'discrepant experiences' of 'Greek' and 'Roman' under the empire.[22]

In the Sebasteion, in particular, existing side by side with panels and reliefs which celebrate the imperial power, a series of fifteen pantomime masks (Jory 2002) adorning a frieze of the Propylon, the cultic complex's gateway, confirm pantomime's perceived role as a fundamental player in the multiple contests over the appropriation, reconfiguration and amalgamation of cultural memories that took place in the imperial East.[23] Moreover, whenever pantomime dancers performed at prestigious festivals or other ritual celebrations intended to integrate the imperial cult into the indigenous religious structures of the Hellenised East (see Price 1984), some strange cultural transactions emerged as a result. The emperor's glorification came to rest on (inter alia) the glamour of that very spectacle which, above all other performative expressions, celebrated the memory of Hellenism, as the dancer led his viewers through the vast landscapes of Greek myth, thereby re-activating a Greek, i.e. pre-Roman, past (see especially Chapter 7).

After the new lease of life offered to pantomime by Bathyllus (I) and

Pylades (I), its flight towards fame and popular acclaim was instantaneous. Apart from periods of trouble, when the dancers were banished from Rome or even Italy on account of the violence and unruly passions generated by their performances,[24] and despite the best attempts of committed moralists and polemicists on the side of the Christian Church, pantomime's success story was phenomenal.

In the West, pantomime is clearly in full bloom not only at the time of the early Church Fathers (e.g. Cyprian, Tertullian, Novatian, Arnobius, Lactantius) but also in Augustine's native Carthage of the fourth and early fifth centuries, and it attracts the opprobrium of Salvian, presbyter of Marseilles in the mid-fifth century. Sidonius Apollinaris, born in Lyon *c.* 430, treats us to a wonderful outline of live pantomime topics interlaced with the praise of contemporary pantomime stars (*Poem* 23.267-99), while in fifth-century Carthage Dracontius composes a poem (*Romulea* 10 [*Medea*]) which professes to 'sing' what the silent pantomime Muse narrates in the theatres (16-18). As late as the sixth century the genre is refracted through the admiring glance of Cassiodorus (*Various Letters* 5.51.8-9), powerful writer and diplomat in the court of Theoderic I.[25]

In the East, the constant fulminations of John Chrysostom (bishop of Antioch and later patriarch of Constantinople) against the paganism and immorality of pantomime dancing as well as the defence of the genre composed by the sophist Libanius (*Oration* 64) confirm pantomime's protagonistic role on the theatrical and cultural stage of the fourth century. Moreover, a precious piece of information from Sozomen's *History of the Church* (*PG* 67.1568), written in the fifth century, reveals that 'public spectacles of mimes and pantomimes' were customary on the occasion of the dedication of imperial statues and portraits in the East. Pantomime performances undoubtedly shaped parts of the late epic poet Nonnus' narrative (second half of the fifth century), but, whereas Nonnus' pen transcribes the marvels of the dancer's art (as experienced in his native Panopolis, in Egypt?), the Syriac homilist Jacob of Serugh, writing from the banks of the Euphrates in the early sixth century, pours venom on the same spectacle, an art he repudiates as the 'miming of lying tales' and the 'mother of all lasciviousness' (*Homily* 3, F7v[b] and F9v[b]; text in Moss 1935). Similarly, in the very last years of the fifth century, Joshua the Stylite is outraged by the sins of the citizens of Syrian Edessa. Assembled at the place 'where the dancer (*orchêstês*), who was named Trimerius, was dancing' at 'the time of that festival at which the heathen tales were sung', as well as 'praising the dancer until morning, with singing and shouting and lewd behaviour', the Edessan flock exhibited provocative impiety, responsible, in the cleric's view, for the calamities that befell the city at the turn of the century. Joshua's fury is levelled at a public entertainment that shows no signs of dwindling, but perpetuates instead the evil 'tales of the (ancient) Greeks'. It is therefore with glee that he mentions the emperor

Anastasius' well-known edict of 502, which banished pantomime dancing from all cities of the empire.[26]

Despite such measures, both mime and pantomime were still flourishing in the sixth century. The former merited the very skilful defence of the sophist Choricius of Gaza, while the latter, owing to its long-standing ability to polarise the emotions of its fans, received occasionally severe knocks, such as the edict of Justin I (524/5), mentioned by the chronographer Malalas (*Chronicle* 17.12), which banished 'all dancers throughout the East ... except from Alexandria the Great in Egypt'.[27] Both genres must have suffered incalculable damage when Justinian withdrew the public funding of theatrical performances in the early period of his reign, initiating for his people what Procopius in his *Secret History* calls 'a mirthless life for everybody'.[28] Pantomime, however, proved spectacularly hard to kill. Although tracing its history becomes more and more difficult as we advance into the Byzantine era, because of minimal differentiation between the theatrical professions and their corresponding genres in our sources (Puchner 2002: 313), some version of pantomime dancing seems to have lingered on even to the end of the seventh century. At that time two canons of the Council in Trullo (691/2) gave it the decisive blow by banning 'dancing on the stage' (*tas epi tês skênês orchêseis*; Canon no. 51) as well as the pestiferous 'public dances by women' and all dances and rites in the name of pagan gods (Canon no. 62).[29]

§3. Peering into the melting-pot

Tracing the linear development of pantomime dancing from the first appearance of an identifiable pantomime dancer to the death pangs of the genre in late antiquity is by no means the sole avenue that promises to lead us to a better understanding of the nature of imperial pantomime. Almost as important as the 'direct' line of descent is what we may call the 'indirect' one, stemming first and foremost from the age-old dance culture of the Greek world. Just as ocurred with many a genre in the history of dancing, it was inevitable that pantomime borrowed substantial elements from many dance languages and styles,[30] even if these continued their independent existence after the emergence of the new genre. Masked dancing, for example, an almost indispensable ingredient of pantomime performances, had been part of Greek cultic dancing from earliest times,[31] while the long tradition of mimetic dancing, both cultic and secular, in the Greek world must have been hugely important in the gradual development of pantomime's corporeal eloquence.[32]

To the first category belong all those dances which were supposed to re-enact a particular episode of myth, such as the *geranos*, a serpentine dance in imitation of the turnings and windings of the Cretan labyrinth: it was believed to have been instituted by Theseus and his companions when they stopped at Delos on their return to Athens.[33] As for secular mimetic dances, they must have been legion, especially those connected with the main events of the agricultural year. Xenophon (*Anabasis* 6.1.8), for example, describes an elaborate dance performed by Aenianians and Magnesians. It seems to have consisted of a judicious blending of a mini-plot (a farmer's armed fight to protect his livelihood) with the mimetic representation of agricultural activities (sowing and ploughing with oxen) and the portrayal of human emotion (anxiety and fear), and was danced rhythmically to the music of the flute. That such dances were entrenched in Greek tradition and continued to exist in parallel with pantomime (perhaps even lending it some of their storehouse of kinetic images) can be gauged from some scattered gems in our literary tradition. A prominent example is the tantalising glimpses into a 'dance of the grape harvest' in Longus' *Daphnis and Chloe* (2.36.1-2), a novel of the second century AD, the heyday of pantomime:

> Sometimes his [i.e. the dancer's] movements were those of someone picking the grapes, sometimes carrying the baskets, then treading the grapes, then filling the jars, then drinking the sweet new wine. Dryas danced all this so gracefully and vividly (*enargôs*) that they seemed to see the vines, the press, the jars – and Dryas really drinking (trans. Gill in Reardon 1989).[34]

Very close to the mimetic core of pantomime was the elusive (for us) *hyporchêma*, presented in some ancient accounts as a kind of musical composition wherein poetry (set to music) and dance are in a relation of 'full communion' (Plutarch, *Moral Essays* 748a), 'as if the words and the parts of the body were connected by strings which the former pulled' (Pickard-Cambridge 1988: 249). The ancient evidence is tangled and often contradictory, but if we were to visualise a performance featuring a separation of singers and dancers, where the latter group's bodily motion represents mimetically through gestures (*dia tôn schêmatôn*, Plutarch, ibid.) the subjects elucidated by the former group's song,[35] we would find ourselves at the very threshold of the pantomime genre. Interestingly, both Athenaeus and Plutarch (or their common source) associate Bathyllus' lighthearted pantomimes with this particular performance medium, saying that they were presented as 'some kind of *hyporchêma*' (Plutarch, *Moral Essays* 711e-f; cf. Athenaeus, *Sophists at Dinner* 20e).

Over and above any other indirect influences on the emergence of the fully-fledged pantomime, however, we must consider the dances that were at the heart of the great mystery traditions, i.e. the initiatory cults of (mainly), Demeter and Core at Eleusis, Dionysus/Iacchus, Sabazius, and Cybele with Attis.[36] Voices from pagan antiquity down to the Christian world speak in unequivocal terms of the quintessential part played by dancing in initiation ceremonies. One cannot find a single 'ancient initiation rite performed without dancing', since Orpheus and Musaeus, foremost dancers themselves, who instituted them, deemed it 'a most beautiful thing to be initiated with rhythm and dancing', claims Lucian (*Dance* 15).[37] But there is a special reason why such dancing may have contributed in a major way to pantomime's development. In many cases, undoubtedly far exceeding our extant corpus of evidence, initiatory dancing consisted of the mimetic re-enactment of a mythical plot undertaken by worshippers impersonating mythical characters with the aid of masks and/or costume. The constituent ingredients of imperial pantomime are not hard to detect, especially when we bear in mind the manifold and versatile Bacchic/Dionysiac mysteries, in connection with which Plato (*Laws* 815c) speaks of the imitation of Nymphs, Pans, Silens and Satyrs in the midst of ritual dancing. Revolving frequently around grottoes (especially in later periods),[38] Bacchic mysteries centred on the ritual re-enactment of the god's sacred legends,[39] such as his double birth (cf. Euripides, *Bacchae* 88-100), a theme inherently connected with mystic initiation (see Seaford 1994: 268), or his underworld search for his mother Semele, which culminated in her 'bringing up' (*anagôgê*) to the upper world, again a typical initiatory scenario.[40] Given the pivotal position of the dance in the Dionysiac world,[41] dancing would have been a sine qua non in the progression of the initiate to the status of the god's mythical companions, that is to say, a satyr, a silen or a maenad. Such is probably the story illustrated in a pictorial triptych on a cup from Oxford (*ARV*[2] 865, 1), where the contrast between pre- and full maenadic status is conveyed through an antithesis in the initiand's dress and bodily motion. To the draped, immobile figure of the first two pictures is opposed the dancing figure of the last, i.e. the same woman now clad in typical maenadic dress and dancing freely among the god's initiates.[42]

During its long evolution pantomime must have assimilated and translated into its own technical language not only a vast number of individual dances (local, national, social or ritual) but also specific features of individual dances. Even when pantomime first emerged as an identifiable genre, it would have found readily available a rich repertoire of dance types that could be incorporated wholesale or slightly adapted in order to satisfy the demands of particular kinds of plots. So, for example, Pollux, Athenaeus and Hesychius refer to dances that are dainty, supple, almost voluptuous,[43] and others that are openly lewd and lascivious.[44] There were dances that were deemed coarse and vulgar,[45] others were registered as terrifying, and Hesychius (s.v. *aposkelisai*) even mentions a dance considered appropriate for children. Given the sheer variety of plot-types reflected in pantomime dancing (see Lucian, *Dance* 37-61), every corner of a mature dance tradition was likely to be explored and put to use. Take the dancer required to impersonate heroes afflicted with madness, such as Ajax (e.g., Lucian, *Dance* 83-4) and Heracles (e.g., Macrobius, *Saturnalia* 2.7.16). For this kind of plot the dancer could have appropriated the cluster of dances which Athenaeus (*Sophists at Dinner* 629d) calls 'frenzied' or 'dances of madmen' (*maniôdeis*), such as the *therma(u)stris*, a vigorous and rapid dance characterised by big leaps during which the dancer, before returning to the floor, repeatedly crosses his legs.[46] A pantomime's Ajax leaping over the plain, sword in hand, might well have employed such choreography, especially as it would have been familiar to a wider audience.

Plots requiring transformation into animals or birds (cf. Lucian, *Dance* 41, 48, 57, 59) might have drawn on dances and dance sequences or motifs under the cluster of *morphasmos*, which was, according to Pollux, 'the dance imitating all kinds of animals' (*Onomasticon*, 4.103). A widespread dance of this kind, referred to in manifold ways in literary texts from the early fifth century BC to the Middle Ages, was 'the dance of the owl', a mimetic dance incorporating many figures or motifs, most characteristically the dancer's twisting and wiggling of the neck and head, in imitation of the bird's behaviour when caught (Pollux, *Onomasticon* 4.103). The choreography for the myth of Polyidus and Glaucus, a pantomime *fabula* according to Lucian (*Dance* 49), might have drawn upon this mimetic cluster, given that an owl plays a prominent part in it.[47] On the other side of the spectrum, for plots of a military type, the 'vocabulary' of the most famous armed dance, the *pyrrhichê*, would have come in useful, with its imitation (*mimoumenên, mimêmata, mimeisthai*) of a warrior's defensive and offensive movements, i.e. all kinds of blows, archery and the hurling of javelins or the characteristic *schêmata* of 'swerving and ducking and leaping up to the side or sinking to the ground' (Plato, *Laws* 815a).

Even beyond the range of entire recognisable dances, the many centuries of dance tradition on Greek soil must have created a vast repertory of dance sequences and phrases, a convenient (and perhaps more broadly recognisable) vocabulary of postures, gestures and mimetic sequences[48] that could be used to convey facets of character or emotional states or even regular activities, such as running, galloping, fighting, harvesting, and so on. In conclusion, even though it is impossible to trace pantomime's linear ancestry any further back than the mid-third century BC, we should imagine the remote origins of imperial pantomime buried in the depths of the many idiolects of Greek mimetic dancing.[49]

2

Pantomime and Other Entertainments: Cross-Fertilisations and Affiliations

We saw in the previous chapter that pantomime was both a radically new aesthetic form and a genre which assimilated multiple layers of an already thriving dance tradition. But just as it is important to acquire a sense, however incomplete, of pantomime's origins and the movement of dance vocabularies *through* time, it is also essential to obtain as clear a view as possible of pantomime's relation to cognate areas *across* time, on the synchronic level. Given that, as we shall see in greater detail in Chapters 9§3 and 11, pantomime was in cut-throat competition with a multitude of other performative genres, we can well imagine the dancer to have been forever on the lookout for innovation and for startling ways to captivate a public avid for spectacle and spoilt for choice. Moreover, the well-documented geographical and social mobility of pantomime dancers must have generated a most fertile cross-pollination between the 'languages' of pantomime and different entertainment traditions in a variety of contexts throughout Rome's vast empire.

§1. Pantomime's lowbrow companions

Immensely formative must have been the kind of interbreeding taking place between pantomime (especially as practised by artists of more modest ability and at non-prestigious, public or private, occasions) and the entire *demi-monde* of subliterary genres and lowbrow entertainers.

The entertainment closest to pantomime throughout its stage history was the mime.[1] Not only did it lay a special emphasis, as pantomime did, upon the value of corporeal eloquence, but it also often partnered the genre and its dancer, especially in the constant fulminations of moralists and Fathers of the Church against the stage's immoral nature.[2] Of equal importance, however, was the overlap between the two domains in performative terms. The Christian Choricius, whose treatise *In defence of those who represent life in the theatre* (commonly known as *Apology* or *In Defence of the Mimes*) offers invaluable insights into the theatrical life of sixth-century Gaza in Palestine, stipulates that a mime 'must know how to dance' (*Apology* 124). Furthermore, with respect to female stage-performers, we hear that it was primarily their dancing skills which placed them in high demand in both types of entertainment. Thus, before converting to Christianity, the flamboyant Pelagia was said to be first among the female mimes in Antioch and first dancer among the pantomime's chorus-girls (Webb 2002a: 289), while Basilla, the female performer commemorated on a stele of the third century AD, must have had skills equipping her for mime (apparently her foremost area of expertise) as well as pantomime (see Webb 2002a: 289 and 301).

Indeed, an area of extreme (albeit gravely overlooked) importance for pantomime dancing was the broad, heterogeneous domain of female dancing, a bodily language built upon the intoxicating syntax of carnal temptation and materialising throughout the empire in dissolute and often exotically tinged private or public entertainment.[3] From the realm of the professional stage[4] to that of social dancing[5] and the array of festive occasions for which entertainers could be privately hired, opportunities for cross-fertilisation between pantomime and the characteristic habits of female movement were legion, and eagerly sought after by a genre in which the male routinely represented the female with an eye to performative verisimilitude (see Chapter 3§4). Although the range of hostile sources (pagan as well as Christian) which construct the pantomime as an effeminate performer have their own axes to grind and should be treated with due care, we may still get closer to the corporeal images a pantomime would have conjured for his original spectators by delving into the (conveniently) hidden world of both professional and demi-monde female movement vocabulary. It was partly the plumbing of that world which would have furnished the dancer with eloquent markers of female expression, such as lascivious gestures (e.g. in Martial, *Epigrams* 6.71.1); the characteristically female swaying of the hips and shaking of the buttocks, shimmying all the way down to the floor;[6] the beautiful rippling of the spine (Apuleius, *Metamorphoses* 2.7); the fluid softness of the arms;[7] the bending of the torso; the 'quivering' or 'soft side' that twists voluptuously in the rhythmical measures of a 'soft' art[8] – in short, all those bodily tropes which cause him to appear 'sinewless' and 'broken up', having forfeited the brawny and erect carriage of a man (see Chapters 5§1 and 9§2). No wonder that some of the 'technical' terms in pantomime dancing, namely the verb *lygizein*, which means 'to bend or twist like a withe', and *lygisma* or *lygismos*, 'sinuous bend, twist', are also staples in the vocabulary of female body-language.[9]

Given pantomime's notorious dramatisation of female mythical narratives (see Chapter 5§2) and its assimilation of female corporeal habits, the so-called *magôidia* should be singled out next among the lowbrow performance genres rubbing shoulders with pantomime. Hesychius (s.v.) glosses it as 'a dainty dance' (*orchêsis hapalê*), and Athenaeus (*Sophists at Dinner* 621c), on the authority of Aristoxenus, qualifies it further as a vulgar performance to the accompaniment of tambourines and cymbals.[10] Clad in female clothing, the actor makes indecent gestures and puts himself completely beyond the pale of good order, impersonating now adulterous women, now drunken men.[11] In addition, the disorderly mix of gender-specific body languages that could have fed into pantomime performances can be gauged equally well from *magôidia*'s cognate genre of *lysiôidia*, wherein the 'lysiodist', a performer of 'female roles in male costume' (*Sophists at Dinner* 620e), could be either male, like 'Metrobius the lysiodist',[12] or female, like the dancer Antiodemis, 'the halcyon of Lysis', whose arms, 'liquid like water', and body, 'without a single bone', moved with intoxicating grace.[13] Generally speaking, contacts between the fully-fledged pantomime genre and a whole series of lowbrow entertainments were manifold, and the 'chemistry' of their interaction merits investigation in its own right. Here, however, I will restrict myself to two further examples, significant because they indicate pantomime's cross-pollination with activities that lie even further beyond a narrowly conceived realm of stage-entertainment.

In the first place, then, we should look at the elusive area of the so-called 'wonder-makers', the *thaumatopoioi*, whose remit encompassed 'conjuring, acrobatics, juggling, and marionette-shows or, in other words, any kind of performance that produced baffled amazement in spectators' (Dickie 2001: 601). From the dancing girl 'skilled in wonder-making,' who went on to dance the role of Ariadne in Xenophon's *Symposion* (see Chapter 1§1), to the dream interpreter Artemidorus, *orchêstai* (pantomimes) and *thaumatopoioi* could be lumped together as belonging to the same class of entertainers (cf. Aelius Aristides, *Oration* 34.55),[14] while in the fourth century AD, Gregory, archbishop of Nyssa, refers to stage-pantomimes as 'the wonder-making actors' (*tous thaumatopoiountas*) (*Letter* 9 = *PG* 46.1040).[15]

Secondly, it seems that dazzling exhibitions of acrobatic brilliance, intended to showcase the performer's physical virtuosity, were regularly incorporated into the pantomime dancer's movement vocabulary. Thus Lucian speaks of pantomime's 'turns and twirls and jumps and back-flung poses' (*Dance* 71), while the second century AD doctor and polymath Galen offers an invaluable snapshot of the pantomimes' 'jerky movements',

> during which they perform the greatest leaps and whirl around as they rotate with the greatest speed and, after sinking down with bent knees, they rise up again and drag their legs forward and to the side and cleave them asunder as much as possible and, in a word, move extremely quickly ... (*On Preserving One's Health* 2.11.40).

Libanius, for his part, in a passage that sheds invaluable light on the pantomime dancer's early training, presents the young boy's teacher (the *paidotribês*) twisting his malleable body into the most convoluted shapes, imposing upon it full spirals, the total curving of the spine, deep arches from fingertip to toe or the painful projection of the limbs past the body's outer edges into space.[16] Besides, many reflections of the pantomime's art in later literature point us in the direction of the kind of breathtaking acrobatics we now associate with the graceful performances of gymnasts at Olympic and other high-profile contests.[17]

In the Greek tradition, dancing had always overlapped with acrobatic exhibition,[18] and a certain tendency towards the acrobat's intoxicating play with the laws of gravity was probably an inherent feature of the genre from the start. At the time of pantomime's heyday, however, when competitiveness was one of the foremost markers of the genre and acrobatic numbers were the stock-in-trade of many other entertainers, a dancer's choices must have been infinitely more self-conscious. It is hard to believe that a pantomime contestant seeking to impress his public with his speedy trajectory across the stage (cf. Chapter 3§2), judiciously interlaced with spins and turns and launches into the air in virtuosic jumps, would not have been looking with the keenest interest at the performances of those for whom such exercises were their livelihood. The closeness of the fields can be seen also from the fact that even fully-fledged acrobatic numbers were sometimes ingeniously combined with dancing. Apuleius' description of a sword-swallower's tricks is the most illustrative example in this case. After having buried a hunting spear into his bowels, death-dealing edge foremost, the fellow exhibited a boy 'of effeminate beauty' who

> rose up [to the other end of the spear] and with sinuous bends unfolded himself into a sinewless and boneless dance, attracting the admiration of all of us present. You could have said the boy was that noble serpent which clings with his slippery embrace to the staff of the physician god (Asclepius) ... (*Metamorphoses* 1.4).[19]

Even if we prefer to think that the refined pantomime of the great public imperial occasions would not have stooped that low for inspiration, it is inconceivable that the street-corner pantomime or dancing-master (cf. Dio Chrysostom, *Oration* 20.9), who might have been sharing his spot with dancing stuntmen such as Apuleius' acrobats, would not have sought to build into his own performance his competitors' crowd-pulling tactics. In any case, describing a game extravaganza provided by Carus and his sons, Carinus and Numerian, in the late third century AD, their biographer mentions in a single breath the 'one thousand pantomimes and gymnasts' hired for the delectation of the public (Flavius Vopiscus of Syracuse, *Carus, Carinus and Numerian* 19.2).

§2. Pantomime's highbrow sibling: tragedy

As we shall see, pantomime derived its special power to haunt the imagination from its pronounced cultural ambivalence: an inextricable part of popular culture, it was nevertheless disquietingly close to up-market cultural domains. The most crucial determinant of pantomime's contiguity with upper echelons of culture was its generic affiliation to tragedy, primarily on account of their shared subject-matter (see Lucian, *Dance* 31), namely plots drawn from myth and legend.[20] The principal piece of evidence for the perceived proximity between the two performance genres is epigraphic. Inscriptions from the Greek and Hellenised East designate the dancer as 'an actor of tragic rhythmic movement' (*tragikês enrythmou k(e)inêseôs hypokritên*) and the entire spectacle as 'tragedy set in rhythm' (*enrythmos tragôidia*) or 'tragic (rhythmic) movement' (*tragikê* [*enrythmos*] *k(e)inêsis*).[21] As for the Latin-speaking West, hard and fast boundaries between different kinds of non-burlesque solo performance of mythological material (e.g. by tragic actors, singers accompanied by the lyre, or pantomime dancers) were often impossible to draw.[22] For example, in a much-quoted passage from Suetonius' biography of Caligula we read that, on the day before the emperor was murdered, the pantomime star Mnester *danced* 'the same tragedy' that the great fourth-century BC tragic actor Neoptolemus had *acted* at the games during which Philip of Macedon had been assassinated.[23] It would seem that one poetic adaptation of a famous tragic role or story could easily be re-adapted to fit another performance medium, so that, ultimately, what provided good acting material for a virtuoso of the tragic stage was also eminently suitable for a pantomime libretto (the so-called *fabula saltica*), destined for the performer eager to exhibit his prowess in dancing style. As Kelly (1979: 27-8) put it in an article on late-antique performances of tragedy, 'the libretto of the pantomime chorus, or *fabula saltica*, was probably not very different from the text used by the tragic singer'.

The most beloved gems of literary tradition and mythology, then, seem to have been rendered in song, in the form of *tragoedia cantata* (tragedy sung) *as well as* dance, in the form of *tragoedia saltata* (tragedy danced). Thus a poet like Statius, who famously sold a brand new composition on the story of Agave to the pantomime Paris (Juvenal, *Satire* 7.87), might also have expected to hear it sung by different virtuoso artists in different generic contexts, in the same way that Macrobius (*Saturnalia* 5.17.5) attests that the love story of Dido and Aeneas is kept alive by the 'perpetual gestures and songs of the actors' and Augustine laments that the misbehaviour of the pagan gods never stops being paraded in song and dance on his contemporary stage.[24] In a most enlightening passage referring to the variety of artistic means (painting, sculpture, pottery, architecture, literature) that exhibit Jupiter's adulteries, Augustine singles out the stage with its three different yet closely intertwined ways of portraying mythical material: traditional (tragic) acting, singing and pantomime dancing (*Letters* 91.5).

As far as cross-fertilisation between tragedy and pantomime in terms of stage-acting is concerned, we are lamentably in the dark, unable to form any but the most tentative conjectures. For example, as pantomime dancing was centrally concerned with the expression of 'character' and 'emotion' (see, e.g., Lucian, *Dance* 67), we may well imagine an exhilarating cross-flow of influences between the silent dancers and their speaking counterparts, the actors on the tragic stage.[25] In particular, the ever-growing expressiveness and affective power of tragic acting[26] (which in pantomime's heyday was mostly concerned with the artful delivery of tragic highlights[27] or the singing of emotionally-laden arias) may have fed into the domain of pantomime, sustaining or even instigating the pronounced emotionality of pantomime dancing (see Chapter 3§4). Moreover, perhaps we should also be thinking of pantomime in its coexistence with a theatrical tradition in which corporeal mimeticism was ever on the increase, not just with respect to actors but, more interestingly still, with reference to other kinds of artists, such as the instrumentalists (who also performed in cognate genres, especially as accompanists in lyric compositions). Already in the fourth century BC Aristotle complained that vulgar musicians, such as incompetent players of the *aulos*, resorted to crude *mimesis* and excessive bodily movement in order to get their point across, for example, rolling their bodies round when imitating a discus, or grabbing at the chorus-leader if their music was meant to represent Scylla, the sea-monster (*Poetics* 1461b 30-2).[28] Even as early as the fifth century BC, star pipers like the celebrated Pronomus seem to have been spicing their performances with the rhythmic movement of their entire body,[29] a developing tradition of performative expressiveness which must have been extremely relevant to pantomime, a genre heavily reliant on instrumental music, especially the *aulos*.

Significantly better, on the other hand, is our position with respect to the relative overall character of tragedy and pantomime as performative genres. The relation of tragedy to pantomime can be epitomised with reasonable certainty as the relation of a 'drama of words' (Burian 1997: 199) to a drama of the body, the antagonism between a highbrow, intellectual aesthetics of verbal brilliance and cerebral power, and an intrinsically sensual genre, chained to 'a narrative aesthetics of embodiment, where meaning and truth are made carnal', to use an eloquent description of eighteenth-century European melodrama (Brooks 1993: 21). This is not to say that the human body and its adventure or rather 'misadventure', as Zeitlin (1996b: 349-50) famously put it, is not the focus of classical tragedy. In the grip of madness or disease, in physical pain or psychological torment, the actor's body in all its corporeal syntax of attitudes and gestures is meant to rivet the audience's attention (cf. Valakas 2002): 'upright or prone, vigorous or weak, alone or assisted, naked or clothed, free or constrained, alive or dead' (Zeitlin 1996a: 209), the body of the tragic actor or the tragic dancer is indispensable and irreplaceable. Yet in tragedy the human body's physical vocabulary plays a clearly supportive role: both the expressiveness of body language and the choreography of bodily deployment in the case of the tragic chorus are there to enhance dramatic meaning, whose irreducible vehicle is the written and spoken word.

2. Pantomime and Other Entertainments

We could not be any further away from the world of pantomime dancing, where a 'poetry of language' has given way to a 'poetry in space',[30] and where the audience is invited to admire 'the position of the feet, the direction of the hands, the harmony ... of the nods, and in general, the graceful elegance of the entire spectacle' (Libanius, *Oration* 64.57). The primary sense-making mechanism is now uncontestably the human body, with *logos* having receded to a place of secondary importance. Inevitably, even the plot-lines that pantomime seems to privilege are perfectly in tune with this heightened bodily and spatial focus. Pantomime favourites are now those plots best able to showcase the evocative, communicative power of the dancer's metamorphic brilliance, the aesthetic (and erotic) thrills of his somatic versatility. To take the most extreme examples, although tragedy often uses the imagery of female labour to emphasise the vulnerability of the male body or underline its torment (Loraux 1981), no tragic plot would have centred on the physical act of giving birth or even on the act of making love on stage. Pantomime, on the other hand, can represent in dance 'the birthpangs of Leto' (Lucian, *Dance* 38), 'the double birth of Dionysus' (*Dance* 39), the 'birth of Zeus' (*Dance* 80) or the amorous adventures of the gods (especially of Zeus; *Dance* 59), the sexual act even giving the impression of being performed on the stage.[31] Violence too, of the kind confined to the interior of the stage-building or, more generally speaking, to the tragic play's 'off-stage' space, seems to be the central focus of pantomime *fabulae*, such as the dismemberment (*sparagmos*) of Iacchus (*Dance* 39), Orpheus (*Dance* 51) and Apsyrtus (*Dance* 53). Similarly, the un-tragic plots of cannibalism and transformation from one register of life to another (or even the passage between life and inanimate nature) appear to be enduring presences in the repertory of danced dramas.[32]

Any attempt, however, to venture beyond the level of such generalities takes us straight into unplotted and (largely) unplottable territory. The most insurmountable difficulty is the complete absence of pantomime libretti, which makes comparative pronouncements on either the narrative or the performative economy of the two genres especially hazardous. We know, for example, that, as Burian (1997: 199) put it, the tragic stage is a space where 'very little "happens" ': 'physical action ... is usually limited in scope and relatively static ... violent events tend to be described in messenger-speeches ...', with the result that 'the confrontations of tragedy are ... essentially verbal'. In pantomime, on the other hand, the 'performance' space is very far from static.[33] It can even be suggested that pantomime turns tragedy's conventional way of linking 'performance space' and 'dramatic action' on its head. Whereas in tragedy it is the 'off-stage' space that features as the space of intense and often violent physical action, in pantomime drama action invades, and becomes the lifeblood of, the performance's 'on-stage' space. Now, if we did have some of the vast number of *fabulae salticae* that were in circulation in antiquity, we would be able to put such a proposition to the test by means of a close comparison of the tragic and pantomimic handling of the same myths. In their absence, however, we have only the precious few insights that can be garnered from literary sources with respect to the pantomime dramatisation of well-known tragic legends. Out of a handful of possible comparisons, I will only take a brief look at the single case linked with Lucian's *On the Dance*, namely a notorious pantomime performance of the quintessentially tragic plot of Ajax's madness in the aftermath of his defeat at the contest for the arms of Achilles (see *Dance* 83-4).[34]

In Sophocles' *Ajax*, the sole extant dramatisation of the story in Greek tragedy, Ajax's slaughter of the Greek army's cattle together with their guardians (*Ajax* 26-7) can be fleshed out only in the audience's imagination. The audience have access to it indirectly, as their knowledge of Ajax's delusional behaviour is mediated by the narrative of those who either saw it themselves (*Ajax* 61-4, 235-44, 296-322) or heard about it, either in the form of rumour (*Ajax* 141-7) or by means of an eyewitness's report (*Ajax* 29-31). At the most, Sophocles' spectators would have glimpsed the acts of Ajax's madness transiently and intermittently through their partial evocation by the gestural language of other stage-characters[35] or the Salaminian chorus. In pantomime's dramatisation of Ajax's *pathos*, on the other hand, Lycinus' comment that the unlucky dancer 'exceeded all bounds of appropriate *mimêsis*', to the extent that 'he might reasonably have given someone the impression that he was not feigning (*hypokrinasthai*) madness but was actually mad himself', suggests a radical recasting of the tragic play's subject-matter. It seems that the part of the tragic action now flipped into prominence is precisely that narrative which in Sophocles' play had been assigned to 'off-stage' space. Reshaped for the needs of the new genre, the role of Ajax consists in *hypokrinesthai*, impersonating, Ajax in his delusion,[36] the enactment of the hero's madness having moved now centre-stage, the sole subject of the dancer's art.[37]

It would therefore seem that, when a myth makes the transition from tragedy into pantomime, the crossing of the border entails the transposition of tragedy's 'invisible' space into the heart of pantomime's 'presentational' space, the space energised by the dancer's movements in the audience's full view. With respect to Ajax's legend in particular, it is easy to see why tragedy's 'backgrounded' space of mad action would have ignited a pantomime's imagination: a choreography of frenzied leaps across the Trojan plain (cf. Chapter 1§3) would have offered the aspiring star a splendid opportunity for self-display and self-promotion. Similar conclusions can be reached with respect to the tragic and pantomimic dramatisation of Heracles' madness and Phaethon's demise.[38] The space and the action which tragedy allows its audience to glimpse only at a second (or sometimes third) remove, through the eyes and perceptual filters of its choruses or other characters, pantomime freely opens up to the spectator.[39] Regrettably, however, the absence of libretti makes it impossible to elevate such suggestions above the realm of the plausible.

2. Pantomime and Other Entertainments

A last word will take us back to the issue of filiation. Aristonicus (in Athenaeus, *Sophists at Dinner* 20e) derives pantomime from the tragic, comic and satyric dances of the fifth-century Athenian stage. Although the case for a straightforward line of descent is implausible, we should nevertheless be more alert to the quasi-pantomimic nature of a substantial part of classical dramatic dancing. The praise of the dancing-master (*orchêsto-didaskalos*) Telesis or Telestes in Athenaeus (*Sophists at Dinner* 21f) for his 'consummate demonstration of what was spoken by means of his hands' highlights the essential skill of the imperial pantomimes (cf. Chapter 3§1). Besides, whatever we may choose to make of Aristocles' puzzling reference to the Aeschylean dancer[40] of such supreme skill that 'in dancing the *Seven against Thebes*, he made the action clear by means of his dancing',[41] it does help focus the mind on the mimetic aspect so deeply ingrained in the chorus' presence in fifth-century Athenian tragedy. For the chorus' dancing-steps and overall movement within the designated performance space of the tragic genre were not abstract or haphazard, but full of specificity and purpose.

There can be no better illustration of this claim than those instances in tragedy where chorus dancers, by means of song and movement and aided by the flights of poetic imagery, help the audience visualise actions taking (or supposed to have taken) place off-stage. For example, when Phaedra rushes into the *skênê* building to hang herself, and the chorus of Troezenian women visualise the imminent fastening of the noose from the rafters and the fitting of the rope to the white neck (Euripides, *Hippolytus* 769-72), it is hard to think that no imitative gesturing is interlaced with their dance (see Kernodle 1957: 2). Similarly, the choreography of the first Ode of Aeschylus' *Agamemnon*, where the chorus of Argive Elders look back to Iphigeneia's sacrifice, must have been such as to enable the entire episode to come to life before the audience's eyes: 'the father's anguish, the daughter's cry, the lifting her up over the altar while the father prays, the appeal of the gagged, mute daughter, and the turning away from the actual sacrifice' (Kernodle 1957: 2; cf. Wiles 1997: 17). In other words, the corporeal evocation of characters and their surrounding spatial milieu that came to be the hallmark of pantomime dancing was already part of tragedy's peculiar magic and inextricably interwoven with the performance of the carefully trained choruses of tragic dancers. Despite continuities, however, pantomime should best be understood as the theatrical form which tore performance aesthetics away from its traditional moorings in the legacy of the classical Athenian drama and steered it into previously uncharted waters. The six centuries of pantomime's reign until the death pangs of the pagan world amply testify to the resounding success of the new direction.

'Technologies' of the Body: The Pantomime's Art

What did pantomime look like as a fully-fledged genre, avidly consumed in both the East and West of the empire? Our first question is already an intractable one: as Edith Hall (2002: 29) sums it up, 'it is clear that there was no single "correct" way to stage a pantomime'. In terms of the 'realities' of its performance, the genre was almost as protean and adaptable as its main artist.

The clearest illustration of this versatility was the fact that a pantomime could be both entertainment on a massive scale, presented in the big theatres and amphitheatres of the late Hellenistic and Roman world, but could also be staged, to similar acclaim, in private venues, the villas of the wealthy and the noble, and even the emperor's palace itself (cf. Chapter 4, n. 8). In the East of the empire, John Chrysostom admonishes his flock unceasingly not to hire mimes and pantomimes for domestic entertainment, e.g. wedding celebrations,[1] while papyri indicate that professional dancers (especially castanet-dancers) as well as pantomimes could be hired for private occasions in Egypt in the first centuries AD.[2] We even get a rare glimpse of dancer and dancing-master performing or teaching on a street-corner.[3] Similarly, we ought to bear in mind that the information we possess about pantomime dancers concerns primarily the genre's mega-stars, the Nureyevs and Nijinskys of antiquity, not the long line of less talented artists who would have been making a precarious living dancing their way from village fair to private wedding in the vast provinces of the empire.

A strange story related by Dio Cassius (*Roman History* 78.21.2) speaks volumes for the different levels of proficiency expected of the artist in the metropolis and in the provinces. The pantomime Theocritus (II), he tells us, an imperial freedman, was unsuccessful when introduced to the theatre in Rome, but, when he performed at Lugdunum (modern Lyon) in Gaul, he delighted his viewers, the reason being, in the historian's mind, that people there lacked urban sophistication – they were 'more boorish'. What is good enough for the country is not necessarily acceptable in the big city, where one might find a supremely knowledgeable, exacting audience, as can be gauged from Lucian's insights into the Antiochean audience's spectating habits (*Dance* 76).[4]

Moreover, there may well have been considerable variation between the choreographic choices prevalent in the great urban centres and the styles of movement more popular in the remote edges of the empire. Local dance traditions (as is the case with folk dancing today) would have been particularly strong and perhaps prominently displayed at events sponsored by local benefactors. More importantly, in those periods when mythological self-definition on the level of entire cities mattered enormously, as it did at the time of the so-called 'Second Sophistic' in the first centuries AD (see Chapter 7), pantomime choreography may have been judiciously adapted to promote local myth or local variants of panhellenic tales. A universal repertoire may have had inexhaustible capacities for cross-fertilisation with both indigenous narrative material and indigenous corporeal dialects.

Crucially, however, we also have to be alert to variations in the way the fictional world of a pantomimic *fabula* would have been created in the course of the performance. For example, we should beware of assuming that the breathtakingly naturalistic set which was supposedly erected in the theatre of Corinth for the dramatisation of the 'Judgement of Paris' legend and described by Apuleius in book 10 of his *Metamorphoses*[5] constituted a representational norm for the genre.[6] To be sure, grand venues for public performances would have been equipped sufficiently well for a basic pictorial evocation of a libretto's imaginary geography – mountains and seas, heaven and earth, even the underworld. Seneca refers to the *machinatores*, the stage-machinists, 'who invent scaffolding that goes aloft of its own accord, or floors that rise silently into the air, and many other surprising devices' (*Letter* 88.22; trans. Gummere, Loeb 1962); Pollux and Vitruvius speak of screens or draperies (*katablêmata*) and curtains (*siparia*), which could be used to indicate the setting, and of three-sided prisms (*periaktoi*) fixed into the ground and turned whenever there was a need to indicate a change in a play's locality.[7] To what extent the *verbal* scenery conjured by the narrative of the libretto and the chorus's songs was actually complemented by a material stage-set is difficult to gauge. But at least we can be confident that it would have been technically perfectly possible for a pantomime audience, informed by the libretto that the story takes place, say, on the heights of Cithaeron, to have been aided by appropriate stage-painting in their transportation to a mountainous landscape.

Even so, state-of-the art facilities for the creation of illusionistic verisimilitude may not always have existed in smaller-scale public venues, such as, for example, the *odeia*, public buildings of more modest size, where pantomimes were sometimes staged, or in aristocratic villas, where pantomime troupes often resided and performed for the entertainment of the rich and powerful.[8] The situation must have been similar in the case of pantomime props. In Apuleius we find an array of individualised items, such as the characteristic emblems of each deity appearing on stage, a variety of head-wear (from tiaras and diadems to military helmets), arrows and wings for little dancing Cupids, full body armour for supporting actors, and so on (*Metamorphoses* 10.30-4). But, to look at the other end of the spectrum, itinerant troupes travelling from one humble venue to another may well have found the cost of both owning and transporting vast amounts of equipment financially crippling. The only relative fixture in a pantomime's gear may have been his heavily embroidered, magnificent cloak,[9] to which Marcus Cornelius Fronto, the second-century AD Roman orator, devotes a distressingly brief aside: in close partnership, so to speak, with this wonderful piece of fabric, dancers are able to represent 'a swan's tail, the tresses of Venus, a Fury's scourge' (*On Orations* 5, p. 150 Van den Hout).[10]

The overall impression created by a pantomime spectacle would have been contingent on a long list of variables, such as the skill of the dancer(s), the composition and wealth of the pantomime troupe, the occasion and venue for the dance, the kind of audience addressed, and so on. A lavishly endowed pantomime show in the capital of the empire, or a pantomime contest forming part of a great imperial festival in the provinces (cf. Chapter 4), would have provided altogether different opportunities for optical extravaganzas compared with, say, a lower-key performance staged by an itinerant troupe in a backwater Syrian village. The only irreducible item in pantomime performances was the dancer's own body, to which we now turn.

§1. Aural and visual signs: song, narrative and dance

Lucius Apuleius, the dazzling second-century AD orator, 'literary showman' (Fantham 1996: 255) and self-styled philosopher from the North African city of Madaurus, whom we shall meet repeatedly in the course of this book, treats his readers to a fascinating description[11] of a festive extravaganza which took place in the theatre of Corinth, on mainland Greece (*Metamorphoses* 10.30-4). The dance adaptation of 'The Judgement of Paris' was enacted by as many as five main dancers (impersonating Mercury, Paris, Juno, Minerva and Venus) and a supporting cast dancing the roles of the deities' attendants, including Castor and Pollux, a whole crowd of little Cupids, and even the Graces and the Hours. In addition, the cast featured female dancers, whose appearance and overall deportment seemed appropriate to the role apportioned to them. Insofar as the protagonists signalled everything by means of gesture, body movement and dance, the spectacle rested on that silent, corporeal eloquence that is the essence of pantomime dancing.[12] Nevertheless, the overall character of that performance was far from what theatre-goers in the imperial period would have primarily understood, if invited to a 'pantomime' entertainment.

The most normative version of the spectacle featured a single, usually male[13] dancer, who acted out[14] successively by means of dancing all the characters in a given pantomime plot (*fabula*), so that, in a danced adaptation of, say, the Dionysiac story dramatised in Euripides' *Bacchae*, he would impersonate in turn Dionysus, Teiresias, Cadmus, the Messenger and the frenzied Agave (Anonymous in *Greek Anthology* 16.289). How exactly the transitions between the roles were effected we do not know,[15] but it is possible that an instrumental and vocal interlude entertained the spectators while the dancer changed his mask in order to 'become' the next character. With the aid of his masks (sometimes as many as four or five in a single plot),[16] the dancer exhibited himself as a single body endowed with many souls (*Dance* 66).[17] As Cassiodorus (*Various Letters* 4.51.9), at the turn of the sixth century AD, verbalises the experience,

> the same body indicates Heracles and Venus, represents a woman in a man, fashions a king and a soldier, renders an old and a young man, so that you would have thought that in one body there are many, differentiated by such a varied imitation.

The most enthralling aspect of the dancer's art is his corporeal eloquence, expressed primarily through his 'wise [i.e. skilled] fingers', 'better than the Muses and the Graces' themselves (*Greek Anthology* 16.283), and his 'most talkative hands' (*loquacissimae manus*, Cassiodorus, *Various Letters* 4.51.8), so indispensable that the dream interpretation manual of Artemidorus records:

> it is, of course, obvious to everybody that, to sailors, pantomimes and illusionists, it is not a good sign to dream of not having hands, for without them they are unable to work (*Interpretation of Dreams* 1.42)

Beyond the dancer himself, one of the most individual features of the genre was the unprecedented variety of instruments uniting their sounds to provide musical accompaniment for the moving figure on the dancing floor (Cassiodorus, *Various Letters* 4.51.9). Lucian mentions the double pipes (*aulos*), the Pan's pipe (*syrinx*), the cymbals (cf. Arnobius, *Against the Gentiles* 7.32) and even the lyre (*kithara*) (*Dance* 26, 63, 68, 72, 83), but there were also castanets (*krotala*), drums (*tympana*; cf. Arnobius, *Against the Gentiles* 7.32) and, above all, the *scabellum*, a loud percussion instrument made of wood or metal and attached to the foot of some of the musicians,[18] the so-called *scabellarii* or *scabillarii*.[19] They operated it by stamping their foot to the ground (*Dance* 2 and 68; cf. *Dance* 63 and 83),[20] an absolutely vital (yet much maligned)[21] component of the whole event, since it helped preserve the rhythm for singers, players and, of course, the dancer himself (see Libanius, *Oration* 64.97).

Now, as already hinted in the Introduction, describing pantomime as simply 'corporeal dramaturgy' or 'silent exposition' (*expositio tacita*, in Cassiodorus, *Various Letters* 4.51.8), without further explanation, is severely misleading because verbal narrative, even if not directly associated with the *orchêstês* himself, was also an integral part of the performance. Lycinus, the pantomime lover in Lucian's *On the Dance*, informs his interlocutor that, in the genre's early days, dancing and narrative were so closely interwoven that 'the pantomimes themselves both sang and danced'. It was thought necessary to end that practice only at a later stage: as the heavy panting resulting from their physical exertion 'disturbed their singing', 'it seemed better that vocal accompaniment should be provided to the dancers by others' (*Dance* 30). Pantomime dancing, then, should not be confused either with classical ballet, which has renounced the spoken word, or with some forms of modern dance, where not even a specific story-line exists, since all that matters is the powerful images created by the dancer's body. In a spectacle that aimed to enact stories from the treasure trove of (predominantly) tragic myth,[22] narrative was of paramount importance in the channel of communication between the stage and its addressees. As Lycinus puts it, the dancer 'promises to demonstrate (*deixein*) by means of movement (*kinêmasi*) that which is being sung (*ta aidomena*)' (*Dance* 62).

Verbal accompaniment took the form of a libretto, a text specifically composed (occasionally by an eminent poet) for pantomime performances. Its lyrics, set to music, were sung sometimes by a solo singer,[23] at other times by a chorus, and were occasionally disparaged for their low musical quality[24] or considered (predominantly by the Church Fathers)[25] partly responsible for the moral pollution emanating from the stage. Encomiastic voices, on the other hand, praised the chorus' richly textured vocalism and its ability to sing rhythmically in pleasing unison (*Dance* 63, 68, 72).[26] Apart from the choir, the pantomime was occasionally supported by the clear, melodious voice (*Dance* 68) of a secondary performer, a non-dancing actor (*hypokritês*, e.g., *Dance* 68), called upon to incarnate the minor figures of the myths enacted,[27] such as Odysseus, opposite the dancer's 'mad Ajax' (*Dance* 83), Ninus, opposite the dancer's Semiramis, or Metiochus and Achilles accompanying the dancer's Parthenope and Deidameia respectively (Lucian, *The Mistaken Critic* 25).[28]

Whether the libretto was usually laconic or detailed we have no means of telling. Besides, no contemporary source exists to illustrate the symbiosis of verbal and non-verbal action in pantomime performances. It is a fairly safe inference, however, that if narrative and dance were 'accomplices' in the creation of meaning, they had to be synchronised in a judicious way, otherwise the total effect would be marred. Just as Quintilian (*Training* 11.3.67) regards the dissonance between facial expression, gestures and speech as a major trap for the orator, depriving eloquence of both authority and credibility, Seneca (*Letter* 121.6) remarks that 'skilled dancers' (*saltandi peritos*) elicit admiration because their gestural discourse 'keeps up with the speed of the verbal narrative'.[29] It seems that an important element in the collaborative effort of word and movement, verbal and somatic action, was their skilful unfolding *pari passu*.[30]

However, even when the verbal and the visual succeeded in producing that much coveted harmony which rendered verbal discourse corporeal and bodily action textual, they did not carry equal weight in the performative event. Although verbal narrative was a powerful cementing force binding together the disparate performative elements and providing the spectacle's logic on an intellectual level, the chief unifying factor was the dancer's constantly evolving, self-creating body. Libanius could not have made it any clearer that the narrative was a subordinate element, ancillary to the dancer's own display of virtuosity – the linchpin upon which the show's success or failure rested:

> For we do not come (to the theatre) to listen and pay attention to noble songs ... but we only insist on this much, that the verbal element supports the dancer's figures (*hypêretêsai tên phônên tois schêmasi*). For it is not the dancing that is made complete by means of the songs, but the songs have been created for the sake of the dance. And it is by the beauty and shameful ugliness of the dance that we judge the day, not by the words or the rhythms of the songs (Libanius, *Oration* 64.88).[31]

In pantomime performances, then, the principal medium of communication was bodily eloquence, a system of signification in its own right, which privileged the physical embodiment of thought and feeling. For this reason, it seems to have been a clever virtuosic move on a pantomime's part to perform his role without any verbal or other accompaniment, simply by trying to affect the viewer through the 'articulate silence' (*Greek Anthology* 9.505, 18) of his gestures, steps and movements. Thus, for Libanius, it is almost part of the course in pantomime performances to stop the voice of the chorus in order to 'instruct the viewer to grasp the plot by means of gestures' (*Oration* 64.113).

As for Lucian, he too tells the story of the Cynic philosopher Demetrius, who criticised the dancer as a mere appendage to the electrifying accessories of the performance (the instrumental music, the melodious singing, the stamping of the feet and the luxurious clothing), but was finally won over when a dancer performed for him pure, elemental dance, unencumbered by either instruments or song:

> having ordered the stampers and pipe-players and the chorus itself to be silent, he danced, entirely by himself, the adulterous liaison of Aphrodite with Ares, Helios disclosing their secret and Hephaestus laying his trap and catching them both, Aphrodite as well as Ares, in bonds, and each and every one of the gods who came upon them; (he portrayed) Aphrodite overcome by shame and Ares cowering and begging for mercy, and everything that belongs to this story, in such a way that Demetrius, exceedingly pleased with what was being performed, lavished on the dancer this mighty important praise. For he raised his voice and shouted out loud: 'I hear, man, the acts you are performing; I don't merely see, but you seem to me to be talking with your very hands (*tais chersin autais lalein*)' (*Dance* 63).

A pantomime could boast of having reached ideal gestural 'clarity' (*saphêneia*) if all his figures had been conveyed intelligibly, 'having no need of any interpreter': he who watches a pantomime must 'understand the mute and hear the dancer, who does not articulate a single sound' (*Dance* 62). One thinks of Quintilian's observation that 'often the dance[32] is understood and works upon the feelings independently of spoken words' (*Training* 11.3.66), as well as of Augustine's remark that the dumb and the pantomimes (*histriones*) 'signify by means of gestures, without words, not only the things which can be seen but more besides, and almost everything we speak of' (*Concerning the Teacher*, 7.19). The forceful impact of the dancer's silent eloquence on the popular subconscious can be gauged from Artemidorus' 'reading' of the dream of the dancing child: it 'indicates that it will grow up to be both deaf and dumb, so that it will communicate by means of gestures whatever it wishes to signify' (*Interpretation of Dreams* 1.76).

§2. Speaking hands[33] and talking limbs: the corporeal eloquence of pantomime dancing

Our sources are unanimous about the pantomime's ability to 'speak', 'display', 'demonstrate' or even 'write'[34] with his hands. The inexhaustible variety of Greek and Roman myths that formed his performative repertoire would come to life through the 'speaking... silence' (*Greek Anthology* 9.505, 18)[35] of 'fingers fitted with a tongue',[36] 'palms that take the place of a mouth' (Nonnus, *Dionysiaca* 7.21), and 'multiply expressive hands' (*Greek Anthology* 16.290, 6).[37] Besides, although his art resided primarily in his ability to 'explain words with his hands'[38] his corporeal language was much more all-embracing. Possessing 'as many tongues as limbs' (Anonymous, *Latin Anthology*, I.1 [Shackleton Bailey] 100, 9), the pantomime communicated 'through nod,[39] leg, knee, hand and spin' (Sidonius Apollinaris, *Poem* 23.270). Every single part of the body, down to 'the clenched fingers of the hand and the nerves and veins which are affected along with them (*sympathounta*)' (Plotinus, *Enneads* 4.4.34), had something to contribute to the overall effect.[40] We even hear of the dancer's meaningful use of his eyes,[41] a piece of information which makes sense only in those cases where the dancer would not have been wearing a mask.

Exactly how the pantomime's body signified the vast array of human and divine characters, animals, events, and even objects of inanimate or sentient nature required by the narrative remains a great puzzle. Theoreticians of the dance and semioticians of gesture have isolated a variety of representational strategies, the commonest being straightforward imitation: the performer aims to portray his object realistically, so that he kneads and moulds his body in the total likeness of whatever image he wishes to portray. As Socrates and his interlocutor agree in Plato's *Cratylus*, if one needed to indicate a galloping horse or any other animal without the use of language, there would be no other way of doing so, apart from making one's body and gestures 'as similar as possible' to those belonging to the object of one's imitation (*Cratylus*, 423a).

Undoubtedly direct corporeal imitation would have been the elemental core of ancient pantomime, 'a science of *mimesis*' (*mimêtikê ... epistêmê*) (Lucian, *Dance* 36), practised by an 'imitative' (*mimêtikos*) agent (*Dance* 62; cf. ibid., 19), who can 'fashion himself into everything by means of his dance' (Plotinus, *Enneads* 6.1.27) and 'takes his name from multifarious imitation' (Cassiodorus, *Various Letters* 4.51.9; cf. *Dance* 67). Lucian even introduces an additional level of *mimesis*, by claiming that contemporary pantomimes 'imitate' (*mimoumenous*) the legendary Proteus,[42] who

> was able to mould himself into any shape (*pros panta schêmatizesthai*) and transform himself, so that, in the intensity of his movement, he could imitate even the liquidity of water and the sharpness of fire, as well as the fierceness of a lion and the rage of a leopard and the vibrations of a tree, and, in a word, whatever he might wish (to represent) (*Dance* 19).[43]

In practice, isolating and projecting the most characteristic properties of a role – swiftness and lightness for Procne changed into a bird, sinuous motion for Cadmus as a snake, the rigidity of tree trunks for a metamorphosed Daphne, the stillness of stones for a petrified Niobe – must have been a fundamental exercise in the pantomime's choreography, insofar as his art consists in 'representing' (*paristas*) 'in and by himself' (*en hautôi*) the entire gallery of characters who populate the Greek mythical repertoire (Libanius, *Oration* 64.116). In addition, a pantomime may well have found himself creating corporeal metonyms in order to express contiguous experiences (signifying, for example, a battle or a war by means of a violent, warlike dance), or adopting a highly symbolic corporeal vocabulary in order to express more abstract concepts, as Lycinus claims with respect to the mysticism enshrined in Egyptian tales (*Dance* 59).

Nevertheless, even if we could somehow tap the performative logic or reconfigure the mechanics of the dancing star's somatic transformations, there would still be unmapped territory ahead. How did the dancer 'translate' the aural into the visual, the libretto's word into the corporeal 'writing' of his voiceless limbs? Once again, Apuleius' description painfully excites our curiosity. How was Minerva able, simply by means of menacing glares, tossings of the head, and rapid, contorted gestures, to indicate to Paris that, 'if he were to assign to her the victory in the contest over beauty, he would become, through her assistance, courageous and famous on account of trophies gained in war' (*Metamorphoses* 10.31)? Or how exactly did the 'effort of her arms' convey Venus' promise that, if proclaimed victorious, Paris would acquire a bride equal in beauty to herself (*Metamorphoses* 10.32)? Only one short narrative among the extant sources addresses such matters in a theoretical, self-conscious way. Here is Macrobius (*Saturnalia* 2.7.12-15), on the antagonism between the famous Pylades (I) (see Chapter 1) and his pupil turned 'equal' and 'rival', Hylas:

> Hylas one day was performing a dramatic dance, the closing theme of which was *The Great Agamemnon* and by his gestures he represented his subject as a man of mighty stature. This was more than Pylades could stand, and from his seat in the pit he shouted: 'You are making him merely tall, not great'. The populace then made Pylades perform the same dance himself, and, when he came to the point at which he had found fault with the other's performance, he gave the representation of a man deep in thought, on the ground that nothing became a great commander better than to take thought for all (trans. Davies 1969).

Even within the relatively unified performative tradition represented by a master and his pupil, then, diametrically different approaches to the method of translating from verbal to corporeal narrative can be seen. Pylades decides to convey the 'character' and unlock the deeper meaning of the verbal text. In this respect, he proves himself equal to the good and sensible orator, who, in Quintilian's view (*Training* 11.3.89), should adapt his gestures to fit his thought, rather than his actual words, a practice attributed even to the 'more dignified' among the stage-performers (cf. Chapter 9§2). Hylas' performative choice, on the other hand, consists in movements which translate the text 'literally' into corporeal images, a tactic most typical of a stage-actor, if we believe the contemptuous remarks of generations of orators practising in Rome. Cicero deprecates precisely that 'stagey gesture' of reproducing the words, instead of conveying the general idea and overall spirit of what is said (*On the Orator* 3.220), while Quintilian (*Training* 11.3.88) pours scorn on those who 'signify things by means of imitation', as people do, for example, when indicating a sick man by imitating the doctor's feeling of the pulse, or a lyre-player by shaping the hands as if they were plucking the strings. Quintilian's frame of reference here is probably the mime, but it is perfectly conceivable that dancers impersonating, say, Apollo, would signal to the audience the god's identity by miming the action of lyre-playing (as the twentieth-century choreographer George Balanchine did, in his *Apollo*). However, if translation from the aural to the visual was a contentious issue, whatever pertains to the relevant debates eludes us. All we can do is be content with the assumption that a truly spellbinding performance presupposed both a narrative providing the overarching framework for bodily excellence, and the display of that excellence in a way closely supportive and illustrative of the sung and spoken word.

Finally, how did the dancer give life to the *fabula*'s fictional universe, its spatial geography? We saw earlier in this chapter that backdrop painted scenery, set, and props must have been among the variables of the production, but, as I have argued elsewhere,[44] the sense of an on-stage fictional place and the particular spatial coordinates of the libretto's mythical world were much more likely to emerge from the currents of energy flowing from the pantomime's body and the 'drawings in space' executed by his nimble limbs and eloquent fingers. This metaphor I use with good reason, for one of the relatively more secure areas of knowledge about pantomime concerns its nature as 'pictorial' dramaturgy (see Lada-Richards 2004b).

Writing in the sixth century AD, Paulus Silentiarius distils a deceased dancer's art as his ability to fashion 'figures (*eikonas*) of men of old with silent gestures' (*Greek Anthology* 7.563, 2), while Plutarch, in the early second century, seems to understand pantomime as a spectacle that integrates the figurative arts, and refers to bodily configurations frozen in space and time, as if incorporated in a 'picture':

> ... when the dancers, having arranged their overall appearance (*schêma*) in the shape of Apollo or Pan or a bacchant, retain these attitudes, like figures in a painting (*Moral Essays* 747c).[45]

Similarly, for Libanius in the fourth century pantomime is a genre that exhibits and highlights both painterly and sculptural features. Having expressed his admiration of the dancer's speedy floating across the stage (*Oration* 64.117; cf. ibid., 28), Libanius draws our attention to the pantomime's transition from dizzingly swift movement[46] to a statue-like stillness that culminates in a veritable tableau vivant:

> What would someone admire more? The continuity of their many pirouettes or, after this, their suddenly crystallised posture, or the figure held fixed in this position? For they whirl round, as if borne on wings,[47] but conclude their movement in a static pose, as if glued to the spot; and with the stillness of the pose, the image presents itself (*hê eikôn apanta*) [i.e. takes shape, emerges] (*Oration* 64.118).

In a genre where the actor incarnates in turn all the characters in the dramatisation of a myth, it is very likely that carefully choreographed moments of suppressed action would also have served as pictorial 'transitions' between the roles of, say, Dionysus, Teiresias, Cadmus, the Messenger, and Agave, in a pantomime re-creation of the story told by Euripides' *Bacchae* (see *Greek Anthology* 16.289). Lying at the intersection of drama and the figurative arts, pantomime dancing seems to have been playing with the juxtaposition of energetic movement and statuesque configurations, as well as exploiting the fascination of frozen pictorialism for maximum dramatic effect.

The full meaning of the pantomime stage as 'gestural' space, that is, space created by the performer's own corporeal presence (Pavis 1980: 156), becomes evident yet again with the aid of Libanius' text:

For what painting, what meadow offers a sight more pleasant than pantomime and its dancer, taking the spectator round into groves and lulling him
to sleep under the trees, as he evokes herds of cattle, goats and sheep and
the shepherds on guard over the nurslings, some playing the pipe and others
the flute, as they are occupied with their diverse tasks? (*Oration* 64.116).

Not only does Libanius' dancer create with his own somatic versatility an
idyllic pastoral landscape, teeming with vegetable, animal and human life,
but the vividness (*enargeia*) of his bodily dramaturgy is such that it even
embraces and involves the viewer, plunging him into the middle of the
action.[48] Rather than watching from a distance, this deeply engaged
spectator makes his way *inside* the pictorialism of the stage-space, takes
an active part into its life, and positions himself at a variety of places in a
constantly unfolding narrative tableau, now ambling through groves, now
sleeping under trees. Independently of an illusionistic setting, which may
or may not be deployed on the stage, the fictional space of a pantomime
fabula seems to be taking shape in that magical grey area that lies
between illusion and reality, at the intersection of the dancer's mesmerising power to 'work' on the audience's 'imaginary forces' (cf. Shakespeare,
Henry V, Prologue 17-18), by means of expressive movement and suggestive figures, and the spectators' willingness to 'collude', 'piece out' the
visual 'imperfections' with their 'thoughts' (Shakespeare, *Henry V*, Prologue 23), so that the bare stage is transformed into the spectacle's
fictional milieu.[49]

§3. 'Body memory' and the question of codification

In Lucian's *On the Dance*, the ability to memorise the treasure-trove of
Greek myth and history down to the time of the Egyptian queen Cleopatra
is hailed as one of the dancer's most essential accomplishments (*Dance* 37;
cf. 36). But while Lucian's Lycinus discusses memorisation as a predominantly intellectual activity (in tandem with his attempt to emancipate
pantomime as a truly educational experience; see Chapter 6§2), social
anthropologists and performance theorists interested in dancing speak of
body memory and 'kinaesthetic' learning (cf. Chapter 9§1). After having
been 'embedded', by means of unremitting physical drills, in the dancer's
'performative, permanent body-consciousness', not only movement patterns but also their accompanying emotions are 'ready-at-hand to be used
"unthinkingly"' at any moment during a performance.[50] Similarly, the
ancient pantomime dancer must have had a 'corporeal' memory of thousands of myths and legends. We might even speculate that, like a Noh
dancer in the Japanese theatrical tradition, he possessed a relatively
limited vocabulary of 'building blocks or performance modules', which he
could then combine and re-combine with limitless variations, in accordance with well established artistic principles. Moreover, it is always

possible that, as in the practice of Noh, so in ancient pantomime the 'underlying rules' were 'subconsciously internalized during the course of training' instead of 'explicitly stated or taught'.[51] Thus the pantomime may have been working with something like a bodily analogue of the formulaic language of archaic epic: just as the epic poet combines his verbal and thematic formulae to compose an infinite number of new poems, the dancer creates each new embodied narrative by modifying a basic performative model. This is similar to classical ballet, where all the roles are created from combinations of a standard set of movements and positions (pirouettes, arabesques, etc.).

However, what is impossible for us to know with any certainty is the extent to which pantomime performances were codified in the ancient world, that is, the extent to which they may have constituted a more or less cryptic and intricate performance alphabet, fully decipherable only by the real connoisseurs of the overwhelmingly popular art. Our scraps of evidence here are conflicting and therefore inconclusive.

Writing at the turn of the fifth century AD, Augustine, bishop of Hippo, records that, when pantomimes first started to perform in his native Carthage (a time still alive, he claims, in the memory of the city's elders), people needed considerable help in order to understand the meaning of their dancing. A herald was engaged to acquaint the audience, by means of his public declarations, with the subject they were going to represent (*On Christian Doctrine* 2.25.38).[52] 'This is eminently credible', Augustine continues,

> for even now, if someone were to come into the theatre uninitiated into such trifles, unless he is told by someone else what those movements [of the dancers] signify, he gives his whole attention [to the spectacle] in vain (*On Christian Doctrine* 2.25.38).[53]

Pantomime spectating, according to this view,[54] requires some kind of code-apprenticeship, and cannot be put in the same category as the contemplation of pictures, statues and aesthetic artefacts. In such cases, Augustine opines, recognition of the subject represented, especially if it has been rendered by skilled craftsmen, is instantaneous: 'nobody errs, but no sooner does he see the likenesses than he recognises what things they are likenesses of' (*On Christian Doctrine* 2.25.39).

At the other end of the spectrum, Lucian's Lycinus emphasises the openness of the spectacle and its appeal to all. In *Dance* 64, as a proof of the lucidity and clarity of the art, we are treated to the story of the noble barbarian from Pontus, who, without any aid from the verbal accompaniment to the performance (for he was only half-Hellenised and could not comprehend the songs), understood every gesture of a leading dancer in Nero's reign. He even asked for him, as a take-away present, so that he might use him as an interpreter in his dealings with neighbours who did not speak the same language: 'this man will interpret every single bit for me through nods and gestures'. Elsewhere, Lycinus harps on the entire audience's responsiveness to the performance's moral content, and interprets collective tears at moments full of *pathos* as an 'indication of the theatre's familiarity with what is going on, as well as of every spectator's ability to recognise what is being displayed' (*Dance* 79). Whether collective understanding is assumed here as the direct result of the spectacle's accessibility or the consequence of the spectators' frequent exposure to a pantomimic repertoire is impossible to tell. In *Dance* 76, where Lycinus attributes exquisite connoisseurship to the 'exceedingly intelligent' and pantomime-honouring city of Antioch, the examples he adduces have very little to do with recognition of particular gestures or accurate readings of movement phrases and everything to do with the search for representational realism. One does not need any special knowledge of pantomime conventions to hiss a very small dancer incarnating Hector (rather than Astyanax), or joke that an excessively fat pantomime must beware of damaging the stage by his leaping.

On balance, any attempt to argue that pantomime was as 'closed' a spectacle as Augustine's passage in *Christian Doctrine* seems to imply would go against what we know about pantomime's breathtaking popularity throughout the empire for nearly six centuries. The wealth of traditional material absorbed by pantomime in the protracted period of its gestation (cf. Chapter 1) must have accounted for a basic level of accessibility. Moreover, it would be inconceivable that pantomime conventions would not have appropriated the rudiments of other gestural languages, 'open' and available to all, such as those of painting and sculpture (cf. Lada-Richards 2004b), for example, or even the sign language of formal oratory.[55] Undoubtedly, however, pantomime would also have developed its own 'idiolect', its own unique performance language, fully intelligible only to informed, competent viewers, whose expertise in the details of dance vocabulary is described (and obviously shared) by Plotinus:

> And the connoisseur of ballet (*ton empeiron orchêseôs*) can say that to fit a particular figure one limb is raised, another bent together, one is hidden, another degraded; the dancer does not choose to make these movements for no reason, but each part of him, as he performs the dance, has its necessary position in the dancing of the whole body (*Enneads*, 4.4.33; trans. A.H. Armstrong, Loeb 1984).[56]

The implication here is not that connoisseurs are the only ones able to decipher a pantomime performance, but that there is a pantomime-specific body of performance knowledge: its acquisition puts those who have managed to master it in a league of their own. Beyond a certain 'ground level' of accessibility, pantomime addicts repeatedly attending such performances would have been able to accumulate pantomime-related 'capital' over and above the occasional spectator (cf. Chapter 10§2). It was certainly that kind of pantomime fan, versed in the secrets of the art, who would have been able to distinguish, in performative terms, the conflagration of Semele from that of Glauce or the tecnophagy of Cronus from the same crime of Thyestes (see *Dance* 80). If a pantomime himself could be confused by similar choreographies, it is unlikely the wider audience would have known any better. Just as in our day everyone can enjoy a televised competition of, say, dancing on ice or rhythmic gymnastics, but only the expert commentators can discriminate corporeal minutiae or use specific technical language confidently, in ancient pantomime too, both enjoyment and a broad-base level of subject recognition may well have been the property of all.

§4. *Mirabilis ars*:[57] the wonders of pantomime dancing

What this chapter has so far thrust into relief is the sheer number of almost intractable questions which torment us on all sides. It is still possible, however, to pull our various threads together, in order to acquire an overall impression of the primary highlights of the dancer's performative technique.

(i) In the first place, the marvels of the pantomime's art must have resided in his own extreme plasticity and mimetic flexibility (cf. *Dance* 71). Although our sources convey the dancer's corporeal ductility in manifold ways, they harp consistently upon the fact that the pantomimic body changes the mode of its integration into its surrounding space at will: now 'loose' and gently undulating, 'pouring itself out'[58] in ripples of graceful vibrations, it can also be a 'mighty, solid mass', rooted firmly in the ground when movement fades into stillness (*Dance* 77). Lycinus sees the uneasy combination of 'strength' and 'liquidness' of limbs as an 'astounding' feature of the art, comparable to the (impossible) amalgamation of Heracles' brawn and Aphrodite's daintiness in a single human body (*Dance* 73).[59]

(ii) A talented performer on the pantomime stage would have been able to captivate his viewer by means of his ability to create 'character' (*êthos*) as well as 'passion' (*pathos*) (see primarily *Dance* 35, 67). Skilful character portrayal must have been indispensable in those among the pantomimic *fabulae* where the realistic, evocative delineation of individual traits, habits and reactions was the linchpin of the show. It must have taken an exceptionally versatile pantomime, for example, to convey persuasively, through body eloquence alone, the clash of characters involved in the exposure of Aphrodite and Ares' adulterous liaison, the *fabula* whose main points are touched upon in *Dance* 63. And, although the majority of pantomime topics we know about today seem to presuppose the fully-fledged enactment of a 'myth with a plot', the pantomime exhibition briefly glimpsed in Nonnus (*Dionysiaca* 19. 210-18) foregrounds the dancer in his rendition of 'character sketches', as he impersonates the entire company of the immortals on Olympus, enjoying, cup after cup, the nectar drawn for their sake by either Ganymedes or Hebe.

Moreover, hand in hand with the fashioning of character goes the representation of emotion. Thus, in a highly polished epigram, Automedon praises a female pantomime's talent in conveying 'all shades of passion' (*hoti panta pathainetai*) (*Greek Anthology* 5.129); Arnobius (*Against the Gentiles* 4.35) rails against the dancing of 'Venus in love', complete with the expression of 'all the emotions of meretricious vile'; Claudian (*Against Eutropius*, 2.405) envisages the dancer as 'Hecuba in tears'; Manilius refers to him as absorbing in his limbs 'all manner of (mis)fortune' (*Matters of Astronomy*, 5.483) and, in an exceptionally nuanced funerary inscription (*IG* 14.2124), a dead pantomime is acclaimed for his ability to 'empathise with' (*sympaschôn*)[60] the characters brought to light in the course of his dancing.

We could justifiably surmise that a highlight of superior quality performances would have been the pantomime's ability to signify a series of *contradictory* emotions. Lycinus, for one, marvels at the excellent dancer's empathic versatility, as he is trained to evoke by means of a corporeal alphabet 'now someone in love, now someone in the grip of anger, this man caught up in a frenzy, another plunged in sorrow' (*Dance* 67).[61] The 'most incredible' part of his art resides in the fact that

> within the selfsame day, he displays himself now as Athamas in the throes of madness, now as a terrified Ino; at other times he is Atreus himself, then, a little while later (he becomes) Thyestes, then Aegisthus, or Aerope. And all these (characters) are (in reality) one man (*Dance* 67).

The ability to project 'character' and 'passion', however, must have been even more important in those instances where the dancer's change of character would not have been effected through the full-scale change of his mask. Apparently, it was also possible for the dancer to 'embed' secondary roles into the flow of his primary impersonation, so that, as Libanius puts it, the audience would be both able to visualise and thrilled to recognise 'Poseidon by way of Athena, and Athena by way of Hephaestus, Hephaestus by way of Ares, Ganymedes through Zeus, and Paris through Achilles' (*Oration* 64.113).

It is precisely this notion of a single body split into a multiplicity of characters emerging *from* and *through* each other in succession that links the ancient pantomime's metamorphic skills with the idiosyncratic art of Emma Hart, mistress and later wife of the eighteenth-century eminent diplomat, art lover and collector Sir William Hamilton.[62] Lady Hamilton took the aristocratic courts of Naples, London, Paris, Geneva, Venice and Rome by storm, especially because of her portrayal, by corporeal means alone, of an entire repertoire of ancient sculptures: in her case, both characters as well as passions were created as a result of her smooth, uninterrupted passage from one pose and role to the next. According to eye-witness accounts, a large part of her success was due to the ingeniousness and skill with which she glided, without an entr'acte, between the various sculptural groups she was enacting, so that, for example, the frightening 'statue' of Medea about to slay her child would melt almost imperceptibly into a mourning Niobe, fighting over the same child 'with the rage of heaven'.[63] Novelli's full-figure drawings of Emma, which captured the essence of her plastic transformations much more vividly than the accomplished products of pictorial art, give us a sense of 'how a lying or kneeling pose could with the slightest movement turn Agrippina clutching the ashes of Germanicus into a drunken bacchante' (Jenkins and Sloan 1996: 258). Moreover, Emma drew gasps of admiration from her viewers for her ability to pass, often in rapid succession, 'from grief to joy, from joy to fear',[64] becoming by turns 'serious, sad, playful, ecstatic, contrite, alluring, threatening, anxious' (Goethe 1982: 208), a skill which brings her perfectly in line with Lycinus' pantomime in *Dance* 67 (quoted above).[65] As Mme Vigée-Le Brun, the fashion portraitist who painted her in Naples, wrote,

> With lively eye and scattered hair she presented a charming *bacchê*; then, suddenly, her face expressed sorrow, and one would see an admirable repentant Magdalene ... (Vigée-Le Brun 1989: 103).

(iii) There is good reason to believe that an important part of pantomime fascination lay in the delights of witnessing the very process of creation, as the dancer's body, in a state of perpetual flux, was continuously remoulded into new configurations. Those moments of 'transition', the mesmerising trajectory from one mythical figure to a series of others, or from one mode of existence to its diametric opposite, may have been more arresting than the finished artefact itself, the pantomime, that is, in the full likeness of the animate or inanimate model of his imitation. Sidonius Apollinaris, in his short yet invaluable excursus on the pantomime's art, provides a most interesting close-up of this sensational process of 'becoming'. We are told that, while impersonating Mars, the dancer gradually transforms himself into a boar,

> roughening his head and back with bristles, curving the smooth ivory upward from his shaggy jaws, and the hairy-backed monster is shown sharpening his up-bent weapons by diligent rubbing (*Poem* 23.291-5; trans. W.B. Anderson, Loeb 1936).

We can offer a real feast to our imagination simply by conjuring up the coiling, creeping, gliding motions of a Cadmus turning into a snake; feet taking root, and arms changing into branches to depict a Daphne slowly changing into a tree; fingers becoming set into hooves to bring Io the cow to life; or stones growing progressively soft, relinquishing their rigidity in order to re-enact Deucalion's re-population of the earth. Is pantomime the 'missing link'[66] in our appreciation of Ovid's literary treasures, in those parts of his *Metamorphoses* where the narrative describes in slow motion a character's somatic transformations?

(iv) The driving force behind the rhythms and figures of the dancer's corporeal imitation may well have been an overall aesthetic of performative verisimilitude. Libanius, who predicates a dancer's success on his ability to imitate, explains that, to be successful in *mimesis*, art must approximate nature, 'come as close to the real thing as possible' (*Oration* 64.62). A couple of centuries after Libanius' time, Choricius too comments on the pantomime's aspiration 'to persuade the audience in the theatre not that he is in the process of imitating others, but that *he really is by nature* (*pephyke*) the object of his imitation' (Choricius, *Oration* 21.1, p. 248 Foerster-Richtsteig).

Most of our informants comment on the pantomime's success in impersonating women, effeminisation by means of performance being the bane of Christians, moralists and satirists alike (see Chapter 5). For John Chrysostom, the pantomime is keen to transgress (*ekbênai*) his own gender, in order to transform himself, by means of facial expression, gesture, clothing and every means at his disposal, into the 'image' (*eikona*) of a 'tender virgin' (*PG* 57.426; cf. 49.195).[67] And yet, despite their biased rhetorical agenda, such texts do dovetail with purely aesthetic appreciations of the dancing soloist as a performer adept at choosing and highlighting the most characteristic properties of his stage-character, be it the rigidity of tree-trunks for the metamorphosed Daphne or the stillness of stones for the petrified Niobe.

Like pigment on the brush or marble under the chisel, the pantomime's body moulds itself into the likeness of the hero or heroine he imitates, the transformation being sometimes so complete that viewers may marvel at a Niobe carved out of stone or a Daphne made of wood:

> The roles of Daphne and of Niobe snub-nosed Memphis danced,
> Daphne as if he were wooden, Niobe as if he were of stone.
> Palladas, *Greek Anthology* 11.255[68]

Having coalesced so deeply with the object of its imitation, the dancer's body finds itself at variance with its own essence. The audience, correspondingly, faced with an aesthetic wonder wherein what 'seems' and what 'is' are almost impossible to disentangle, is entranced by the thrills of a naturalistic art. With their sensory faculties pleasantly hovering in the flickering twilight between belief and disbelief, where one fancies that the imitators really 'are' what they merely represent, pantomime viewers stand 'thunderstruck', their eyes 'deceived' (Columella, *On Agriculture* 1, Preface 15) by an art which elides the boundary between itself and nature. 'We seemed to see Iobbachus himself', asserts an anonymous epigram in the *Greek Anthology* (16.289, 1). Or, as Apuleius comments on the aesthetically pleasing mergings of signifier and signified, 'you might have said that those smooth, milk-white little boys were real Cupids, opportunely flown in from the sky or the sea' (*Metamorphoses* 10.32).

(v) As the greatest pantomimes were in cut-throat competition with each other for the favour of a volatile public, their dancing must have been full of figures and movements designed to highlight their dazzling balletic accomplishments. The genre's emphasis on the interior world of character and passion notwithstanding, a pantomime star's choreography cannot have failed to provide brilliant showpieces of pure dance, scintillating displays of virtuosity, with no direct point of contact with the story and with the sole aim of eliciting applause. Part of the difficulty of such a form of dancing must have resided in the need to present the most intricately woven gestural architecture in a way that would appear flowing, effortless and natural.

(vi) Finally, pantomime was not just about movement, but also about the pictorial quality of movement held in abeyance. Whether the dancer's statuesque configurations of which Libanius speaks (above, §2) formed themselves with such frequency as to make his performance 'a perpetual succession of striking pictures', as was said in nineteenth-century England of Edmund Kean's Richard the Third (see Hazlitt 1930-4: vol. 5, 184), we cannot tell. With the aid of Plutarch and Libanius (above, §2), however, we can easily imagine that one of the high points of pantomime entertainment would have consisted in watching the dancer's flowing movement stilled for a second, melding imperceptibly with its surrounding space, then artfully resumed. Punctuating the narrative continuum at the appropriate junctures, those static spatial compositions of compressed narrative would have been vital in eliciting affective audience response, especially the voyeurism of male spectators.

To conclude: our rare glimpses into 'pantomime in action' lead us to visualise a display of exceptional precision, dexterity, and agility, offered by a human body trained to respond with marvellous plasticity to the requirements of the diverse reincarnations inscribed in the mythical plots. As an artist controls the clay under his fingers, rounds a hip, slopes a shoulder, folds an arm, until the sculpture truly represents its model, so the accomplished pantomime would have been taught how to discipline every limb, control the flesh down to the most imperceptible quiver, guide the face (when maskless) through successive tides of passion, until his body language would answer to his inner world and that inner world would find itself in full accord with the dramatic character created. Combined with the virtuosic brilliance of pure dance, the naturalistic expressiveness of gestural and body language must have produced a truly haunting spectacle. It is now time, however, to turn our attention to the political and social aspects of pantomime dancing, that is, to pantomime as a socially 'embedded' art.

4

Pantomimes and their Body 'Politic'

We tend to imagine dance as a quintessentially apolitical domain, operating through pure bodily configurations, divorced from debates and conflicts over authority and power, and insulated from political anxieties or social ferments. In fact, nothing could be further from the truth. An ever-growing body of research into the anthropology of dance is shedding light on the many ways in which human movement, such as that expressed in dancing, becomes embroiled in a range of cultural expressions, including politics, national identity and relations of power between different social groups.[1] Dance may *appear* apolitical but, like all performative expressions, it neither exists nor develops in splendid isolation from broader concerns located outside its artistic realm. Its politics may be 'invisible', but they run through the dancer's very body (see Washabaugh 1996: 1), so that dance styles can be embodiments of political positioning, and movement vocabularies promote political agendas by physical (albeit no less effective) means.

Thus, in the Renaissance and early baroque periods, court ballets in France expressed the nobility's resistance to an increasingly absolutist monarchy, while in early twentieth-century Spain, flamenco-style dancing was associated with resistance to Franco's dictatorship.[2] As for the National Socialist Party in Germany, immediately after its accession to power in 1933 it systematically appropriated the post-modernist and liberalist dance that was known as *Ausdruksdanz* (Expression dance) in the inter-war years, forced it into an alliance with the Ministry of Culture's nationalist ideals (significantly renaming it 'German Dance') and twisted it into an organ of political propaganda. Eminent dancers complied, like Mary Wigman, who, 'from 1934 to 1936 ... received Nazi subsidy to choreograph group dances, staging the body politic envisioned by fascist ideology' (Manning 1993: 170). The overarching ideals of the Nazi party were now expressed in bodily form by means of choreographic patterns that dramatised the individual's subordination to the group, while Wigman's choreography for the 'opening-night spectacle for the 1936 Berlin Olympic Games explicitly celebrated Olympic symbolism and implicitly glorified the presence of the Führer, who reviewed the spectacle from the stands' (Manning 1993: 3).[3] During the Cold War, dance intersected with diplomacy and played an important part in the fashioning of cultural images on the part of the USA as well as the USSR. To the technical sophistication and complexity of the Bolshoi ballets, America counter-posed all kinds of popular dance as well as small dancing companies like Martha Graham's, in order to showcase the individual artist's freedom in the United States. Dance was treated as a source of international power, almost on an equal footing with military might and economic productivity (see Prevots 1998). Even heavily marginalised forms of dancing, such as the lambada or break-dancing, become a means of articulating political attitudes and social affiliations (cf. Desmond 1993-4), a way for the body itself to speak 'its pain, its oppression, its needs and dreams' (Levin 1990: 232).

§1. Pantomime politics?

The dance's subliminal yet potent relationship to politics and power is also the story of ancient pantomime dancing. The most overt manifestation of pantomime's political involvement was the notorious case of the so-called pantomime riots, whose complexity and changing nature over the centuries precludes even a cursory discussion here.[4] Nevertheless, disturbances revolving around pantomime dancers (whether instigated by the competitive element built into the genre from the start and the concomitant animosity between the rival dancers' supporters, or tangled up with imperial policies, often even directly concerning the provision of public entertainment in Rome) demonstrate that pantomime performances did matter on the political front. From the reign of Tiberius onwards, they were feared by many an emperor as explosive sites where potentially dangerous counter-narratives could be spun and spiral out of control, especially with respect to public order and morality.[5] And by the time of John Chrysostom and Libanius in the fourth century AD, what was originally a 'fan club', 'whose business it was to stimulate and maintain applause for theatrical performers', had acquired a formidable political role, seeking to guide and channel political feeling, put pressure upon officials by means of well-rehearsed slogans chanted in the theatre, and ultimately provide professional leadership for political demonstrations (Browning 1952: 16-17).

Later developments aside, pantomime did matter politically from the time of its Roman (re)birth, for the craze for dancers was never the exclusive vice of mindless, impressionable and volatile masses, as some of our sources sneeringly imply (cf. Chapter 9§3). Base-born and aristocrats alike were wholly captivated by star dancers.[6] Admiring and envying them (Plutarch, *Moral Essays* 473b), supporting pantomime troupes on their estate,[7] and re-enacting their voluptuousness on private stages 'throughout the city' (Seneca, *Natural Questions* 7.32.3),[8] senators[9] and knights behaved (in the eyes of their less enthusiastic peers) as if they were 'the pantomimes' slaves' (Seneca, *Letter* 47.17).

Tacitus' account of the measures taken in 15 AD by Tiberius to limit expenditure on public entertainments and check partisan violence related to pantomime performances (*Annals* 1.77.4) is very informative with respect to the upper-class practices he wished to eradicate. Senators were in the habit of visiting the dancers' dwellings and knights used to take part in their processions when they appeared in public (cf. Pliny the Elder, *Natural History* 29.5.9) – undoubtedly hoping that an appearance in the entourage of the day's greatest stars would boost their own public image. In that same period of Tiberius' reign, moreover, pantomimes seem to have had a staunch ally in the imperial court itself, namely the emperor's son, the dissolute Drusus, whose backing may well have been responsible for the minimal impact the legal measures of 15 AD had on pantomime-related disorder.[10] But the political roots of pantomime went even deeper than one particular supporter, no matter how prominent, in the imperial court, for the dancers seem to have enjoyed close personal bonds of friendship with both senators and knights.[11] As Slater (1993, 1994), expanding on the seminal work of Morel, has argued, it was especially those belonging to the latter group, and in particular the young men (*juvenes*) among the equestrians who were most likely to find their path intersecting with that of pantomime dancers. How?

Bringing social disgrace (*ignominia*) upon oneself voluntarily through condemnation in a public court, so that one would be expelled from the upper orders and hence acquire the freedom to perform for fame and money on the professional stage, was one of the tactics of the Roman aristocracy of rank that went long undetected, until specific legislation (in several waves) was brought in to curb it (unsuccessfully).[12] Suetonius (*Life of Tiberius* 35.2) believes that Tiberius' harsh measures of 19 AD [13] were specifically aimed at 'aristocratic renegades' (Edwards 1997: 89), the most profligate equestrian and senatorial youths who, 'contrary to the dignity of the order to which they belonged, were appearing on the stage or at games or were pledging themselves to fight as gladiators' (*Senatorial Decree from Larinum*, 5; trans. Levick 1983). Equestrian stage-dancers had actually made their appearance as early as 23 BC at the games put on by Augustus' nephew Marcellus (Dio Cassius, *Roman History* 53.31.3), just at the time when pantomime was taking flesh as a new form of entertainment thanks to the talent of Bathyllus (I) and Pylades (I).[14] Because of their equestrian provenance, such dancers contributed immeasurably to the spectacle's politicisation, especially by means of their complex interactions with the various 'Associations of Young Men' (*Collegia Juvenum*) in the auditorium, associations presided over by prominent young knights and, in their turn, lending their support to individual pantomimes' fan clubs – such as, for example, the 'Paridiani' and 'Anicetiani' (supporters of Paris and Actus Anicetus respectively), known to us from graffiti in Pompeii (see Franklin 1987). In this respect, then, applause for the pantomime's undulating body, expertly orchestrated by claqueurs whipping up support for a particular dancer, had less to do with proficiency in dancing and much more to do with an entire nexus of tensions and alliances, a 'network of relationships' which 'bound together the performers and their friends in the front fourteen rows and the orchestra' (Slater 1994:143). Besides, as Edwards (1993: 133) notes, 'by becoming an actor (or a gladiator) a Roman senator or equestrian was questioning the value of the official hierarchy the emperor controlled, even questioning the emperor's authority to control it' (cf. Edwards 1997: 89).

Of even greater consequence for pantomime's political entanglements may well have been the common athletic ideals binding gymnasium-trained youths with pantomime dancers. Under the increasing influence of Greek practices, upper-class youths had the opportunity to learn (as amateurs, of course) in the *gymnasia* rhythmical and callisthenic dance exercises similar to those constituting the staple of pantomime training. From there it was but a short step for the willing and talented upper-class man to seek perfection in the realm of dancing eloquence and bodily grace, as opposed to building the masculine body required by the Roman army. This seems to have happened, for example, with Titus' childhood boy-friends, 'so proficient in dancing that they later took to the stage', i.e. became pantomimes by profession (Suetonius, *The Deified Titus* 7.2). In any case, having not only tasted but even possibly acquired a taste for pantomime skills (cf. Chapter 6§4, on *cheironomia* in the *palaestrae*), privileged youths felt a natural closeness to pantomime performers, the affinity between the two groups sometimes materialising in exceedingly eloquent social gestures, such as the acceptance of pantomimes into 'youth associations', organisations whose various social privileges were jealously guarded.[15]

Moreover, the fate of pantomime became entwined from the start with the very heart of imperial power, as the dancers became the lovers of the most powerful at court, starting with Maecenas' notorious infatuation with Bathyllus, one of the reasons, according to Tacitus, why Augustus was especially tolerant of the new genre.[16] The dancer's erotic allure (see Chapter 5§2) was directly convertible into political capital, whose highly prized 'value' did not escape the arrows of contemporary satire. The pantomimes' fixed presence in the close company, villas, courts and even beds of Roman dignitaries informs the claim in Juvenal's *Satire* 7.88-92 that the road to imperial favour passes directly through the pantomimic body:

He's (i.e. the pantomime Paris II)[17] the one who generously hands out positions in the army and puts the gold ring on the fingers of bards after just six months. A dancer gives what the great men won't. ... It's *Pelopea* that appoints prefects and *Philomela* tribunes[18] (trans. S. Morton Braund, Loeb 2004).

Although it is unlikely that any Paris or Pylades ever wielded such power in imperial Rome, Procopius in sixth-century Constantinople explicitly remarks (*Secret History* 9.5) that it was directly in the gift of a top pantomime (or rather imperial ballet-master) to appoint or not appoint someone to a job; in the case Procopius discusses, the job is bear-keeper to the faction of the Greens (see Cameron 1976: 220).

Last but not least, it should be borne in mind that the pantomime's very body was an excellent (because highly visible) site for the emperor's display of the asymmetry of power between himself and even the most highly acclaimed among his subjects. So, for example, Augustus was quick to inflict humiliating bodily punishment on pantomimes perceived to have defied authority,[19] while Caligula, himself excessively fond of 'the theatrical acts of dancing and singing',[20] proclaimed an emperor's freedom from all rules by openly indulging his own libidinous desires, infamously aroused by Mnester:[21]

> He used to kiss the pantomime actor Mnester even in the middle of the games. And if, when Mnester was performing, anyone made the slightest noise, he had him dragged from his seat and flogged him himself (Suetonius, *Life of Caligula* 55.1; trans. Edwards 2000).

Abstention from the pantomime body, correspondingly, was meant to be constructed as an act of responsible statemanship. Titus, for example, upon his accession to the throne, ceased even to watch the public performances of his boyhood friends who had made the transition to pantomime professionalism (Suetonius, *The Deified Titus* 7.2).

The last word in this section belongs to anecdotes – not a reliable source about what really happened, to be sure, yet a window on what people in the teller's own world thought *could* plausibly have happened (cf. Edwards 1993: 11), and hence a powerful indicator of wider cultural perceptions. Thus, according to a story related by Dio Cassius and Macrobius, the most acutely conscious of pantomime's political import seem to have been the pantomimes themselves. When Pylades (I) was rebuked by Augustus, on account of the troubles caused by his rivalry with Hylas (or Bathyllus), he boldly replied:

> 'It is to your advantage, Caesar, that the people wear themselves out wrapped up in our affairs' (Dio Cassius, *Roman History* 54.17.5).

Just as in eighteenth-century Britain balls and masquerades and tales about them could be said to occupy 'people's thoughts full as much' as politics and national events,[22] *pantomania* was credited with such a hold on people's minds that it could even deflect their attention from serious political concerns (therefore becoming all the more intensely political through its seemingly de-politicising power). Dio couples the anecdote with his belief that the crowds turned a blind eye to the strictness of Augustus' moral legislation because the emperor, alongside allowing greater expenditure on public festivals, restored to them the exiled Pylades (*Roman History* 54.17.4). What Pylades (I) pointed out to Augustus,[23] then, was pantomime's formidable diversional quality, its ability to collude subliminally with the ruling classes by helping quash public dissatisfaction with imperial measures. Far from constituting a self-contained aesthetic realm, pantomime was the kind of political capital an emperor could neglect only at his peril.[24]

§2. The 'embodied' politics of pantomime dancing

If pantomime-related troubles and the enigmatic lure of pantomime *infamia* politicised the genre, so did the lustre of pantomime glory, which can be best recaptured with the aid of a substantial corpus of inscriptions, recording in a factual and formal manner the privileges extended to the most popular performers by an impressive list of cities.[25] It is primarily on the basis of such non-literary, official documents that the 'market value' of successful pantomimes appears staggering, especially in the East of the empire.[26] Invariably granted honorary citizenship and/or bouleutic status, the erection of honorific statues and sometimes *proxenia* (public guest-friendship) or even *ateleia* (freedom from civic obligations),[27] they emerge as individuals commanding extraordinary wealth[28] and power, and as holders of municipal offices, priesthoods and much-coveted honorary posts. If their victory was in the extra-prestigious category of the 'sacred and iselastic contests', their 'package of honours' even included 'the right to a cash pension and a triumphal procession (*eiselasis*), the financial burden in both cases ... falling on the home-cities of the *hieronikai*', the 'sacred victors' (Spawforth 1989: 193). It would be safer, however, to assume that the upward mobility Dio Cassius (*Roman History,* 78.21.2-4) records for the pantomime Theocritus (II), the imperial freedman promoted 'from a slave and a dancer ... to commander of an army and a prefect' (cf. Chapter 10§1), was relatively rare.

The professional pantomime's body emerges as 'body politic' par excellence on several counts. As the star attraction of the innumerable agonistic festivals (of international, provincial or local status),[29] processions, communal celebrations and public dinners which punctuated urban life under Roman rule even at the remotest fringes of the Greco-Roman world, a pantomime would be regularly hired to 'please' the crowds[30] with his unrivalled ability to offer *psychagôgia* and aesthetic delight (*apatê*).[31] But within the value-system of a fiercely competitive world, where wealthy local notables struggled for enhanced status and cities vied for increased standing against their neighbours, the provision of a glittering festival with all the trimmings of carnivalesque and fashionable displays – all the 'hired performances' which 'entertain the city', as a famous inscription from the Lycian city of Oenoanda puts it[32] – was one of the quickest routes for the attainment of recognition, power and prestige,[33] that is, precisely what a *philotimos* (covetous of honour) aristocrat and an ambitious city were bound to desire.

Being the first to display at the theatrical shows of one's native city the best and most fashionable spectacles (*ta prôteuonta ... akroamata*) in the entire province was prime cause for public commemoration, as we can see on an inscription from Aphrodisias honouring 'with the highest honours' an 'ambitious' and generous priestess of Hera.[34] More specifically, with explicit reference to pantomime, we can turn to an inscription from Lagina in Asia Minor recording the 'pious' and 'honour-loving' way in which a priest of Hecate and his mother performed their service to the goddess and the people. Their claim to honour is corroborated by the fact that they had 'hired a pantomime dancer for 6 days', a performer who pleased (*aresanta*) everybody, and whom they rewarded with a sum of money delivered in the theatre itself.[35]

On Italian soil one could hardly find a more revealing document than the funerary inscription of A. Clodius Flaccus (*CIL* 10.1074d; from Pompeii), a magistrate of the highest standing, who, on his tombstone, chose to highlight as a matter of pride the fact that the Apollonian games he financed in his first duoviral year included 'every entertainment and all the pantomimes and Pylades' (lines 6-8). Securing those pantomimes who had reached the apex of the performing hierarchy as prime entertainers in one's shows must have been a matter of the greatest urgency for the Roman aediles charged with the organisation of official games. With rapid promotion along the traditional *cursus honorum* often linked to the sponsorship of lavish spectacles,[36] the skilful pantomime, who helps make an event outstandingly memorable, becomes directly tied up with individual struggles for political advancement.

To turn the spotlight exclusively on the East of the empire, when we consider that the overall prestige accruing to the city hosting the event and the local benefactor who finances it is proportionately analogous with (inter alia) the event's duration and magnificence, as well as the number of spectators and the broadness of their geographical provenance,[37] a VIP dancer's ability to attract vast crowds from the corners of a province and beyond is not a trifling matter. With imperial festivals being prime avenues for élite self-fashioning and civic self-definition, the passionately adored and crowd-charming dancing body should be seen as an important factor in a never-ending political quest for influence and power. Besides, insofar as all agonistic festivals – both the 'sacred crown games', granted directly through imperial munificence, as well as the lower status, local 'prize games'[38] – 'formed the essential framework of the imperial cult' in the Roman cities and provinces (Price 1984: 102), the pantomime dancer of international renown was part of an event which led directly to the emperor's glorification. So, for example, a Greek inscription from the Lydian city of Thyatira honours the pantomime Paris (III), for during his stay in the city his dancing helped to 'adorn' the epinician feasts in honour of the co-emperors Marcus Aurelius and Lucius Verus.[39] And, to the extent that cities were engaged in an unremitting effort to outstrip each other in the founding of new festivals or the upgrading of existing ones as 'sacred', the pantomimes who graced such events were inevitably caught up in the maelstrom of civic contests for increased political, economic and cultural prestige. As Slater (1995: 290) writes, performers like the celebrated Tiberius Iulius Apolaustus 'were undoubtedly as important to representatives of the imperial cult as they were to the emperor'.

Of course, it cannot be stressed too strongly that in the Eastern part of the empire pantomime long remained peripheral to the agonistic programme of the great festivals.[40] Our earliest evidence of pantomime competitions can be dated to between 176 and 180 AD, most probably in connection with the sojourn of Marcus Aurelius and Commodus in Asia during the summer of 176.[41] To a significant extent, however, the lateness of official recognition is irrelevant, for the 'symbolic' capital enclosed in the dancer's body was the same even when that body was simply exhibited as a 'spectacle' (*akroama*), an appendage to the festival rather than an integral part of its agonistic kernel. One could reasonably argue that the dancer's body was all the more open to political appropriation when it was directly 'answerable' to the local notable hiring its performance and, presumably, reserving the right to request the dancing of those myths and legends which best served particular agendas, personal or even local.

In conclusion, then, despite its surface political detachment, pantomime dancing is a prominent example of 'embodied' politics: while verbalising stories essentially devoid of contemporary political content,[42] the pantomime's own body becomes an important instrument for the signalling, construction and enactment of social and political meaning. Moreover, insofar as they received the sponsorship of governors and rulers and were included (albeit relatively late) in the agonistic agenda of civic festivals, pantomime performances existed in tandem with dominant ideologies, and were integral to civic ceremonial as well as inextricably tangled up with imperial cult and social identity formation.

Pantomimes and their Body Dangerous

Let us take a momentary step back into the cultural tradition of Greek and Roman dancing. Greek culture was first and foremost a culture of *mousikê*, that almost untranslatable term which must be understood as the close-knit combination of instrumental music, poetic word and dance – in Greek mythical terms, the province of the Muses.[1] And as all significant private and public events, from weddings and funerals to the celebration of victory in war, were marked by choral performances in the Greek world, it is difficult to overestimate the irreducible centrality of dancing, especially in the form of collective, choral dancing, in the life of Greek cities from the archaic period onwards. Such was the importance of 'dance literacy' that the 'Athenian' in Plato could assert that lack of experience in choral dancing is tantamount to lack of education (*ho men apaideutos achoreutos*), while the educated man can be defined as the one 'adequately versed in choral dance' (*Laws* 654b). Preserving and transmitting the riches of collective memory, participation in choral dancing was 'both a principal means of education and the medium through which mortals can relate to the gods and affirm and share with each other the values of their society' (Bacon 1995: 14).[2] Besides, an education in dancing was not so much a matter of proficiency in graceful body movement, but a young boy's or girl's initiation into the entire complex matrix of social and cultural practices whose mastery would turn them into accomplished men and women (see Calame 1997: especially 222-38). In Rome, however, things were different. Despite the fact that, as we have seen, pantomime was warmly embraced by some of the foremost figures of Roman power, starting with Augustus and his closest entourage, there were fundamental problems for pantomime's neat assimilation into the Roman social fabric.

In the first place, the theatre itself did not have an easy relationship with Roman culture. Singled out by jealous guardians of cultural boundaries and indigenous morality as an 'imported licentiousness', it was feared as the abominable offshoot of foreign (Greek and Etruscan) decadence, which had the power to 'overthrow ancestral morality from its foundations', and cause the youth of Rome to degenerate into lovers of indolence and disgraceful erotic passion (Tacitus, *Annals* 14.20.4). As for actors, they too led an existence balanced on a razor-sharp divide between prejudice and admiration, hostility and utter fascination. Even though they clearly commanded the attention of the entire body politic, their own bodies bore the indelible brand of *infamia*, 'lack of public honour', and their social status was for all legal purposes equivalent to that of convicted criminals, soldiers dismissed from the army in disgrace, gladiators, prostitutes and pimps.[3] Not a propitious start for a new genre which inevitably became suspect on both counts, theatricality and Eastern provenance alike.

Secondly, although dancing, as we have already seen in Chapter 1, was part of a well-developed Roman ritual, ceremonial and entertainment tradition, it also carried a trail of negative associations: a fear of dancing as a symptom of and incitement to a corruption of cataclysmic proportions is very palpable within the context of traditional Roman *mores* and society. We need only to look into the Ciceronian corpus to get a flavour of what dancing could be made to symbolise in the generation before the Pyladean revolution took place. As Corbeill (1996: ch. 4 and 1997) has shown, moral profligacy, perverse sexuality and lust, diminished control over one's self and one's emotions belong to a broad conceptual matrix which ties dancing with all manner of evils that lie beyond the pale of social propriety. In Cicero's defence of Murena, for example, a speech of 63 BC, dancing is highlighted as the climax of debauchery (*On Behalf of Murena* 13), and glossed further as a vice which cannot exist in isolation but is inescapably attended by luxury, sensuality, lasciviousness and riotous behaviour – a dissolute and reprehensible life-style. Not surprisingly, an expertise in dancing, including the art of dancing naked at banquets, is also claimed to be a marker of Catiline's most intimate friends, gamblers, adulterers and lechers, protagonists, as Cicero puts it, in contests that pit justice, moderation, bravery, wisdom, and all the virtues, against injustice, intemperateness, cowardice, folly, and all the vices (*Against Catiline* 2.22-5).

The best insight into the uncertain cultural standing of dancing practices in Rome can be gained from the late fourth-century AD writer Macrobius, insofar as some of the interlocutors of the third book of his *Saturnalia* turn their gaze backwards to the period between the Second and Third Punic wars, a time of proverbially staunch morals. In a speech attributed to him by Furius Albinus in Macrobius' text, Scipio Africanus Aemilianus, the famous conqueror of Carthage, professes himself shocked at the sight of boys and even girls 'of good family' attending a dancing school 'in the company of effeminate fellows' (*cum cinaedulis; inter cinaedos*), and learning the kind of dances that would have been 'improper for a shameless little slave to dance' (*Saturnalia* 3.14.7). The noble families themselves, however, whose conduct sparked off Scipio's vociferous disapprobation, must have entertained completely different ideas as regards the role of dancing in the strategies of upper-class self-fashioning. Despite the stigma of incompatibility with desirable élite deportment, they clearly regarded excellence in dancing as the kind of kinaesthetic literacy from which their offspring, whether male or female, could not afford to be excluded. Within the fold of élite Roman morality itself, then, dancing was ambivalent coinage, *both* a potential source of social embarrassment, and therefore a 'vice' to be kept under control, *and* a highly prized cultural asset, most probably a way of demonstrating urban refinement and sophistication.[4]

Notwithstanding the fundamental differences between the Greek and Roman traditions vis-à-vis dancing, the story of pantomime's resounding success on *both* sides of the Mediterranean for a period of about six centuries is also the story of an uneasy, ambivalent affiliation to mainstream cultural norms and to the centres of political power. Throughout the empire's geographical territory, the privileged classes responded to pantomime with a mixture of fascination and outright hostility, and all shades of grey in between, so that the adulation and even fetishisation of the dancer went hand in hand with imperial edicts banning him from Rome and other major cities as well as with colourful calumniations of the genre, not only from the Christian pulpit but also from the pens of prudish moralists and snooty pagan intellectuals. This chapter, then, partners Chapter 4 by choosing a different point of entry into the world of pantomime dancing. This time we shall follow the thread provided by the hostile voice of Crato, the anti-pantomime interlocutor in Lucian's *On the Dance*, a dialogue which, while attempting to rebuff the major charges against dancing, inscribes – and thus offers invaluable insights into – some of the vital ingredients of anti-pantomime mentality.

§1. In search of pantomime's transgressiveness

Radically incommensurable evaluations of pantomime dancing are pitted against each other early on in Lucian's *On the Dance*. What is for Lycinus, the dialogue's pantomime addict, a performance full of clarity (*saphêneia*; *Dance* 36, 62, 64), celebrating rhythm, harmony and order (*Dance* 7, 72), is for his opponent Crato chaotic, meaningless, disorderly activity. Dissonant movements and random gestural articulations accompanied by the monstrous thumping of the feet (*Dance* 2) to wanton songs (*Dance* 2) amount to a performance alphabet in total disarray. The interweaving of diverse modes of representation (dancing, singing, instrumental music), praised by Lycinus as a rich and varied spectacle (*Dance* 68, 72), is for the sceptic a hybrid composition, devoid of refinement and unworthy of a self-respecting intellectual's attention (*Dance* 1-3). Moreover, what Lycinus celebrates as an arduously trained body, perfectly conditioned to appear decent, well-ordered and comely (*Dance* 29), appears to Crato's eyes unbridled and unmanageable, the filthy instrument of 'some noxious fellow' (*Dance* 5), whose depravity corrupts the theatre in its entirety, so that the body-politic itself is open to infection. Pantomime spectacles infest their viewers like a a disease (*Dance* 6), the infestation running so deep that those contaminated are oblivious to their own predicament:

5. Pantomimes and their Body Dangerous

By Heracles, how badly you have been affected, Lycinus, since you are not even ashamed of your deeds and sayings, but give the impression of being proud of them as well! And this is actually the most terrible thing, that you do not show me even a glimmer of hope that you may be cured, daring, as you do, to praise things that are so shameful and despicable (*Dance* 4).[5]

Most crucially, however, pantomime's enchantments are pervasive. Assailing the spectator's mind and eradicating his sense of separate identity, the dancer can sap that complete command over the self which befits a man of education and status (*Dance* 2-3) and ultimately drag the unsuspecting viewer all the way down to madness (*Dance* 5, 6).[6] Even a man 'who has been brought up with letters and holds moderate converse with philosophy' (*Dance* 2) can degenerate into an idle aesthete, happy to turn his back on intellectual labour and abandon himself to the allurements of pleasure:

So I, for my part, when I learnt that you are wasting your time on such spectacles, not only felt ashamed on your account, but also vexed at your sitting there unmindful of Plato and Chrysippus and Aristotle and getting treated like those who have their ear tickled with a feather (*Dance* 2).

The ignominy of pantomime seduction becomes all the more disturbing when the dancer's victim is of high intellectual calibre. Given that *pantomania* rivals not just the delights of philosophical discourse but also noble entertainments such as tragedy and comedy (*Dance* 2), the male who declares himself a pantomime addict displays a lack of discernment and sophistication serious enough to imperil his membership of the cultural élite.

For Crato, then, conversion into a lover of the dance entails a contemptible cultural leap in terms of gender, status, sanity of mind, and purity of intellect. It is up to the man of sense to guard against the lure of the theatrical, recoiling from such a spectacle with the same horror that makes the Euripidean Pentheus in the *Bacchae* cringe at the thought of wearing female garb:

May I never reach ripeness of years, if I ever endure anything of this kind, as long as my legs are hairy and my beard unplucked! For now, to be sure, I already pity you; to our sorrow, like a bacchant, you have gone completely out of your mind (*Dance* 5; trans. based on Harmon, Loeb 1936).

The spectacle a pantomime presents threatens to unman his male viewer, by dislocating him to the farthest possible extreme of socially acceptable male roles:

Beware, lest you become some Lydian woman or a bacchant, you, who were hitherto a man (*Dance* 3).

67

In sum, from the standpoint of a sceptic like Crato, pantomime viewing leads to a sweeping disempowerment of the spectator on a multiplicity of levels. Besides being feminine in gender, the pleasure one derives from the spectacle (cf. *Dance* 1) belongs to the realm of the mentally unhinged and the barbarian (*Dance* 3, 5, 6), and is culturally aligned with servility or, at the very least, unworthy of the status of a free-born male (*Dance* 2), whose recreational activities should be starkly divorced from the sensual and bodily element that pantomime dancing represents (cf. Chapter 9§3).

Crato's hostile voice is by no means a solitary one. His most powerful allies in decrying the pantomime are the Fathers of the Church, for whom the stage in general is 'the place where public morality prostitutes itself' (Novatian, *On the Spectacles* 6.2), 'the private home of unchastity, where nothing is deemed good, unless it is elsewhere judged unworthy of approval' (Tertullian, *On the Spectacles* 17). Pantomime dancing, in particular, 'a spring of licentiousness' and 'a net which ensnares boys in the ways of a vicious life' (Jacob of Serugh, *Homily* 3, F9v[b]; text in Moss 1935: 105), becomes synonymous with all-pervasive evil[7] and galloping decadence. 'And then, what a profound decline of morality', exclaims Cyprian, bishop of Carthage, 'what an incitement towards unchastity, what a nourishment for vices it is to become polluted by the pantomime's gestures':

> What is such a man[8] [i.e. the pantomime] incapable of recommending? He galvanises the senses, he sweetens the feelings, he takes by storm the steadfast conscience in a good man's breast (*To Donatus* 8).

The very vices bred inside the theatrical enclosure, where he reigns supreme, are so corrosive that no spectator (especially no woman) can remain pure (Cyprian, *To Donatus* 8). As Jacob of Serugh puts it, 'Who can bathe in mud without being soiled?' (*Homily* 5, F20r[a]).[9] The mere mention of pantomime dancers in casual conversation is a means of 'defiling one's hearing, corrupting one's soul, stirring one's nature up to frenzy, introducing into the mind every kind of wickedness through such discourse' (John Chrysostom *PG* 59.119). All in all, the verdict of the Church is scathing, for every single aspect of the pantomime's terrain, words and songs, clothes, movements and 'satanic gestures', the twisting of the dancer's limbs and the rolling of the eyes, alongside the flutes and pipes and the plays themselves with their (indecent) plots, are 'full to the brim with the worst kind of licentiousness' (John Chrysostom, *PG* 57.426).

Interestingly, although the harshest indictment comes from the quarters of the early Church, Christians find themselves in strange alliance with many a pagan intellectual in condemning spectacles and their pernicious effects on individual and public morals, as Tertullian observes (*On the Spectacles* 10).[10] So, for Lucian's exact contemporary Aelius Aristides, the sophist whose anti-pantomime mentality is the avowed target of Libanius' *Oration* 64, pantomime dancers are nothing less than a cause of 'disease' and 'ruin' for their viewers (9), the 'defilement of households and cities' (31; cf. 83). 'Leading lewd lives themselves', they 'destroy besides those who watch them (37),[11] on the basis of that deep-seated anti-theatrical prejudice which wants the viewers turned into replicas of the performers, that is, inescapably assimilated to whichever spectacle they witness on the stage (60, 61).[12] And if Cyprian believes that being willingly 'stained' by the pantomime's gestures heralds a more general collapse of morals, Aristides is also keen to underline the virulent power of the dancer's body-language, claiming that pantomime infestation is effected primarily through the dancer's movements: 'a nod of theirs wields greater power for corruption than do the siege-machines of others in capturing a city' (Libanius, *Oration* 64.59).

Above all, the dancer is berated for his dubious sexual identity: 'fitting a pliable sex to both his flanks' (Anonymous, in *Latin Anthology*, I.1 [Shackleton Bailey] 100, 2), he excels in a language of movement and gesture that becomes by turns both male and female. As Gregory of Nazianzus puts it, pantomimes, blurring all notion of sexual differentiation,[13] hover between the gender (male) which their chosen way of life (*tropos*) prevents them from sustaining, and the one (female) which their anatomy (*physis*) precludes them from acquiring.[14] Predictably, the result of such a daring tampering with gender is not only a 'sinewless' body (*enervatum corpus*)[15] deprived of the vigour of manly nature, but also a 'broken', enfeebled body. Thus an ubiquitous marker of the dancer in polemical narratives is the notion of his body as 'fractured', 'broken into bits', 'fragmented', 'snapped off', invariably carrying the connotation of effeminacy.[16] In the same vein, the pantomime stage is condemned as a discourse of *mollitia*, 'effeminate softness',[17] manifesting itself on all levels, from the performer's mind to his body, 'softened up to a feminine gait and carriage' (Lactantius, *Divine Institutes* 6.20.29), and from his moral disposition to the mellifluousness of the choir's songs or the noise of the *scabellarii*.[18]

The dancer himself, 'a man utterly dissolved in feminine softness' (*vir ultra muliebrem mollitiem dissolutus*) (Novatian, *On the Spectacles* 6.6),[19] is often presented as the epitome of foppishness:

> No sooner has the tongue uttered the pantomime's name than the soul has moulded anew the face, the hairstyle, the delicate clothing, the man himself, softer (i.e. more effeminate, *malakôteron*)[20] than even these (John Chrysostom, *PG* 59.119-20).

Throughout antiquity, the perceived link between effeminacy and pantomime remains strong enough for pantomimes or 'dancing-masters' (*orchêstodidaskaloi*) to be persistently associated with *cinaedi* (passive homosexuals)[21] and for Firmicius Maternus to conflate the two in his early fourth-century AD compendium of astrological knowledge:

> If the moon, Saturn and Venus are in the seventh house ... they fashion sexual perverts (*cinaedos*) with the softness of an effeminate body; these, forever dancing, imitate in the theatres the outcome of the ancient fables (*Mathesis* 6.31.39; cf. 8.23.3).

In a world where élite education was so obsessively geared to the construction of manliness and in a symbolic gender-economy wherein 'each man was forever trembling "on the brink of becoming womanish" ' (P. Brown 1988: 11), the pantomime's constant oscillation between male and female roles could only serve to reinforce one of imperial and later antiquity's most obsessive anxieties: the danger of the male relapsing into a state of undifferentiated sexuality, reversing and undoing all that had been painfully attained by strict schooling and vigilant social grooming.

Travelling effortlessly between Athamas and Ino, Atreus and Aerope (*Dance* 67), the skilled pantomime falsifies gender in a twofold way. On the one hand, being a 'womanish' creature (*thêlydrias*, *Dance* 2) instead of a real man, his imitation of male heroes on the stage is a counterfeit. It puts him on a par with fraudulent pretenders to masculinity, those well-rehearsed sham-men, whose show of ruggedness may even fool the expert in the audience, the physiognomist who makes it his business to diagnose a 'soft' unmanly man (see Gleason 1995: 76-81). Being anatomically a man, conversely, he is again a counterfeit when he plays at being female. As Columella moans about pantomime addiction,

> As if struck by thunder, we are lost in admiration of the gestures of effeminate males (*gestus effeminatorum*), the reason being that with their womanish motion they feign (*mentiantur*) the sex denied to men by nature and (thus) deceive (*decipiant*) the eyes of the viewers (*On Agriculture* 1, Preface 15).[22]

In the eyes of theatre's detractors, then, *pantomania* worked as a destabilising agent, signalling the onset of an accursed era of effeminacy and undermining the very fabric of society. As for the pantomime, he was invariably troped in polemical narratives as deeply deviant from the dominant cultural parameters defining masculinity, so much so that to reverse successfully the overwhelming tide of femininity engulfing performer and audience alike, one would have needed to put on a formidable show of defence on many intertwined fronts, performative no less than moral – a rhetorical path never taken by Lycinus.

§2. Firebrands on the stage: pantomimes, erotic dancing and the perils of the 'gaze'

Apart from seeing the pantomime stage as reprehensible, moralists and Christians alike object to its eroticism, inscribed first and foremost in pantomime's passion-filled repertoire. Our sources are unanimous on this one matter: erotic stories, some of them revolving around the impersonation of the 'lewdest women of old legend, those Phaedras and Parthenopas and Rhodopas' (*Dance* 2), hold pride of place in pantomime's thematic range. From Lucian to Libanius and Choricius of Gaza, and from the epigrams of the *Greek Anthology* to Sidonius Apollinaris, we hear of a pantomimic repertoire brimming with female roles[23] and offering the dancer ample scope for the expression of amorous passion, as he engages now in realistic imitation 'of the desirable daughter of Briseus and Phaedra in love',[24] now in the suggestive and even lustful re-enactment of Zeus' erotic escapades. Lycinus, whose summary of pantomimic themes (*Dance* 37-61) is full of erotic narratives, stipulates that the aspiring dancer needs to know 'above all, the love stories of mythical characters, including those of Zeus himself' (*Dance* 59), while Cyprian complains:

> They portray the shameless Venus, the adulterous Mars, and Jupiter himself – excelling more by his vices than by his reign – burning in earthly love affairs together with his thunderbolts, now turning white in the feathers of a swan, now flowing down in gold rain, now leaping forth to snatch pubescent boys with the aid of birds (*To Donatus* 8).

Nor did this thematic range change over time. Writing in Carthage at the turn of the fifth century AD, Augustine, bishop of Hippo, attests that Jupiter committing his countless adulteries is the subject of actors, singers and dancers alike, the acting and dancing of these stories being so popular that the rich cannot resist pouring out their patrimonies on stage-folk (*Letters* 91.5). Jacob of Serugh, writing his homilies in late fifth- or early sixth-century Syria, bemoans the dancing of Zeus' erotic transformations, and considers 'famous among spectacles' the danced representation of Zeus' 'immorality with men and women'.[25]

The erotic subject-matter goes hand in hand with the perceived erotic impact of the dancing body, that is, the pantomime's own ability to ravish the senses and throw his audience into raptures. Under the formidable eye of the theatre's detractors, the aesthetics of pantomime dancing appear dangerously conflated with sizzling moments of erotic passion, with both stage and auditorium being transformed into a zone of filthy visceral transactions, where a 'multifarious flame of carnal pleasures is being kindled', and where everything conspires for the fanning of 'the sparks of lust'.[26] While Lucian's Crato does not expound on the subject of eroticism, theatrophobic narratives construe pantomime performances as sensually explosive,[27] and the experience of pantomime viewing as closely analogous to sexual consummation:

> When soft Bathyllus dances Leda, with sinuous gestures,
> Tuccia cannot control her bladder,

is Juvenal's satirical rendition of the genre's chemistry of elemental passions (*Satire* 6.63-4; trans. Rudd 1991). Shimmering and undulating in flowing lines and delicious curves, the dancer, himself 'embellished with the charm of seductiveness' (Firmicius Maternus, *Mathesis* 6.31.85; cf. ibid. 8.28.11), instils in the entire body politic 'a crazed desire for libidinous spectacle'[28] or, as Minucius Felix (*Octavius*, 37.12) puts it, 'while he feigns love, he inflicts the wounds of love'.

Far more than any other stage-performer, including the female dancers of the mime shows against whom John Chrysostom and others rail, it is the pantomime who embodies theatre's immense and lethal physicality. The greatest source of public danger and fascination is located in his sexual indeterminacy, the lure of a body that emits conflicting gender-signs. Having learnt 'how … his sex can be modified by means of his art' (*quemadmodum … sexus arte mutetur*) (Cyprian, *Letter* 2.2.1), and thus constructing and de-constructing the categories of male and female in performance, he treats his audience to an unrivalled diversity of erotic titillation. The entire complexity of pantomime viewing informs Ovid's *Remedies for Love* 753-6, a wonderful insight into the erotic polymorphy of the genre and its dancer:

> Lutes, flutes and lyres enervate the mind,
> as do the voices and the arms moving to their own rhythms.
> Here fabled lovers are constantly portrayed in dancing:
> the actor teaches (you) with his art how alluring is the thing that you
> must guard against.

Instrumental music, the chorus' melodious voices and the dancer's rhythmical figures 'emasculate' the viewer.[29] But this very same dancing virtuoso is also able to kindle the viewer's languishing erotic flame[30] by taking part in highly eroticised narrative discourses which turn his pliant body into an instrument of captivation and seduction.[31]

How dangerous it is for the spectator to identify vicariously with male/female subject-positions, in tandem with the pantomime's oscillation between male and female parts and their concomitant emotions, cannot be overstressed. The agent who causes 'the entire city' to be 'thrown into a whirlpool of desire' does not even have an undisputed place on either side of the great divide:[32] 'men among women (*andres gynaixi*) and women among men (*kai gynaikes andrasin*)' in their erotic drives, 'a puzzle of lasciviousness and riddle of carnal passions' (*asôtias ainigma kai griphos pathôn*),[33] pantomimes act as the catalysts for 'a universal effeminization' in the auditorium, to borrow from Orgel's brilliant reading of cross-dressed performances on the Elizabethan stage.[34] Eroticised signifier of a woman, and hence bombarding the spectator with unquenchable desire of the female form, the dancer *playing-at-being-a-woman* turns his male viewer into a 'sissy' and a 'pansy', a *gynaion* in Crato's words (*Dance* 5), for unrestrained lust is thought to sap a man's virility. As the embodiment of male allure in the dancing of male roles, correspondingly, he yet again causes male viewers to become 'replete with femininity' (Libanius, *Oration* 64.74), for now he elicits the abominable, forbidden and unmanning homoerotic love. Yet even so, the narrative of pantomime seduction is infinitely more complex.

A cultural logic deeply ingrained in patriarchal structures aligns the action of seeing with the enactment of power. Being at liberty to deploy one's gaze wherever and for as long as one wishes is co-extensive with a position of dominance and superiority, while being transfixed by another's eyes implies subjection and reification. The human body in particular, when scrutinised by a sustained and avid look, is turned into 'a disposable term – object to be held in position, term of subservience, submission' (Bryson 1983: 152). Independently of its provenance, the action of gazing is gendered 'male', while the passive position of 'being looked-at' is reserved for the 'female'. This alignment of vision with the articulation of masculine control turns the privilege of sight into a privilege of erotic appropriation, so much so that, as Kramer (1990: 273) writes, *scopophilia*, the pleasure of looking, 'can plausibly be said to rival physical penetration as the chief means of satisfying sexual desire'.[35] Exposed to the male libidinal gaze, the body on display is feminised, eroticised, laid bare and avidly consumed.

'Darling and sweetheart of the city', the epitome of *erôs* and desire,[36] the pantomime's dancing body is a perfect illustration of what feminist critic Laura Mulvey (1975: 11) famously termed female 'to-be-looked-at-ness'. Nevertheless, the fetishised pantomime, who draws his audience's voluptuous gaze like a magnet, not only proves admirably resistant to any confinement to a subordinate position, but also turns the power differential between the bearer and the object of the gaze on its head. Like the dancing temptress Salome, from whose body 'invisible sparks shot out, firing the men with excitement',[37] the pantomime's bodily trajectory across the stage is an explosive firebrand of sexual energy. But like Salome, who, while being the sole object of Herodes' scopophiliac look, 'usurps control of it' and 'subjugates the eye that subjugates her' (Kramer 1990: 274), the pantomime's erotically desired body reigns supreme: instead of *being* possessed, it is the centre of a spectacle that 'takes possession of' the audience's soul (Aristides in Libanius, *Oration* 64.61).[38] Broken by and through his own gaze, the pantomime viewer 'appear[s] utterly enslaved', as Crato says of Lycinus in *Dance* 3, to charms that soften the mind to the point of complete seduction.[39]

The pantomime's dangerous control over the gaze of his onlookers is so haunting that theatrophobic narratives articulate their fear in the related images of military aggression and captivity. For Aristides (in Libanius, *Oration* 64.59), the channel of communication between dancers and spectators can be compared to military attacks (cf. John Chrysostom, *PG* 59.333), while Christian sources in particular construct the spectacle's delights as sensual gratification that incarcerates and entraps. 'Prisoners of pleasure', the victimised viewers find themselves pulled along 'like grazing animals', wherever the wolf may chance to lead (John Chrysostom, *PG* 58.490), or 'dragged off captive as booty' (Tatian, *Address to the Greeks* 22.13), with ears as well as eyes 'detained' (Novatian, *On the Spectacles* 8.2). Wherever pantomimes dance, gender-hierarchies become embattled. Rather than asserting their phallic domination and the privileges of their class, even educated males choose to spend their life in the pantomimes' thrall, 'serving them, obeying them, flattering them, courting them, paying honour to them, depending upon them, neither doing nor knowing anything else' (Libanius, *Oration* 41.7). Baring his soul 'melted' (cf. Libanius, *Oration* 64.70) and dissolved, the pantomime addict ends up assimilated to the very femininity that he beholds.

Finally, bastions of masculinity are not the only social bedrock that finds itself under attack. Among the pantomime's hysterically devoted fans, women are a sizeable proportion. And while from a Christian and a moralising perspective their theatrical experience leaves them defiled and polluted, from the point of view of patriarchal structures female fans become the dangerous usurpers of privileges and pleasures jealously guarded by the Male. Looking at their idols in a covetous way, they exchange their socially obedient gaze, always expected to be lowered in response to the desirous looks of others, for the kind of gaze strictly reserved for the Male. And, all the while they watch, and are inflamed by, the pantomime's sensuous dancing, they undergo a kind of mental cross-dressing, slipping out of their role of passive and desired objects into the impermissible domain of male active and desiring subjects.

§3. Body matter unbridled and unmanageable

If for the spectating masses the dancer's endless transformative capacity is a liberating and empowering principle, a locus of fantasy, desire and inspiration, for a society's moral guardians it is often a force that must be curbed, policed and regulated. Such is the case with pantomime dancing. From the vantage point of the hegemonic classes, setting great store by social stratification and the preservation of the status quo, the dancer can offend by means of his shape-shifting, 'protean' nature. In a culture built upon the rigid separation of human, bestial and divine, the pantomime who, like the mythical Proteus or the multiform Empusa (*Dance* 19), becomes all creatures of sentient and non-sentient life in a swift succession of roles, masks and costumes – now a river, a serpent or a tree, now a god, an outcast sinner, a sceptred king or woman in exile – could be taken to exemplify the chaotic and unclassifiable, the single body that invalidates all distinctions.

Nevertheless, the real danger inherent in the pantomime's defiance of structural classification could be seen to reside in his performance's infectious nature. The tides of emotion generated by the spectacle are so immense that what seems to be an innocent, almost 'carnivalesque' release from boundaries within a single, endlessly mutating self risks sparking off a much more general fluidity of social norms within the wider body politic. Sharing vicariously in the dancer's own psychic and somatic tribulations as he travels between a host of different personae, the audience-body too enacts the perilous journey between modes of existence that a neatly ordered society strives to keep apart.

The pantomime's transgressive body, then, could be felt to hybridise not merely itself but also its viewers, inviting them to take part in chaos-building spectacles and luxuriate in those emotional experiences that dominant discourses fiercely disown. As we have already seen in §1, in Crato's theatrophobic world even an educated man like Lycinus risks degenerating into a grotesque compound wherein, to borrow the words of Stallybrass and White (1986: 193), 'self and other become enmeshed in an inclusive, heterogeneous, dangerously unstable zone'. Besides, the pantomime's body could be deemed subversive by means of glorifying the negation (or, even worse, the undoing) of the idealised body each and every élite youth should be aspiring to acquire and struggling to preserve.[40]

During each show of dancing virtuosity, the élite male body, complete and closed, residing within its own limits, ever on the guard against the merest transgression, and fiercely 'walled off' against invasion, is put in contact with a body that is fluid and formless, forever fashioning itself, and with no fixed semiotic status. With limbs so soft and liquefied that, like molten bronze or wax (cf. Libanius, *Oration* 64.104), they can be poured out to fill an endless repertoire of stage-figures, the dancer's body constantly outgrows itself, forever reaching out of, and ultimately violating, its own limits. The violence of the clash between the 'normative', the socially prescribed body, idealised by the upper classes, and the 'anarchic' body pantomime represents may best be conceptualised with the aid of Bakhtin's (1984: 29 and 317) well-known opposition between the body of 'classical' aesthetics and that of 'grotesque' realism. To the body as a 'strictly completed, finished product ... fenced off from all other bodies' is counterposed a body 'in the act of becoming ... never finished, never completed ... continually built'. Like the ever-shifting costume of the eighteenth-century masquerade, which, 'freighted with disturbing symbolical potential', 'bespoke the possibility of astonishing transfigurations, and of a world perennially open to reconstitution' (Castle 1986: 55), the pantomime's body could be seen as a perilous site of taxonomic failure, a negative example of confusion and disorientation. Needless to say, its greatest crime concerns its deviant modelling of gender-matter.

Viewed from lookout posts firmly anchored in conservative élite territory, pantomime dancing could not be neatly accommodated into the imperial social fabric without breaking the seams. A French critic's tirade against the ballerinos of mid-nineteenth century Paris (well before the explicit and provocative eroticisation of the male dancing body through Diaghilev's innovations) turns the spotlight on a gulf between dancing and established social structures no less formidable than that which separates pantomime from élite conceptualisations of Roman *virtus*, morality and military tradition:

> But a man, a frightful man, as ugly as you and I, a wretched fellow who leaps about without knowing why, a creature specially made to carry a musket and a sword and to wear a uniform. That this fellow should dance as a woman does – impossible! That this bewhiskered individual who is a pillar of the community, an elector, a municipal councillor, a man whose business it is to make and above all unmake laws, should come before us in a tunic of sky-blue satin, his head covered with a hat with a waving plume amorously caressing his cheek, a frightful danseuse of the male sex, come to pirouette in the best place ... this was surely impossible and intolerable ...[41]

In the Roman world, as much as in nineteenth-century Paris, the social 'text' created by the dancing body could be 'read' as anti-conformist. In both cases, being 'a pillar of the community' and being a male 'danseuse' were deemed mutually exclusive ways of belonging to the body politic.

§4. Conclusion

This chapter has argued that, by appropriating the voice of a sceptic, Lucian's *On the Dance* aligns itself, in part, with narratives which (a) locate the pantomime dancer beyond the pale of culturally dominant definitions of masculinity and acceptable standards of morality; (b) identify the pantomime viewer with forms of un-assimilable, un-masculine 'otherness' in terms of gender, culture and rationality; and (c) lock together stage and auditorium as willing accomplices in an erotically charged discourse. From the vantage point of self-proclaimed watchdogs of élite morality, the pantomime's cultural 'otherness' was readable in an array of deviant corporeal signs (neck bent, body 'fragmented', 'sinewless' movements, languid gestures, etc.), all threatening to undermine the behavioural models designed for ambitious upper-class males. In particular, the ease with which the dancers shaped and re-shaped their gender in the course of their performance was received in some corners of imperial society and culture as openly provocative, raising the possibility of similar arrangements in real life. Before proceeding to Lycinus' elaborate reply to Crato's accusations (see Chapter 6), however, a final note of caution is in order. For, as the reader will notice, I make no attempt to tie up loose ends by means of reconciling either the conflicting viewpoints emerging from Chapters 4 and 5 or those that will subsequently emerge from the juxtaposition of this chapter with its sequel. This lack of a desire to intervene in the discrepant stories provided by our sources has sound justification.

Pantomime was construed in diametrically different ways in different contexts and by different interpreting agents, groups and individuals alike (see Introduction). But no matter how fervent is our wish to uncover the 'real' pantomime underneath the many layers of appropriation and concomitant distortion, we shall always stumble on a hard and stubborn inner core which cannot be peeled away, because it is part and parcel of pantomime's very essence. I mean the genre's intrinsic power to polarise opinion, to generate competing accounts of itself, almost alternative histories of what it was and what it represented. The story of imperial pantomime was inextricably interwoven with the tensions it created within those very frames which hosted and sustained it. Given that imperial culture was not a monolith, but a diverse, versatile, ever-changing conglomerate of values, practices, beliefs and attitudes, it is perfectly plausible that the same spectacle which sent shock-waves through the ranks of Christians and moralists throughout the empire could be incorporated in traditional frameworks of political practice. Irreconcilable tensions were in themselves an ineradicable part of pantomime's meaning – or, to put it another way, pantomime existed as the sum total of its ambiguities.

The dancer could be honoured and extolled as an outstanding individual just as readily as he could be vilified as a good-for-nothing, 'sinewless' fellow; and the genre itself could be exploited as an essential part of institutionalised celebrations of Roman power just as zealously as it could be repudiated as an explosive force, striking at the vitals of Romanness itself. It is precisely because of pantomime's balancing on the fragile equilibrium of the diametrically opposed forces it unleashed that contradictions in our evidence should not be viewed with frustration as thorns to be eradicated. Both sides of the pantomime 'narrative' existed simultaneously, and neither cancelled the other out, despite the fact that conflicting forces strove to project their own meaning onto the genre. Any attempt to 'legislate' in retrospect on whether in its own time the image of the genre as supportive of or colluding with dominant structures was more 'authentic' than the picture of a challenging, destabilising pantomime is dangerously reductive. It introduces an additional layer of mis-representation: the elimination of pantomime's inherent doubleness, ambiguousness, controversiality. Just as, in terms of literary criticism, to privilege one particular inroad into a literary text while barring others is tantamount to 'abusively closing off the plurality of codes' (Barthes 1975: 206), so in the case of pantomime, to decide that one set of narratives must be preferred to others is an arbitrary interpretative act, which must be

77

avoided at all costs, even at the risk of preventing the construction of an homogeneous, self-consistent picture. While the ironing out of panto-mime's ambiguities in the hope of presenting it as a uniformly noble genre is precisely what Lycinus sets out to do in Lucian's dialogue (see Chapter 6), we ought to know better. Besides, if pantomime truly was the seething site of cultural ferment suggested by the conflicting narratives of our sources, this very fact alone is significant. It indicates to us the genre's irreducible centrality in the many and tangled debates over issues fraught with cultural anxiety, such as gender-fashioning and power; ethics and morality; education, and the negotiation of the boundaries between refined and vulgar (or licit and illicit) entertainment with respect to an urbane, cultured citizen-body.

Emancipating Pantomime: Lycinus' Speech in Lucian's *On the Dance*

The previous chapter, dwelling on the negative, disparaging views of pantomime and its dancer, may well have created the impression that the rehabilitation of the genre in the face of so much anxiety and outright hostility would have been a near impossible task. Yet Lucian's *On the Dance* undertakes to do just this, putting together a case for pantomime as a learned and educational spectacle (§1-2 below), with ample moral essence (§3), superior to other institutions (see §4 on athletics) and rival entertainments (see Chapter 9§3 on tragedy), and addressed to a sophisticated and appreciative audience. Against a background of undisguised calumny, then,[1] Lycinus, the pantomime defender, treats the genre's corporeal dramaturgy not as an impediment to cultured aesthetics, but as a highly valuable system of signification. In the same breath, and fully in line with the tradition of encomiastic speech-writing, the praise is transferred from the art of dancing to those who actually practise it (see especially *Dance* 74-81), so that the pantomime dancer may be elevated from the level of an amateur, effeminate and brainless sensualist to the pedestal of a professional, masculine and erudite performer of an intricate art.[2] Far from being engaged in disjointed reckless movement or luxuriating in euphoric abandon, the pantomime's body, disciplined, creative and self-critical, is now celebrated as the marvellous instrument of an intelligent, instructive spectacle. It is therefore the aim of this chapter to examine the strategies Lycinus uses to achieve the genre's and the dancer's ultimate legitimation.

§1. Pantomime and its 'sister arts'

When Leonardo Da Vinci set out to legitimise painting as a liberal art in Renaissance Italy, his primary concern was to prove its semantic and structural analogies with rhetoric and poetry. Similarly, in his unremitting struggle to emancipate theatrical dancing as an independent art form, Jean-Georges Noverre, the foremost choreographer and dance theoretician of the eighteenth century and father of the modern ballet (conceived as a revival of ancient pantomime dancing),[3] called upon the accrediting powers of cognate arts:

History, legend, painting, all the arts may unite to withdraw their sister art
from the obscurity in which she is shrouded; and it astonishes one that *maîtres
de ballet* have disdained such powerful assistance (Noverre 1930: 11).

Not unlike their European counterparts, ancient apologists for manual
arts countered the disdain of their detractors by claiming for their own
craft the kind of respectability enjoyed by loftier creative practices or more
commendable pursuits.[4]

The Elder Philostratus, for example, in the Preface to his *Images*,
introduces an influential analogy between painting, truth and poetic
wisdom, bestowing thus upon the fashioner of shapes and colours the
credibility attached to the creator of words (*Images*, Proem 1).[5] In another
treatise of the early third century AD entitled *On Athletic Training*, the
same author takes it upon himself to compose the defence of the art of
exercising the body (*gymnastikê*), proclaiming it as 'not inferior to any art
with respect to wisdom' and arguing for its particular affiliation to medicine and the art of the physical trainer (*paidotribikê*): it is a part of the
former, and superior to the latter.[6] In the Latin-speaking West, Vitruvius,
author of a celebrated treatise on the art of architecture, takes pains to
link architectural expertise with 'many disciplines and varied learning'
(*On Architecture* 1.1.1), including draughtsmanship, mathematics, history, philosophy, music, medicine, law and astronomy (*On Architecture*,
1.1.3). Even the exponents of the élite, but often maligned, art of rhetoric
justify its position of supremacy among the 'high' arts not merely by
harping on its reliance on universal knowledge, rigorous training, and
unceasing practice but, most impressively, by claiming that no estimable
art or branch of knowledge falls outside its range.[7]

It should therefore come as no surprise that, in his attempt to guarantee
for pantomime a place among respectable pursuits, Lycinus adopts a
comparable licensing approach. For this fictitious defender of the pantomime's art, emancipation of the genre seems to be intricately braided with
demonstration of its links with a range of more highly regarded spheres of
expertise. Like Cicero, keen to emphasise the 'incredible vastness and
difficulty' of the art of rhetoric (*On the Orator* 1.5.16), Lycinus is anxious
to impress upon his interlocutor that the pantomime's *technê* is 'not one of
the undemanding arts or those easy to master, but has reached the very
summit of all education', not only in the sphere of music but also in the
arts of rhythm, metre, philosophy (both natural and ethical), rhetoric, and
even the plastic arts (*Dance* 35). 'Education' (*paideusis, paideia*) is actually
the keyword that unifies several of Lycinus' legitimising tactics in his
speech. In a world where the possession of *paideia* accounts for the
difference between 'leading or being led, wielding power or being power-
less, being in a position to help others or being in need of help, being
counted as blessed or complimenting others' (Libanius, *Oration* 35.8), it is
only natural for Lycinus, as an encomiast, to take pains to endow his

subject with a share of educational capital, portraying him as a man 'deeply learned' (*tên paideian bathyn*) (*Dance* 81).[8]

This strategy is neither new[9] nor unlinked to the circles within which we imagine Lucian moved. In his attempt to validate architecture, Augustus' contemporary Vitruvius stakes almost everything on the ideal architect's breadth of education, his command of 'varied and numerous branches of knowledge' (*On Architecture* 1.1.11). As Masterson (2004: 393) puts it, it is the 'authorizing power' of education that makes the architect look 'impressive intellectually', assimilates him 'to his social betters' and consolidates 'his claim to be an estimable personage'. In the intellectual climate of the second century AD in particular, we find Lucian's contemporary Maximus of Tyre casting his net widely over poetry, oratory and political science in his urge to defend the value of philosophical discourse. In the philosopher's instruction, he claims, the aspiring student will discover the eloquence of an orator, the multi-coloured brilliance of poetic style and all the trappings of the politician's art (*Oration* 1.7).[10]

Lycinus' overarching plan for pantomime's accreditation, then, is the generous embedding of the genre into the fabric of high culture: having spun with the aid of intellectual disciplines and loftier aesthetic practices a powerful legitimating web, Lycinus placed pantomime at its very centre. Alongside claiming for pantomime the mantle of a dignified art, Lycinus also stakes for the dancer a claim to professional respectability by emphasising the complexity, difficulty and all-encompassing nature of his training. By the time Lycinus has brought his exposition to a close, pantomime has been fashioned as a noble and ennobling form of cultural capital.

§2. The dancer's intellectual gear

Which other *technai* are congenial with pantomime and how their mastery contributes to the genre's respectability, Lycinus expounds to his interlocutor in 45 long paragraphs, starting with his preamble in *Dance* 35:

> What qualifications the dancer himself must have and what training he should have received and what he should have learnt and by what means he ought to strengthen his work, I will now tell you in detail.

To start with, then, the dancer must be armed with extensive learning (*polymatheia, Dance* 37; cf. Chapter 7), in order to be able to command the vast swathes of mythical/historical material contained within the genre's usual repertoire:

> Commencing straightaway with Chaos and the first beginnings of the universe, he must know everything down to the stories that concern the Egyptian Cleopatra (*Dance* 37).

And, as no amount of knowledge is of any use unless one's memory is strong enough to keep it readily available (see, e.g., Cicero, *On the Orator* 1.5.18), Lycinus is especially keen to prioritise the genre's affiliation to the powers of memorisation, Mnemosyne and Polyhymnia, who are themselves envisaged as 'kindly disposed' towards an art that 'strives to remember everything' (*Dance* 36). These, however, are no modest claims[11] and beg for further exploration.

Control of 'the past history', to the extent that it becomes 'the whole equipment for the pantomime's task' (*Dance* 36), makes the dancer a match for the historian. If the historiographer's words reveal to the reader or the listener 'the panorama of the distant past', all the while allowing him to learn 'of a vast mass of events concisely, Assyrian, Egyptian, Persian, Median, and Greek' (Maximus of Tyre, *Oration* 22.5; trans. Trapp 1997), the pantomime dancer fulfils the same purpose to a superlative degree, 'presenting in his own body' (Libanius, *Oration* 64.116) the history of the past on stage. Moreover, when stipulating that the pantomime himself must be 'retentive of memory' (*mnêmonikon*) (*Dance* 74), Lycinus barely refers to the corporeal or 'kinaesthetic' memory that lies at the core of every dancer's art (Chapter 3§3). For him the issue at stake is intellectual memory, the acquisition of which is, as rhetorical manuals tell us, a matter of industry, devotion, toil and care (see, e.g., Anonymous, *Rhetoric for Herennius*, 3.24.40).

Such an ability, however, puts the dancer on an equal footing not merely with the speaking actor, who is expected to remember the dramatist's own words, but, more provocatively, with the pupils of grammarians and rhetors. For the latter the development of a strong memory was the foundation of all knowledge acquisition, 'from learning to speak, learning to read and write, learning canonical and ethical literature and the elements of rhetoric to memorising a speech for delivery'.[12] As Quintilian (*Training* 11.2.1) puts it, 'the entire body of rhetorical education rests on memory, ... the treasure-house of eloquence' (cf. Anonymous, *Rhetoric for Herennius* 3.16.28). Even accomplished declaimers and the great display-orators needed to be able to memorise their extempore speeches verbatim, without a single error.[13] And, just as the incredible memory of Porcius Latro, a friend of Seneca the Elder, enabled him to have at his fingertips and activate at will his vast historical knowledge (*Legal Disputations* 1, Preface 18), the pantomime's mnemonic wealth must always be *procheiros*, 'at hand' (*Dance* 37). As Lycinus explains, all the information pertaining to the pantomime's repertoire must be 'provided for and stored away in good time', so as to lie 'ever ready for recall' (*procheira*), as each occasion for performative display arises (*Dance* 61).

The predominantly legendary nature of the knowledge involved in the pantomime's repertoire (*Dance* 37-61) elevates the pantomime into a repository of cultural tradition and mythical memory:

And surely, in the manner of the Homeric Calchas, the pantomime must know 'the things that are and those that will be and those that were before', so that nothing escapes him,[14] but their memory is readily accessible to him (*einai procheiron tên mnêmên autôn*) (*Dance* 36).

The genre's affiliation to Mnemosyne almost sanctions the performer as the heir to the archaic Muses, who also know things present, future and bygone (Hesiod, *Theogony* 38). Preservers of the epic past, the Muses protect a hero from the danger of becoming *amnastos* ('with no reason to be remembered'), without the privilege of being easily 'accessible' in a community's collective consciousness. The pantomime, for his part, striving to ward off oblivion and remember all the legends from the beginning of the universe to the time of the Egyptian Cleopatra (*Dance* 37), not only appropriates the historian's goal of guarding and transmitting human history (see, e.g., Maximus of Tyre, *Oration* 22.5) but, like the archaic Muses, guarantees the everlasting 'presence' of the characters he incarnates.[15] 'Teaching a great deal of what pertains to generations of old' (*Dance* 72), the pantomime genre becomes some kind of embodied myth-and-history, while the dancer himself, impersonating a whole gallery of gods and heroes, emerges as that marvellous site where past and present meet, and where the distant, abstract shapes of myth can be transformed into the reality of flesh. In Lycinus' construction of the genre, pantomime literalises a recurrent metaphor in the historian's trade, the notion whereby the good historian's narrative itself becomes a visual image, replete with characters and passions, as if it were a painting (see Plutarch, *Moral Essays* 347a). If the historian's raw material can be conceived as a 'grand spectacle' (Polybius, *Histories* 1.2.1) and the finished product of his labour as an illustrious visual artefact, a 'monument' for public contemplation into which readers, like privileged viewers, are invited to peer,[16] the pantomime dancer is himself a living *monumentum*, exemplifying the notion of the past 'made visible'. What the historian's reader is likely to see, with the aid of literary vividness, in his mind's eye, transmuting *logos* into vision, the pantomime enables his audience to perceive through physical sight. Linking together the totality of time, both pointing backward to the past as well as signalling towards the future (*Dance* 36), the dancer seems to approximate the historian's task of 'bringing into comprehensive view' (Polybius, *Histories* 1.4.2) the vast chronological expanses condensed in the act of his narration.

Moving beyond Lycinus' understanding of the dancer as a guardian of historical memory and mythical tradition,[17] a major art invoked in the process of pantomime's validation is Rhetoric.[18] Nothing can be more critical than Lycinus' success in establishing the genre's share in such a key accomplishment, the most enduring 'correlate of power' (Morgan 1998: 235), a trusted avenue for social mobility and a most effective weapon in an individual's quest for fame, wealth, social influence, authority, and prestige. In consonance with other literary voices positioned within the fold of élite culture, the apologist compares the pantomime to the orator,[19] on the basis of their common preoccupation with clarity (*saphêneia*)[20] and the display of *êthos* and *pathos*:

> Dancing has not held itself apart from Rhetoric either, but has a share even in this art, insofar as it displays character and passion (*êthous te kai pathous epideiktikê*), which is also what orators long for (*Dance* 35).

In Lycinus' words, the principal point of contact between dancing and oratory is *hypokrisis*, that is, role-playing, impersonation:

> As I have said, the chief occupation and the aim of dancing is impersonation (*hypokrisis*), which is cultivated in the same way by the rhetoricians, particularly those who recite these pieces which they call 'declamations' (*meletas*);[21] for in their case also there is nothing that we commend more highly than their accommodating themselves to the roles that they assume, so that what they say is not inappropriate to the princes or tyrant-slayers or poor people or farmers whom they introduce, but in each of these is presented what is individual and distinctive (*Dance* 65; trans. modified from Harmon, Loeb 1936).

Both orator and pantomime are in the business of creating and sustaining personas, 'plausible' and 'appropriate' characters with whom they strive to align themselves as closely as possible.[22]

Rhetoric is closely followed by philosophy in Lycinus' treasure-trove of the dancer's desirable qualifications. Problematising the relationship between philosophy and dance has a notable pedigree in Xenophon's *Symposion*, a philosophical treatise in which 'philosophers dance and dancing becomes a topic of philosophical discussion' (Wohl 2004: 337), especially as Socrates 'draws dance – with all its pleasure and corporeality – into philosophy, and makes it both an element and a symbol of the healthful regimen of a philosophical life' (Wohl, ibid., 346, on *Symposion* 2.17-19). Lycinus himself signals (albeit not by name) the *Symposion* as an intertext of far-reaching implications for his own claims, when he refers to Socrates' desire to be indoctrinated in the rhythm, grace and harmony of dance movements, and Socrates' belief in the intrinsic value of dancing as a field of study (*Dance* 25; cf. *Symposion* 2.15-20). But, although in the Xenophontic dialogue the contest staged 'between the pleasure of dance and the pleasure of philosophical discourse' (Wohl 2004: 343) is inconclusive, with no theoretical viewpoint triumphing over its rival, in Lycinus' 'apology' the pantomime-lover is resolved to demonstrate that nothing prevents the man of letters from enjoying philosophy *as well as* dance. In *Dance* 69 Lycinus invokes the testimony of the learned Timocrates, who, on seeing by chance 'just one single performance ... of a dancer going through his repertoire', is alleged to have said: 'What a spectacle my respect for philosophy has deprived me of.' Moreover, although he couches his assertion very carefully in qualifying adjectives, Lycinus ventures the idea that pantomime *is* a kind of philosophical exposition, its silence 'hinting at some Pythagoric doctrine' (*Dance* 70).[23] In any case, this same section of the apologist's speech is a brilliant example of Lycinus' bold construction of the genre as an activity compatible with, or illustrative of, philosophical discourse:

> If Plato's arguments about the soul are true [cf. Plato, *Republic* 436a-441c], the dancer illustrates well the soul's tripartite division: he exhibits the soul's wrathful part when he presents a man in rage, its desirous part when he impersonates characters in love, its reasoning part when he keeps a tight rein on each of the different passions. This last one, in fact, is besprinkled over all parts of the dance just as touch is disseminated in the other senses. And as he plans in advance the pulchritude and comeliness of his dance-figures, what else does he achieve but verify the words of Aristotle, who praised beauty and deemed it to belong to the third part of his notion of the *agathon*? (*Dance* 70).[24]

History, rhetoric and philosophy are not the only unfamiliar and élite territories the 'written' pantomime is presented as invading. Insofar as he creates visual compositions with his own body, the literary construct of the skilful dancer is not unlike a painter or a sculptor[25] (cf. Chapter 3§2). Aristaenetus (*Letters* 1.26, 7-11) hails the dancer as a painter ('Shall I address you as a painter?'), albeit one who substitutes bodily *schêmata* for the artist's pigment ('You draw actions, ... using instead of colours ... a hand that creates many a figure'), while Lycinus claims that the dancer's art can be explicitly compared to painting and sculpture:

> Pantomime has also a share in painting and sculpture, manifestly imitating their sense of rhythm above all else, so that neither Pheidias nor Apelles seems in any respect superior to it (*Dance* 35).[26]

As Plotinus (*Enneads* 5.9.11) explains in more objective (as opposed to encomiastic) terms, painting and sculpture, pantomime dancing and the art of hand-gesture, coupled together as mimetic arts, imitate shapes and movements, taking their models from the world of the senses.

Finally, insofar as Lycinus maintains that the pantomime ought to be

> capable of judging poetry (*kritikon* ... *poiêmatôn*), distinguishing (*diagnôstikon*)[27] the best of songs and melodies[28] and criticising (*elenktikon*) bad poetic compositions (*Dance* 74)

the dancer even appropriates the functions of a literary critic and a musicologist.[29] Critics of literature (*kritikoi*) and music (*mousikoi*) and discussions of problems in music and poetry (*logoi peri mousikôn kai poiêtikôn problêmatôn*) are also joined together in Plutarch (*Moral Essays*

1096a and 1095c), while 'poetic criticism' seems to have been an integral part of the art of grammar (*grammatikê*) (see, e.g., Sextus Empiricus, *Against the Grammarians* I.93). The scope of such critical activities was said to include the pronouncement of definitive judgement (*krisis*) over 'healthy' and unsound expressions as well as the distinction of genuine from spurious works (*Against the Grammarians* I.93). According to the *Art of Grammar* attributed to Dionysius 'the Thracian', 'criticism of poetry' (*krisis poiêmatôn*) is the 'finest part of the entire art' (*Art of Grammar* 1) or, in the words of one scholiast, its 'crown'.[30] In the Hellenistic world there were even those who deemed that a *kritikos*, in whose cognitive field lay experience 'in the whole science of speech', was as superior to the grammarian as a 'master builder' is to an 'underling'.[31]

In reality, the shades of different pantomimes' musical and literary activities may well have been as numerous as individual dancers but, be that as it may, the claims made on their behalf are clearly immense. On the one hand, it is very unlikely that dancing virtuosi would have had much (if anything!) to do with matters of style, composition and literary technique.[32] Yet if we imagine the pantomime not as the counterpart of a contemporary 'first dancer' but as the closest analogue to a choreographer or Jean-Georges Noverre's 'ballet-master', Lycinus' stipulations can be more easily appreciated. As the leader of the troupe, the pantomime ought to boast a keen eye (as well as ear) for those compositions most likely to achieve a mass audience's *psychagôgia*, enthralment being much of the time dependent not on noble ideas and lofty moral content, but on such formal matters as word selection and word order, beauty of diction, or the artful combination of more and less euphonic sounds. Maybe Lycinus here envisages his pantomime performing a popularised or watered-down version of the kind of criticism maligned by Philodemus, that is to say the literary activities of those who believed poetic beauty to reside in the aural, euphonic qualities of verse and be discernible by the recipient's ear rather than the mind.[33] Whatever (if any) aspects of (quasi-)literary criticism the dancer may have practised, what is of primary importance is that in *Dance* 74 Lycinus ascribes to the pantomime functions clearly belonging to educated circles. In his summary of the plots that fall within the range of a pantomime's repertoire, Lycinus requires of the dancer the kind of knowledge that liberal education can offer: 'he will not be ignorant of anything narrated by Homer and Hesiod and the best poets, in particular, the tragic poets' (*Dance* 61).

I hope to have thrown sufficient light on the principal emancipating strategy followed by Lycinus in this dialogue, that is, the building of strong bridges between pantomime and a range of arts, disciplines and intellectual pursuits. Whenever pitted against those, the genre is proclaimed of comparable or even higher value. We never hear Lycinus expatiating on the logic of this strategy, but we do find it nicely expounded by Noverre: the more intimate the link between the dance and a family of cognate arts, each having a need of the others 'for their mutual elevation, embellishment and continuation' (Noverre 1930: 37), the greater its immunity to slander and derision. To use one of Lucian's expressions, whoever sets out to disparage pantomime will have to 'pull down with himself' (*synkataspan, Nigrinus* 11) a whole array of established professions, rendering his own position problematic or untenable. Furthermore, all the while Lycinus reframes pantomime's artistic experience by breaking down the barriers between the genre and other cultural forms or aesthetic practices, he erects by implication an impassable boundary between the real, professional pantomime artist and the unskilled, amateur pretender to pantomimic glory. Just as ignorance of the different components that assist the acquisition of rhetorical excellence can reduce this distinguished art to 'a ridiculous flow of words without any substance' (Cicero, *On the Orator* 1.5.17), Lycinus' sustained foregrounding of the need for an educated dancer implies that, if deprived of the refinement afforded by a varied education, the pantomime's exhibitions may indeed be nothing more than a set of 'purposeless', 'irrational' configurations, as pantomime critics were all too eager to assume (Lucian, *Dance* 63).

§3. The moralising discourse of pantomime dancing

There is a second pressing reason why the pantomime *must* be presented as an educated man. In the upper-class circles of the first centuries AD, possession of education went hand in hand with the underlying assumption that the educated man was also morally superior, success in education presupposing as well as spawning virtue and integrity. As Kaster (1988: 27) writes, 'literary culture in itself guaranteed virtue', an equation that formed the basis of Apuleius' self-defence against the charge of sorcery in his *Apology* (cf. Too 2000: 119). It cannot be stressed too strongly that any art aspiring to the prestige of high culture had to make a concerted effort to appropriate a didactic, especially a moralising, function. 'Even the musicians', Strabo argues, 'when they teach singing and the skill of lyre and flute-playing, lay claim to the ability of imparting moral wisdom; for they maintain they are skilled in teaching and can restore morals' (*Geography*, 1.2.3). Insofar as pantomime inscriptions too stress the praised dancer's virtuous disposition in life,[34] it is only to be expected that Lycinus would not have missed the chance to invest his favourite pastime with the prestige and dignity of moralising discourse.

The beleaguered and maligned pantomime, excoriated and lambasted on grounds of morality as an ethically repugnant spectacle (cf. Chapter 5), is now accorded the wholesome and character-building mission of high literature: having experienced the dance, Lycinus argues, the viewer will return from the theatre 'a better person' (*beltiôn*) (*Dance* 69), with his character 'improved' (*ameinôn to êthos*) (*Dance* 72). Just as the *logoi* of a poet or philosopher, if read for the sake of instruction as opposed to pleasure, lead to the redressing of one's moral constitution (see, e.g., Plutarch, *Moral Essays* 79c), pantomime encompasses a manifest reformative dimension:

> I leave aside how much better you will become in terms of character by being conversant with such a spectacle, when you observe the theatre having a strong aversion to wrongdoings [on the stage], weeping for those who are being wronged, and in general, guiding the viewers' moral disposition (*ta êthê tôn horôntôn paidagôgoun*) (*Dance* 72).

Shaping and moulding 'character', the most invaluable of human assets, pantomime is presented as aligned with the dominant, controlling forces of society and culture. In *Dance* 81, Lycinus draws on a hodge-podge of ethical, philosophical and performative traditions to argue that the experience of pantomime viewing provides the audience with a marvellous instrument of self-exploration and self-revelation:

> In fact, only then is the praise that he [i.e. the dancer] gets from the spectators complete, i.e. when each one of the beholders identifies his own characteristic traits or rather when the beholder sees in the dancer, as in a mirror, his own self and (recognises) his habitual passions and actions. For then the spectators cannot even restrain themselves for enjoyment and all together give themselves up to praise, as each one of them sees the likeness of his own soul and recognises his very self. Really, then, that Delphic saying 'Know thyself' (*gnôthi seauton*) is accomplished for them on account of the spectacle, and they leave the theatre having learnt what they must choose and what they must shun and having been taught what they hitherto ignored.[35]

Instead of a voluptuous or penetrating gaze, eyes that can ravish or consume, or even eyes that can be wounded, Lycinus ascribes to the dancer's audience the most sublime kind of gaze, the wise, introspective eye. To use a metaphor borrowed from the Polish director and producer Jerzy Grotowski (1968: 37), Lycinus conceives of a performance that can serve as 'a surgeon's scalpel', enabling the viewer to 'dissect' himself until he ultimately exposes to his own gaze his hidden, innermost core, the ever-elusive object of the Delphic admonition. Taking introspection to its furthest limits, Lycinus interlaces with his argument the all-important concept of the mirror as an instrument of moral self-reflection. *Dance* 81, therefore, leads us straight into the philosophical tradition of self-knowledge (and, potentially, self-improvement) attained via a mirroring process, a tradition stretching at least as far back as Plato and with milestones in the work of Plutarch, Seneca, Apuleius and the Neoplatonists.[36] In Lycinus' idealised presentation of the pantomime stage-audience interaction, returning from a pantomime performance becomes equivalent to coming out of a philosopher's lecture hall, where, as Plutarch (*Moral Essays* 42b) contends, the gaze should ideally be bent back on itself, subjecting the soul to the kind of specular self-scrutiny the physical body undergoes in a real mirror hanging in a barber's shop. By virtue of the same analogy, pantomime viewers can almost be imagined as a philosopher's pupils, allegedly admonished by Socrates to make constant use of the mirror for the purposes of self-inspection and correction,[37] or even philosophers themselves, insofar as they would be ready to defend the mirror, as Apuleius did, as a a sine qua non of philosophical inquiry.[38]

Moreover, if in moralising discourse the mirror-like reflective surface tends to be located in the soul of the sage or the lives of illustrious individuals or even the lucidity of the philosopher's own *logos*,[39] in Lycinus' construction of the reciprocal relation between the audience and the play, Socrates and the line of eminent men have been upstaged by the dancer: it is the pantomime, as opposed to the wise man, who can delight and educate his audience by virtue of a body that becomes a magical kaleidoscope of individual self-reflections. Finally, Lycinus' insistence that the spectator departs having learnt what he must choose and what he must avoid links pantomime as a spectacle to the very cornerstone of Greek and (especially) Roman moral training, that is, the education of the young by means of positive and negative 'examples' (*paradeigmata*; *exempla*).[40] As Livy puts it in the Preface of his history, the value of his narrative resides in its provision of a treasure-trove of *exempla*, some inspiring imitation, others begging for rejection (Livy, *From the Foundation of Rome*, Preface 10).

The instruction offered by pantomime, then, cannot be said to be exhausted in the viewer's passively absorbed knowledge about heroes and legends of a hallowed past. Aided by the figurative mirror that Lycinus seems to envisage as almost an extension of the dancer's own limbs, pantomime viewing has clear-cut, practical implications for the better steering of one's everyday life. Offering its viewer much coveted self-knowledge as well as admonition, the pantomime genre is brought on a par with an array of authoritative discourses (from poetry to history and biography and from elementary school teaching to rhetoric and philosophy),[41] whose privileging of instruction by *exempla* sanctifies them as character-shaping and so, potentially, life-changing for their addressees. The prestige of pantomime dancing could not have been staked any higher.[42]

§4. Athletic pantomime

We have so far examined those among Lycinus' tactics that place the dancer at the centre of the many strands of literate education. Yet although, far and wide over the intellectual landscapes inhabited by the dominant classes in the Hellenistic and imperial world, literacy was largely deemed to represent 'the *only way* in which the mind can be altered' (Morgan 1998: 131), there was no single, uncontested path leading to the acquisition of a universally accepted version of *paideia*. As Whit-marsh (2001: 5) writes,

> The precise nature of the ideal 'education' was a subject of ongoing debate. *Paideia* was not a single, doctrinally coherent system, but the locus for a series of competitions and debates concerning the proper way in which life should be lived.

An endless line of professional rivals were all too eager to fight it out for a share in educational legitimacy or, even more aggressively, for educational primacy: philosopher took up arms against philosopher, grammarian lashed out against music teacher, orator denigrated sculptor, physiogno-mist challenged sophist, and medical practitioner inveighed against ath-letic trainer.

It is precisely this last category of self-proclaimed educators that we must look at more carefully in connection with Lycinus' claims on behalf of pantomime dancing. For Lycinus recommends the genre as 'the most beautiful as well as most rhythmical of gymnastic exercises',

> making the body soft and flexible and light and teaching it to change its shape with ease and procuring for it no small amount of strength (*Dance* 71).

Taking his argument a step further, he claims that not only is pantomime on a par with athletic training but that it improves on it, constituting an option significantly preferable to the conventional path athletics offer. Like the poetry of Propertius and Tibullus, which sets up the provocative ideal of a *militia amoris* (soldiery of love) as a rival and more fulfilling alternative to the life of civic *militia* with its misery and carnage, Lycinus extols pantomime as a spectacle 'much more pleasant to watch' than an athletic contest's ugly bundle of blood, dust and peril:[43] it offers a superior kind of *thea*, which 'displays' the dancers in a manner that is 'often safer as well as more beautiful and more enjoyable' (*Dance* 71; cf. Libanius, *Oration* 64.119). But why should Lycinus feel the need to include athletics in the 'web of power' called upon to legitimate pantomime dancing? The answer surely lies in the fact that the Greek tradition of athletic education and athletic excellence continued to thrive even under Roman rule.

As van Nijf and, more recently, König have amply demonstrated,[44] following a line of inquiry that goes back to Louis Robert, athletic educa-tion and the ideal of the well-trained body had a key role to play in the manifold strategies of male élite self-fashioning in the first centuries AD. Flying in the face of the much better known discursive documents that forge an indissoluble association of élite identity with literary *paideia*, the frequently under-valued material record tells a different story. The urban upper classes expended both funds and energy in order to record the athletic achievements of themselves and their offspring, turning physical prowess into 'a major source of masculine identity' and an 'essential vehicle of elite self-presentation' (van Nijf 2003: 265, 267). Reflecting both an older (Platonic and Isocratean) model for the holistic development of soul-and-body as well as contemporary trends in encomiastic literature, a wealth of honorific inscriptions and funerary epigrams claim for their subjects moral *and* bodily *aretê*, routinely turning each athlete or deceased young notable into 'a classy combination of brawn and brain' (van Nijf 2003: 282; 2004: 222). The good citizen, an honour to his family and benefit to his city, is perceived as having both culture and athletics under his belt, linked together as 'two sides of the same coin' (van Nijf 2003: 282). Even beyond the politics of élite commemoration, in the *gymnasion*, that central hub of the élites and 'most important educational institution of the Greek east within the Roman Empire' (König 2005: 47), 'physical skills were taught alongside intellectual qualities' (van Nijf 2004: 206-7),[45] while school-teachers (*grammatikoi*) and athletic trainers (*paidotribai*), the joint 'products' and 'producers' of *gymnasion*-culture, could both bear the title of *paideutai*, 'educators' (van Nijf 2004: 209).

That Lycinus should take care to situate the genre in the circles of literate as well as somatic education,[46] then, stipulating for the dancer not only intellectual and moral assets but also a body of perfect physical proportions (see *Dance* 75; cf. Libanius, *Oration* 64.103), is an entirely intelligible move. Besides, given the uncontested status of athletics as a hallmark of Greek culture, demonstrating pantomime's affinity with forms and ideals of athleticism was tantamount to proclaiming the genre's outright affiliation to Greekness. Granted, Lycinus has already done this by means of annexing pantomime to such impeccable markers of Hellenism as philosophy and rhetoric. However, as van Nijf (2001: 334) has argued persuasively, not only was athletic excellence 'an alternative passport to Greek identity' in the imperial East but, outside the narrow realm of a 'small and hyper-literate élite', it may well have seemed to the privileged classes 'a more attractive way' of being Greek: 'many may have felt it easier to achieve social status, Greek identity and manhood through the training of their bodies than through the arduous route of literary education' (ibid.: 329). It is to such segments of his audience that Lycinus' fashioning of a bond between athleticism and pantomime would have seemed particularly attractive.

Interestingly, on the subject of the interface between dancing and gymnastics/athletics, Lycinus is not a lone voice. In Plato's *Laws* (813b), dancing is coupled with bodily gymnastics as part of a young boy's or girl's physical education and, although the spatial complexity of the pantomime's dancing figures cannot be reconstructed, our evidence suggests that these must have included acrobatic numbers of extreme difficulty (cf. Chapter 2§1), comparable to the training some athletes were subjected to. Libanius, for example, for whom the early stages of a pantomime's education start in the hands of the gymnastic trainer, the *paidotribês*, reports that this teacher will twist his charge into more numerous bends and spirals than a wrestler (*Oration* 64.104), the accomplished dancers outperforming even the pentathletes in leaping (ibid., 68-9). Polybius (*Histories* 9.20.7) observes that those who wish to be indoctrinated in pantomime dancing consent to acquire even some of the skills of the *palaestra*, while in a difficult passage Athenaeus (*Sophists at Dinner* 629b) remarks that, in the times of old, figures and postures were carried over from statuary to dancing, and from the dancing floor 'into the wrestling schools'.[47]

The grey area that pantomime and athletics were supposed to share can best be glimpsed through the slippery semantic field of *cheironomia*, on which pantomime lays, according to Lycinus, a legitimate claim.[48] Its primary sense being the rhythmical movement of the hands (Pollux, *Onomasticon* 2.153), *cheironomia* was nevertheless a versatile term, belonging to dancing in general[49] as well as to the world of the *gymnasion* and *palaestra*. Pantomime dancers in particular could be called *cheironomoi* and their dance *cheironomia*,[50] while, as Dickie demonstrated, 'under the Roman Empire dancing was one of the activities of the palaestra or gymnasium', indeed 'one of the ways in which *eurhythmos kinêsis* [rhythmical movement] was inculcated in the gymnasium' (1993: 114).[51] Generally speaking, symmetry of bodily form, rhythm and grace of movement seem to have played almost as prominent a role in *palaestra* training as they did in the realm of pantomime dancing (see Dickie, ibid.), and similarities in the language and movements used in both areas[52] may well point in the direction of clear links between 'the training of pantomimes and the gymnasium exercises of the Greeks' (Slater 1994: 134). What is more, the Greek custom of 'elegant callisthenics and dance exercises in the gymnasium' may well have been 'discovered' by the Roman youth 'by the late Republic' (Slater 1993: 211), so that upper-class young Romans would be 'skilled in the techniques of Greek chironomy' (Slater 1994: 136) (cf. Chapter 4§1).

Lycinus' presentation of pantomime as a gymnastics of the body would have been infinitely more persuasive than his rhetorical construction of the genre as a 'gymnastics of the mind' (see Chapter 8§1). Even so, I very much doubt that 'heavy' athletes could have been won over by Lycinus' claims. In Aelius Aristides' (deeply biased) perspective, the victors in the Panhellenic games have nothing in common with effeminate bodily poses, the poses that belong to the realm of *orchêsis*:

> Come, let us consider the athletes at the crown contests, such as Dorieus of Rhodes and Glaucus of Carystus and Milo and Polydamas, and all those in whose honour bronze statues are erected. Which of these two things happened? Did those in charge of the contest for Olympian Zeus crown them for being unmanned and drunk and twisting about like dancing girls or because they exhibited admirable endurance and bravery of both soul and body, qualities which generate the greatest and most abiding pleasures both for

those who possess them and for those who share in the knowledge of such things? (*Oration* 34.23).

Pitted against the professional athlete, who has been trained to assert his painstakingly attained virility through displays of physical fitness in all kinds of contests, the pantomime, who has adulterated his Heraclean bodily strength with the full dose of daintiness that is proverbially the domain of Aphrodite (*Dance* 73), can only be transgressive, non-assimilable material. His deviance challenges the established link between full-blown masculinity and traditionally defined athletic prowess. Just as Rudolph Valentino found it very difficult to counteract the stigma of effeminacy by actively taking part 'in the cult of physical fitness, with scores of publicity stills showing him working out in seminudity or boxing, fencing, or lifting weights' (Hansen 1991: 265), a pantomime could have certainly expected comments of the kind: 'this athlete possesses strength, but it does not originate in the wrestling ground'.[53]

§5. Enchanted *and* instructed: a wise audience for an intellectual genre

Finally, no redemption of the pantomime genre would have been possible without a parallel redemption of its viewing public. Although Lycinus never wages systematic war against Crato's multiple assumptions concerning half-witted pantomime audiences, driven out of their senses or possessed by Bacchic frenzy (e.g. *Dance* 3 and 5), and even takes over (*Dance* 85), albeit momentarily, Crato's fixed idea of the viewer's irrational emotional response, he does make a concentrated effort to dissociate the picture of the pantomime addict from the stereotypes of spellbinding and fascination prevalent in Greco-Roman texts.[54] The apologist's model of pantomime spectating is presented instead as a wonderful amalgam of *thelxis* and mental alertness, enchantment[55] intertwined with critical discrimination. With the exception of one notorious tale of an audience thrown into raptures (*Dance* 83-4), internalised audiences embedded in the treatise set forth a way of viewing primarily dependent on intellectual appreciation (see, e.g., *Dance* 76). We are not far from Bertolt Brecht's (1964: 14) ideal of a 'quick-witted audience that knows how to observe, and gets its enjoyment from setting its reason to work'.

Yet while for Brecht emotional involvement precludes intellectual insights and rational judgement, in Lucian's treatise the pantomime spectator is being fashioned as *both* potentially entranced *and* in possession of his critical faculties. As Lycinus puts it in the conclusion of his speech to Crato,

So, I will have no need at all to repeat Circe's saying to you: 'I am amazed that, although you drank these drugs, you remained unenchanted.' For you

93

will be enchanted (*thelchthêsêi gar*) and, by Zeus, you will not have a donkey's head or a pig's heart, but your mind will be more firmly set and, wallowing in your delight, you will not offer even a tiny part of the brew to anyone else to drink (*Dance* 85).

The spectacle on offer may well be a *thelktêrion*, an enchantment as powerful as Circe's evil drugs (Homer, *Odyssey* 10.236), but the outcome of such bewitchment is the complete opposite of the loss of one's humanity or the obscuring of one's reason:

Dancing effects just this: it charms (*thelgousa*) the eyes as well as causing them to be wide awake and stimulates the mind, so that it can take in every single bit of the action (*Dance* 85).

Rather than blunting critical awareness, pantomime enthralment goes hand in hand with knowledge, perspicaciousness and wisdom. As Lycinus verbalises his experience,

I am not standing about in forgetfulness of my domestic situation nor in ignorance of my own affairs but, if I may offer my opinion without any trepidation, it is as a much wiser person and far more discerning with respect to what is happening in life that I have come back to you from the theatre. Or rather, it is fitting to borrow Homer's very phrase, that whoever has seen this spectacle 'returns home having enjoyed himself as well as knowing more' (*terpsamenos neitai kai pleiona eidôs*) [*Od.* 12.188] (*Dance* 4).

In other words, Crato's disparaging equation of the dancer (and, by extension, the entire genre) to the sensual destructiveness of the Homeric Sirens (see *Dance* 3) is now being turned on its head: in pantomime audience-response, pleasure (*terpsis*) comparable to that bestowed by the supreme enchantresses of legend is inextricably interwoven with enhanced knowledge and 'beneficial education' (*Dance* 23). The genre therefore teaches *through* (rather than *despite*) enchantment – that is to say, through its infinite capacity to charm the viewer's eyes and ears alike (*Dance* 72).

Given that, by Lucian's time, 'enjoyment' (by means of fiction) and 'instruction' (based on the imparting of knowledge and truth) are almost ubiquitously understood as the exclusive and non-negotiable functions of poetry (especially tragedy) and history, and therefore forced into a rigid, indissoluble polarity,[56] Lycinus' claims have much broader implications. By showcasing so prominently the instructional aspect (*didaskousa*) of pantomime pleasure (*terpousa*) and harping so obsessively on it, Lycinus not only grants the genre the quintessential mission of (at least) two qualitatively different discourses, but also places it provocatively and programmatically within the noble tradition of performative didacticism, such as we know it, most notably, from a range of fifth-century comic texts.[57] Closest to Lycinus' formula detailed in Lucian's treatise comes the comic poet Timocles' claim on the psychagogic/educational value of the tragic genre: 'enthralled by another's *pathos* | the mind goes away full of pleasure spliced with instruction' (*Women at the Dionysia*, fr. 6 K-A, 6-7).

Thelxis and *psychagôgia*, however, are not the sole attributes of poetry[58] that pantomime usurps. Bestowed generously upon the genre is also poetry's most distinctive property from the archaic epics onwards, namely its unrivalled ability to assuage the soul:

> he who is afflicted by grief comes out of the theatre more cheerful than before, as if he had drunk a drug (*pharmakon*) inducing forgetfulness (*lêthedanon*) and, according to the poet, grief-removing (*nêpenthes*) and anger-reducing (*acholon*) (*Dance* 79).

The poet invoked at this juncture is Homer, and the grief-allaying *pharmakon* is the magic drug Helen had famously mixed up with wine, before pouring it out to Telemachus and the other guests in Menelaus' palace (*Odyssey* 4.219ff.).[59] Possessing the qualities of *logos* and of bardic song, whose listener 'forgets his anxious cares and does not give a thought to his own griefs' (Hesiod, *Theogony* 102-3; cf. 55), Helen's fortified potion was associated ever since antiquity (Plutarch, *Moral Essays* 614) with the story she herself proceeded to narrate for the distraction of her guests in *Odyssey* 4.238-9. By equating pantomime, then, with Helen's drug-and-tale and pantomime's viewer with the Homeric banqueters who drank-and-listened to it in Sparta, Lycinus claims for the mute, sub-literary dance poetry's own peculiar power to beguile and to charm, especially by setting its enchantments at work upon the passions.[60] Besides, fixing our eyes on the stage, Lycinus' claim bestows on pantomime the pacifying (or, as Brecht would say, narcotic) influence sometimes attributed to tragedy, a genre that could be constructed as enabling one's mind to 'forget its own troubles' (Timocles, *Women at the Dionysia*, fr. 6 K-A, 5) through witnessing the tragic hero's predicament, invariably more serious than the kind of calamity befalling the average mortal (*Women at the Dionysia*, fr. 6 K-A, 8-19).[61] Flying against all notion of the genre as a disease (*Dance* 6) that needs a cure (*Dance* 4), Lycinus boldly foists on it the therapeutic qualities traditionally ascribed to *logos*, the drug par excellence for the afflicted soul.[62]

§6. Conclusion

As we have seen in this chapter, Lycinus attempts to reposition pantomime on the cultural map by creating a complex network of affiliations to anchor it in the seas of high culture.[63] At the end of the dialogue, Crato declares himself fully persuaded and eager to allow his eyes and ears to become immersed in the spectacle's delights:

And be sure to remember, my good friend, whenever you happen to go to the theatre, to reserve a place for me as well at your side, so that you are not the only one returning to us wiser from that place (*Dance* 85).

Whether Lycinus' 'naturalisation' of the dancer in the realm of high culture could really have persuaded a hardened, deeply prejudiced intellectual in the mould of Crato we shall examine in detail in Chapter 8. But, even if Lycinus' exposition is considered only self-referentially with respect to its own arguments and its internal logic, flaws abound.

Quite apart from never addressing head-on some of Crato's key objections to the spectacle (primarily those centring on the dancer's own morality and gender-bending), there is a strong sense that Lycinus' apology has not entirely broken free from the language, mentality and terms of his antagonist's polemical discourse. To mention only a very few examples, mirrors, Sirens, drugs, and even Proteus himself are treacherous allies in the face of Crato's accusations. The swirl of their potential connotations can turn them very easily into precarious signifiers, able to plunge the dancer even deeper into the murky grounds of femininity,[64] seduction or moral duplicity.

As for the greatest faux-pas, this is certainly *Dance* 83-4, relating the story of the unlucky pantomime who, while dancing the episode of Ajax's madness, became so imbued with his part that 'one could reasonably have got the impression that he was not feigning madness but was raving mad himself'. His *pathos* spilled over and engulfed the viewers, who 'went mad collectively together with Ajax and were jumping and shouting and flinging their garments about' (*Dance* 83). Lycinus seems to be narrating the story while thinking of it as little more than a spectacular technical lapse, on a par with ignorance, senseless movements incompatible with the accompanying music or sheer confusion of cognate pantomimic themes, such as the dancing of Thyestes' tecnophagy, instead of that of Cronus, or the representation of Glauce's death, instead of that of Semele (*Dance* 80). However, what is actually at stake in this passage is much more important.[65]

In the first place, if reality and fiction, professional artists and their *dramatis personae*, can blend as deeply as the Ajax anecdote suggests, Crato may be right in perceiving the pantomime himself as a 'pernicious', 'lethal' man (*Dance* 5), no different in moral substance from the characters that populate the lewd legends he enacts (*Dance* 2): the more intimate the fusion between the actor/dancer and his part, the greater the danger of contamination by the vices of his fictive characters. Secondly, Lycinus' vivid pictures of a whole auditorium infected by the dancer's 'performative' insanity corroborate Crato's deep-seated preconceptions about pantomime audiences given over to collective frenzy (cf. *Dance* 5 and 3) and pantomime spectacles unworthy of a self-reflecting intellectual's attention (cf. *Dance* 2-3). If the currents of energy released by pantomime are such that dancers can be turned into their characters, and viewers into a replica of the dancing soloist, the 'self' being subsumed in both cases into the 'other', pantomime can no longer be the urbane and educational spectacle of Lycinus' apology. Stage and auditorium become instead immoderately joined up in one continuous flow of indiscriminate emotion, exposing the genre as anarchic, uncharted and dangerous terrain. Seen through the lens of *Dance* 83-4, pantomime theatre cannot be said to represent a prized instrument for the inculcation of knowledge and moral instruction. Rather than bolstering the apologist's general case, the story of the mad dancer rehearses, vindicates and heightens some of the prejudices and reservations expressed by Crato (and similarly-minded sceptics).

Yet what might such blots on the canvas of Lycinus' narrative mean? The question is inextricably interwoven with the stubborn issue of Lucian's own attitude to the genre and its artist – a question that will be revisited in Chapter 12. It is nevertheless already possible to claim that, if holes (no doubt, deliberately planted) do exist in Lycinus' fine-honed rhetoric, they signal to us loudly that the dialogue's dominant voice should not be taken as gospel truth. Not only Crato's but also Lycinus' perspective has to be taken with a pinch of salt, set within quotation marks, understood as ironised. In this respect, *On the Dance* is in many ways similar to Lucian's equally witty *Anacharsis*, where the juxtaposition of Solon's traditionalist perspective and Anacharsis' inquisitive, almost subversive stance throws sharply into relief 'a sophist's awareness of the potential incongruity of any single way of seeing a subject' (Branham 1989: 104). Employing rhetorical tactics reminiscent of those in *Anacharsis*, Lucian 'ingeniously undermines the certainties of both of his interlocutors' and, whether readers are in sympathy with Crato or Lycinus, he nags and challenges them 'to re-examine the significance of their own pre-conceptions' (König 2005: 95, on *Anacharsis*; cf. Branham 1989: 88).

Lucian's *On the Dance* or
The Sophist's Pantomime

We saw in the previous chapter that Lycinus located the dancer firmly within the orbit of liberal education, placing him at the crossroads of all the avenues through which symbolic capital could be accumulated in the second century AD: rhetoric, philosophy, music, poetry and even athleticism (cf. Whitmarsh 2004: 144). This chapter suggests that in fact Lycinus went much further, for the dancer fashioned by his exposition is moulded in accordance with the age's predominant mentality, more specifically, in accordance with the cultural preoccupations of the Second Sophistic. As we shall see in Chapters 11-12, this 'extraordinary phenomenon', consisting of a culture of erudite display-oratory and 'found over all of the Greek-speaking parts of the Roman empire' (Whitmarsh 2005: 3) during the first three centuries AD, provides the broader intellectual milieu for Lucian's own literary activity.[1]

To start with, *polymatheia* (great learning) as a legitimating principle and an empowering force in the career of ambitious male élites achieves its highest currency in the first centuries AD. Some of the most successful men of letters are now praised for their exceptionally wide-ranging wisdom or the versatility of their manifold mental skills and intellectual accomplishments. So, for example, the erudite guests at Larensis' dinner party, the subject of Athenaeus' *Sophists at Dinner*, can be described as 'most experienced in all branches of liberal education' (1a), and Apuleius can boast that he has drunk 'the specially made wine of poetry, the clear white of geometry, the sweet muscat of music, the dry red of dialectics, and the never-sating nectar of universal philosophy' (*Flowery Excerpts* 20.4; trans. Hilton in Harrison 2001).[2] But if a sophist can be compared to a 'breathing library and a walking museum' (Eunapius, *Lives of the Philosophers* 456, on Longinus), it is not difficult to see that Lucian's pantomime has been fashioned as a 'dancing' library, the knowledge carried within the sophist's head now ingrained in the dancer's body.

Paideia, however, was not in itself a notion without multiple and interlocked qualifiers in the period of the Second Sophistic. Quite apart from being gendered 'male', insofar as only men (and men of privilege at that) could ever hope to attain it, it was also deemed the surest indicator of a specific cultural tradition, that belonging to the Greeks.[3] This is the reason that in this period, *hoi Hellênes*, 'the Greeks', means primarily 'the

educated', those partaking of *hellênikê paideia*, as Isocrates had so pro-
phetically declared in the fourth century BC, with respect to the paideutic
role of the classical Athenian *polis*.[4] The slow, painful process of acquiring
an education was the most highly respected way of *becoming* Greek,
constructing an Hellenic identity despite one's actual ethnic provenance,
which might well be non-Greek.[5] A note of caution is nevertheless in order
at this point, because the 'Greece' that mattered at the time of the Second
Sophistic was not the conquered Greek land under the sway of Rome, but
the *idealised* Greece at the height of its glory, the Greece of the luminous
classical past. In truth, the pantomime constructed by Lycinus could not
have borne more clearly the marks of the period's multiple engagements
with all aspects of the classical past.

If the sophist, by virtue of his possession and public display of an
impressive knowledge of all things Greek, becomes the guardian of Hellenic heritage in the Roman political present (cf. Russell 1983: 84 n. 51),
the pantomime too, by virtue of the vast swathes of Greek mythology and
history 'sedimented' in his body,[6] emerges from the dialogue as a treasure-
trove of Greek cultural patrimony. His genre, correspondingly, becomes a
theatre of Greek memories, a theatre for the display of 'the tales of the
(ancient) Greeks', as the sixth-century AD Syrian homilist Joshua the
Stylite puts it.[7] By preserving and re-inscribing figures of Greek history
and legend in the 'here and now' of his performance, the pantomime
materialises the most characteristic cultural obsession of the Second
Sophistic: the collective desire to 'repossess – even reactualize – in a new
age the heritage of a long-vanished past' (Zeitlin 2001: 207).

There was, however, another equally important way of 'being' or 'becoming' Greek in the heyday of the Second Sophistic. In the first centuries AD,
individuals and cities alike went to great lengths to establish or promote
their personal or collective standing in the present by claiming direct
descent from the remote Hellenic past. As Swain (1996: 411) writes, 'the
concept of descent through historical or mythological figures of the Old
Greek world' became a vital way of 'ensuring genuine contact with Greek
antiquity among Greeks and those who claimed to be Greek'. With respect
to cities in particular and, most critically, the cities whose cultural affiliation to Greekness seemed tenuous,[8] their fate 'in terms of imperial
recognition and favour' was often tied up with their 'mythic genealogy and
history' (Alcock 2001: 331): it was contingent on their success in staging
compelling narratives of continuity with the political, historical and
mythological 'hard core' of the Hellenic world, the great ancient civic
centres of mainland Greece.[9] Despite the fact that, even in the Hellenistic
world, 'the right to privilege, the very right to existence, increasingly had
to be demanded upon historic grounds' (Alcock 1997: 33), descent as a
touchstone of Greekness on the level of civic self-definition was never a
matter of greater urgency than in Lucian's own time, in the early second
century AD, when the so-called 'Panhellenion', the Emperor Hadrian's new

organisation of Greek cities, was created in 131/2.[10] In this particular case, 'being Greek' in terms of culture only was no longer adequate, for membership of the prestigious institution was 'restricted to cities that could establish impeccable credentials of Greek descent'.[11] Predictably, a whole cultural industry of civic genealogies (real or invented) emerged, with men of standing and *paideia* determined to leave no stone unturned in their antiquarian searches. Mythology (the pantomime's own home turf) no less than history was harnessed to the task of preparing on behalf of a commissioning community the kind of claim that would be able to withstand the 'test of Hellenism' (Woolf 1994: 129), and thus provide access to the much-coveted right to be called 'Greek'.[12]

How does Lucian's dialogue relate to such genealogical preoccupations? Despite Lycinus' insistence that he does not purport to offer a dance genealogy himself,[13] he does acknowledge the existence of such material,[14] and actually *attempts* pantomime's accreditation 'by means of pedigree',[15] that is, by means of fashioning for it a long line of illustrious ancestors running back into the prehistoric and classical Greek past. As if pantomime were a city on the outer margins of the Hellenised world, vying for admission into Hadrian's Panhellenion, Lycinus proposes for the genre a mode of self-definition that spotlights its glorious Hellenic lineage.[16] In *Dance* 8-32, in a sometimes tedious digression into myth, history, socio-religious and performance practice, Lycinus anchors pantomime in the mists of cosmogonic time (*Dance* 8),[17] his various narrative stopovers[18] being highlighted as the 'roots, so to speak, and the foundations' (*Dance* 34) for the contemporary flourishing of the genre. Although his account does not unfold in any precise chronological order, it does posit, as other dance genealogies seem to have done (*Dance* 7), a clear first beginning (*Dance* 8), and seems to have been conceived as the showcasing of several incremental steps (see *Dance* 7) towards the perfection that takes shape in the imperial present (see *Dance* 7 and 34). Moreover, Rhea and the Couretes, Neoptolemus and his pyrrhic dance, Pollux and Castor with their Spartan dances, alongside so many other legendary figures that people Lycinus' narrative, are meant to provide the pantomime with distinguished mythical forebears, capable of sanctioning him as a rightful inheritor of the Hellenic world. As for Homer and Hesiod, who 'praise dancing' (*Dance* 23-4), they too are intended to lend the genre the kind of respectability that only Greek lineage can ensure.[19] In line with the mentality of the Sophistic era, Lycinus claims for pantomime an entitlement to special respect by offering abundant proof of its undeniable Greek ancestry.

An inextricable part of the spinning of genealogies was the demonstration of sound and often multiply intertwined 'links of filiation', the so-called *syngeneia,* twinning the candidate for membership into the Panhellenic league with notable centres of the old (i.e. pre-Roman) Greek world.[20] Lycinus devotes chapters 38-53 to a narrative that maps pantomime's best-known stories onto the geographical grid of mainland Greece, a significant move both in terms of how the Panhellenion operated[21] and with respect to the ubiquitous implication of regional lore (be it mythical, historical or ritual) in Greek narratives of local self-definition.[22] Like an erudite sophist/genealogist of the mid-second century AD, Lycinus composes for the genre its own 'foundation story', affiliating pantomime in its contemporary form to famous mainland Greek places (Attica, Megara, Thebes, Corinth, Mycenae, Nemea, Sparta, Elis, Arcadia, Aetolia, Thessaly), just as much as anchoring it firmly, as a form of dance, into the Hellenic cultural universe from the dawn of time to the present. In other words, the 'kinship ties' Lycinus hammers out between pantomime and 'Greekness' are not merely bonds with geographical locations but also links with social and ritual practices powerful enough to integrate the genre into the cultural matrices of the Greek world.

Indeed, Lycinus' literary 'genealogy' may well be much more factual than many politically traced genealogies in the real world of the second and third centuries AD. Where so much was at stake, it is only to be expected that neglected local traditions would have been flipped into prominence or imaginatively embellished, decisive details tampered with or mythical links invented. So, for example, as Curty (1995: 205) suspects, Tabenos, the otherwise unknown Argive hero who allegedly founded the Cilician city of Tabae, must have been created to serve the needs of a claim to Greekness. As both *polymatheia* and rhetorical ability were undoubtedly crucial to success in such enterprises, the whole business of *genealogein* (tracing by way of pedigree) would have been the special province of sophists or, more broadly, men of education. Lycinus declares himself sensitive to the possible charge of 'ignorance or lack of education' that may attach to his cursory foray into the forebears of pantomime dancing, while in the same breath professing his indifference to the glory accruing to displays of *polymatheia*:

> But I, for my part, deeming that overzealousness about such things (sc. *genealogein*) is vulgar, pedantic and, as far as I am concerned, out of place, I pass it by (*Dance* 33).

In reality, however, such disclaimers are a covert way of drawing attention to Lucian's actual desire to be admired for the thoroughness of his *paideia*, as was, for example, the sophist Publius Antius Antiochus, whose success in demonstrating the 'ancestral link' (*syngeneian*) between his own city of Cilician Aegeae and the Peloponnesian Argos was commemorated by means of an Argive decree carved in stone.[23]

So, with an eye fixed on what counts as especially significant in the intellectual quarters of the Second Sophistic, Lycinus presents his pantomime as 'Greek' on account of *both* descent *and* culture – ironically, the doubly powerful credential that Lucian, himself a Syrian, partly lacks (see Chapter 12§2). To the radical discontinuity feared by Crato between pantomime and the manliness of Greek *paideia* (cf. *Dance* 3), Lycinus' apology opposes an argument of unbroken continuity: the silent dancer is as legitimate a mouthpiece of the Hellenic past as are Crato himself and his educated friends. One can even detect conceptual similarities between Lycinus' defence of pantomime and Pausanias' contemporary understanding of the Greeks 'as united by a continuous culture stretching from the era of Deucalion and Minos down to his own time' (Bowie 1996: 208). Like Pausanias' description of the Greek world, Lycinus' pantomime offers the intellectually minded viewer a representation of 'all things Greek' (Pausanias, *Description of Greece* 1.26.4). And just as Pausanias brings 'all the separate *hellenika* ("worlds of Greece") into one Greece' (Elsner 1992: 14), the pantomime fashioned by Lucian's pen amalgamates all the separate Greek microcosms with their dance-narratives into his own corporeal, 'mobile' architecture, an embodied mythological-and-geographical compendium which, like Pausanias' text, can be 'read' as a guidebook of Hellenism. Watching the totality of a pantomime's available repertoire, such as that laid out by Lycinus, an educated pantomime lover is able to navigate the whole geographical territory of the old Greek world,[24] the glory of 'free' Greece which, as a political entity, can now exist only at the intersection of collective memory and individual imagination. Lycinus' paragraphs on pantomime geography are the vantage points from which the suitably equipped second-century AD viewer could take a plunge into the deep pools of Greek cultural identity.

Most importantly, if the dancer *was* actually perceived by some in the way suggested by Lycinus, that is, as a storehouse of Hellenic memories, pantomime viewing would emerge as one of the manifold ways in which one could engage with the classical past in the period of the Second Sophistic, 'swim[ming]' in it as 'fish do in water', as Hobsbawm (1972: 17) would put it. The *pepaideumenos* who enjoys listening to the classically inspired verbal pyrotechnics of sophists (cf. Chapters 8§2, 9§1 and 11); the citizen or visitor who takes a stroll in an imperial city's streets or *agora*, teeming with classical presences, and the pantomime addict absorbed in 'reading' the narrative of Greekness etched on the dancer's bodily discourse, are all locked into the same cluster of 'backward-looking practices', that cultural archaism which, although 'far from unprecedented in earlier Greek self-perception and self-presentation' (Alcock 2002: 39), was the hallmark of the Second Sophistic in the imperial East.[25]

There is no doubt that this dazzling construct of the genre as a splendidly Second Sophistic product did not really form part of the experience of the man in the street, the non-urbane, uncultured spectator. It is, nevertheless, of no inferior value, being a brilliant illustration of the genre's chameleon nature, its adeptness at modifying its colours to reflect the hues of whichever narrative provides it with a literary home (cf. Introduction). Just as the author (most probably Lucian) of the remarkable treatise *On the Syrian Goddess* 'translates the strange practices and attitudes (strange, at least, to Greeks) of late-antique Syrian religion into the thought-structure and conceptual frame of Greco-Roman culture in the imperial period' (Elsner 2001: 125), the author of *On the Dance* translates the alien (at least to the élites) mentality of pantomime dancing into the most quintessentially upper-class idiolect of the first centuries AD, namely the cultural language of the Second Sophistic.

Pantomime, the Intellectual's Equal?
The Genre Through the Eyes of
the Cultural Élites

We saw in Chapter 4 that the socio-political élites throughout the empire not only embraced pantomime as a spectacle and graced its performers with gifts and honours but, most importantly, used the dancer as a major asset in their own agonistic or other performative events: the star panto-mime's ability to 'please the people' was easily convertible into political and economic capital as well as social prestige for a festival organiser or civic benefactor. But while the élite experience as lived in real life proved often tolerant or even enthusiastic towards pantomimes,[1] the picture changes dramatically when we take into account élite life as 'lived largely in the imagination',[2] that is to say the élite not in its state of 'being' but in its state of *'being-perceived'*[3] – crucially, by itself. Whenever the politically dominant classes chose to redraft themselves in a different capacity, as *intellectual* nobility, they also tended to reinvent themselves as over-zeal-ous guardians of cultural boundaries and arbiters of cultural authentic-ity.[4] Investing themselves with the power to pronounce definitive judgements on the value of different cultural expressions, they foisted on pantomime dancing 'signs of vulgarity' rather than 'signs of distinction' (Bourdieu 1984: 483). It is first and foremost this élite as an 'imagined'[5] or symbolic community, as the product of its own language-structures and as it emerges from its own strategies of textual self-representation, that will preoccupy us in this and the following chapter. Was there any chance that élite mentality as a carefully self-constructed subject-position would have been prepared to endorse Lycinus' fashioning of pantomime as a highly polished, educated genre? Was there any possibility that it might have been willing to accept the dancer himself as the intellectual's equal?

One preliminary clarification is in order. In our attempt to reconstruct aspects of upper-class attitudes to pantomime, any use of the binary high/low and élite/popular culture includes invisible quotation marks: all these terms must be understood as shorthand for socio-cultural formations that were neither static (and therefore easily definable) nor even homoge-neous. In the higher and the lower social registers alike, 'culture' was an ongoing process, 'continually to be renewed, recreated, defended and modified' (Williams 1977: 112). Furthermore, on each side of the slippery divide, élite and popular culture in themselves were hierarchically structured and ranked. A multiplicity of socio-ideological 'languages',[6] belonging to different professions, vocations and moral inclinations, literary and entertainment genres, or even educational discourses, vied for supremacy in areas irreducibly plural and varied. Élite and popular alike were extremely volatile, unstable constellations of 'cultural performances' articulated in a bewildering range of discursive complexity. Finally, both domains existed in a state of constant interaction, high culture in particular finding (or presenting) itself forever challenged, threatened and even haunted by elements of the subaltern.[7] Pantomime-related struggles were merely one element in the endless dialogic confrontations between different levels and notions of cultural legitimacy and illegitimacy that were played out in the post-classical world. The vestiges of such (often messy) negotiations are still visible in our texts to date.

§1. *Paideia* embodied and the intellectual's sneer

Let us start by casting a critical eye over the cultural terrain of the late Hellenistic and Roman world that pantomime was poised to infiltrate. As the centuries rolled by, élite texts became increasingly obsessed with the erection or preservation of impermissible boundaries between the imaginary landscapes inhabited by those in possession of education and the territories that housed those deprived of it. Beyond the area circumscribed by Education, an educated man could (and should) discern nothing but an intellectual wasteland, stretching out as far as the eye could see, and populated by 'slaves and scum', ants, ground-crawlers and creatures smaller than the Pygmies (Lucian, *Hermotimus* 81 and 5), in view of their lack of the up-market educational capital that was the near-exclusive property of the élites.[8] The Preface to Aulus Gellius' *Attic Nights* is typical of the many self-conscious cultural positionings enacted by élite texts in the first centuries AD. It expels forthrightly the uneducated throngs from the author's literary endeavours, with a passion openly compared to the religious fervour of the mystic Chorus in the Aristophanic *Frogs*, initiates anxious to exclude those uninitiated into their Eleusinian rites.[9] When so many of our texts yield the impression of a total impasse in the communicative channels linking the high and the low on all conceivable registers[10] or brim with the educated man's delight in fashioning himself as the jealous guardian of intellectual pleasures not meant to be wasted on the vulgar many, it becomes hard to see how pantomime, even supported in practice by some of the most powerful among the Greek and Roman upper classes, could have made a credible bid for acceptance as an edifying mouthpiece of élite cultural traditions. Indeed, in outright negative representations of the genre, the pantomime experience was categorically denied any claim (of the kind envisaged by Lucian's Lycinus) on didactic discourse.

Rather than propagating education and culture, pantomime was fashioned, by both Christians and a substantial concentration of pagan voices, as an alternative, subversive locus of authority, a force that threatened to disrupt instructional activities or, even worse, antagonise the voice of God. Libanius, for example, his long defence of dancing (*Oration* 64) notwithstanding, never misses a chance to stress the incompatibility of pantomimes with the study of rhetoric (e.g. *Oration* 35.17), even if only to complain that his students rudely exchange glances about charioteers, mimes and pantomime dancers while he is trying to declaim (*Oration* 3.12).[11] And who can forget the charming story Pliny the Younger tells (*Letter* 7.24) about society lady Ummidia Quadratilla, who would always send her grandson Quadratus away to his studies before allowing herself to watch her private troupe of pantomimes perform in her own house (5). Quadratus never laid eyes on those dancers till after his grandmother's death, when they danced in public at the Sacerdotal Games (6).

On the Christian front, John Chrysostom fulminates unceasingly against those who, while unable to recite a psalm or a portion of the Scriptures or even to remember the names of the holy books, prove marvellously retentive when it comes to matters of the stage, and impressively eager when a pantomime or other entertainer invites the city to a *thea* (see *PG* 59.320; cf. 57.22, 57.30). If to the pagan intellectual the pantomime is merely an inferior purveyor of knowledge, to the Christian he is the 'black double' of an educator: a teacher of lessons which corrupt or lead to death (Cyprian, *Letter* 2.1.1 and 2.2.3), as well as 'an instructor of passive homosexuals' (Tatian, *Address to the Greeks* 22.1), the pantomime has turned his teaching trade into 'a study of adultery, a gymnasium of prostitution' (John Chrysostom, *PG* 60.301) and a 'common and public school of licentiousness' for those who attend it.[12] Such acts of exclusion, bold and unforgiving though they seem, are neither unintelligible within their own context nor entirely unpredictable. In a world where all cultural interfaces constituted slippery and heavily contested ground, the frictions between pantomime and high culture were bound to be multiple as well as complex. It is precisely because of such complexity that pantomime's precarious balancing act between élite sophistication and the modalities of popular, mass culture demands a harder look.

The upper classes of Hellenistic and imperial times reproduced themselves primarily (although not exclusively; see Chapter 6§4) through the acquisition of literacy and the achievement of textual competence, which led to the most coveted mastery of the art of *logos*. More specifically, in Lucian's world, the Eastern half of the empire, being fully educated entailed the ability to write Attic Greek in imitation of the most acclaimed authors of fifth- and fourth-century BC Athens[13] as well as the internalisation of the themes and tropes of the great canonical mastertexts.[14] Insofar as the pantomime's 'teaching' (see Chapter 6) was non-literary and non-textual, he had virtually no hope of being validated as an 'educator' in the strictest sense of the term, that is, as a purveyor of literate *paideia*. Even the grammarian, that 'pivotal figure' (Kaster 1988: 18) standing on the lowest threshold of literate education and setting his pupils on the path of social differentiation by teaching them the rudiments of language, numeracy and literature, might well have been unwilling to concede educational capital to a 'teacher' whose only articulate utterances were based on a 'grammar' and a 'syntax' of the flesh.

A rare exception, which does not change the overall picture, can be found in the voice of Cassiodorus (sixth century AD), a Christian of noble lineage who reached the highest echelons of government in the courts of Theoderic and Anastasius. In one of many letters he drafted for Theoderic in his capacity as Quaestor, pantomime is discussed in an entirely positive light and the dancer's bodily writing is singled out for special praise. While the alphabetic record of literary writing merely 'declares', the pantomime's hand itself becomes a living piece of script: 'with signs arranged in order, as if they were letters', it 'educates the spectator's sight'. In it are read the highlights of pantomimic plots, so that 'without writing, it performs (*facit*) what writing has declared (*quod scriptura declaravit*)'. What a written text can only 'enunciate' in abstract terms, the pantomime's corporeal writing 'fashions' or physically accomplishes (*Various Letters*, 4.51.9).

Furthermore, despite the practice – widely established among the local élites of the Roman East – of commemorating athletic victories and physical prowess with prominently placed honorific monuments or funerary inscriptions (Chapter 6§4), the relation between high culture and 'body matters' was not unproblematic. Influential voices (more loudly heard in the Western part of the empire) disparaged obsession with body-building as inferior or 'animalistic'[15] and forged a link between the care of the body and cultural inadequacy.[16] If, however, the physical education of the body could be so ardently belittled in some intellectual circles as something utterly worthless or even dangerous, Lycinus' model of an all-round, up-market education emanating from the dancer's *body* and reaching out to the spectator's *mind* was infinitely more problematic. Training the body with a view to achieving physical excellence (as is the case in athleticism) or even policing the body with a view to imparting on it the markers of élite deportment (as is the case with rhetorical education) is one thing. Marketing the body's corporeal eloquence as *an alternative route* towards the high-status goals which are normally achieved via the 'intellectual gymnastics' of literate educational practices is one step too far in the direction of implausibility.[17] While even school-children are taught that 'those on the road to becoming great men must train the body with exercises (*gymnasiois*), but exercise their soul with discourses (*logois*)',[18] Lycinus promises excellence in the frightfully complex 'gymnastics' of the viewer's 'mind' or 'soul'[19] through mere participation in the spectacle of a gymnastics of the body (see *Dance* 71). From the standpoint of élite notions of pedagogy and ideological self-definition, the dancing body of the educat*ed*

107

and educat*ing* pantomime fashioned by Lycinus' admiring *logos* must have seemed a preposterous intruder into upper-class mechanisms of knowledge production and dissemination and a hopeless claimant to educational legitimacy in the fiercely competitive arenas of imperial cultural politics.

§2. The intellectual's *paideia* vulgarised

Taking a broader sweep over the Greek and Roman world of the first centuries AD, a performative genre would have seemed a very unlikely candidate for the dissemination of educational legitimacy, as performance culture had started counting for much less than the 'textual' or 'book' culture which the élites appropriated for themselves and used to mark themselves off from the vulgar 'theatrical' habits of the lower classes. Although the upper classes availed themselves liberally of the 'uneducated pleasures' (Quintilian, *Training* 1.12.18) offered by theatrical spectacles, in 'the portrait of itself which the élite wished to present' (Hunter 2002: 195), it preferred to define its link to culture through more intimate means, such as 'reading or listening to readings of "the literary classics", including drama', as opposed to the public consumption of literature as members of a vast audience.[20] The thriving Roman institution of the *recitatio*, in particular, 'textualised' élite performance, since the reciter replicated orally a text already committed to the page (see Dupont 1997).[21] Talking up a performative genre as a conveyor of public education was not as easy in Lucian's time as it had been in the classical Athenian city, when the Aristophanic Aeschylus could declare that poets are to adults what a teacher is to young children (*Frogs* 1054-6). Even so, further clarifications are in order.

As we shall see in greater detail in Chapter 11, the élite culture in the time of the Second Sophistic was very much a 'rich and vibrant oral culture of debate, criticism and rival schools' (Webb 2002b: 198), with the fame of intellectual celebrities still firmly anchored in their dazzling performative displays, and 'almost in inverse relationship to the extent of their surviving texts' (Fantham 1996: 230). Reputations were constantly made and un-made 'by means of performance', as the most insatiable social climbers 'acted out' their own prestige and power through a vast array of delivery tropes borrowed from the otherwise maligned domain of the stage (see Chapter 11§3-4). Nevertheless, a pantomime's dancing exhibition could never be seen as 'educational' in the way an élite declaimer's performance could. Even though the grand orators staked their stardom on their ability to circumvent the written page, 'performativeness' and lack of textuality did not hamper their legitimacy as educators: the flamboyance of their *extempore* speeches was validated through its systematically flaunted indebtedness to textual culture. In the case of the sophists, more specifically, *paideia* was disseminated precisely by means of their displayed interaction with the literary and historical thesaurus of a glittering Hellenic past. And this leads me straight on to my next point, concerning the difficulties of emancipating pantomime dancing from the perspective of high culture.

We have already seen in Chapter 7 that Lycinus' expansive treatment of pantomime's wide-ranging repertoire, extending from the origins of the world to the time of Cleopatra, could be better understood in the light of the Second Sophistic's all-pervasive concern to recreate the glorious classical past, a Greece re-defined and idealised through the double agency of learned memory and nostalgic desire. From a practising sophist's vantage point, however, similarity of subject-matter would have been as far as the analogy would go. While he, the proud guardian of Hellenic heritage, sweats out his linguistic skills in order to bring forth a verbal pageant of past glories, the pantomime lives the past *within and through his body*: silencing its distinctive Attic voice, the dancer acts out a classical inheritance 'made carnal', an image of Greekness reduced to flesh. Translated into the mute, primeval language of vitals, veins, limbs and muscles, and tainted by the fluids of physical exertion, the pantomime's 'Greece' is forged upon the anvil of a degraded and degrading corporeal process. To borrow Lucian's language, a self-consciously superior, arrogant *pepaideumenos* would have thought the dancer's bodily vocabulary as closely related to the sublimity of a 'Greek' vision as the proverbial 'ass of Cumae' was related to the lion whose likeness he had somehow appropriated (Lucian, *The Dead Come Back to Life* 32). 'When soft Bathyllus dances Leda', moans the satirist's persona in Juvenal's *Satire* 6, no cerebral spark is ignited between the stage-performer and the audience's mind. The connection between dancer and spectator is visceral and synaesthetic, instead of intellectual, and any 'chemical' reactions are located within the viewer's very body: 'Tuccia cannot control her bladder' (*Satire* 6.63-4; cf. Chapter 5).

Finally, although the great, open-air performances offered by eminent sophists may well have been attended by crowds similar to those at a pantomime exhibition (cf. Chapter 11), the display-orator's linguistic and thematic recreation of a distant past was intended as an act of cultural distinction and exclusion. In a really learned performance (as opposed to the theatricalised camouflage of ignorance that Lucian satirises in, say, his *Professor of Rhetoric*) only the *pepaideumenoi* were able to decipher the speaker's intricate web of allusions to a variety of texts, genres, figures and episodes from the inexhaustible resources of Hellenic culture.[22] Showing off their ability to share fully in the picture of Greekness constructed by the sophist, the educated listeners forged with him what Bailey (1994: 151) calls (with respect to nineteenth-century music-hall audiences in England) 'a select conspiracy of meaning', segregating and insulating them from the ignorant masses. Relishing the opportunity to 'live out' their hard-earned knowledge, such listeners seemed to derive special pleasure from affirming and consolidating their possession of the precious 'cultural status of Greekness' (Goldhill 2002: 75). However, if in sophistic displays the verbal evocation of 'Greekness' acted as 'a badge of elite identity and exclusion' (Goldhill 2002: 92),[23] or as a deeply polarising force binding those proudly 'in the know' into a close-knit, self-congratulatory circle, in pantomime performances the enactment of a version of Greekness on the dancing floor was the potential catalyst for a wholesale dissolution of class-consciousness into the dreaded melting-pot of libidinal fire and elemental passion. To be sure, agonising with Medea, Niobe or Phaethon was still a vastly different cognitive process for *pepaideumenoi* and ignorant spectators (cf. Introduction), but, unlike sophistical show-rhetoric, the pantomime spectacle itself made no attempt to appear more meaningful to a select bunch of literate viewers. On the contrary, pantomime could pride itself on making the cultural inheritance of the élites more widely accessible, thus bringing down the multiple barriers erected during a sophist's lecture. As we have seen in Chapter 5, for literati in the mould of the Lucianic Crato, the social and cultural contamination of the educated viewer (cf. *Dance* 2-3) was the inescapable result of such a process of intellectual trivialisation and sweeping eroticisation.

Pantomime's double sin of embodying as well as popularising the rudiments of high culture, then, seems to have condemned the genre to a subordinate position in terms of educational value. The notion of '*paideia* embodied' emerging from Lycinus' construction of the genre was not valid currency in the highlands of imperial culture. And yet the very fact that pantomime's stock-in-trade was material which, when clothed in the legitimising armour of the Attic dialect, could be transformed into a prized model of instruction, places the genre considerably higher than, say, the 'absurd exhibitions of jugglers' (Basil of Caesarea, *To Young Men, on How they Might Derive Profit from Pagan Literature* 9.7), pole-bearers or contortionists, whose function is to merely 'astound' the crowds. Lycinus' dancing master could be described more realistically as the most licit denizen of an illicit cultural world, the world of non-literary and therefore non-élite spectacles and institutions. Just as British nineteenth-century working- and lower middle-class audiences with 'little or no formal training in Latin or Greek' secured some access to classical material through theatrical burlesques (a genre 'providing entertaining semi-musical travesties of well-known texts and stories, from Ovid to Shakespeare and the *Arabian Nights*'),[24] a large proportion of imperial audiences would have derived their mythological staples (or furthered the elementary knowledge provided by the grammarian) from the *fabulae* danced on the pantomime stage.

Together with visual art (images and sculpture), which was the common property of all, and the mythical plots of the elementary 'school exercises' in composition (*progymnasmata*), pantomime would have been the chief exponent of a widespread 'mythological *koinê*', a 'language' carrying its own educational value and accessible to all but the completely boorish.[25]

8. Pantomime, the Intellectual's Equal?

As Morgan (1998: 150) puts it, 'even a limited acquaintance with the characters of myth and history or some of the famous first lines of books endowed the learner with a basis on which to identify with powerful and high-status Greek or Roman socio-cultural groups'. Libanius comes much closer to expressing pantomime's intermediate educational position when arguing for the genre's power to 'redress' the lack of education of the masses:

> So, up to the point where the race of tragic poets was in bloom, they continued to come into the theatres as universal teachers of the people. But when, on the one hand, tragic poets dwindled and, on the other hand, only the very rich could participate in the instruction offered in the schools of art and poetry, while the majority of the people were deprived of education, some god took pity on the lack of education of the many and, to redress the balance, introduced pantomime as a kind of instruction for the masses (*didachên tina tois plêthesi*) in the deeds of old. Consequently, a goldsmith now will do not badly in a conversation with a product of the schools about the house of Priam or of Laius (Libanius, *Oration* 64.112).

In the reckoning of a *pepaideumenos*, this cultural veneer provided by the dance would certainly have been derided as inadequate. What Libanius' 'not badly' might mean in practice can be gauged from the freedman Trimalchio's ridiculous confusion of the best-known heroes of the Trojan war in Petronius' novel (*Satyricon* 59), while, as Morgan (1998: 270) argues, in Hellenistic and Roman texts 'the partially educated are described as being as far from the perfectly educated in information, behaviour, language and cognitive development as they are from the illiterate'.

Moreover, the beneficiaries of pantomime education, as envisaged by Libanius, are only passive recipients of the spectacle's instructive subject-matter. Their relation to the spectacle's educational treasures can be paralleled, at best, with the tenuous 'degree of complicity' that links a grammarian's pupil at an early stage of education to his literary texts: he can read them aloud, but he is not yet able to act upon them, 'restate what he reads in his own words' (Morgan 1998: 224 and 225). How much this difference between active co-operation and passive acquiescence mattered could perhaps be gleaned from the way Aulus Gellius approaches his painstakingly compiled compendium of knowledge, the *Attic Nights*: its value resides in its ability to inspire the mind to further learning and the study of the useful arts (*Attic Nights*, Preface 12). Whereas the compilation's learned reader, having been shown the right path, may follow up the leads provided with the aid of either books or teachers (*Attic Nights*, Preface 17), pantomime-inspired learning stops by definition at the very threshold of active education: the 'stimulation' and 'sharpening' of the mind (see Libanius, *Oration* 64.113) by the spectacle on offer. Besides, mythical education in itself, the indispensable ingredient of pantomime teaching, carries little weight in a hierarchy of educational pursuits. In an

111

important passage, Strabo makes both mythology as well as poetry subordinate to history and philosophy: the latter disciplines are only for the few, while poetry is addressed to the many and 'draws full houses' (*Geography* 1.2.8).

Pantomime dancing, then, could not have been what Lycinus wanted it to be. Even in the eyes of those *pepaideumenoi* who did deign to pay attention to its charms, pantomime would have been an aesthetically pleasing encounter with mythical and literary traditions, yet unable to substitute literature's role in the acculturation of the dominant classes or rival the educational capital disseminated by the parchment in the library or the *logos* in the mouth of the declaiming sophist.

9

A 'Margin of Mess': Pantomime and the
Strategies of Élite Cultural Self-definition

The previous chapter argued that, confronted with pantomime in their own *cultural* backyards, the imperial élites tended to fence themselves in, shutting the door in the dancer's face; deprived of markers of *paideia* that the upper classes could sanction as 'legitimate', the pantomime could never hope to be accepted as one of their number. If left unqualified, however, such a statement becomes an oversimplification of the way in which the systems of power operating on behalf of high culture reacted to the growing impact of pantomime dancing.

The upper classes may well have denied to pantomime a place of its own within the fold of dominant culture, but they did not altogether expel it beyond their line of mental vision. Rather than ensuring the dancer became untraceable by their cultural antennae, they made sure he was stationed *no further than* the perimeter of their cultural concerns. With respect to two important areas represented in Lucian's *On the Dance,* this chapter argues that imperial élites invested pantomime with formidable 'relational' value, embroiling both the genre and its artist in their own strategies of cultural self-definition. More specifically, taking its cue from Bourdieu's (1984: 57) assessment of the 'function' of the working classes 'in the system of aesthetic positions', it proposes that one of pantomime's multiple social roles was 'to serve as a foil, a negative reference point', in relation to which high-class discourses defined themselves through a series of 'successive negations'.

§1 below revisits Lycinus' proposed link between pantomime and declamations (cf. Chapter 6§2), while §2 problematises further the embattled zone of overlap between rhetoric and dance by looking at the ways their relationship was conjured from the perspective of rhetorical legitimacy, such as it was entrenched in the systems of oratorical training which have come down to us.[1] §3 suggests that pantomime's aesthetic denigration was an integral aspect of much broader struggles, in a world where some of the most heavily contested issues revolved around the privilege of leadership in the playing fields of performance culture. Lycinus may well have extolled pantomime's entertainment value as above that attached to spoken drama (*Dance* 26-31), but his attempt would have carried minimal weight in intellectual circles that prided themselves on defining their own essence in contradistinction to the cultural profile they ascribed to the

113

dancer's art. In this, as in the previous chapter, I am concerned not with the way the élites actually lived their lives, but with the way they perceived and displayed themselves to the world.

§1. 'Just as in declamations ... ' (*Dance* 65)

As we have already seen in Chapter 6§2 with respect to *Dance* 65, Lycinus' comparison of pantomime and rhetoric focuses on *hypokrisis* (role-playing) as the most important element that dancers and orators share. On one side of the cultural divide, the dancer recreates mythical figures in the flesh, often giving the impression that he truly 'is' Orestes or Andromache, Pentheus or Agave (cf. Chapter 3§4). On the other side of the boundary, both the so-called *progymnasmata* (basic exercises in speech-making) and the fully-fledged declamations of accomplished public speakers (*meletai*, to which Lycinus refers in *Dance* 65) demand a degree of 'impersonation or creative mimetism', involving 'the composition of imaginary speeches or scenes in keeping with the presumed character of long-vanished figures of both history and myth' (Zeitlin 2001: 208). In the time of Lucian especially, the heyday of the Second Sophistic, around the middle of the second century AD, declamation was first and foremost an oratory of role-playing.[2] Putting the self in an endless variety of fictitious situations derived from Greek history or myth, this most fashionable kind of public oratory in the imperial East involved the quintessentially dramatic acts of 'pretending to be someone else and composing imaginary speeches in character' (Russell 1983: 1).[3]

As a *composer* of such speeches, the display-orator had to 'feel himself', much as an actor does, 'into' the consciousness and frame of mind of his projected characters, before he would be ready to endow them with the most befitting *logos*, such as 'the kind of speech Andromache would make over Hector's body' or 'a husband about to go abroad would address to his wife'.[4] As the *performer* of the characters he had created, the declaimer had to call upon his own acting prowess (*hypokrisis*) to incarnate them in the most engaging way, by granting them the most appropriate utterance in terms of tone, pitch and vocal modulations, emotions, facial expression and bodily deportment.[5] Most crucially, in pantomime, just as in sophistic declamations, the performer appeared in the guise of another. As Schmitz (1999: 78) writes on sophistic declaimers:

> in their declamations, they actually embodied the great figures of the past; at least for the duration of their speeches, they turned into these classical authorities. Every sophist had many times enacted the role of Demosthenes, had spoken before King Philip of Macedonia or the Athenian assembly.... in these speeches, the personality of the sophist would completely disappear behind the figure he was embodying; when he said 'I,' this pronoun referred to, say, Demosthenes, not to himself.[6]

9. A 'Margin of Mess'

In sixth-century AD Gaza, Choricius, most probably the most talented declaimer in later antiquity, sets his own profession, demanding transformations of character and intellectual perspective, against the background of the corporeal transformations taking place on the pantomime stage:[7]

> You have already, I am sure, been spectators of choruses in the festival of Dionysus, where, I suppose, you have seen some pantomime (*orchêstên*) now enchanting the stage with masculine bodily configurations, whenever he dances the Thessalian or the Amazon's young lad or some other male figure, now imitating most skilfully the much-desired daughter of Briseus and Phaedra in love, and attempting to persuade the audience in the theatre not that he is in the process of imitating others, but that he really is by nature (*pephyke*) the object of his imitation (Choricius, *Oration* 21.1, p. 248 Foerster-Richtsteig).

To some extent, then, insofar as it refers to the declaimer's and the dancer's preoccupation with playing at being 'other' than themselves, Lycinus' twinning of pantomime and rhetoric neither seems nor is entirely misplaced.

Nevertheless, while *Dance* 65 lends the dancer yet another helping hand for his 'naturalisation' in the upper-class man's world, supercilious intellectuals could only have recoiled in outrage in the face of the apologist's comparisons. Restricting my discussion to the rhetor's and the pantomime's evocation of characters from history and myth,[8] any non-satirical portrait of élite *paideia* would have presented the *pepaideumenos'* encounter with such figures as a purely intellectual affair, an erudite symbolic journey to the imaginary time and space of a distant past. Élite mechanisms of self-perception would have understood Andromache or Socrates, Demosthenes or Hecuba as useful fodder for the aspiring performer's tongue and mind. For the pantomime, however, instead of representing storehouses of narrative patterns and rhetorical techniques, mythical and historical *personae* were live figures, whose likeness he wore in the form of a mask; they were primarily emotional landscapes, whose innermost recesses his dancing sought to illuminate and, ultimately, 'body-texts', whose fleshly grammar he had learnt to graft upon his very own skin. In other words, if projected onto the (often distorting) mirror of élite self-presentation, the gap between speech-making and pantomime dancing would have appeared unbridgeable.

On the one hand, the grammarian's pupil or the orator-in-the-making rehashes the range of ideas, sentiments, subject positions and linguistic tropes traditionally associated with Medea, in order to construct, ideally in the crispest Attic idiom, his exercise on 'What would Medea have said at the point of murdering her own children?' (e.g. Libanius, *Preliminary Exercises*, 11: 'Characterisations' 1).[9] The pantomime dancer, on the other hand, can only absorb the elemental 'essence' of Medea into his body, and allow the intoxicating concoction of her swirling passions (injured pride, betrayed love, heroic vengefulness and motherly grief) to pulsate through his veins and muscles, now slumbering in blood-curling stillness, now bursting out in violent bodily contortions. The young boy's toil, while scribbling in his exercise book, we can somehow reconstruct, on the basis of tantalising ancient evidence.[10] But the physicality and naked passion of a pantomime's Medea we can seek only in modern analogues, as, for example, in Martha Graham's danced dramatisation of Medea's myth, her monumental *Cave of the Heart*. As choreographer and dance historian Agnes de Mille (1992: 295-6) describes it, the ballet

> contained Martha's lengthy and frenetic solo of devouring jealous passion. It was a dance of such animal anger and frustration as to defy sense and sensibilities. It almost evoked disgust. And it was done on the knees, long pas de bourrée on the knees, including a passage of quivering, carnivorous rage in which Martha would half squat, half kneel, and vibrate the knees in and out like a hungry insect in spasms of evisceration and digestion – an effect which made the blood run cold.

Even the pantomime's much-praised mnemonic power (as we saw in Chapter 6§2, yet another point of contact between dancing and oratory) is in reality corporeal (cf. Chapter 3§3), as dance training aims to inculcate choreographical repertories in the performer's 'muscular memory', so that they can be ' "spontaneously" reactivated in the present moment of performance' (Reynolds 2002: 8). Martha Graham's dancers, to take just one example, underwent specific exercises to ensure that new movement experiences could be felt 'muscularly' and become in due course firmly incorporated into 'physical memory' (Reynolds 2002). Once again, pantomime dancing comes close to aspects of high culture, but a crucial twist makes complete dovetailing impossible: 'body' memory is not the equal counterpart of 'intellectual' memory, the concept praised so profusely in élite discourses.

§2. Pantomime and the orator's body

Preliminary exercises and declamations aside, the relation between oratory and pantomime is by no means as straightforward as Lycinus' 'apology' suggests. The boundary that separates oratory from dancing, alongside that which insulates the orator from the more general realm of stage-acting, is one of the hardest to define, police or negotiate. Although techniques for arousing or calming the passions in oneself and in the judge can be profitably learnt from actors, the entire range of artistic expertise in bodily deportment, vocal modulations and mastery of feelings is not suitable for the orator's imitation. The art of acting should be adopted only up to a certain limit (cf. Fantham 2002: 371): gestures should be used without excess, delivery (*actio*) should always be kept under control. Above all, on no account should the stage as a source of learning become easily identifiable.[11] Thus, Seneca the Elder praises the orator Cassius Severus for a delivery which 'could have been the making of an actor, yet could not have seemed to belong to an actor' (*Legal Disputations* 3, Preface 3) – 'a fine distinction', as Richlin (1997: 103) puts it.[12] Too zealous a quest for the theatrical performer's elegance may lose the aspiring rhetor the authority of the 'good man' (Quintilian, *Training* 11.3.184). In other words, rhetorical education aims to demarcate that thin zone of legitimacy between the boorishness of uncouth, uneducated hyper-virility[13] and the hyper-sophisticated, almost effeminate elegance associated with theatricalised declamation or the stage.[14]

There can hardly be a better indication of the tense relationship between oratory and pantomime dancing than an extended passage in Quintilian's first book (*Training* 1.11.15-19), where the master-rhetorician commends '*cheironomia*' (understood as the 'law of gesture', *lex gestus*) as an acceptable part of oratorical training.[15] As the 'legitimating' authorities and practices he cites either sanction an education in dancing (Socrates; Plato; Chrysippus) or situate dancing at the heart of civic life and rituals, there is no doubt that the instruction meant in *Training* 1.11.18 is the kind of bodily régime we should imagine as lying at the root of pantomime education. Quintilian strictly prohibits exercises of this sort beyond the years of boyhood, and yet would like to *preserve* the charm and grace they bestow – unobserved, it goes without saying:

> Indeed, I do not want the orator's gestures to be composed in imitation of the pantomime's gestures, but (I would like) something of these puerile exercises to remain palpable, so that the grace bestowed on us, as we were learning them, may accompany us unnoticed, while we are pursuing other things (*Training* 1.11.19).

All the while avoiding looking like a dancer (cf. Richlin 1997: 105), an orator must possess a speck of dancing elegance, a most delicate balance between distance and appropriation. Precariously poised between the beauty and grace of the pantomimes and the impeccably masculine dignity of public speaking, he must always make sure he stops *just* short of being a dancer in his gesture (cf. Quintilian, *Training* 1.12.14).

Most interestingly for our inquiry, the penalty in store for those who do 'cross over' is the social stigma associated with dancing.[16] So, we are told that the orator Sextus Titius, a tribune of the plebs for 99 BC, was so 'loose (*solutus*) and soft (*mollis*, i.e. effeminate) in his gesture' that he started a trend for a 'kind of dance' (*saltatio quaedam*) to which his own name was given: 'the Titius' (Cicero, *Brutus* 225).[17] Or, as another tresspasser found out to similar cost, the flouting of rhetorical prescriptions in terms of gestural eloquence, the special province of pantomime dancing, entails one's expulsion to the dancer's illegitimate domain. Thus Quintus Hortensius, a foremost orator, endured many a jibe in court for resembling an actor/pantomime (*quasi in histrionem*), on the basis of his excessive employment of gestures.[18] Lucius Torquatus, one of his detractors, went one step further, calling him not just an actor/pantomime (*non iam histrionem*), but a 'female pantomime' (*gesticulariam*) and 'a Dionysia', 'which was the name of a most famous dancing girl' at the time (Aulus Gellius, *Attic Nights* 1.5.3).[19]

However, if we move beyond those grey areas of rhetorical propriety where, as we have just seen, dancing is held at arm's length, while still remaining within the speaker's line of vision, we shall find the voices of moralists and supercilious intellectuals all too keen to undercut the pantomime-orator pact promoted by Lycinus. Messalla, in Tacitus' *Dialogue on Orators*, forges a link between histrionic tropes and the decadent oratory of the empire. Reporting as a common remark the view that 'orators speak voluptuously and actors dance eloquently', he is appalled at many speakers' boast that 'their speeches can be sung and danced to', as though that were a mark of praise, fame and a sign of genius (Tacitus, *Dialogue* 26.3). For him, the fashion of producing 'the rhythms of stage-dancing' in one's speech not only 'does not befit an orator', but is 'scarcely worthy of a man' (*Dialogue* 26.2).

The mutual exclusiveness of a declaiming and a dancing body is most dramatically fleshed out in Seneca the Elder, who declares any alliance between oratorical eloquence and effeminate bodies impermissible: 'Go then and look for orators among those who are plucked and smooth, men in no other way except their lust' (*Legal Disputations* 1, Preface 10). Men deprived of firmness and sinews (*emolliti enervesque*) (*Legal Disputations* 1, Preface 9) and competing with women in bodily softness (*mollitia corporis*) are not fit for oratorical delivery, but only destined for the lubricious study of singing and dancing (ibid., Preface 8).[20] Even Cicero and Quintilian, who are so acutely aware of the slippery interface between pleading and dancing and expend considerable energy on demarcating the area of legitimacy between the two, can at other moments posit the farthest possible distance between orator and dancer[21] and codify the respectable speaker's bodily deportment in a way that makes it fundamentally irreconcilable with the pantomime's:

> He will use movement in such a way as to avoid any excess: he will stand erect (*erectus*) and lofty in his posture ... there will be no (effeminate) softness (*nulla mollitia*) in the neck,[22] no quick movement of the fingers, no finger joint moving in time with the rhythm (Cicero, *Orator* 18.59).

The 'soft', 'bent', 'fragmented', undulating pantomime (see Chapter 5§1) incarnates the very faults a budding speaker is taught to eradicate, for the whole rationale of pantomime training, aspiring to a body that can mould itself into any conceivable configuration, flies in the face of rhetorical education, wherein a strict regime of constant vigilance aims to produce a body that knows how to deploy itself within 'a carefully circumscribed space' and along 'a stable and upright line' (Gunderson 2000: 80). It therefore seems that the only analogy that would have happily aligned pantomime and oratory in the perspective of élite mentality was unqualifiedly *negative*.

The body that élite narratives attribute to the pantomime – boundless and effervescent, multiple and metamorphic, loose and loinless, effeminate, sinuous and luxuriously adorned (see Chapters 5§1, 5§3, 11§4) – is in complete contrast to the strictly disciplined body of the good speaker: virile and upright, 'bounded by lines of decorum defining, constraining, and restraining' it at all times (Gunderson 2000: 78), resplendent without ostentation, always true to itself, and unfailingly integrate.[23] To put it another way, when moulded with the tools of the élite rhetorical orthodoxy, the 'soft' and 'enervated' (albeit lustful) pantomimic body (cf. Chapter 5§1-2) is constructed as the mirror-image of the ambiguously gendered, incontinent body ascribed to the *lapsed*, the *degenerate* orator.

In rhetoric, however, it was not just the physical self of the performer that could be treated as 'corporeal'. His style too could have a 'body', so much so that the 'real' and the 'insubstantial' could sometimes overlap, turning the condemnation of one's style into an indictment of the orator's very self, in line with the principle that 'such is a man's style as is his way of life'.[24] Insofar as transgressive eloquence is 'broken'[25] and 'soft',[26] 'delicate and flowing' (Seneca, *Letter* 114.21), 'translucent' (Quintilian, *Training* 8, Preface 20), 'loose',[27] 'lascivious' and 'effeminate',[28] 'sinewless' and 'jointless',[29] and opposed to a 'straightforward speech' (*sermo rectus*, Quintilian, *Training* 2.5.11), the pantomime's deviant body becomes a metaphor for the depraved orator's expressive tropes.[30] Indeed, Longinus ventures an open parallel between the 'broken', effeminate and hurried style and the usual rhythms of dancing:

> Nothing damages an elevated passage so much as effeminate and agitated rhythm, pyrrhics, for instance, and trochees, and dichorees, which fall into a regular dance rhythm [...] over-rhythmical prose gives the audience the effect not of the words but of the rhythm. Thus, they sometimes foresee the due ending themselves and keep time with their feet, anticipating the speaker and setting the step as if it were a dance (*On the Sublime* 41.1-2; trans. Fyfe, revised by Russell, Loeb 1995).

As for Quintilian, he perceives the style of many an orator as effeminate and enervated (*compositionem ... effeminatam et enervem*), the kind that dances to the 'most lascivious rhythms' of castanets (*Training* 9.4.142).[31] Within the cluster of mainstream élite assumptions, then, the only plausible link between oratory and pantomime dancing can be located in that transgressive, undisciplined mode of public speaking whose most prominent 'corporeal' signs are fragmentation, sinewlessness and dissolution. The pantomime's body is co-terminous with the *unruly* rhetor's body.

Yet, from the rhetorical theorist's viewpoint, the pantomime interloper was neither useless nor expendable. On the contrary, he was extremely 'good to think with'. Standing on the outer rim of rhetorical propriety (alongside the stage-actor, the woman and the slave; see Connolly 1998), he gave a name and a shape to that furthest outpost of legitimacy, the point beyond which rhetoric was believed to collapse into another kind of discourse: female doublespeak or illiberal and lowly stage-mimicry. In practice, as we shall see in Chapter 11, pantomime dancing shared much of its territory with rhetoric – the epideictic, 'display'-branch of rhetoric in which the sophists in particular excelled.[32] In theory, however, the genre served to flesh out the 'illegitimate', 'unauthorised' body against which the good orator could and should define his own legitimate *eloquentia corporis*.[33]

§3. Pantomime in the élite cartography of entertainment

As we have seen, a major cause of élite anxiety is the ever-dreaded dissolution of the boundary between the manly, rhetorical act of the forum or the lawcourt, and the popular or lower end of the performance spectrum, i.e. the vast realm of theatricalised entertainment. It is therefore time to revisit pantomime dancing with an eye on the heterogeneous entertainment culture of the Hellenistic and post-Hellenistic world.[34] For one of the chief characteristics of performance history, from (broadly speaking) the third century BC to the fifth century AD, is the multiformity of voices in a motley cultural universe, where spectacles abound.

At public festivals, communal events and private occasions, mime actors and pantomime dancers, miracle-workers, conjurers, jugglers, marionette-players, acrobats, stuntmen, street-performers and rope-dancers, jockey for position against the chief exponents of 'legitimate' performance, such as virtuoso tragic singers, soloists of the lyre, or performers of Homeric epics.[35] And when the more intriguing, lettered breed of public entertainers is taken into account, such as the itinerant sophist, whose declaiming habits are just as sparkling and 'theatrical' as those of a real actor (see Chapter 11§3-4), or even the philosopher performing in his lecture-hall to a circle of select admirers and disciples, not only does a performance culture of the broadest possible variety emerge, but also a dynamic arena for the rehearsal of some of the most passionate discourses of self-definition in the ancient world.

The plurality of entertainment traditions bred antagonism and wars for the demarcation of cultural territories. No type of performance rejoiced in an unassailable position. Poetry was not immune from oratory's attack;[36] the rhetoric of the forum could be pitted against that of the declamation hall (e.g. Pliny the Younger, *Letters* 2.3.5-7); indigenous Roman declaimers might be unable to hold their ground against dashing travelling sophists from the East. In short, even the upper-class topography itself was not free from vitriolic discord, as its educated 'inhabitants' engaged in bitter fighting with a view to canonising their own mode of performative expression as unquestionably superior.

Pantomime's position in the ever-shifting entertainment hierarchy was hardly a matter of individual voice-contests: belittlement of the genre as a form distinct from Culture was a much more complex and broad-ranging phenomenon, part and parcel of the regular 'pigeonholing' exercises of those preoccupied with the construction of ever-fresh taxonomies of erudite pursuits. It cannot be emphasised too strongly that in such labelling practices, 'inferiors'/losers were even more eagerly sought out than 'superiors'/winners: before a particular genre could be deemed of higher rank, a number of subaltern realms were needed, spectacles that could be berated for their affiliation to the small and petty. Élite re-mappings of the geography of entertainment culture in the Greek and Roman world of the first centuries AD provided ample space for the accommodation of vulgar and uncultured 'outcasts', the better to showcase by comparison their own chosen bastion(s) of refinement and culture. Like all pronouncements on taste, verdicts on wholesome entertainment expressed themselves in a negative fashion or, as Bourdieu writes, through 'the refusal of other tastes'.[37]

The blasting or praising of pantomime, then, was an essential element in the strategic moves made by the élites as part of the unremitting battles *they* waged for the consolidation and expansion of *their* intellectual hegemony. In fact, pantomime offered its élite detractors a formidable *casus belli*. Sexy, vibrant and all-inclusive, as it happily annexed elements from many a cultural backyard and danced its way even to the very heart of a senator's or emperor's banqueting-hall and bedroom, the genre must have pressed hotly on the neck of those trying to make it big on the performative arenas of high culture. To be sure, some individual members of the educated classes felt 'maverick' enough to cross the impermissible divide. Enlightened and nonconformist, bold and versatile, a small minority of eccentric performers, whom we shall meet again in Chapter 11, appropriated elements of the pantomime's (or, more generally, the stage-actor's) winning portfolio of techniques in order to enhance their own crowd-pulling rates. But the collective reaction of those who made it their business to police the borders of élite performative expressions, or legislate on what is worthy of being seen and heard, was a jealous (even fearful) closing of ranks – after all, any generous acknowledgment of value in popular culture entails a subtle or open questioning of the supremacy or relative value of one's own, 'higher' culture. In their attempt to cordon off the culturally 'profane', the educated upper classes fitted out their own territory with the most rigid, impermeable contours. A couple of examples will suffice to corroborate this point.

When Plutarch (*Moral Essays* 711b-13f; cf. 710b-11a) fences in the entertainment space of the *symposion* and legislates on the aural and visual delights that should be admitted to or excluded from a civilised drinking party, he trenchantly bans vernacular practices and lowbrow pastimes. No excess flow from below the 'great divide' is allowed to seep through any fissures in the edifice of culture. Thus, popular genres related to the mime are vilified as so 'full of scurrility and scandal' that they 'ought not to be seen even by the slaves who fetch our shoes, if their masters are in their right minds':[38] the more 'open' and 'accessible' a spectacle is, with respect to the demands it makes on its audience, the more certain its banishment to the remotest outskirts of the cultural playground becomes.[39] As Bourdieu (1984: 60) notes, 'those who intend to mark their difference' ought to be particularly vigilant with regard to the vulgar and the universally popular. Striking a very typical note of intellectual élitism, Horace spurns any contamination of the lofty tragic stage by what we might call a 'pantomime' aesthetic: pantomime's lifeblood, somatic transformation, is one among the mythical staples that must not be enacted before his audience's eyes.[40] As for Seneca (*Letter* 52.12 and 13), he stipulates that there should be an obvious disparity between the applause given in the theatre and that lavished on the philosopher performing in his school: histrionic outcries befit the arts and artists that aim to please the crowds, while on the side of true philosophy and the *pepaideumenoi* one should expect to find worshipful silence.[41]

Back in the East, exercising a *pepaideumenos'* self-acquired right to adjudicate between the high and the low, Aelius Aristides attempts to drive a wedge between élite and popular entertainment cultures by assigning to each part of the divide its own model of performer/audience interaction:

> And this other thing as well: it is not fitting, I think, for the orator and the philosopher and all those involved in liberal education to please the masses in the same way that these servile fellows do, the pantomimes and mimes and jugglers (Aelius Aristides, *Oration* 34.55; cf. Plutarch, *Moral Essays* 46c).

Rebuffing the possibility of intellectual parity between the pleasures offered by low-class entertainers and those dispensed by reputable minstrels of high education, Aristides dictates that élite performers are above all need to cater to low tastes. Predictably, in his attempt to ensure that no exponent of high culture defects from party lines to pander to his public's whims, Aristides tramples the dancer and his cultural brethren underfoot, and marks them out as dwellers of an intellectual netherland, the province of servility and non-urbanity.[42]

Erection of boundaries, however, goes hand in hand with even more complex mechanisms for the distancing of the 'self' from the attitudes and idiolects of the subaltern. In a dangerously fragmented post-Hellenistic world, where a multiplicity of attractions tugged at the edges of fragile classifications, a rhetoric of polarisation became the inescapable corollary of any battle to construct a closed system of intellectual nobility. On the side of the *pepaideumenoi* and their world, there is refinement, taste, educational discourse, and intellectual pleasures providing a feast to delight the rational part in man.[43] On the side of the ignorant, the inferior pretenders to cultural capital, reign the sensational and the electrifying, the cheap and mindless delights of the eye or the sensual and senseless pleasures of the ear which, as Maximus of Tyre puts it, 'have no significant contribution to make to the entertainment of the soul, because they have no meaning and no rational content, and cannot speak to us' (*Oration* 22.3; trans. Trapp 1997).

To restrict discussion to those areas in which theatrical or theatricalised forms of culture are involved, a fully-fledged rhetoric of cultural differentiation can best be seen at work in some of the writings of Dio Chrysostom, a typical exponent of upper-class traditions and aesthetics. In his oration to the people of Alexandria, for example, legitimate tastes in the world of public entertainment become more rigorously defined through their emphatic severance from a host of low diversions, consisting in noise, ribaldry and scurrilous jesting (*Oration* 32.4). Spectacles whence one might gain intelligence or prudence or a commendable moral disposition are presented as diametrically opposed to those that give rise to ignorant strife, unrestrained passions and senseless emotions (32.5). Respectable spectators are pitted against those addicted to popular pastimes, men devoid of seriousness, devoted to childish play, sensual pleasure and laughter (32.1). There is no doubt that Dio meant pantomime to be relegated to the negative side of his pairs of opposites. About a century earlier, Philo Judaeus had contrasted commendable leisure, occupied 'by the pursuit of wisdom only', with the kind of leisure that is filled 'with the show-displays of mimes or pantomimes, on account of whom theatre addicts become sick at heart and die a lingering death'[44] (*Moses* 2.211): it is during such spectacles that the senses of sight and hearing 'enslave' the soul, by natural right their queen (211).

In the Latin-speaking world, Pliny the Younger and Juvenal's literary *persona* in *Satire* 11 make it clear that their house is closed to buffoons and clowns or attractive girls dancing immodestly with castanets and wanton songs, for the feasts which they provide instead are adorned by epic recitations, readers, musicians or professional actors.[45] As for the politics of verbal versus visual communication, textual culture versus spectacular performance culture (where pantomime obviously belongs), the polarisation of tastes is nowhere more graphically portrayed than in Horace's *Letter to Augustus*, where the poet's literary voice is drowned by the din of the *plebs* (compared to the moaning of the Apulian forest or the Tuscan sea), the 'stupid', 'illiterate' masses 'calling for bears or boxers in the middle of a play'.[46] In social circles that take obvious delight in pitting the body against the mind, the sensual against the intellectual, the reasonable and edifying against the dumb, the foolish and the whimsical, and even, as Horace does, literature against the *ludi* and writing against performance (see Habinek 1998: 99), the cultural demotion of pantomime dancing seems inevitable. In the philosopher Demetrius' words, as rehearsed by Lycinus, the pantomime makes meaningless and pointless movements with no sense in them whatsoever (*Dance* 63), while, as Pliny the Younger declares, a self-respecting intellectual sees no attraction of any sort in the soft gestures of a dancer (or in the mime's cheek and the clown's folly; *Letters* 9.17.2).

In the Eastern part of the empire in particular, one of the fiercest battles for mastery over the performance-world is played out between traditional drama and pantomime dancing. How come you are wasting your time on dancers, Crato lashes out at his friend, when

> there are millions of other dignified auditory and visual spectacles, if one wanted to have recourse to them, ... especially solemn Tragedy and the most joyous Comedy,[47] which have moreover been deemed worthy of inclusion into an agonistic context? (*Dance* 2).

Marshalled against tragedy and comedy is the undifferentiated torrent of newer or derivative dramatic forms flooding into the sphere of cultural legitimacy;[48] neither peace nor treaty can exist between this motley bunch of quasi-theatrical attractions, a constellation of inferior 'languages' that mesmerise the gaping crowds, and the serious, refined literary production of the educated few.

There is little doubt that the legitimate 'technologies' of culture felt under attack from an art form that was spreading like wildfire. But there is equally little doubt that the 'imaginary' community of the élites became adept at exaggerating the pantomime threat, which quickly took the face of a cultural monstrosity, poised to strangle all liberal pursuits. We can still hear Seneca's moan as he vents out his frustration over the boorishness and immorality of his contemporaries, who indulge themselves in the cruder pleasures of pantomime shows, while the halls of professors and philosophers are deserted (and, by implication, their livelihood threatened; cf. Chapter 11):

> Who respects a philosopher or any liberal study except when the games are called off for a time or there is some rainy day which he is willing to waste? And so the many schools of philosophy are dying without a successor. The Academy, both the Old and the New, has no professor left.... But how much worry is suffered lest the name of some pantomime actor be lost for ever! The House of Pylades and of Bathyllus continues through a long line of successors (*Stat per successores Pyladis et Bathylli domus*). For their arts there are many students and many teachers (Seneca, *Natural Questions* 7.32.1-3; trans. T.H. Corcoran, Loeb 1972).

In élite literary constructions, the knife-edge between the high and the low, where the descendants of Pylades (I) and Bathyllus (I) danced, becomes a menacing crevasse, while the genre's popularity swells up as a hideous tide of aesthetic, moral and intellectual degeneration. Magnifying devices of this kind were not the product of irrational, impulsive fear, but inextricably interwoven with well-calculated games of cultural self-definition. Claiming with Seneca that pantomime is rising from the ashes of the philosopher's trade makes as little sense as claiming, with Allan Bloom (1988: 73), that rock music 'has risen to its current heights in the education of the young on the ashes of classical music': rock and classical music still exist side by side, just as pantomime and philosophy continued to do for centuries. The important point is that Seneca (and any other who sounds the alarm against what is presented as galloping cultural decadence) carves out for himself a markedly distinctive space and promotes his own profession as a terrain of unsurpassable intellectuality.

§4. 'Othering' the dance

We can now understand more fully what may have been at stake in ancient *anti*-pantomime discourses. Independently of whether they attended the spectacle or not, the educated classes in both Greece and Rome preferred to declare their intellectual dissociation from the pantomime addiction of the crowds, treating the genre as a blot on their cultural landscape. The pastime of the brainless, the immoderate and the effeminate, the physical, somatic pantomime, a most licentious and polluting form of recreation, was alleged to infect even the refined, educated viewer. As often happens in the processes of collective cultural self-fashioning, pantomime, the perceived threat to cultural normality, was invested with all the properties and values that the élites, as the legislating cultural core of the imperial era, found abominable: irrationality, disorder, uncontrollable emotion, gender-instability or outright femininity, voluptuousness and carnal passion, opulence and splendour, moral incontinence and licence, and so on (cf. Chapter 5). In the language of cultural theory, Greco-Roman pantomime was gradually moulded into the shape of the negative 'Other', that most useful of dialogic partners for delineating the edges of the defining subject's own world.

There is no doubt that simply taking this cluster of negative polarities at face value, as a set of descriptive categories which could help position pantomime objectively in the symbolic economy of the imperial world, is gravely misleading. Ignoring them, however, is equally short-sighted, for stereotypes reveal a great deal about those who fashion them. In this case, what the culturally displaced pantomime represents is nothing short of the emotional residue of the legitimating centre, the most haunting fears and hopes, fantasies and dreams of the self-appointed intellectual élites. In the ambivalent landscape the pantomime 'Other' represents, élite culture could rehearse not merely what it *could not* contain within its bounds but, most importantly, what it *would have dearly loved to have been able to embrace*, as pantomime distils the élite male's dream of indulging in sexual, moral and emotional licence all the while keeping his upper-class body and upper-class identity intact. Turning the 'Othered' pantomime's unflattering tags on their head, one can gain spectacular insights into the very core of the 'legitimate' culture of Lucian's time.

In any case, insofar as they conceptualised the hodge-podge of pantomimes and similar inferior entertainers as an unlawful 'Other', and all too carefully landscaped an ineradicable difference between their own entertainment or educational practices and the illegality of pantomime-land, the intellectual élites of the imperial world not only reinforced the boundaries between the spheres of the high and the low, but also deepened their own sense of themselves as an homogeneous and superior cultural community. As anthropologist Barbara Babcock (1978: 28) put it, 'We seem to need a "margin of mess," a category of "inverted beings" both to define and to question the orders by which we live.' Pantomime was very 'good to think with' in the ancient world, for it could easily be made to play the role of that 'margin of mess' necessary to define both the core and the rim of cultural legitimacy.

Dancing on the Brink: The 'Hybrid' Discourse of Pantomime Dancing

§1. The special in-betweenness of the pantomime ground

Chapters 8 and 9 have brought us back to the cultural paradox that was first highlighted in Chapter 5. While Lucian's Lycinus endeavours to demonstrate an uninterrupted continuity between pantomime discourse and élite modes of cultural production (see Chapters 6-7), a multitude of self-conscious images belonging to the cultural profile of imperial élites register a radical discontinuity by highlighting the fissures and cracks, the crucial junctures where pantomime diverged from perceived standards of legitimacy or social propriety. As demonstrated in Chapters 8-9, from the vantage point of the upper classes as an 'imagined' community of intellectual stardom, pantomime was decidedly non-assimilable (even though not totally expendable)[1] material. Taken in splendid isolation, none of the conflicting snapshots we have encountered so far offers a reliable impression of pantomime's actual cultural standing. Yet the irreconcilable rifts that run throughout the body of our existing evidence reveal something of extreme importance about the genre's position in the symbolic topography of imperial culture: like many other highly successful forms of aesthetic dancing throughout Western performance history, pantomime experienced a turbulent, uneasy 'marriage' with many dominant parameters of social, political and intellectual life.[2] 'Insider' and 'outsider' at once, flirting with the outskirts of legitimacy without ever holding a secure place within its compass, the genre became indelibly marked by the precariousness of its position with respect to the competing orthodoxies of mainstream imperial culture. Beyond the range of material already discussed in Chapter 5, an interstitial quality flavoured most aspects of the pantomime experience throughout the empire.

The poet of standing, for example, who, like Lucan and Statius, lends his talent to the pantomime stage,[3] is caught in a dangerous double bind. While he is all but guaranteed to earn good money for selling his work to the star dancers and may even 'captivate' the ruler's eyes in the process,[4] he can be perceived at best as 'deserting' and 'polluting' his great talent,[5] at worst as being on a par with a pimp, who hires out his 'virgin' girl to clients and brothel-keepers.[6] The fact that not a single pantomime libretto has survived testifies to the contempt of ancient critics for this kind of enormously popular literary output.[7] Pantomimes were, as we saw in Chapter 4, part and parcel of imperial celebrations, yet Pliny the Younger (*Panegyric Oration* 54.1) recalls with horror the times when imperial panegyrics were disgracefully unmanned (*frangerentur*) by pantomime antics (*saltarentur*), effeminate voices, rhythms and gestures, and Dio Chrysostom (*Oration* 2.56), wearing the mask of Alexander the Great, offers his opinion that a king ought to banish public *orchêseis* (which, in Dio's time, could be translated only as 'pantomimes'). Pantomime addiction and pantomime-related connoisseurship can be admitted in polite conversation and, in the same breath, referred to as a *morbus*, a disease,[8] just as every stage-performer (along with gladiators, athletes and charioteers) is an object of amazement as well as dread, fascination inextricably interwoven with revulsion (e.g. Tertullian, *On the Spectacles* 22, with Barton 1993: 12-15).

Even the openly adoring crowd's pleasure could be constructed as ambivalent, a relationship of love and hate, adulation and contempt, spontaneous emotional proximity and calculated social distancing. 'Let us also consider this', Aelius Aristides insists,

> that not even the masses wholeheartedly love and welcome those spectacles [i.e. mimes, pantomimes, wonder-workers] to which one could say they are above everything else enslaved. For who is there who does not claim for himself to be better than every pantomime dancer (*orchêstou pantos*)? Or who would accord a mime the right to speak off-stage?[9] But while they are titillated for the moment (i.e. during the performance), once they have left the theatre they immediately pour scorn on what they saw, or rather, even during the show, they feel pleasure of the kind experienced by those who are in jest (Aelius Aristides, *Oration* 34.57; cf. ibid. 55).

As John Chrysostom focuses on the paradox with Christian eyes,

> If anybody calls you a charioteer or a pantomime (*orchêstên*), you claim to have been insulted and you move heaven and earth to shake the insult off, but if he lures you to see the spectacle itself, you do not turn away from it. The art whose name you avoid, you pursue almost wholesale (*PG* 59.320).

Like most tragic and comic actors on the Roman stage, or like gladiators, the pantomime dancer lives his life on a social brink, adored and despised, lauded and reviled (cf. Chapter 5§4). Even at the peak of his power, while he enjoys unmitigated imperial favour and sometimes the privileges of a high position in the imperial administration, the 'pantomime' tag is always there to haunt and taunt him, as Theocritus (II), an imperial freedman who became extremely powerful at the beginning of the third century AD, found out. As he leapt to his sword and brandished it menacingly against a man who had offended him, his adversary was unable to suppress the gibe that cost him his life: 'even this you did like a pantomime' (*kai touto … hôs orchêstês epoiêsas*), he sneered, whereupon Theocritus ordered him to be killed (Dio Cassius, *Roman History* 78.21.4).

Most importantly, however, it was with respect to the opposites of high and low culture that pantomime dancing displayed the features of a 'middlebrow' art. Even the cruellest remonstrations of intellectual purists have not obscured the fact that pantomime was not a total write-off with respect to the regions of the mind, but possessed instead sufficient trappings of sophistication to enable someone skilled with words to pass it off as educational. Despite Lycinus' efforts to annex the dancer's art to high culture, conversely, the genre could do little more than hover on the edges of cultural respectability. As we saw in Chapter 8§2, while pantomime's use of myth, that staple of literary discourse, gave it its most conspicuous share in high culture, its complete reliance on the body, with its carnal, biological rhythms of expression, kept it firmly in the terrain of the low and the popular. We could profitably apply to the genre the Bakhtinian concept of a 'hybrid' construction, a form that 'contains mixed within it two utterances, two speech manners, two styles, two "languages", two semantic and axiological belief systems', in such a way that there are no formal boundaries between them (Bakhtin 1981: 304).

Finally, although we can almost take it for granted that the dancer himself would have been desperate to see the moral stigma and aesthetic disrepute attached to him and his profession lifted, it should not be as readily assumed that a pantomime of, say, Lucian's time, would have craved for his full assimilation into the tropes and patterns of high culture. Pantomime's popularity was inextricably linked with deviation, its power fuelled by a fire that could only burn beyond the bounds of cultural propriety. Even before the emergence of pantomime as a fully identifiable art form, an epigram of Dioscorides from the third century BC (*Greek Anthology* 11.195; cf. Chapter 1§1) makes it clear that what transforms the dancer's body into an object of aesthetic fascination is precisely its much maligned ability to transcend the dominant culture's gender-norms: the masses will not go to the theatre to watch a dancer re-enact the deeds of war-loving heroes, an unnamed proto-pantomime complains. What they crave is the effeminate and the exotic, both of which are spliced in the role of the *galli*, Cybele's eunuch priests. Centuries later and viewed from a different perspective, the thorny issue of the dancer's gender-indeterminacy emerges yet again as the most powerful magnetic pull (cf. Chapter 5§2). In Cyprian's eyes, a pantomime's glory is commensurate with his encroachment on feminine ground:

men are emasculated (*evirantur*), the entire honour and vigour of the male gender melt because of the dishonour of a sinewless (*enervati*) body, and whoever goes to greater lengths in order to break down virility into womanishness (*quisque virum in feminam magis fregerit*) gives the greatest pleasure in that matter (*To Donatus* 8).

129

Neither pantomime's hybridity, however, nor the 'forbidden' joys of its transgressiveness are anywhere in evidence in Lycinus' discourse, which appears totally oblivious to the genre's nature as a sensual and middle-brow art. Perhaps more clearly than any other ancient text, Lucian's *On the Dance* demonstrates how pantomime, perched like a Siren (cf. *Dance* 3) on the high rock that separates the popular from the élite, could be easily 'pulled over' towards either side of the cultural divide, in accordance with the appropriating subject's rhetorical agenda.

§2. Lycinus' 'designer brand' of pantomime dancing

We can now take some more sure-footed steps towards appreciating the peculiar nature of Lycinus' speech. An art which built its reputation on a blurring of the lines between the high and the low, he chose to anatomise as if it were a fully-fledged product of high culture. Instead of assigning it grounds of its own and celebrating it as a 'space apart', he laboured to enmesh it in networks of legitimate cultural expression into which neither the genre nor its artist could happily fit. By lavishing the trappings of high culture so liberally upon the dance, Lycinus ultimately detracted from it attributes that were inherently, even exclusively, its own: he dissociated the dancer from the real roots of his power, the physicality of his performance and the raw visceral appeal of his electrifying body-rhythms.[10] For, although the individual or collective, conscious or unconscious impulses that ancient pantomime as a genre satisfied are still matter for scholarly debate, voyeuristic pleasures would certainly have ranked very high among the thrills experienced by pantomime addicts. Both the serpentine delights of the dancer's undulating body and the elegant configurations of his limbs must have provided a real feast for the viewers' avid stares, especially in a visual economy where the pleasures of ocular contemplation were deemed to rival the joys of erotic consummation (cf. Morales 2004). Travelling from Athamas to Ino or from Aegisthus to Aerope (*Dance* 67), the pantomime not merely constructed a fantasy of many bodies tantalis-ingly fused into one, but also a living kaleidoscope of gender-positions that bombarded his audience with ever-fresh matter for desire (cf. Chapter 5§2). Freed from the limitations and emotional narrowness of his social role as a citizen and as a man, the élite male spectator enjoyed roaming the vast landscapes beyond reality, where without fear of repercussion he could both explore non-normative configurations of desire and delve into the hidden depths of the female psyche. In other words, what the élite male fan could not experience in the culturally sanctioned language of unadul-terated masculinity, pantomime allowed him to experience in the socially marginalised dialect of femininity, a mode of speech whose multi-hued emotional vocabulary was made so readily available to him through the silent dancer's 'eloquent' limbs and 'speaking' fingers.

Contrary to what Lycinus claims for the genre, then, for most imperial pantomime fans, deprived of liberal education as well as the sophisticated tastes that go with it, pantomime's special pleasures did not lie in the domain of intellectual consummation. Pantomime must have been a genre that clamoured to be experienced by means of what Bourdieu (1990: 166) calls

> a way of understanding which is altogether particular, and often forgotten in theories of intelligence: that which consists of *understanding with one's body* [my italics]. There are heaps of things that we understand only with our bodies, outside conscious awareness, and without being able to put our understanding into words.

The occasional glimpse afforded by a miscellany of sources into the bodily response of audiences to pantomime-shows encapsulates the kind of contact forged between the dancer on the boards and his entranced auditorium far better than Lycinus' sophisticated anatomy of pantomime viewing. Whether the viewer leaps 'higher than the dancers', as Dio Chrysostom sneers, or re-enacts mimetically the pantomime's gestures, as Aristaenetus admiringly recounts,[11] it is through the vibrations of his own body, linked by means of an affective sympathy to the performer's every twist and turn, that the spectator understands the dancing body's speech, its fantasies and its desires, its pain and its oppression. As Tatian says in his anti-theatrical tirade, being a pantomime spectator is a matter of a bodily response, whether that means sitting open-mouthed while the chorus sing, or arranging oneself in the same corporeal (and, undoubtedly, emotional) disposition (*syndiatithesthai*) as the 'dancer, who gesticulates and moves in an unnatural way' (*Address to the Greeks* 22.2).[12]

Finally, there is yet another sense in which pantomime's cultural profile is misrepresented in Lycinus' speech. Although Lycinus *does* appreciate very keenly the singular impact of pantomime's non-verbal language,[13] he is primarily concerned with demonstrating a lower-key proposition, namely that the dancer's silent eloquence *does not lag behind* the complexities of articulate speech. It is true that comparisons with language are suggested by the genre itself, since the pantomime, unlike the ballet artist or the modern dancer, is supposed to 'show' the actions and the passions contained in the sung libretto. Nevertheless, a dance addict of any period would be able to affirm that dance's unique value as a communicative channel transcending social and linguistic, political and cultural barriers resides precisely in its ability to touch upon, illuminate or bring to life those ineffable and inaccessible regions of feeling and experience that verbal language can never reach. Dance simply eschews the possibility of a complete translation into the linguistic mode, for it enters the area of its highest affective potency only at the point where spoken-and-written language leaves off, or is strained to its utmost limit. As Sheets-Johnstone (1979: 62) writes about Martha Graham's 'Lamentation', any verbalisation of this stunning piece 'is in no way equivalent to the import of the dance itself'.

Cassiodorus, the high-ranking Christian official we first met in Chapter 1§2, grasped this dimension of pantomime infinitely better than Lycinus: explaining the designation of pantomime as a 'mute' art, he points out that 'with closed mouth, it speaks with the hands, and, by means of certain gesticulations, it renders intelligible what could hardly be expressed by means of oral narrative or written text' (*Various Letters* 1.20.5).[14] Ironically, Church Fathers were the quickest to grasp the insuperable power of corporeal language: 'you did not say it in words', preaches John Chrysostom,

> but you did say it by means of gestures (*tôi schêmati*); you did not utter the
> sounds with your mouth, but you did mouth them with your way of walking;
> you did not summon by voice, yet you did summon with what is clearer than
> voice: the eyes (*PG* 47.515).[15]

What it all amounts to is that Lycinus' attempt to dislodge the genre from its middling ground by pulling it unequivocally into the fold of high culture came dangerously close to falsifying its essence, and may well have frustrated the pantomaniac in the streets just as much as it frustrated Lucian to find his own homeland, Samosata, transposed, 'acropolis and all', to Mesopotamia, instead of being recognised for what it really was: a Syrian town on the west bank of the Euphrates (see Lucian, *How to Write History* 24). By turning the dancer into a *pepaideumenos*' ideal spectacle – *in him you have the quintessence of all knowledge and all the arts collapsed upon each other* – Lycinus very nearly transformed him into something he was not.

And yet the strongest note of caution is in order here, lest the transformation is thought to be as ludicrous as the masquerade of monkeys, who can be trained to dance and even keep the time, all dressed up in purple mantles and impressive masks, but are immediately exposed when their simian nature is offered the chance (in the form of a nut or a fig) to shine through.[16] Lucian's *On the Dance* is neither a spoof, like his playful attempt to elevate the ways and tactics of the sponger to the level of an art (see *On the Parasite*), nor a mere jeu d'esprit, absurd verbal pyrotechnics, like his *Encomion of a Fly*. Nor do we find in *On the Dance* the same kind (or the same extent) of the clever 'metaliterary' game we encounter in Lucian's contemporary *Portraits*,[17] where the two interlocutors agree to 'put together' artificially (*systêsômetha*) the image of Panthea's[18] physical, intellectual and moral excellence by synthesising select ingredients, 'images' culled from rhetoric, poetry, history, philosophy and the mimetic arts (e.g. *Portraits* 16).

Sure enough, the tone ascribed to a work defending pantomime is largely dependent on the predisposition of the addressee, so that what would sound like an *endoxon* encomium (the praise of honourable things) to a pantomime fan would seem to the disdainful intellectual[19] an *atopon* or *paradoxon* encomium (the empty rhetorical praise of trivial objects and slight themes or the arguing of prima facie indefensible cases).[20] But even though hardened opponents of the dance would certainly have thought Lycinus' claims preposterous (see Chapter 8) and his entire *apologia* ludicrous, pantomime enthusiasts would have been perfectly able to recognise the spectacle they loved amid the many layers of embellishing sophistication – unlike the co-emperor's mistress Panthea, who declared herself unable to appreciate the encomiasts' images as congenial or 'similar' to herself (*In Defence of the Portraits* 10).

If the benchmark for a non-embarrassing encomium is the ability of the person praised to truly see him/herself in the encomiast's compliments (cf. *In Defence of the Portraits* 2), it is important to keep this in mind: all the *realia*, that is to say, the objective, non-value-laden hallmarks of the pantomime genre featured in Lucian's *On the Dance*, are not fanciful constructs but can be easily corroborated from a variety of other sources (cf. Jones 1986: 72-3),[21] thus belying G. Anderson's (1977: 286) assertion that Lucian wrote this dialogue 'for an occasion with neither knowledge nor interest in his subject'. In addition, a sympathetically-minded intellectual may well have been culturally predisposed to see the dancer in the way indicated by Lycinus, namely as the epitome of Greekness, a treasure-trove of Hellenic memory and glory (cf. Chapter 7).

What is dubious in this dialogue is the sheer *weight* of the dancer's intellectual panoply, whether understood as a prerequisite and asset of a good performer or as a cluster of knowledge and moral values that can be transmitted from the stage to the genre's addressees. In his attempt 'to justify the art in terms acceptable to cultured society' (Jones 1986: 74), Lycinus went a step too far in two directions: first in 'glossing over' the spectacle's less dignified aspects;[22] secondly in his more than generous raising of the genre to the rank of an educated and educational pastime (cf. Chapter 8). What this dialogue represents is neither a window on the genre (in any case, as I have already pointed out in the Introduction, such windows do not exist) nor a wilful or clumsy distortion of its traits. The brand of pantomime dancing advertised by Lycinus is merely a genetically modified version of the genre: substantially true to form, but artificially enhanced, with wrinkles smoothed and shades toned up or down, as required on each occasion. Having shied away from staring the real-life pantomime in the face, Lycinus set out to validate a substantially tamer and more refined version, a mode of entertainment tinged by the apologist's preferred rhetorical colouring. For it would be reasonable to claim that the pantomime-related knowledge which the vast majority of pantomime fans would have accumulated through their long exposure to the genre would have had nothing to do with pantomime's entanglements with élite cultural pursuits, such as rhetoric or philosophy.

The kind of topic pantomime addicts would have been debating in the Roman alleyways of Lucian's time (cf. Lucian, *Nigrinus* 29) or in Libanius' classroom in fourth-century Antioch (see Chapter 8§1) would have been each individual dancer's beauty and allure, the strength of his leaps, the grace of his pirouettes or, to put it in John Chrysostom's words, the pantomimes' lineage, their country of origin, their upbringing and all kinds of similar matters (*PG* 51.188). According to Libanius (*Oration* 64.57), the joy (*terpsis*) of pantomime viewing lies in the ability to exercise one's gradually acquired dance-related knowledge: audiences relish the chance to scrutinise 'the position of the [dancer's] feet, the direction of the hands, the harmony of the gestures … and, in general, the comeliness of the entire spectacle'. The invaluable fictitious letter to the pantomime Panarete penned by Aristaenetus is most eloquent in this respect, since it turns the spotlight on the fans as they resume their seats after the end of the performance to reminisce over the spectacle's highlights. Engaged in detailed conversation among themselves, they eagerly go over the 'movements' of the dancer's 'multifarious silence' (*Letters* 1.26, 15-17), those 'in the know' enlightening those who are not, and all together prolonging the delights of the performance by reliving in their own body the pantomime's bodily eloquence (ibid., 17-18). And, as becomes immediately clear from the equally invaluable musings of the third-century AD philosopher Plotinus on pantomime dancing (a spectacle he clearly appreciates and knows well), pantomime connoisseurship is a thoroughly 'technical' stockpile of knowledge, enabling the expert viewer to understand the manifold configurations of the dancer's body, how, for example, 'one of his limbs is pressed hard down, another relaxed, one works hard and painfully, another is given a rest as the figuring changes' (*Enneads* 4.4.33; trans. Armstrong, Loeb 1966), and so on.

Lycinus, then, failed to teach us (alongside Crato, his 'built-in' addressee) how to appreciate a pantomime show *on its own terms*, without first relating it to, or feeling obliged to translate it into, the tropes and languages of a different register of culture. Consequently there is a real sense that, rather than empowering the dancer, Lycinus' apology subtracted from his power, for the construct of a 'fully integrated' pantomime, speaking from the same subject-position as any minstrel of élite educational practices, could only be a pale imitator, a bungler of cultural discourses in which other agents were far more likely to excel. What never emerges from Lycinus' construction is the pantomime's dwelling in a zone of cultural ambivalence and contradiction, his body being the site where two worlds fused and merged in a powerfully explosive single substance. On the other hand, this 'intellectualisation' of the dancer was most probably the price that had to be paid if the genre was to be made palatable to a refined and open-minded audience, which may well have been Lucian's ultimate target.[23] Lucian has produced the perfect alibi for the pantomaniac of social and intellectual standing who wants to feel good about his socially suspect pantomime addiction.

134

11

Who is Afraid of Pantomime Dancers?

Time now to visit the single real-life battlefield where, as already indicated in Chapter 9, talented pantomimes and a relatively small but prominent section of the upper classes collided in 'contests' whose prizes were no more and no less than an even greater share in the kind of fame and power that a public performance could bestow on individual agents. Pantomime may well have played the role of a larger-than-life enemy in the many tangled strategies of élite self-presentation (Chapter 9, especially §3), but it was a far from imaginary threat. For at least one segment of the educated élite, the breed of public declaimers or 'show orators' of all colours and denominations,[1] the dancer was not a mirage but a frustratingly palpable presence in the cultural playgrounds whose mastery they greedily coveted. Needless to say, our own perceptual filters, conditioned by our present cultural perspective, must first be blocked before we can appreciate this statement to the full.

While we would be hard-pressed to imagine a social context wherein, say, world famous rock-stars and university dons (good modern equivalents of pantomimes and élite declaimers) could find themselves performing side by side and in intense competitive spirit for the plaudits and affections of a single audience, there was an ample 'zone of contact', where electrifying pantomimes and sophists, as full of pride as 'many-coloured peacocks' and 'carried aloft, as on wings, by their fame and students' (Dio Chrysostom, *Oration* 12.5), saw their career paths cross and fame charts in conflict. Such 'contact zones' were primarily the great theatres of the imperial world, where the pantomime industry flourished and where élite declaimers displayed their talents in the broader context of the numerous fairground-style *panêgyreis* (public assemblies) and *agônes* (agonistic festivals) which punctuated civic life in the empire (see Chapter 4§2). If the model of Caius Iulius Demosthenes, the wealthy second-century AD benefactor who instituted the 'Demostheneia' festival in the Lycian city of Oenoanda, is anything to go by, such festivals could even set apart ring-fenced time for what van Nijf (1999: 193) very aptly calls 'real popular entertainment', namely the displays and spectacles 'that please the city', pride of place among which would have been assigned to pantomime dancers (cf. Chapter 4§2). In other words, sophists, just as much as pantomimes, displayed their intellectual or corporeal 'wares' to mass audiences in those ambivalent terrains of Greco-Roman life where

135

heterogeneous elements converged and a plurality of cultural 'languages' cross-fertilised each other in a forever-sizzling melting-pot.

Splendid insights into the atmosphere of such events can be gained from Dio Chrysostom. His vivid pictures of quarrelsome sophists and their disciples rubbing shoulders not just with lawyers, writers and reciters but also with jugglers, fortune-tellers and peddlers of all sorts[2] indicate that one of the reasons that the pantomime lingered persistently in the élite declaimer's mental field of vision was that, more often than not, he also hovered at the edge of his physical vision, being occasionally a stubborn speck in the declaimer's own eye. This much at least we can surmise from Apuleius, illustrious public lecturer in North Africa.[3] Despite his fame, Apuleius seems acutely conscious of the fact that even an eminent orator in his league does not perform inside an insulated bubble, but shares his venues, sometimes as imposing as the Carthaginian theatre, with his sub-cultural showbusiness rivals. As he puts it in one of his speeches,

> here [i.e. the theatre of Carthage] the mime indulges in idle talk, the comedian engages in conversation, the tragedian bawls, the rope-dancer takes risks, the miracle-worker steals, the pantomime displays his gestures (*histrio gesticulatur*), and all the other players demonstrate to the people whatever art each of them possesses (*Flowery Excerpts* 18.4).

The reference to other entertainers can be easily mistaken for a dispassionate aside, yet tension simmers beneath the calm surface.

Put on a par with the material adornments of the 'performance space' (such as the marble pavement, the pillars of the stage, the panelled ceiling, etc., in 18.3), popular entertainments are deemed equally 'external' to the real business that takes place in a venue of this kind, namely the bond forged between enthusiastic audiences (such as Apuleius' own, of course!) and the speech of the declaimer (18.5). Supercilious dismissiveness is deftly spliced with the orator's calculated meanderings via the territory of his opponents. Apuleius' look in the direction of pantomimes may be an undercover, 'silent' killer but, above all else, it is the very necessity of casting this 'Medusa' look in the first place that matters. A high-powered cultural player, who feels his own pre-eminence not only unassailed but even unassailable, is unlikely to stop and notice the rabble under his feet. The fact that Apuleius *both* notices *and* cares, his glances condescending and at the same time anxious, speaks volumes. 'Beggars' on the threshold of high culture they may well have seemed to be, but pantomimes were also formidable presences in the world of imperial performative displays. In the East of the empire, Dio Chrysostom harbours no illusions about who is really in control of theatre space in Alexandria: it is those whom he sneeringly enumerates, by means of a Homeric pastiche, as 'mimes and pantomimes (*orchêstai*), best of men in beating the ground with their dancing, and the riders of swift horses' (*Oration* 32.4). It is *they* who rule the roost and it is over and against the crowd's applause for *their* talents that he, the wise intellectual, must strive to be heard.

As a last stop, then, on the cultural map of imperial and later antiquity (albeit with a sharper focus on the Eastern side of the Mediterranean), this chapter probes the problematic coexistence of pantomimes and élite declaimers in the performative arenas of their world. Understanding the relationship between these two categories of public entertainers in the way it was shaped not in the 'life of the imagination' (cf. Chapters 8 and 9) but on the real-life battleground where their fortunes intersected is essential for a deeper understanding of the exchanges between pantomime as a genre and high culture.

§1. Living life on the brink

Sophists and pantomimes were not as odd bedfellows as it might seem. Epideictic declaimers just as much as pantomime dancers were crowd-pleasers and public entertainers, single-mindedly wedded to the pursuit of fame. As Cribiore (2001: 239) writes (cf. Horrocks 1997: 80),

> Panegyrics and declamations on judicial and especially historical topics became very popular forms of entertainment. The most brilliant sophists were the idols of the educated public. They commanded high fees, were disputed among the cities, and attracted vast, frenzied audiences. They were the athletes of the word, the adored heroes with whom their fans identified and whom they tried to imitate.

When successful, dancers and sophists were lavishly rewarded with fabulous wealth and public honours, a life of glitz and glamour.[4] However, the standing of both within their own performative milieu was equally precarious. In the first place, both professions were highly competitive, hotbeds of antagonism and power-struggles, where the destruction of a rival was as indispensable as the direct promotion of oneself.[5] We have already seen Macrobius' anecdotes on the rivalry between Hylas (I) and Pylades (I) (cf. Chapters 3§2 and 4§1), the latter missing no opportunity to deprecate his gifted ex-pupil's performance. And Lycinus himself tells the story of the unlucky pantomime who, after an unfortunate performance of 'Ajax mad' was pained above all by his 'antagonist and rival in the art' (*antagônistês kai antitechnos*), who performed the same role with an eye to his predecessor's mistake (*Dance* 84).[6] In the world of declaiming intellectuals, correspondingly, the antagonism between eminent performers was a 'zero-sum' game, predicated on the idea that 'for one man to triumph, all his rivals had to lose' (Gleason 1995: xxiii).[7] For this reason, the mere thought of a rising star rapidly making a name for himself in the sophistic circuit, can make the more established declaimer frightfully uneasy, his heart and mind 'palpitating', as he realises how many admirers the potential usurper of his own glory can already boast (see Philostratus, *Lives* 525, on Dionysius of Miletus in awe of the young Polemo).

Secondly, not only did their performance venues sometimes overlap,[8] but they often played host to an equally fickle and excitable public, unevenly composed of intellectually-minded viewers avid for cultured, sophisticated performances, and vulgar, rowdy crowds with their 'souls all but hanging on their lips' (Dio Chrysostom, *Oration* 32.50), greedy for spectacular attractions. It was before such audiences that both dancer and élite declaimer lived their lives on the brink, deriving their frisson of pleasure from constantly teetering between public adulation and damnation, for merciless ridicule was the inevitable price of failure.[9] Neither the sophist nor the pantomime was forgiven any lapses, but lived for the sake of a reputation that might die 'every day and on the spot' (Aelius Aristides, *Oration* 34.58). As Apuleius points out to his audience,

> ... who among you would forgive me for a single solecism? Who would allow me one ignorantly pronounced syllable? Who would permit me to jabber any wild and uncouth words like those that well up in the mouths of the insane? ... You examine every word of mine keenly, weigh it carefully, subject it to the file and the rule, and compare it with the products of the lathe or productions on the stage (*Flowery Excerpts* 9.7-8; cf. 6; trans. Hilton, in Harrison 2001).[10]

As for pantomime spectators, those best initiated in the conventions of the dance (cf. Plotinus, *Enneads* 4.4.33) derive special pleasure from 'judging' the performer's bodily technique,[11] never overlooking a 'solecism' of movement (see *Dance* 80) and ever-ready to denounce the smallest faux-pas (e.g. *Dance* 76). Much like eighteenth-century audiences in England who, according to one observer, came along 'with ears of moles and eyes of cats ... to pick up a false emphasis, or a reading contrary to their opinion',[12] the Antiocheans described by Lycinus are obsessed with keeping such a close eye upon the stage-world 'that nothing escapes the notice of a man of them' (*Dance* 76).[13] In a fascinating passage John Chrysostom highlights 'scrutiny' as the one common characteristic that unites the behaviour of audiences at spectacles of mass entertainment (e.g. instrumental music or singing) and sophistic displays: 'for these too (i.e. sophists) have theatres, and listeners and applause and noise and the utmost scrutiny (*basanos ... eschatê*) of what is said' (*PG* 59.25).

It therefore seems that, for both dancer and sophist, each individual performance was a fresh battle for their reputation, a huge 'risk' in Apuleius' words, as even the most illustrious among them was only as good as his latest appearance.[14] Like the precariously poised pantomime, his fame resting on the dubious balance of his every twist and leap, the sophist too was exposed, his every word and gesture putting his image at every moment to the test.[15] The magnitude of the declaimer's agony is well conveyed by the star sophist Polemo, who, on seeing a gladiator dripping with sweat before the life-or-death combat facing him, remarked: 'you are in as great an agony as if you were about to declaim' (Philostratus, *Lives* 541). Sophist and pantomime alike were fully at their public's mercy – in Libanius' expression, they were 'enslaved' to that public. Dancer and orator could feel secure in their rule only to the extent that thousands of eyes remained avid to 'consume' their bodies and hordes of fans craved a morsel of their glittering success. Of their own accord, neither perfect bodily training nor exquisite learning nor faultless eloquence could guarantee fame – the ultimate judge and guarantor of immortality was the spectating public.[16] As Libanius (*Oration* 25.50-1) brilliantly argues, when the moment of reckoning draws near, it is the crowd's voice that decides all, turning the sophist into the slave of every creature who possesses hands and tongue. To make matters worse, every pair of hands and every mouth in the audience carry the same power in making or breaking the sophist's reputation, irrespective of whether they belong to the professor or the labourer, the educated few or the illiterate many. The teacher of rhetoric may believe he is a free man, but fails abysmally to realise that he is ultimately enslaved to the innumerable throng, 'each of the listeners leaving the lecture-hall as master of the one who has declaimed' (25.51).

§2. Formidable rivals

Sophists and pantomimes, then, were undeniably twin stars on the horizon of imperial performance culture. If the crowds flocked to the theatre to watch the dancer's bodily contortions and exertions, they ran, just as eagerly, to feast upon the visible signs of agony imprinted on the sophist's body: his panting and his sweating, his nervous pacing back and forth, his all too palpable anxiety to win the favour of his public. In both cases, fame could not persist unless it was made at all times 'visible': constructed and enacted every time *in* performance, their brilliance was offered up for visual consumption to a public expecting to be dazzled and seduced first and foremost by the sight. Nevertheless, for all their equally resplendent radiance, they were also formidable opponents, whose rivalry in the performance field has left its mark[17] on a variety of Greek and Roman texts. Philostratus, for example, deems it thoroughly fitting to magnify the reputation of the illustrious Hadrian of Tyre by recording that, whenever the herald announced his epideictic declamations in Rome (he held the chair of rhetoric there), the crowds would abandon their lowbrow entertainments, 'predominantly consisting in the shows of pantomimes' (*orchêstôn... to epipan*), and run to the performance venue 'full of enthusiasm and reproaching those who kept a walking pace' (*Lives* 589).

Pantomimes may well have been the losers in the popularity 'contests' referred to by Philostratus, but at the same time they were not to be ignored. In his mordant satire *On Salaried Posts in Great Houses*, Lucian ridicules the intellectual who, on top of all the humiliations he endures while in willing servitude to some wealthy Roman patron, must even put up with being 'overtaken in reputation' (i.e. in the favour of his boss) by 'some lewd fellow (*kinaidos*) or dancing master (*orchêstodidaskalos*)' residing in the house: though theoretically inconceivable that an educated man could be 'held in equal honour' with such a creature, grim reality dictates otherwise (*On Salaried Posts in Great Houses* 27). Beyond satirical snapshots, Athenaeus pays tribute to the excellence of Memphius, Lucius Verus' freedman and 'philosopher-dancer' (*philosophon orchêstên*),[18] by pitting him directly against his brainy rival, the teacher of the art of *logos*:

> [the pantomime] demonstrates (*epideiknysin*) the nature of Pythagorean philosophy, making everything manifest (*emphanizôn*) to us with silent gestures more clearly (*saphesteron*) than they who purport to teach verbal eloquence (Athenaeus, *Sophists at Dinner* 20d).

To be sure, such a comment tells us about the possible rhetorical constructions of a pantomime's appeal more than it testifies to any extraordinary knowledge or skills mastered by a particular exponent of the art. Its value resides in its bold visualisation of the pantomime as a winner in a totally uncongenial contest, falling exclusively within the remit of a culture he is not supposed to possess: an intellectual contest of *saphêneia*, the clarity and vividness of narrative that can be acquired only through years of practice and painstaking schoolroom learning.

Even from the viewpoint of the sophist sitting on the highest throne of literary culture, the silent pantomime was a 'voice' to be reckoned with. Only posthumously could he be safely hoisted to the lofty heights of the élite declaimer's line of vision. As Libanius very interestingly records, the same Hadrian of Tyre, whom Philostratus' narrative presents as a greater crowd-puller than his lowly antagonists in Rome, delivered such a magnificent funeral oration in honour of the pantomime Paris (probably L. Aurelius or Paris III) that it could have been meant as a farewell to a fellow sophist:

> What is more, the dancer whose star once shone bright among us and had the same name as that herdsman of old before whom the goddesses were judged with respect to their beauty, that dancer the Tyrian sophist, whose tongue possessed Poseidon's strength in shaking and brandishing everything, lamented so much as he was lying dead and offered to him such a magnificent shroud in the form of a speech that I do not know what greater honour he would have sought to bestow if he were honouring a departed sophist. Indeed, he deemed the pantomime worthy of being called exactly that (i.e. a sophist) (*Oration* 64.41).

Sophist and dancer, then, were not merely engaged in 'deep play' vis-à-vis their public, that is, performances in which their reputations could be built, affirmed and celebrated just as easily as torn in tatters.[19] They were also engaged in 'zero-sum' games played out against each other, as neither side could claim for itself an uncontested lead in the perilous performative arenas of imperial culture.[20]

In truth, upper-class performers suffered from a serious disadvantage in comparison to their pantomime rivals: while the pantomime was supported in his efforts by an array of sensational paraphernalia ('the silk robes and beautiful masks, the double pipes and trillings and the pleasing voices of the singers', *Dance* 63), the orator was solely responsible for 'stage-managing' his one-man show, with all its special effects. As mass audiences are wooed more easily by the flamboyant and spectacular, the élite declaimer was painfully aware that his intellectual pre-eminence alone was unable to secure an uncontroversial lead on his behalf:

> It is not easy to cope with the din of so great a crowd nor to stand face to face with countless myriads of human beings without (the support of) song and a lyre; for this is indeed the antidote (needed) against the people of your city,

admits Dio Chrysostom in his famous speech to the Alexandrians (*Oration* 32.20).[21] All the while the bearer of up-market education was looking down on pantomimes as inferior, crude and ignorant pretenders to educational capital, he must have known full well that even the flashiest of declaimers might run the risk of being outshone by the collection of electrifying items which accompanied a dancer's show.[22] Once again, Dio's side-glances at musicians and hired dancers (e.g. *Oration* 32.24, 55, 62) are instructive. Himself deprived of the sweetness of song (32.22), he views them with contempt and trepidation. Desiring nothing more than to triumph over them, he is nevertheless astute enough to realise that the mere suggestion that his audience should turn their back on lowly pleasures would be tantamount to madness on his part (32.5).

§3. Spicing up élite performance

If I am right in my contention that a serious asymmetry of power existed between the most successful exponents of popular entertainment culture and élite declaimers of all kinds, it must also be conceded that élite performers would have felt the need to develop strategies for their defence. Although 'Othering' the vulgar arts and their performers (see Chapter 9§4) or ignoring their existence[23] were frequent tactics, when tested in the fray they proved to be allies of little strength, unable to secure a crowd's rapturous applause or, at least, prevent it from shouting: 'When will the guy shut up? When will the juggler come on?', as Dio Chrysostom (*Oration* 32.7) complains. What was vital was the ability to beat the enemy at his own game, thrash him with his own weapons. Indeed, élite performers who were not content with small-scale gatherings,[24] and sophists who, avid for disciples, money, renown, rewards and power, set out to make a name for

141

themselves by captivating the crowds in the various 'theatres of the Greeks', as Themistius puts it (*Oration* 24.304a), were quick to identify and respond to the need to develop expansive histrionic gestures. Orators understood that, without an impressive array of eye-catching and ear-seducing mannerisms of all kinds (with respect to voice, bodily deportment, dress, manner of acting), they had no hope of riveting a mass audience's attention, let alone of holding it for the duration of performance.

In the first place, unaided by the illusion-conducive ambience of the dramatic stage, the display-orator must have been eager to prove himself at least as intensely theatrical as stage-actors/dancers, in order to convey in an entertaining manner the mental attitudes or passions of the *dramatis personae* populating his *meletai* (declamations). So, for example, the sophist Scopelian, who in Philostratus' opinion far exceeded his fellow-sophists in the way he interpreted epideictic plots drawn from the Persian wars,

> acted out in them (*hypekrineto*) the arrogance and the empty-mindedness intrinsic in the character of the barbarians. And people say that in those declamations he would sway his body to and fro more than usual, as if he were possessed by bacchic frenzy... (Philostratus, *Lives* 520; cf. ibid., 588 on Hadrian of Tyre).

As for the 'scenic effects' (*skênên*) developed by his younger rival Polemo of Laodicea, they are said to have included a calculated ascendance to a pitch of excitement, a most spectacular 'jumping up' (*anapêdan*) from the lecturer's chair at the conclusion of a powerful argument, a histrionic smile at the rounding of periods to underscore the effortlessness of his delivery[25] and the occasional stamping of the ground 'with no less vigour than the horse in Homer' (*Lives* 537). Both '*hypokrinesthai*', in the sense of acting out a role, playing one's part as if on stage,[26] and '*skênê*', in the sense of 'stage-effects', 'theatrical properties', are recurrent terms in Philostratus' narrative (e.g. *Lives* 537, 541, 595), underlining the extent to which display-performers sought to be the stage's equals in the areas where stage-performers (especially pantomimes) were thought to be unequalled: impersonation and physical dramaturgy, the gestural vocabulary of bodily communication.[27]

Secondly, of momentous import for their self-presentation was, to borrow Greenblatt's (1994: 44) felicitous expression, the 'privileged visibility' of their own fame and power. Epideictic declaimers chose to encode their cultural supremacy in strikingly visible signs, ranging from the effeminate hyper-elegance of personal appearance[28] to such perennially trusted crowd-pullers as extravagant splendour and pomp. The ostentatious display of magnificence, whether in the form of priceless gems and clothes or carriages and chariots with silver-mounted bridles and baggage animals, horses, slaves and hunting dogs in tow (Philostratus, *Lives* 587 and 532, on Hadrian of Tyre and Polemo respectively), was meant to astound the audience on top of (or even in lieu of) the oratorical display itself. So, for example, Philostratus records that when Alexander 'Clay-Plato' first addressed the Athenians in their city, his dress seemed to them so exquisite that, even before he had uttered a word, 'a low buzz' (*bombos*) shot through their ranks in commendation of his elegance (*Lives* 572).[29] The anecdotal flavouring of Philostratus' narrative notwithstanding, it dovetails to perfection with Lucian's satire of the successful (albeit ignorant) sophist's style:

> as for the crowds, it is your dress and voice and gait and walking about, your tune and your sandal and your use of 'sundry' that they will admire; what's more, when they catch sight of your sweat and your labouring breath, they won't harbour the merest doubt that you are some terrible opponent in the contests of words (*Professor* 20).

The charge that orators, pinning their hopes on a 'mellifluous voice' (Philostratus, *Lives* 593), indulge in a seductive 'sing-song' style, thereby infusing their speech with 'rivulets of sweetness' (*Lives* 592), is pervasive in élite texts. From the eccentric eunuch Favorinus, ridiculed on account of 'the enervated quality of his recitatives',[30] to Dionysius of Miletus, whose teacher Isaeus disparagingly denied ever having taught him to 'sing' (*aidein*),[31] and from the West to the East of the empire, orators, responding to their audiences' craving for a sung style, exhibit an impressive array of enchanting vocal flourishes and acrobatics. As Plutarch (*Moral Essays* 41d) puts it,

> sweetening their voices with harmonious modulations and soft tones and rhythmic cadences, they become possessed by bacchic frenzy and carry their listeners along, offering an empty pleasure and reaping an even emptier fame in return.[32]

From the sophists of Lucian's and Philostratus' day to the élite performers of later antiquity, this particular picture of transgressive rhetoric seems uniformly constant in the competitive epideictic performances of the Second Sophistic: it informs Lucian's second-century AD satirical brushstrokes in his *Professor of Rhetoric* no less than Themistius' fourth-century AD portrayal of pretend philosophers (i.e., in his view, sophists) who

> often bring their eloquence out to theatres and festive assemblies, adorned in gold and purple, exuding the smell of perfumes and painted and rubbed with cosmetics all over and crowned with garlands of flowers[33] (*Oration* 28.341b-c).

One cannot stress strongly enough that such 'assessments', no matter how neutral they seem, cannot be taken at face value, for the entire matrix of deviant behaviour with respect to the canon of élite manly deportment is to a very large extent a rhetorical construct: declaimers impugn the personal dignity and paideutic authority of their opponents by relegating them beyond the pale of legitimate speech-making.[34] Moreover, we should never imagine the entire 'rank and file' of upper-class declaimers as challengers of social expectations by means of dabbling at stagy or effeminate modes of rhetorical self-presentation.[35] If the threat of the sub-cultural was great, greater still was the opprobrium that could be aroused by a clumsy mixing of the codes, a half-hearted or botched attempt to maintain one's élite masculine status while experimenting with what the oratorical handbooks condemned (cf. Chapter 9§2). Notwithstanding Lucian's and Aelius Aristides' caricatures, which concede that the 'depilated', effeminate type of rhetoric is more successful (see Gleason 1995: 129), plunging into the underside of the 'great divide' between élite/manly and vulgar/unmanly culture and re-emerging not only unscathed but with an enhanced reputation is precisely the kind of act that would have required decisiveness and guts,[36] with versatility, originality, talent and brilliance of tongue to boot. How wrong the experiment could go we may gather from the narratives of disaster, such as Philostratus' tale about the Thessalian sophist Philiscus, a capable orator of solid Greek *paideia*, who nevertheless fell foul of the emperor's tastes when his effeminate mannerisms of gait and dress, rather than lending him glamour, happened to work against him (*Lives* 623). And Aelius Aristides records the plight of the declaimer who, to gratify his audience, added the same refrain to each of his sentences, *hôsper en melei*, as if in a song. His listeners, however, were far from mesmerised: chanting back at him, ahead of schedule, his catchy little phrase, they mortified the sophist by making his risk-taking strategy of '*bel canto* rhetoric' (Gleason 1995: 130) backfire (*Oration* 34.47).

If one of the most pressing problems was how to 'vanquish one's rivals in a manly fashion without making oneself appealing to one's audience in a feminine way' (Gleason 1995: 129), we have to imagine that the 'lesser lights' (cf. Gleason 1995: xxii) who studied, taught and performed rhetoric in the imperial East continued to operate till the end of pagan antiquity by means of barricading themselves behind the conventional, orthodox image of *paideia* as the expression of a dignified and self-controlled élite manhood. Even *within* the cultural terrain of sophistic superstardom, not everyone followed the example of the provocatively theatrical and androgynous style of rhetorical performance satirised in Lucian's work. Marcus of Byzantium, to take the most frequently discussed case, cultivated a rustic and uncouth appearance, with beard and hair always squalid and unkempt (Philostratus, *Lives* 529). So did Onomarchus of Andros, whom Philostratus openly compares to Marcus (*Lives* 599) and, undoubtedly, a great many others, who would have succumbed to the temptation to 'insulate' themselves from censure 'by adopting a rigidly "correct", hyper-masculine, performance style' (Gleason 1995: 161).[37] As for Dio Chrysostom, the élite declaimer who, as we saw earlier in this chapter, bemoaned the plight of unadorned philosophy in the face of the corrupt tastes of the masses, he built his entire self-dramatisation around manliness (*andreia*) and paraded his oratorical virility in contrast to the castrated type of education put 'on sale' by his opponents, that is, the sexual deviance and licentious unmanliness of the performers he berated as 'sophists'.[38] The citizens of 'Sophistopolis' (Russell 1983: 21), in other words, whose manifold practices are colourfully reflected in Philostratus' work, neither were nor should be treated as a uniform entity (Whitmarsh 2001: 238).

However, despite all the caveats one may wish to keep in mind, the fact remains that, over and above the slipperiness of oratorical constructions of the 'self' and 'others', some scintillating mega-stars of the élite performative horizon, men of the calibre of Herodes and Hadrian of Tyre, Scopelian and Favorinus, opted to fashion themselves as cultural rebels, *enfants terribles* of declamatory performance. Although theatricality was an intrinsic dimension of the upper-class man's *meletai* (declamations) inasmuch as 'being a sophist entailed the creation of a public *persona* in a histrionic display' (see Chapter 9§1),[39] daredevil sophists went considerably further than their contemporaries in the practice of adopting 'exaggeratedly theatricalized qualities in their oratory and daily lives' (Connolly 2001a: 94), treating their everyday sophistic 'act' self-consciously as theatre, 'complete with dramatic entrances, flamboyant dress, interpretative gesturing, careful modulation of voice, and, of course, a shrewd sense for the audience's expectations' (Branham 1989: 3). Dio Chrysostom's picture (*Oration* 12.2-5) is most telling at this point: such sophists offer themselves up to their audience's gaze surrounded by their lavish 'plumage', just as a peacock spreads his tail around him 'like some fair-shaped theatre'. Moreover, alongside forging a disquietingly close partnership between theatre and oratorical performance, these valiant trend-setters launched a new fashion line predicated on the treacherous notions of sensual over-refinement, androgynous grace and the erotic excitement associated with a doubly-gendered performing body. Could we perhaps pinpoint a generating force behind such a feminised 'aesthetic of performative excess' (Connolly 2001a: 77)? The quest for it would catapult us into the very heart of the cultural battlefields of the empire, and would expose that bubbling epicentre of performative discourses, where the 'rhetorical' and the 'histrionic', the two cognate yet diametrically opposed ways of 'staging' the self in public in the ancient world, fought it out relentlessly for cultural supremacy.[40]

As has been demonstrated in this section, by peppering old-fashioned rhetorical tradition with frivolity and eccentricity, a taste of the bizarre, the exotic or even the forbidden 'alien', adventurous sophists crossed over into the domain of the theatrical in an attempt to safeguard, and even increase, their own portion of cultural capital vis-à-vis the rapidly accelerating hold of stage-attractions.[41] For, although not as lethal to the upper-class performer as some sources liked to portray them (see Chapter 9§3), theatrical or theatricalised entertainers of all shades, from the intolerably vulgar rope-dancers and contortionists to the exquisitely graceful, mellifluous *tragôidoi,* were bothersome enough to generate in their opponents the desire to ensure that their ascendancy was kept in check. So, when the speaker in Lucian's *Professor of Rhetoric* introduces the teacher as a foppish fellow, who, with respect to the 'softness of his voice', styles himself in the manner of the famous courtesan and comic heroine Thais, satire goes far beyond the dandy's questionable conception of 'virility as boorish and not befitting the dainty and desired orator' (13). Above anything else, it indicates that the sophist's gaze is firmly fixed on the 'black double' of oratory, the theatrical 'beyond': the stage is what he imitates, the stage is what he seeks to rival.[42] How? Lucian's very same treatise holds the answer: by putting on his own *counter*-theatre, a 'one man band' designed to eclipse the glitz and plaudits of the shows.

This élite 'response' to popular theatrical attractions could not have materialised overnight, but must have been a messy and protracted process of cultural cross-pollination. As the lines of sophists became more thickly populated in the first centuries AD, and as the fame of entertainment heroes rose ever higher, along the whole length of the explosive battlefront one would have seen not only competitive encounters but also progressively abundant signs of interbreeding. Amid the sparks of the collisions, a new cross-breed of cultural performers was taking shape: turning male rhetoric into an embattled gender-ground, the site of heightened eroticism and histrionic antics, a monstrous, hybrid progeny of public declaimers gradually emerged, the outlandish product of a quirky cultural amalgamation. What remains to be seen is where such negotiations between the 'high' and the 'low' leave our story of the pantomime dancers.

§4. Fame in transgression: maverick declaimers and pantomime dancers

Pantomime dancing was a powerful catalyst, quickening the pace of the various 'chemical' reactions taking place at the slippery interface between 'high' and 'low' in imperial performance culture.[43] Given its centrality in the entertainment life of the empire and its formidable hold on public imagination, pantomime was uniquely poised to become a model for anyone craving success and power with the masses. For a start, it may well have been the dancer's own exceptional mimeticism and versatility, combined with the sheer attractiveness and *poikilia* (variety) of what was put on show in pantomime performances, that sparked in dissident declaimers the desire to create the kind of expressive vocabulary that would be able to transcend the communicative range of verbal language.

Sophists like Herodes, whose rhythms are said to have rivalled the variegated tones of flutes and lyres, or the declaimers whom even Philos-

146

tratus deemed beyond the pale, 'intoxicated' as they were with the voluptuous condiments that seasoned their speeches (*Lives* 573 and 522), were clearly keen to redefine élite performance as a spectacle that holds the crowds in thrall by 'pantomime-style' seductions of the eye and ear. Antagonising the dancer, who was able to enchant without words, with the silence of his 'speaking' fingers, the crowd-pleasing rhetor developed the art of entrancing even those ignorant of his declamatory language, that is to say, independently of intellectual comprehension (e.g. *Lives* 491 [Favorinus], 589 [Hadrian]).[44] 'Singing songs full of pleasure, like Sirens' (Themistius, *Oration* 28.341c), nonconformist orators must have hoped to silence the 'theatrical Sirens' who captivated their audiences in pantomime shows (cf. Crato's comment in *Dance* 3 that Lycinus might fall under the spell of the theatre's Sirens). Traces of contamination are discernible even in external appearance, insofar as those sophists who chose to deviate 'from the leonine norms of masculine public deportment' (Gleason 1995: 74) dressed elegantly, luxuriously and ostentatiously,[45] as if measuring themselves up against the alluringly attired pantomimes.[46]

The roaring success of pantomime must have made it clear that the unsettling of gender-norms through the practice of corporeal dialects of sexual ambiguity as well as the eroticisation of the male body were not so much 'high risk' investments for the astute performer as potentially astronomical high earners. How close to one another came the dancer's and the sophist's versions of gender-bending in performance we can gauge from Lucian's own *Professor of Rhetoric*, where the market-wise rhetorician is introduced as

> an exquisitely beautiful fellow, a man with a shimmy in his walk,[47] with his neck bent (*epikeklasmenon*), with a womanish (*gynaikeion*) look in his eye, ... an altogether soft (*panabron*) guy, a Sardanapallus or Cinyras or the very picture of Agathon himself, that lovely composer of tragic poetry (*Professor* 11).

All the ingredients of pantomime appearance are tightly packaged in this passage: beauty and elegance, erotic allure, the gift of Aphrodite and the Graces, effeminate mannerisms, a body that twists and sways far more than masculine *habitus* allows. The body of the rule-breaking sophist, whose meteoric rise rests on an assortment of verbal and corporeal digressions from ethical legitimacy, bears the hallmarks of the dancer's body (cf. Chapter 9§2). If one had to pinpoint a single calling sharing most manifestly with sophists 'a temptation to appropriate characteristics of "the other" as a way of gaining power from outside the traditionally acceptable sources' (Gleason 1995: 162), that would certainly have been the art of pantomime dancers. Undoubtedly, the fashioning of male selves as 'sexual suspects' (Straub 1992), adept at flouting upper-class expectations concerning the proper ways in which manliness should be embodied, was the most troubled meeting point between polishers of words and fashioners of bodies. Gender-bending sophists and pantomime dancers were united in their construction of femininity as a cultural category available to both sexes, rather than restricted to the biologically female. In response to the dancer's unbeatable appeal by means of his departure from the physical deportment of unadulterated masculinity, maverick sophists became experts in styling themselves in mental attitudes and corporeal poses which their societies calumniated as 'unmanly'.

And there is more. If pantomimes became the object of the crowd's erotic fascination (cf. Chapter 5§2), sophists could also be presented as aiming to forge a libidinal channel of communication with their spellbound public; the apogee of their success was marked by audiences turned into celebrity-worshippers, and given over to fantasies of erotic reciprocity. In Lucian's satire the sophist must take particular pains to promote himself as the focus of female adoration:

> It must be your desire to look beautiful and you must make it your concern to create the impression that you are being earnestly pursued by women. For the masses will attribute even this to your rhetorical prowess (*Professor* 23).

Besides, just as the pantomime becomes particularly attractive because of his ambivalently gendered sex-appeal (cf. Chapter 5§2), the sophist too is advised to build an image of himself as capable of answering the dreams of both genders:

> And this other thing as well, do not feel ashamed if you seem to be also loved by men ... in fact, let some stand around you to create this very impression[48] (*Professor* 23).

Finally, the most valuable lesson that eccentric declaimers could have learnt from pantomime dancers was how to build one's personal renown deliberately on deviance. If pantomimes owed a large part of their attractiveness to their incessant flaunting of those qualities and values which were alien to (male) cultural legitimacy, why should élite performers not aspire to capitalise on the rich rewards potentially afforded by 'the play of limits and transgression' (see Foucault 1977: 33)? As Aelius Aristides (by no means an unbiased source) paints his opponents, the practitioners of emasculated rhetoric,

> they claim to transgress (*ekbainousi*) the line which circumscribes order and correctness for the sake of this, namely to enable themselves to please (*aresai*)[49] as many as possible (*Oration* 34.1).

'Willing sin' and 'deliberate transgression' in the name of public entertainment are notions that toll like a bell throughout Aristides' polemical discourse against those he perceives as unbearably eccentric.[50]

11. Who is Afraid of Pantomime Dancers?

Similarities, however, should not overshadow the differences between pantomimes and grand sophists in the entire concept of eccentric self-fashioning and self-representation. While the pantomime, in any case *infamis* by means of his profession, had practically nothing to lose by plunging into the forbidden 'Other', it was of the utmost importance for the rule-breaking declaimer to play with fire *while avoiding getting burnt*. And that was never easy. For rhetoric, especially the entertaining branch of declamation favoured by the sophists, tied its practitioner with a double bind: while proficiency in it was judged by elegance, elegance itself was considered unmanly (see Connolly 2003: 315). Thus, even in the midst of exhilarating breaches of the code, the trend-setting virtuoso sophist was required, unlike the pantomime, to pull the trickiest of tricks. Over and above eccentricities, he had to ensure that his 'effeminate' discourse came across as irreproachably manly: 'depilated' just enough to convey pleasure, yet 'hairy' and austere enough to command authority. As Connolly (2003: 315) writes, such declaimers ' "redescribed" their practices as *andreia*'.[51] The most 'theatrical' and most 'effeminate' among VIP sophists were no exception.

Flaunting and manipulating his unique position as a congenital eunuch (which gave him, inter alia, the shrill, high-pitched voice of a woman), Favorinus nevertheless took care to prove himself 'so fervid in love-affairs that he was charged with adultery' (Philostratus, *Lives* 489). As for his arch-antagonist Polemo, he ensured that his provocatively luxurious (and hence precarious in gender terms) life-style was counterbalanced by his self-appointed role as an arbiter and guarantor of gender-correctness. In his practice of physiognomy, the science that revealed a man's inner nature on the basis of physical traits and bodily habits, Polemo posed as the male above suspicion, whose job it was to separate the real men from the effeminates.[52] Individual star sophists, to be sure, negotiated the frictions of virility and femininity in their performance in their own way, but, once again, what put them on a par with pantomimes was their remarkable ability to translate prominent markers of their deviance into *insignia* of glory. As Aelius Aristides puts it, no doubt with an eye on Favorinus, who famously turned his paradoxical conflation of two sexes in one body into the cornerstone of his promotional self-definition (see Philostratus, *Lives* 489),

> they behave in a manner very similar to that of some hermaphrodite or eunuch (*androgynos ê eunouchos*), if he were to abstain from blaming either his body's disability or fate but would claim instead that he acquired such a nature through providence (*Oration* 34.48).

As for pantomimes, their danced forays into femininity strike the deepest chord in the tastes of their public. As we saw in Chapter 10§1, in Cyprian's perspective, public appeal is inextricably interwoven with the lure of ambivalence, controversy, the crossing of the barriers: the dancer 'grows in fame in accordance with his crime, and is judged so much more skilful as he is more disgraceful' (*To Donatus*, 8).

To emancipate pantomime, then, in the first centuries AD, one would have needed to address the very same tensions brewing at the heart of some nonconformist élite performances, in particular the wounds inflicted by elegance and grace upon the élite orator's manliness. By means of a different route and with our focus more firmly set on the sophistic circus of the Eastern part of the empire, we come back to the relationship between perverted oratory and dancing that was first sketched out in Chapter 9§2: in their opponents' eyes, maverick declaimers could be painted as the prime agents in an élite choreography of shame. Thus, for Aelius Aristides, crowd-pleasing orators were nothing but turning-and-twisting 'female pantomimes' (*orchêstrides*), 'dancing out' with mimetic gestures the mysteries of a hallowed, age-old art.[53] Varo of Laodicea, whom Philostratus deems worth mentioning for negative reasons only, allegedly degraded his calling by 'tarnishing' the beauty of his voice with 'turns of song which could be even danced to (*hais kan hyporchêsaito tis*) by one of the more wanton speakers' (*Lives* 620). As for the speaker in Lucian's own *Mistaken Critic*, anyone witnessing a career-leap between a secondary (i.e. non-dancing) role in pantomime-shows and a low-quality performance in sophist-type displays would think the two professions mirror-images of one another, like Euripides' 'two suns' or 'twin cities of Thebes' (*The Mistaken Critic* 19, quoting from Euripides' *Bacchae* 913). Even more shamefully than Heracles, who, as legend had it, danced against his will among the Lydians, corrupt orators of Aelius Aristides' time 'dance out (*exorcheisthe*) daily their oratorical burlesque before the whole of mankind' (*Oration* 34.60).

§5. Conclusion

If pantomime's influence was immediately obvious in the case of those who were sexually attracted to the dancer's undulating limbs, this same influence was much more 'underground' and subtle in the case of the intellectual élites who came in direct contact (and confrontation!) with the dancer's formidable appeal. As we have seen in Chapters 8 and 9, the upper classes were obsessed with keeping vigil by the heavily patrolled frontier that separates high and low cultural manifestations, lest what they considered as trite and 'subcultural' should infiltrate and pollute their own domain. Nevertheless, they either failed to notice or failed to contain some of their own numbers who defected from the ranks, i.e. those *pepaideumenoi* who chose to borrow, rather than shun, the tropes of self-presentation that held sway 'across the border', in areas which their peers calumniated as an educational and moral underworld. Despite attempts to sequestrate itself from pantomime, high culture became oddly saturated by it – and that in ways we may not yet be in a position to assess.

Most importantly, as this chapter has argued, it was the intellectually restless 'avant-garde' of the élite that became embroiled in, even conditioned by, pantomime culture. Opening up to hybrid tastes and making complex adjustments to their own position, code-breaking public lecturers used pantomime's success as a yardstick by which to re-configure the terms of their cultural dominance and renegotiate the markers of their own intellectual distinction. Far from being an isolated phenomenon, pantomime spawned a promiscuous intermingling of high and low culture, its most active cultural progeny being the brilliant but maverick élite show-speaker, mostly to be found among the ranks of those that Philostratus deemed (or would have deemed) to be 'sophists'. Complementing the conclusions of Chapter 9, then, this discussion demonstrates that, as well as defining itself by means of a *contrast* to the cultural 'Otherness' that the dancer's body represented, imperial high culture also enriched itself through its selective and targeted *appropriation* of the pantomime 'Other'.

Controlling Theatre in the Imperial East: The Sophist and the Pantomime

§1. Lucian's many masks

The previous chapter suggested that in the heavily contested playing fields of imperial culture the chance for peace or treaty between pantomime dancers and élite declaimers was surprisingly slim. The value of such forays into the broader social context of Lucian's time as a way of acquiring a better understanding of the complex cultural dynamics that undergird *On the Dance* can be hardly overestimated. Yet no sooner do we realise that the treatise must be set against the real-life background of competitive encounters between rival categories of entertainers in the second century AD than fresh interpretative problems emerge. How can we explain the unexpected literary alliance between orator and dancer which seems to inform Lucian's dialogue, a text composed by a professional show-speaker, an 'accomplished', 'a practised sophist',[1] in praise of pantomime as a genre and the pantomime artist?

On one level, the particular problem of consistency evaporates once we liberate ourselves from the assumption that the dominant voice in the text – in this case, the voice of Lycinus – carries the full weight of the real-life author's sentiments and thoughts. Advances in literary theory have resulted in much more sophisticated ways of approaching a literary (or any) text. So, just as authorial purpose has been generally understood as only *one* among the many and equally valid ways to access a text, no point of view enshrined *in* the text can be uncritically (if at all) equated with the author's own voice. This is particularly true in the case of a satirist like Lucian, whose merciless arrows against social practices and institutions or individuals and their habits are shot not in propria persona but with the aid of a colourful array of masks, 'a dazzling repertoire of strategies for manipulating and ironizing the performance of self-presentation' (Goldhill 2002: 82). As students of Lucian have argued persuasively in recent years,[2] nowhere in his extant works can the satirist's own voice be positioned with any certainty on the game board between his various fictional contestants, interlocutors, narrators.[3] Even 'perfectly transparent' pseudonyms (S. Saïd 1993: 253), like 'Lycinus' [Lukinos], only two vowels short of 'Lucian' [Loukianos], or 'The Syrian' (see below), pose formidable problems, for they too cannot be taken as straightforward projections or reflections of the authorial ego.[4] In dialogues and narrative pieces alike, Lucian 'teases and taunts the reader with flashes of the face beneath the mask', so that the reader can gain pleasure from the very act of 'testing the simultaneous embodiment and evanescence of the author's ego' (Whitmarsh 2001: 274). We may sense Lucian's presence at many moments in the text but, as Bakhtin (1981: 314) would put it, he so deftly 'utilizes now one language, now another', switching abruptly between belief-systems and cultural accents, that he ultimately 'avoid[s] giving himself up wholly to either of them', remaining 'as it were neutral with regard to language', a 'third party' (even when biased) in a medley of dissonant voices.

Most importantly, however, Lucian is a professional declaimer and, as such, he lives and breathes within a world of contrived poses, made-up speeches, and apportioned roles – everything is 'stage' and 'tragedy' to him, to borrow from an interlocutor's insight in *Nigrinus* 12.[5] Like all trained public orators of the Second Sophistic, it is his job to link fictitious characters with fictive situations, so that the most appropriate, becoming speech is assigned to each speaker on each occasion.[6] What such an understanding of the essentially 'theatrical', 'performative' nature of Lucian's writing (cf. Branham 1989: 18-20) implies for our dialogue is acceptance that the conflicting viewpoints expressed in it may have no more to do with Lucian as their creator than wicked stepmothers and outlandish pirates have to do with the 'real' self of the teacher or practitioner of epideictic rhetoric in the classrooms and theatres of the empire. Just as the student of rhetoric or the accomplished declaimer are called upon to compose and perform the kind of speech a given mythical, historical, or imaginary character would have been expected to deliver in a well-defined set of circumstances, Lucian can be deemed to have equipped his pantomime fan not with his own personal views, but with the kind of arguments which, although bold and unorthodox, might conceivably have been articulated by a deliberately provocative, open-minded *pepaideumenos*, an eccentric member of the lettered élites swept away by the genre's charms.

In this respect it would be justifiable to think of 'Crato' and 'Lycinus' as witty declamatory positions in an imaginary rhetorical scenario necessitating the attack on or defence of such controversial practices as pantomime dancing and pantomime viewing. Experienced speaker that he is, Lucian is able as well as eager to 'speak eloquently both for and against' a given case, much as his own personification of the 'Academy' does in his *Doubly Accused* (15). Once the bait is proffered in the form of a (fictive or real) calumniation of the dance, we can well imagine Lucian experimenting with several lines of defence (much as he does, to our amusement, in his *Apology* 8-11), before settling on the particular set of tactics we have analysed in Chapter 6. And we ought not to be surprised if we find one day among the Lucianic corpus a completely different rhetorical construction, an anti-pantomime tirade of the kind launched by Aelius Aristides and rebuffed by Libanius in his *Oration* 64, *On Behalf of the Dancers*. Lucian could just as breezily have turned Lycinus' arguments upon their head, perhaps taking a line similar to that informing his caustic satire *The Ignorant Book Collector*: *You*, a mere dancer, with a 'crippled and fig-wood understanding' (cf. *Book Collector* 6) of the myths and legends you enact, 'barbarising' them in the process, 'disgracing' them and 'warping' their meaning (cf. *Book Collector* 7), claim to be a man of learning? What can *you* know of rhetoric and philosophy, painting and sculpture, poetry and metre (cf. *Dance* 35)? Even mentioning the Muses would be impious (cf. *Book Collector* 3), let alone claiming they are favourable to *your* bogus art (cf. *Dance* 36).

Insofar, then, as it is accepted that 'Lycinus' *need not* express the 'real' Lucian, we need no longer worry about the oddity of the 'sophist supporting pantomime' scenario (cf. Chapter 11) with respect to rivalry between the two professions at the performance level. Similarly, to the extent that we are prepared to accept that our satirist, in the manner of the 'Protean' dancer with his awe-inspiring transformations, delights in occupying multiple and shifting vantage points at will,[7] there is no need to be alarmed at inconsistencies between the encomiastic view of pantomime presented in *On the Dance* and either Lucian's silence on the genre in the rest of his work or some of his random pejorative comments. Far from emanating from deeply-held personal views or feelings of the author, what Lucian's various characters say at various junctures in his writings is dictated by the needs of the argument, the rhetorical necessity of the moment.[8]

§2. Lucian and Lycinus: a pantomime lover and his mask?

The better understanding of Lucian that has been achieved in recent scholarship may enable us to go one step further. I mean here first and foremost the understanding that, although groomed and moulded by the sophistic milieu of Asia Minor and subsequently Athens (cf. Bompaire 1958: 153, and n. 1 to this chapter), Lucian never became a truly representative product of the second-century AD 'sophist-mill', while his relation to the classical tradition venerated by the sophists of his age was by no means easy and straightforward. A Syrian from Samosata in the small kingdom of Commagene[9] on the very edge of the empire, not only was he initially alien to the rich storehouse of Greek literary *paideia* and the entire cluster of perceptions and assumptions underpinning the framework of Hellenic culture, but he also grew up speaking some thickly accented, provincial, uncultured version of Greek (if not some Syrian or Aramaic dialect), before purifying his tongue of 'barbarism' by means of his rhetorical education.[10] Sure enough, Lucian's ultimate accession to the ranks of Greekness was, by any yardstick, eminently successful. Not only did he distinguish himself as one of the most accomplished and elegant Atticists in the empire[11] and become 'enfranchised' among the Greeks (*Doubly Accused* 31), but he also travelled far and wide, acquiring fame and money to boot. Rhetoric, however, is adept at strategies of self-aggrandizement. As Jones (1986: 12) cautions, Gaul, where the speaker in *Apology* 15 boasts of having been counted among the 'high-earning sophists' (cf. *Doubly Accused* 27), 'was far from the great centers of rhetoric ... and as a place of residence seems only to have attracted lesser lights'. Even some of Lucian's other lecturing stopovers were, as Lightfoot (2000: 269) nicely puts it, 'not the big time for a sophist'. Nor does Lucian feature in that exclusive 'hall of fame' constructed by the third century AD grandee Flavius Philostratus, who bequeathed to us invaluable (even if heavily biased) biographies of the most stellar (in his judgement) figures of the sophistic orbit (cf. Chapter 11).

Hard and hazardous though it is to make biographical assumptions about an author such as Lucian, 'one of the most curiously elusive of ancient authors' (Branham 1989: 11), it is a fair conclusion that, insofar as the VIP circle of star sophists was concerned, Lucian was never a 'part of the club' – in fact, he may well have been, as Branham (1989: 34) put it, 'the odd man out'.[12] It is extremely unlikely that the gilded youth of either Athens or ancient Ionian cities such as Ephesus, Pergamum or Smyrna, would have welcomed with open arms the 'young lad' (*meirakion*) coming from nowhere, or even worse, coming from beyond the pale.[13] To borrow from Lucian's own language, there must have been at least 'two octaves' (*A Literary Prometheus* 6) separating the typical second-century AD sophist or public declaimer from one of the best and wealthiest families of the great urban centres (see Bowersock 1969: 17-29), exuding self-confidence and seeing the world as his oyster, and the migrant from Samosata, with neither glorious ancestors nor even a prestigious fatherland to speak of nor piles of money[14] to help him 'buy' his way into a coterie of important power-players.

It cannot have taken Lucian too long to realise that, although he became perfectly able to 'write in Greek as an insider to the culture of his audience' (Elsner 2001: 128), from the vantage point of this audience's contemptuous trend-setters some 'Greeks' were judged better than others. Although to the eyes of those totally deprived of Greek paideutic capital he may have seemed happily ensconced 'within the protected circle' of sophistic power,[15] he must have been acutely conscious that, to the real hard core of the sophistic super-league, he could not help 'seeming a barbarian' (*Doubly Accused* 34), only 'irregularly' enrolled[16] as a citizen of the age-old Hellenic culture. On several occasions in his work he allows us to glimpse his indelible (and proud) consciousness of his non-Greek, 'Syrian', 'barbaric' origins,[17] a geographical and cultural provenance which branded him as ineradicably 'Other' with respect to an 'intensely discriminating literary culture' (Branham 1989: 32) and a fiercely chauvinist Greek tradition.

What does all this have to do with Lucian's possible attitude to pantomime dancing?[18] In the first place, the realisation that no love-affair existed between Lucian and the sophists can save us from grave errors. To claim, for example, that *On the Dance* strikes a discordant note in the

Lucianic corpus (and is therefore potentially spurious) because, by endorsing a non-canonical and non-Hellenic[19] cultural product, it goes against the grain of the 'pious classicism' (Branham 1989: 34) of the sophistic movement[20] is to misunderstand Lucian's unique position on the outer rim of the sophistic merry-go-round. There is absolutely no reason to assume that Lucian would have instinctively reacted to the pantomime genre in accordance with the *habitus* of his performance brethren, the sophists and other élite public declaimers, or even, more generally speaking, in uncritical compliance with the aesthetic tastes of the wider body of contemptuous well-born *pepaideumenoi*.

'Both fully saturated in Hellenic *paideia*' as well as its detached observer (Whitmarsh 2001: 125); endowed with a 'bifocal' (Whitmarsh 2001: 124) perspective on his adopted culture, 'that peculiar view of the inside that only an outsider can have' (Branham 1989: 32),[21] Lucian was unencumbered by the deeply ingrained assumptions or biases to which the fully-fledged 'Greeks' (by birth no less than education; cf. Chapter 7) were naturally prone. It is precisely as a result of his liminal position with respect to Hellenism, then, that Lucian was exceptionally well-placed to discover as well as endorse cultural worth wherever that appeared to lie, either inside or outside the 'magic circle' of traditional Hellenism.[22] Indeed, as Branham (1989: 35) has put it, in ridiculing so mercilessly 'the intellectually limited, if popular, practice of forensic and epideictic rhetoric, Lucian could hardly distinguish himself more emphatically from the mainstream of sophistic performers as we see them in Philostratus'. In this respect, *On the Dance* may well have been yet another tangible act of differentiation, provocatively distancing its main speaker from the prejudices of a Hellenised and educationally snobbish cultural milieu. Needless to say, the gesture of disassociation would have been even more poignant if the dialogue was Lucian's response to his exact contemporary Aelius Aristides' heavily biased dismissal of the pantomime genre.[23] In fact, of all second-century AD declaiming intellectuals, Lucian was the most likely to have experienced some kind of psychological congruity with pantomime, an empathy, that is, with its precarious cultural positioning and its largely irrational marginalisation at the hands of overbearing cultural snobs.

If pantomime hit the cultural scene of the Hellenised East as the new theatrical attraction, an outsider to the central circuit of agonistic spectacles, so Lucian came upon the land of declaimers and sophists as the 'new kid' in their playground. What is more, if pantomime suffered humiliation initiated by those who considered it 'ludicrous', devoid of intellectual substance, 'womanish' or just too trivial for an intellectual's attention (cf. *Dance* 1-3), so did Lucian experience disdainful dismissiveness, among other things because his new expressive medium, the comic dialogue, was spurned by those either too proud to descend from their lofty literary heights – 'come off their elephants', as the narrating voice puts it in *Dionysus* 5 – or too stupid to uncover the seriousness lurking beneath a comic mantle. Most interestingly, Lucian composed for pantomime the kind of 'self-advertisement posing as self-defence' (Branham 1989: 32) that we also see him constructing for himself in his *Apology* and *Doubly Accused*. Rather than eliciting from his antagonist the relatively restrained rhetorical tropes befitting an *apologia* (defence), Crato's calumniation of the genre spurs Lycinus on to an enthusiastic mapping of pantomime's territory and an almost aggressive staking of its claims to performative and cultural excellence. Pantomime is not merely defensible – it is 'the greatest of all the good things in life' (*Dance* 1), the *agathon* that a stubborn critic like Crato would brush aside only to his own disadvantage.

Finally, considering the dialogue is in all likelihood the work of Lucian, we must imagine his own satisfaction subsequent to composition and (perhaps) oral delivery as proportionately analogous to its amusingly destabilising effect. True, Lucian revels in an audience's applause and praise (cf. *The Dead Come Back to Life* 25). We can nevertheless imagine him as enjoying even more the ripples he can stir up on the smooth surface of received cultural wisdom or unquestioned Greek tradition. Much as a cheeky academic today would relish the shock-waves travelling the length of Oxbridge high tables in response to the suggestion that, say, *Harry Potter*'s literary merits rival those of fifth-century Athenian drama,[24] Lucian may have derived special pleasure from unleashing his own 'cat among the pigeons': an intellectual dancer, hewn from the venerable stock of the Second Sophistic (cf. Chapter 7), and transmitting the Hellenic cultural lore with as much clarity and erudition as the high-minded Hellenes themselves. A shockingly nonconformist stance? So much the better, for thus it would be all the more purely 'Lucianic'. If nothing else, the chance to propose that a fiercely vilified genre did deserve an educated man's attention in the theatre must have felt for Lucian almost as good as it obviously felt to relate the victory of Dionysus against the haughty Indians who 'learn by experience not to despise those who appear ludicrous and strange' (Branham 1989: 46).

Yet if there is nothing preposterous in claiming that a dose of the real-life 'Lucian' peppered the exposition of Lycinus in *On the Dance*, not a single shred of solid evidence exists to support this proposition either. Beyond the excitement of speculation, there is simply no methodologically foolproof way to establish with any certainty what the historical Lucian would have told us about the pantomime genre and its artist, had he resolved to speak to us 'with facial features exposed' (*Nigrinus* 11), without a rhetorical mask. In any case, even if the real Lucian had been favourably disposed towards pantomime (or at least had failed to find in pantomime the abominations which horrified some of his fellow intellectuals), this would still be no reason to assume that he also underwrote the stream of claims on behalf of pantomime made in Lycinus' speech. In other words, even in the case of a broad-based consonance between the author and the main speaker in the treatise, 'Lycinus' should still be seen as a mask, albeit a truly complicated one. Rather than obfuscating the author's supposedly anti-pantomime sentiments, it could be said to fine-tune and modify his basic impression of pantomime dancing, re-calibrating a spectacle the author knows as raucous, raw and explosive in its emotional substance (cf. Chapter 10, with n. 10) so as to suit the persona of an open-minded man of letters (Lycinus) and the tastes of intellectually refined addressees (his 'intended' audience?). With no shortage of ironic glances at the subject of his declamation, Lucian/'Lycinus' offers us an 'apology' whose tone, as Elsner (2001: 144) remarks on a similar Lucianic text, 'is poised with a breathtaking deftness on the very edge of irony and sincerity', speaking to us 'with both voices at once'.

I will close this section with one of the few fixed points we have left. Towards the middle of the second century AD, pantomime's fortunes were undeniably on the up. For one thing, Lucius Verus, co-emperor of Marcus Aurelius from 161 to 169 AD, was a notorious pantomime addict who, on his return from Syria after the end of the Parthian war, led star pantomimes (and other similar performers) into Rome like trophies and 'in such numbers that he seemed to have concluded a war against scenic artists rather than against the Parthians' (Julius Capitolinus, *Verus* 8.10-11). Sincere or insincere, flattery or genuine appreciation, a speech on behalf of pantomimes may have been exceptionally opportune in mid-second-century Antioch – the seat of Verus in the East for the greatest part of the anti-Parthian campaign (162-166 AD) and a city mad about dancing (cf. the compliments of Lucian in *Dance* 76). If scholars have been right in linking the dialogue with Verus' sojourn in the East (*c.* 163-166 AD),[25] *On the Dance* extols the pantomime art roughly at the time when the genre celebrates (at very long last) its admission as an agonistic spectacle to the great festivals of the imperial East (see Chapter 4§2). Moreover, it is in the late second century AD that membership of the *Parasiti Apollinis*, the guild to which mimes and pantomimes had belonged since the first century BC, 'could vie with membership of the worldwide Guild of Dionysiac artists for a place of honour in the career records of public entertainers' (Jory 1970: 242, with n. 2).[26] In other words, Verus' flamboyantly advertised support for the dancers coincided with (or, in some respects, inaugurated) a period of increased prestige for the maligned genre, so that the oratorical praise of pantomime might even have seemed a shrewd tactical move in some circles. While patting the emperor on the back for his refined choice of entertainment, such praise might also have seemed likely to repay the author's cultural investment at an amazingly fast, advantageous rate: a pantomime encomiast could be hailed as a bold path-maker and reliable taste-maker, a wielder of true power, actively shaping and guiding, rather than *being* shaped and guided by, current perceptions of the boundaries between cultural legitimacy and illegitimacy. And this final remark brings us to the last vantage point from which Lucian's experiment with pantomime can be looked at.

§3. Domination and subordination

In eighteenth- and nineteenth-century Europe not only was Lucian's *On the Dance* received as a hugely positive document (see Postscript) but, in periods highly formative for the rehabilitation of the stage as a mode of urbane and wholesome entertainment, it also provided the basis for several attempts to emancipate the stage-performer's art. As far as the treatise's immediate reception is concerned, the details elude us completely. It must have nevertheless propelled the dancer up to the intellectual's line of vision and given the genre a tremendous boost by designating it as the sole focus of an intellectual's attention. The meticulous research into pantomime's thematic range and, most crucially, the pioneering exposition of the requisite qualifications for the building of the perfect dancer imply and project a recognition that *orchêsis* is neither a derivative art, a second-rate substitute for the old and venerable tragedy, nor a haphazard exercise in gravity-defying leaps, but a worthwhile spectacle deserving even a wise man's respect on account of its complexity.

Simultaneously, however, we cannot escape the feeling that we have in this treatise a coexistence of two incommensurable systems of communication, a co-presence of two 'languages': the socially superior, 'dominant' language of rhetoric, the legitimate performative discourse of upper-class *paideia* on the one hand, and the allegedly inferior, non-verbal language of pantomime dancing on the other. The fact that these languages are not paraded side by side, but configured in such a way that the latter can only reach us *through the mediation of the former*, i.e. after it has been reconstituted and remoulded within the cultural/linguistic consciousness of the literate élites,[27] sends out an important message as to their relative standing: there is, after all, a palpable asymmetry of power between the medium of dance and that of oratorical performance. To put it in another way, Lucian's *On the Dance* encodes the voice of an intellectual (Lycinus in the text) in the act of 'giving voice' to the pantomime's voiceless body. In a world where voicelessness is tantamount to powerlessness and the ability to 'lend one's voice' implies a position of control and superiority, speaking *for* and *on behalf of* pantomime ultimately destabilises its authority. By the end of the dialogue pantomime has been described, anatomically dissected, coloured and judged – in fact it has been totally objectified and launched back into the world as material that the educated man can study. Lycinus' and Lucian's intellectual authority over the genre has been thereby unequivocally established.

The previous chapter did suggest that, with respect to matters of performance, the flamboyant pantomime clearly had the upper hand. Yet when it comes to the equally important matter of self-fashioning and public identity construction, it is the pantomime who finds himself a poor match for the élite declaimer. The dancer's art, co-extensive with his body, both flourishes and perishes with it. If a dancer's body in performance creates a 'text', this can only be a *metaphorical* text, leaving no written trace. While the enunciators of literary discourse – in our case the élite declaimers/sophists – are adept at fashioning their own self-presentation, a *real* text over which they have reasonable control, the dancer, master of corporeal eloquence, has only the ephemeral 'writing' of his moving limbs. Modern dancers and choreographers do pen their own memoirs, and hence are able to control the politics of their commemoration. But this would not have been the norm with ancient pantomime dancers, who, with rare exceptions,[28] seem to have had no access to a mode of self-fashioning more nuanced than that provided by their own dancing (or, in the case of masterful performances, the series of honorific inscriptions erected in public places). Their limited ability to fix their own preferred version of their public image meant that ultimately they had no choice but leave it to others to create an identity for them and their profession. As complex and elusive as their own metamorphic powers, pantomimes were fashioned and un-fashioned, adulated or condemned in accordance with the ebb and flow of the narrative which gave their body a literary home. The sophist, by contrast, was able to manipulate body language as well as speech, the emotional as well as the cerebral, passion as well as intellect, in the game of self-presentation.

To return for the last time to Lucian's text: if pantomime can be granted a legitimate existence within the performance field occupied by high culture, this existence must be, at the very least, 'contained' and containable, subordinate or, to use Bourdieu's terminology, 'dominated'.[29] Posting himself at the gates to that élite landscape which pantomime can gaze at only from the outside, the sophist appropriates and exercises the right to define and defend its boundaries, handing out, generously or thriftily, tickets of admission to cultural legitimacy. To put it another way, Lucian's *On the Dance* constructs rhetorically a frame wherein Lycinus, qua open-minded intellectual, lays claim to 'the monopoly of legitimate discourse' (Bourdieu 1993: 36) on pantomime dancing: all the while waxing lyrical upon his pet distraction, he also internalises and re-calibrates the (silenced) voice of the pantomime himself. As for Lucian, the real-life sophist, even as he elevates the dancer to a live embodiment of acclaimed artistic and cultural values, he towers far above him by turning himself into a custodian and guarantor of those same values. Lucian's dialogue is only ostensibly composed for the unconditional benefit of pantomime dancing. What it really represents is a cultural conquest, namely the sophist's ultimate victory in a contest whose top prize is the right to entertain, the right to control the politics of a multi-coloured performance culture.

Epilogue

It has been a central contention of this book that we can have no pure unadulterated view of ancient pantomime dancing. Yet, just because pantomime itself did not weave the narrative of its own self-presentation, we must beware of succumbing to the naive assumption that the genre existed as a passive social agent, soft wax to be shaped and inscribed at will by a confluence of forces situated within the matrices of dominant culture. I hope this book has succeeded in showing that the range of relations forged between pantomime and the diverse manifestations of the cultural mainstream in the life of imperial and later antiquity was much broader, more complex, intriguing and therefore interesting than previous scholarship had given us reason to believe. Chapters 8-12, in particular, should make subsequent debate more sensitive to the dynamic processes of interaction between an ever-popular genre and those segments of high culture that had an active interest in the campaign for pantomime's marginalisation.

From the Roman *plebs*, who, gathered on the banks of the Tiber, rehearse during the festival of Anna Perenna the songs they have picked up at pantomime performances (Ovid, *Fasti* 3.535-8) to the slave boys in Libanius' fourth-century Antioch, who, on errands on their masters' behalf, sing through the narrow alleyways whatever pantomime ditties they happen to have memorised in the market (Libanius, *Oration* 64.93), our sources have preserved the vestiges of an extraordinary spectacle which completely saturated the mental and emotional topography of imperial subjects. When Juvenal (*Satire* 6.67-70) casts a satirist's eye on the ladies of the Roman aristocracy who spend the long winter months fondling their favourite dancer's mask, thyrsus or tights, kept as a fetish; when Galen (*On Precognition*, 14.632 Kühn) recounts the story of the upper-class woman whose mysterious illness he successfully diagnosed as unrequited love for the pantomime Pylades; or when John Chrysostom (*PG* 50.682) deplores the lethal imprint deposited deep within the viewer's soul by the twisting, swaying and gyrating bodies of the pantomime dancers, they each offer invaluable testimony to the fact that, throughout the centuries, pantomime existed as a privileged site for the enactment of secret desires, longings, fantasies and pleasures. The more forcefully pantomime was relegated to the fringe of subcultural 'Otherness', the more vehemently it

161

returned to haunt its audience's imagination, a realm wherein the dancer took hold as did no other ancient theatrical performer.

Reading against the grain of ancient prejudices, then, this book has demonstrated that pantomime was symbiotically linked to both the higher and the lower cultural strata of the imperial world. Indeed, it is impossible to separate it from either. By means of its appropriation of the educated narrative of the 'ancient fables of the Greeks', in particular, pantomime was uniquely positioned to act as a conduit for the easy passage of elements across cultural frontiers, from the highlands of *paideia* to the lowlands of popular culture and back. And just as high literature (stripped of its philosophical subtleties and linguistic sophistication) meandered into pantomime libretti and songs (sometimes penned by leading intellectuals, such as Lucan and Statius), deviant, non-élite conceptions of the body, gender and sexuality found their way into élite male culture, unsettling its rules and gratifying its desires. In other words, pantomime should be seen as one of the many social catalysts whose dynamism and broadbased appeal locked the high and the low into patterns of reciprocal borrowing and mutual contamination. To employ a term used by folklorists, pantomime appropriated 'sunken cultural heritage', trickling down, as it were, from the realms of the élite, just as much as it injected back into the upper classes 'rising cultural heritage' (Birkhan 1989: 1 and 3), mainly consisting in its own imaginative (re)constructions of gender and 'performance', desire and sexuality. At the same time, this book has also shown that pantomime inhabited and defended its own unique and independent territory. Although it occupied the ever-shifting borderland between the popular and the élite and was constantly entangled in a mutually enriching discourse with both domains, it piggybacked on neither. In fact, pantomime not only possessed but also defined and created its very own distinct form of 'cultural capital' (see Chapter 10§2), an idiolect enormously influential in its time, though only partially recoverable today.

A genre long neglected in modern scholarly debates, pantomime deserves a closer look as a phenomenon of tremendous potency and far-reaching repercussions. It quickened the pace of cultural formations and shaped aesthetic sensibilities, moral categories and modes of understanding of the self and others in ways we have only very recently begun to (re)assess. Even the mere 'idea' of the pantomime dancer, with its attendant connotations of disorder and licentiousness, eroticism and riotous passion as well as its intoxicating play with multiple identities thrillingly fused into a single protean body, proved polarising with respect to issues at the very heart of Greco-Roman culture. Although my discussion in this book has been far from exhaustive, it has placed the genre and the artist back onto the map of the imperial and later antique world as powerful and central elements of the political, social, intellectual and symbolic orders.

Postscript

The Afterlife of Ancient Pantomime and Lucian's *On the Dance*

Ancient pantomime breathed its last some time in the seventh century AD, yet the fascination that had always surrounded pantomime dancers lived on. Smouldering under the ashes, the secret that some time in the past there existed a wonderful stage art, 'which shews how to speak without opening the mouth, to express every thing by gestures, and even to render intelligible by certain movements as well as by different attitudes of the body, what we should find very difficult to communicate by a continued discourse, or a whole page in writing',[1] was never extinguished.

'Where could you find today a dancer or a mime who would know how to narrate whichever stories you want solely by means of bodily movement (*solo corporis motu*), who would expound things one by one through mere nods and physical gestures (*solo nutu et corporis gestu*) no less clearly than some eloquent orator, so that he would seem to have as many tongues as limbs (*quot membra totidem quoque linguas*)?', cries the seventeenth-century philologist Isaac Vossius (1673: 135), appropriating a line from the anonymous Latin epigram that has already served us so well throughout this book (*Latin Anthology* I.1 [Shackleton Bailey] 100, 9).

Against a background of theatrical dancing that was simply ornamental[2] and ballet-masters who cared only for the showcasing of the performers' technical virtuosity or the display of symmetrical floor-patterns, early in the eighteenth century there were increasing calls from those who wanted the dance to become more expressive, narrate a story in mute gestural language in the manner of the ancients, and paint vivid, striking pictures on the stage.[3] In England and France, erudites like Michel de Pure, the Jesuit Père Ménestrier, Nicolaus Calliachius, Octavius Ferrarius, Jacques Bonnet, and the influential Abbé Dubos wrote at length about the ancient pantomimes,[4] while men of the theatre, like the librettist, choreographer and dance historian Louis de Cahusac, the dancing-master John Weaver and, after the middle of the eighteenth century, Jean-Georges Noverre, called, each in their own way, for a reform of current practices in theatrical dancing.[5] What they deplored in particular was the dance's lack of meaningful content and narrative coherence and the loss of its ability to be a 'faithful imitation of nature' (Gallini 1772: 95),[6] the dancer even 'becom[ing] what he performs' (Weaver, in Ralph 1985: 662). As Noverre (1930 [1803]: 55) explained, 'those figure dances which express nothing, which present no story, which have no character, which do not sketch for me a connected and logical plot, which possess nothing dramatic and which fall, as it were, from the skies, are only, in my opinion, ... simple dancing *divertissements* which merely display the limited movements and mechanical difficulties of the art.'

Despite individual differences, 'for almost every author, the most significant moment in the development of dance, the dancing against which all subsequent dances would necessarily be compared, occurred in the ancient Greek and Roman amphitheaters' (Foster 1996a: 13). From the last decades of the seventeenth and throughout the eighteenth century ancient pantomime was seen as the 'pinnacle of choreographic achievement' (Foster, ibid.), a phenomenon 'which still astonishes the imagination' (Noverre 1930: 10) and can be believed only because of the overwhelming nature of the ancient evidence.[7] Compared with the clarity of the gestural eloquence achieved by Pylades (I), Bathyllus (I) and their breed, contemporary dancing was found wanting, still 'in its infancy' (de Cahusac 2004 [1754]: 134; Gallini 1772: 235, 56-7). As Weaver wrote, 'It must indeed be granted that our modern Manner of *Dancing* ... falls infinitely short of that agreeable and surprizing Variety which was to be seen in the *Representative Dances* of the *Mimes* and *Pantomimes*' (in Ralph 1985: 681).

Sure enough, optimistic notes concerning the potential of theatrical dancing to match the achievements of the 'century of Augustus' (see de Cahusac 2004: 230) are not absent, and the ultimate aim is to bring the art 'in as flourishing a condition as pantomime was in the time of the ancients' (Noverre 1930: 88). But even as late as the 1770s, after decisive steps in the direction of fully-fledged ballet-pantomimes had already been taken, a columnist could exclaim: 'Oh Pylades! Oh Bathyllus! ... how far we still are from your talents!',[8] and the dancer, choreographer, impresario and writer Giovanni Andrea Gallini could renew the call for 'a revival of the taste of the antients for the pantomime branch', on the basis that 'as hitherto the composers of the dances of action have not been able to recover that height of perfection to which the antient pantomimes carried their art'.[9]

The sheer volume of ancient sources on pantomime dancing that eighteenth-century writers were conversant with is staggering.[10] Favourites like Macrobius' anecdotes on the rivalry of Hylas and Pylades and their different rendition of the 'great Agamemnon' *canticum* (cf. Chapter 3§2) are endlessly retold in almost every treatise.[11] A clear winner, however, with innumerable 'protean' transformations, was Lucian's *Dance* 63-4, namely Demetrius' praise of the dancer who 'spoke' with his hands and thus enabled him to 'hear' the voiceless action, followed by the anecdote about the barbarian prince who fully appreciated the gestures of that same dancer without being able to understand the accompanying choral songs.

Even beyond the range of straightforward retellings and paraphrases from Lucian,[12] the idea of a performance that translates vision into hearing permeated eighteenth-century theatrical discourse. Thus, without the merest mention of Lucian, Gallini (1772: 245) refers to the ancient pantomimes as masters of 'an expression so natural ... a *pathos* so moving, ... that people imagined they heard the actions they saw' (cf. de Cahusac 2004: 107). In his *Letter on the Deaf and the Dumb*, composed in 1751, the very year of David Garrick's sensational visit to Paris, the eminent French philosopher and writer Denis Diderot speaks of his practice of blocking his ears with his hands when going to the theatre, so as to test whether the actors' gestural language would enable him to 'hear' (and 'understand', as the French 'entendre' signifies both) by means of seeing.[13] As for the many fans of David Garrick himself, the most 'pantomimic' actor of the eighteenth-century London stage, they were tireless in stressing the eloquence of his corporeal acting, so evocative that even non-English speakers could achieve a perfect understanding of his performances: 'He was so natural, his expression was so lifelike, his gestures, features and glances were so eloquent and so convincing, that he made the action clear even to those who did not understand a word of English' (Noverre 1930: 82).[14] Reminiscing on Garrick's dumb-show displays in the Parisian salons, a later French mémoir comments thus: 'One felt tempted to call out to him at every moment, as to those mimes whose gestures vied in eloquence with Cicero's speech: 'You speak to us with your hands' [cf. Lucian, *Dance* 63]. His gestures made one shudder, his looks and his tones drew tears' (quoted in Hedgcock 1911: 219).

Most importantly, specific ancient narratives aside, the dance reformers of the eighteenth century reconstructed with the aid of the ancient sources and embellished further in accordance with prevalent aesthetic trends an 'idea' of ancient pantomime as a genre of 'mute Rhetoric' (Weaver, in Ralph 1985: 423) that substituted gestures for speech (cf. Gallini 1772: 76) and 'expresse[d] to the eye the sensations of the soul' (Gallini 1772: 69), all the while 'painting by one single movement a multitude of thoughts' (de Cahusac 2004: 234). As for the pantomimes themselves, '*Imitators of all Things*' (Weaver, in Ralph 1985: 591), who 'spoke while they were silent' (Dubos 1748: 215), they were seen as experts at '*copying* all the *Force* of the *Passions* meerly by the *Motions* of the *Body* to that degree, as to draw *Tears* from the *Audience* at their *Representations*' (Weaver, in Ralph 1985: 684).

In perfect accordance with the all-pervasive eighteenth-century aesthetics of 'sensibility' as well as the theatrical practice of treating the audience to spectacular 'transitions' between a series of different emotions, dance theorists found in the ancient pantomime's art the precious ingredients for a full-scale revolution. Thus, the pantomime's ability to incarnate in his single body a variety of characters and act out even diametrically divergent emotional responses[15] was hailed as a noble prototype for a modern dancer, who would 'successively represent all the gradations' of a given passion, 'whether of fear, revenge, joy, hatred ... by the quick shift and succession of steps, gestures, attitudes and looks' (Gallini 1772: 111-12). Above everything else, however, it was the distant echo of a lost corporeal language, more thrillingly suggestive than articulated speech, that fascinated the progressive spirits of the eighteenth century and resonated admirably with the intellectual preoccupations of Diderot and the Encyclopaedists. Diderot, in particular, not only saw in gesture the universally comprehensible primordial language of mankind, but also called for the greater use of corporeal dramaturgy on the French stage, hoping for plays that would exploit the expressive depths of bodily eloquence and rediscover the secrets of that pantomimic art 'whose resources were well known to the ancients'.[16]

A masterfully developed gestural 'language' was already in full bloom in the several fairgrounds of the French capital, which hosted an unlimited variety of corporeal entertainments, including dancing acts. It was also phenomenally successful in the various London theatres, especially the rival playhouses of Drury Lane and Lincoln's Inn Fields, which staged 'pantomime'-shows reliant on dance, music and sensational spectacle. Dance reformists, however, sought to ennoble the profession by giving to it as a legitimating pedigree not the popular *Commedia dell'Arte* tradition but the sublime dancing of the Greeks and Romans, which had the patent of antiquity and the support of a respected literary tradition (cf. Foster 1996a: 45-6).[17] The most incisive commentary on the perceived asymmetry of cultural capital between the corporeal dramaturgy of Italian and French performers and that of ancient pantomime dancers can be found in what was to become the most influential acting manual in the first half of the eighteenth century, i.e. Charles Gildon's *Life of Mr Thomas Betterton*: 'Were our modern Dancers like the *Mimes* and *Pantomimes* of the *Romans* ... our Dotage on them might have been thought more excusable; since one of them, as I have shewn from *Lucian*, by the Variety of his Motions and Gesticulations, would represent a whole History, with all the different Persons concerned in it so plainly and evidently, that every body, that saw him, perfectly understood what he meant. In this indeed it might be pretended, that there was something to strike the Mind, and rationally entertain it, every Action depending on the other, and all directed to one End' (Gildon 1970 [1710]: 144-5).

Turning now very briefly to individual dance practitioners, the real catalyst for the popularisation of the ideal of the Greco-Roman pantomime in the early eighteenth century was John Weaver. A dancing-master from Shrewsbury, whose professional assignments as a theatrical dancer brought him to London by 1700, he published in 1712 his landmark *An Essay Towards an History of Dancing*. With that and subsequent treatises, Weaver aimed to restore theatrical dancing to the standing of ancient pantomime as 'a Science Imitative and Demonstrative' (in Ralph

1985: 597 and 741), capable of explaining 'Things conceiv'd in the Mind, by the *Gestures* and *Motions* of the Body, and plainly and intelligibly representing *Actions*, *Manners*, and *Passions*; so that the Spectator might perfectly understand the *Performer* by these his *Motions*, tho' he say not a Word' (in Ralph 1985: 652). Two years after the publication of Weaver's *Essay*, the first practical experiment for the revival of ancient pantomime took place in France, under the influence of contemporary works on ancient dancing (see Winter 1974: 47-8).

The cultured and extravagant Louise, Duchesse du Maine, married to one of the sons of Louis XIV and residing in the magnificent Château de Sceaux, 'had a mind to see an essay of the art of the ancient pantomimes, in order to acquire a clearer idea of their representations than that which she had conceived by reading' (Dubos 1748: vol. 3, 220). She therefore asked the first dancers of the Paris Opéra, Jean Balon and Françoise Prévost, to dance in mute, gestural language and to the accompaniment of specially composed instrumental music, the fourth act of Corneille's *Horace*, in which the young Horace kills his sister Camilla. According to Dubos (ibid.), the dancers, 'our two new Pantomimes', stimulated each other so effectively, that they brought themselves to the point of shedding real tears. Thus, the first modern-age conscious attempt to revive Pylades' marvellous art took place on the Fourteenth Night of the so-called *Grandes Nuits de Sceaux*, the festive nightlong entertainments staged by the Duchess from April or May 1714 to May 1715. Although the experiment at Sceaux had no immediate sequel, it attracted considerable attention as part of Dubos' *Critical Reflections*, a work extremely fashionable in high intellectual circles and with multiple editions throughout the eighteenth century.

The second practical experiment followed relatively shortly afterwards. It was John Weaver's *The Loves of Mars and Venus*, first performed as an afterpiece at Drury Lane Theatre on 2 March 1717 and described in the scholarly programme accompanying the production as 'A Dramatick Entertainment of Dancing, Attempted in Imitation of the Pantomimes of the Ancient Greeks and Romans' (in Ralph 1985: 737). Praising his dancers[18] for their willingness to enter 'into a Design so entirely novel and foreign to their present Manner of Dancing' (in Ralph 1985: 739), Weaver could not have emphasised more strongly that his danced drama was only meant as a first step in the direction of a new era of theatrical dancing: 'this Performance was design'd only as an Attempt to encourage others more capable of bringing it to its ancient Perfection' (in Ralph 1985: 743-4). Putting theory into practice in unprecedented ways, Weaver produced two further dance-dramas in the same vein: *The Fable of Orpheus and Eurydice* (Drury Lane, 6 March 1718), advertised as 'Attempted in Imitation of the Ancient *Greeks* and *Romans*', and *The Judgement of Paris* (Drury Lane, 6 February 1733), described as 'A Dramatic Entertainment in

Dancing and Singing, After the Manner of the Ancient *Greeks* and *Romans*'.[19]

John Weaver's theatrical creations were not the enduring crowd-pullers that the Drury Lane management had hoped for, primarily because the public's appetite, whetted by the ingenious mélange of slapstick and seriousness provided by John Rich at the rival playhouse of Lincoln's Inn Fields, inclined towards the more traditional types of pantomime entertainment, consisting either in undiluted grotesque dumb farces or in a marriage of classical myth and *Commedia dell' Arte* characters.[20] Being well ahead of their time[21] in terms of general vision and sophistication, Weaver's attempts to revive ancient pantomime by combining dance and mute, expressive acting had no immediate impact on theatrical dancing. In reality, however, Weaver was the first to fully recognise 'the sufficiency of bodily movement to communicate plot, character, and emotion' (Cohen 1960:43), and the first to present his effort at composing dances 'altogether of the *Pantomimic* Kind' (in Ralph 1985: 752) as an attempt to resurrect and rescue from oblivion the lost pantomime art of Greco-Roman antiquity. Even within a decade from Weaver's retirement from the London scene, Colley Cibber, the influential playwright, actor and manager of Drury Lane from 1704 to 1733, acknowledged that Weaver's *Mars and Venus*, 'form'd into a connected Presentation of Dances in Character', succeeded in establishing the art of dancing as 'something more than Motion without Meaning': 'the Passions were so happily express'd, and the whole Story so intelligibly told, by a mute Narration of Gesture only, that even thinking Spectators allow'd it both a pleasing, and a rational Entertainment' (Cibber 1968 [1740]: 279). Besides, particularly significant is the fact that, very quickly, ancient pantomime broke free from the narrow confines of scholarly research and was brought to the attention of the wider public, as testified by the contemporary press. On 6 April 1723, for example, *The Weekly Journal* praised John Rich's *Jupiter and Europa*, staged at Lincoln's Inn Fields, as being 'after the Manner of the *Pantomimes*, a kind of Actors amongst the *Grecians*, who made themselves understood by Dance and Gesture, without speaking a Word' (quoted in O'Brien 2004: 90). The legacy of the ancient art was matter relevant to all.

After Weaver's productions, the next link in the ballet-pantomime tradition of the eighteenth century was the dancing of Marie Sallé, member of a dynasty of well-established French fairground performers. A pupil of Balon and Prévost, the two dancers who took part in the pantomime experiment at Sceaux, and a performer (as a child prodigy) at Lincoln's Inn Fields in the seasons of 1716-17 and 1718-19, i.e. precisely when the rival playhouse of Drury Lane was staging Weaver's innovative dance dramas, Sallé developed a 'lyrical expressiveness' (Vince 1957: 11) in dance and gesture which had a catalytic influence on both David Garrick and the man considered as the 'father' of the modern ballet, namely Jean-Georges Noverre. Nevertheless, what was exceptionally influential in the long process of dance-reform spawned by the treasured 'idea' of Greco-Roman pantomime was Sallé's radically innovative staging of Pygmalion's story at Drury Lane theatre (14 February 1734), her choreography invoking corporeal eloquence 'as the principal medium for sustaining a coherent exchange of thoughts and feelings among all those onstage' (Foster 1996b: 133). Sallé herself does not appear to have made a conscious connection between her own endeavours and the lost ancient art, but her 'ability to integrate representations of the passions into the danced actions' and her creation of a dancing body 'enmeshed in a sequence of causally linked emotions' (Foster 1996b: 142 and 144) were such as to take choreography one step further along the line starting from antiquity and culminating in the later formation of the 'ballet d'action' or 'pantomime ballet'.

In any case, back in France, Sallé's own native ground, the Parisian public became enraptured by the spectacles 'of unparalleled magnificence' mounted in the impressive Salle des Machines of the Palace of the Tuileries by royal painter, architect and stage-designer Jean-Nicolas Servandoni in the 1740s and 1750s (see Guest 1996: 15 n. 1; Goodden 1986: 96-7). Servandoni not only produced a series of classically inspired pieces (relying much more on the techniques of the 'tableau vivant' and pantomimic action than virtuoso dancing), but he also prefaced the most outstanding of these productions (*The Adventures of Odysseus*, 1741) with a brochure. In it he included a short dissertation on the ancient art (drawing on Lucian) and prided himself on having renewed the public's taste for a spectacle so famous in antiquity yet so neglected for many centuries.[22]

It was in Vienna, however, that two enormously cultured choreographers, Franz Hilverding and his pupil and successor Gasparo Angiolini, took the first systematic steps towards the revival of the 'speaking dance' of the ancient Greeks. Hilverding, whom Angiolini considered 'the true restorer of the pantomimic art',[23] experimented successfully for almost two decades (starting in the 1740s) in the direction of expressive, 'character' dancing and emotion rendered by the movement of the entire body.[24] Angiolini, for his part, brought together theory and practice in the hope of succeeding 'one day ... in producing the same marvellous effects produced by the ancient pantomimes'.[25] What he understood by this was the staging of a complete and uninterrupted dramatic action communicated to the spectator by means of 'speaking gestures' in the manner of Pylades' and Bathyllus' art. His *Don Juan, ou le Festin de pierre*[26] he styled 'a ballet pantomime in the taste of the ancients',[27] while in his *Dissertation on the pantomime ballets of the ancients*, a manifesto possibly co-authored by the poet Calzabigi and serving as a programme for the 'tragic ballet' *Sémiramis* (31 January 1765), he asked the 'sensible and educated public' to applaud his endeavour as a means of silencing those who have 'no taste for Antiquity'.[28]

Yet, despite the many isolated steps down the path to a complete reform of theatrical dancing, the single choreographer who ultimately 'succeeded in breaking the mould of performing style in ballet', and therefore removed the genre 'from the non-dramatic realms which dance had previously inhabited' (Goodden 1986: 137), was the French ballet-master Jean-Georges Noverre (1727-1809). After a period in England in the close company of David Garrick, Noverre expounded his thoughts in a series of fifteen interrelated letters (first published in Stuttgart and Lyon in 1760), a manifesto with 'immediate repercussions on the art of ballet throughout Europe' (Guest 1996: 8). As Beaumont writes in the prologue to his translation of the 1803 enlarged edition of the *Letters*, 'no book has exerted so incalculable an influence for good on the manner of production of ballets and dances' (Noverre 1930: xi). What is of particular consequence in the context of the ancient genre's afterlife is that Noverre himself thought of his *Letters* as 'the first stone of the monument which I desired to erect to that form of expressive dancing which the Greeks called pantomime' (Noverre 1930: 2). As for his entire momentous contribution to his art, no less than 'a revolution in dancing' (Noverre 1930: 2), he regarded it as the first modern attempt 'to re-discover ... or, so to speak, to create ... a second time' the lost pantomime language of Pylades and Bathyllus (Noverre 1930: 10).[29]

Heavily influenced by Diderot's writings and Garrick's excessively physical acting, Noverre called for the re-unification of dancing and mimed action. His hope was to create an 'imitative art' which would at last be free to achieve the lofty aim of 'speaking to the heart' (Noverre 1930: 11), a potential integral to dancing yet never actually unlocked since the age of Augustus. Armed with a self-consistent, linear plot, a ballet could become powerfully evocative, since 'a step, a gesture, a movement, and an attitude express what no words can say' (Noverre 1930: 4). In fact, Noverre determines the point of perfection in pantomime ballet[30] as the moment when 'Words will become useless, everything will speak, each movement will be expressive, each attitude will depict a particular situation, each gesture will reveal a thought, each glance will convey a new sentiment' (Noverre 1930: 53). Fully in the spirit of ancient pantomime, he wished to see in choreographic creations the kind of gestures that are 'the offspring of feeling and the faithful interpreters of every mood' (Noverre 1930: 15), capable of expressing successive stages and gradations of the passions (cf. Lucian, *Dance* 67). Thanks to his innovations, he boasted, dance 'learned to speak the language of the passions which before it had not even lisped' (Noverre 1930: 2). All in all, Noverre was profoundly indebted to Garrick's pantomimic style, which he described, in terms reminiscent of ancient discussions of pantomime dancing, as 'so eloquent and so convincing' with respect to gesture mannerisms that it could make 'the action clear even to those who did not understand a word of English' (Noverre 1930: 82).

A milestone in the attempted revival of ancient pantomime and 'the greatest example' of the choreographic principles set down in his *Letters*, was Noverre's *Médée et Jason*, first performed at the court of the Duke of

Württemberg in 1762, then at the Hoftheater in Stuttgart in 1763, with the celebrated Gaëtan Vestris in the role of Jason (see Macintosh 2000: 4). By 1776, when one of its many subsequent versions was performed to great applause at the Opéra in Paris, the public was ready to appreciate panto-mime's 'extraordinary potential' to stir 'the emotions much more powerfully than any throbbing declamation in blank verse'.[31] The *Journal des théâtres*, moreover, was calling for the Opéra to fully embrace ballet-pantomimes on the grounds that it is 'a shame... that a form of spectacle that was held in such high regard in antiquity is lost to us and relegated to the fairground theatres' (quoted in Guest 1996: 80). As for Noverre himself, he could be styled 'the greatest composer of ballet-pantomimes since the Renaissance of the Arts, and the worthy rival of Pylades and Bathyllus in the art of speaking to the eyes and the soul through gesture and movement'.[32]

By the end of the century, then, the silent art of Pylades and Bathyllus had acquired the aura of a legend and had inspired an entire generation of historians, philosophers and theatre-practitioners, who, frustrated by the non-narrative nature of contemporary theatrical dancing, urged the formation of a new genre that would combine imaginatively the expressive possibilities of dance and mime. From learned connoisseurs to columnists of minor journals, the belief was ripe that contemporary dancing could only legitimise itself as a liberal art worthy of study and esteem by re-establishing the broken link with its remote ancestor, Greco-Roman pantomime dancing. As a result of these ferments in which the 'idea of the ancient pantomime' played a catalytic role, the 'romantic' or 'classical' ballet gradually emerged as an entirely distinct art-form, wherein a self-consistent plot was conveyed through danced movement. In other words, with the aid of ancient pantomime, the eighteenth century redis-covered dance's ability to narrate a story. By the beginning of the nineteenth century, ancient pantomime *together* with its modern off-spring, the pantomime-ballet, could be jointly evoked as legitimating powers: 'Gesture is in itself capable of being used as the sign of ideas, and therefore of being substituted for language. The excellence of the art of the ancient pantomimes, and that also of the modern pantomimic dances evinces this power of gesture' (Austin 1806: 449).

The last word in this epilogue has been reserved for Lucian. For Lycinus' attempt to free the dancer from the stigma of practising a trivial, brainless, entirely corporeal art by arguing that pantomime is neither 'light' as a discipline nor 'easy to master' (*Dance* 35) had innumerable reverberations, especially in a century highly alert to dance's potential to become an autonomous, respected art. Tract after tract repeat with end-less variations that dancing is not the mindless work of legs and arms, divorced from judgement, intellect and sense,[33] and should therefore not be deemed 'too mean a Subject for the Ingenious Labours of Men of Letters'.[34] In its reformed state, such as conceived by the pioneers of the new 'ballet d'action', the dance is not to be seen as 'trifling' but as attainable only with 'great *Difficulty* and *Application*'.[35] As we saw in Chapter 6, Lucian's Lycinus attempted to claim for pantomime parity with the liberal arts or some better accredited professions. Eighteenth-century dance-writers for their part, resolved to prove that choreography and dancing practice were 'not unworthy of being introduc'd among the liberal Arts and Sciences' (Weaver, in Ralph 1985: 873), and expressed the hope that they would see theatrical dancing receiving 'at last ... that praise and applause which all Europe accords to poetry and painting, and the glorious rewards with which they are honoured' (Noverre 1930: 20). Following closely on Lucian's footsteps, Weaver, Noverre and others rehearse Lycinus' assertions that 'To arrive at a Perfection in this Art ... a Man must borrow Assistance from all the other Sciences' (Weaver in Ralph 1985: 595), including music, arithmetic, philosophy, rhetoric, painting and sculpture (see especially *Dance* 35 and Chapter 6§2).[36] Noverre (1930: 32-3) advises his addressee to consult Lucian directly, so that he may enlighten himself: 'If you consult Lucian, you will learn from him, Sir, all the qualities which distinguish and characterise the true *maître de ballet*, and you will observe that history, fable, the poems of antiquity and the knowledge of past times demand his whole application. In fact, it is only after an exact knowledge in all these spheres, that we can hope to succeed in our compositions.'[37]

Most importantly, the influence of Lucian's treatise was not confined to theatrical dancing. Weaver himself very astutely realised that the best modern analogue of the Lucianic 'model pantomime' would have been a stage-actor rather than a dancer: 'But should we form our Notions of these *Pantomimes* from those Representations we have among us, we should be apt to imagine an *Actor* rather describ'd here than a *Dancer*. And indeed the whole Course of the Praise is giv'n them for the Excellence of their *Imitation* of the *Manners* and *Passions*, and not from their *Agility*, their fine *Steps* or *Risings*, which only now seem to distinguish a *Dancer*' (in Ralph 1985: 632). Besides, two years before the publication of Weaver's first theoretical work, Charles Gildon had drawn very liberally on Lucian for his own mapping of the 'Qualities and Qualifications of a *complete Actor*'. His ideal stage-player ought (a) 'to understand History, Moral Philosophy, Rhetoric, not only as far as it relates to Manners and the Passions, but every other Part of it'; (b) 'not to be a Stranger to Painting and Sculpture, imitating their Graces so masterly, as not to fall short of a Raphael Urbin, a Michael Angelo, &c.'; and (c) 'be a good Critic ... in the Poetical Performances, that he may choose the Good, and reject the ill'.[38] Fully conversant with Gildon's manual, Weaver hails the author's exposition as 'so exact a Draught of the Virtues and Qualifications of a *Pantomime*, as far as it relates to the *Player*, that his Rules ought to be the Measure of Excellency in both'. Most tellingly, he recommends Gildon's re-appropriation of Lucian's text to 'the Perusal of all who take any Delight in so noble a Diversion as the Stage; by which they would be render'd more capable of judging of the Performance of both Actor and Dancer, than they usually are' (Weaver, in Ralph 1985: 704-5).

Throughout the eighteenth and for a good part of the nineteenth century, remoulded versions of Lucian's treatise became the ultimate template for the arguments of those who wished to raise the actor's social standing and the character of his profession to the ranks of a liberal art. It would be hardly an exaggeration to claim that Lucian's *De Saltatione* is the first full-scale apology for the theatre and the first systematic rehabilitation of the stage-performer as the intelligent and broadly educated practitioner of a legitimate and beneficial art form in the Western theatrical tradition. Kept alive primarily in the pages of Lucian's treatise, the 'idea' of the pantomime catalysed a twofold revolution in the theatrical world of early modern Europe: the birth of the classical ballet as well as the start of the professional emancipation of the actor's trade. Whatever Lucian himself thought he was doing while composing *On the Dance*, he could never have imagined the far-reaching consequences of his own incisive wit. As cultural historian Roger Chartier (1984: 234) puts it, 'cultural consumption' always 'creates ways of using that cannot be limited to the intentions of those who produce'.[39]

Notes

Introduction

1. Despite the fact that the word *pantomimos* is Greek (he who *mimeitai*, imitates, *panta*, all), it does not appear either in Greek literary sources or on Greek inscriptions, apart from two early cases discussed by Robert (see Chapter 1§1). Lucian (*Dance* 67) attributes the use of *'pantomimos'* to the Greek or Greek-speaking people of Italy ('they call the dancer *pantomimon*'), while Greek speakers in the East indicated the panto-mime dancer by the general term *orchêstês*, i.e. dancer, or by titles underlying his affiliation to the tragic genre (see Chapter 2§2 with n. 21). *Pantomimos* is the term canonised in Latin inscriptions, with Latin texts also using *saltator* and *histrio* to refer to pantomime artists. In English, it should be noted that the term 'pantomime' refers to both the genre and the dancer.

2. Kokolakis (1959) is the first scholarly study of pantomime with a specific focus on Lucian's *On the Dance*. Fundamental too is Jones (1986: 68-77).

3. For collections of ancient sources on pantomime dancing, see primarily Bonaria (1955-6) and Rotolo (1957), the latter with mostly outdated interpretative material. The section on mime and pantomime in Csapo and Slater (1995: 369-89) made available for the first time crucial, yet not easily accessible, Greek and Latin texts in English translation. On individual dancers, see Bonaria (1959), with selective coverage; Stephanis (1988); Leppin (1992), with important discussions of primary sources. On pantomime in the Byzantine period, see Puchner (2002); important source material, especially regarding pantomime's condemnation by the early Christian Church, is scattered in Theocharidis (1940) and Pasquato (1976). Among early discussions, funda-mental are still Weinreich (1948), with plentiful insights into the genre's early history, and especially Wüst (1949), still the most informative general study of pantomime to date. A meticulously documented introduction to the genre prefaces Molloy's useful commentary on Libanius' *Oration* 64 (*On behalf of the Dancers*): see Molloy (1996: 40-79). Good popularising accounts are: Friedländer (1908: 100-17); Beacham (1991: 140-53) and (1999: 141-7); Lawler (1964: 138-44). Scholarly work of incalculable impor-tance for the reconstruction of the genre in its performative and socio-political aspects has been carried out by Jory (1981), (1984), (1995), (1996), (2001); Slater (1993), (1994), (1995), (1996); Morel (1969). Epigraphic evidence has been studied (from different perspectives) by Robert (1930), (1936) and Roueché (1993). Invaluable from the point of view of locating the genre into the broader context of imperial theatrical performances are: Kelly (1979); Jones (1993); Easterling and Miles (1999); E. Hall (2002). More recent contributions, marking a resurgence of interest in ancient pantomime, are: Montiglio (1999); Vesterinen (2003), (2005); Garelli-François (2004); Lada-Richards (2003a), (2003c), (2004b), (2005). Female dancing and pantomime have been expertly discussed by Webb (1997) and (2002a), who is also completing a much awaited book-length study of mime and pantomime in late antiquity. A vital moment in the turn of the tide in pantomime's favour will be the publication of Hall and Wyles (forthcoming), an edited volume covering a very wide range of aspects (including masks, costume, iconography) and marking 'new directions' in the study of the genre.

4. It is undoubtedly this lack of textuality which condemned the genre to neglect at the hands of generations of scholars who, eyes and minds detained by the literary specimens of the ancient performative traditions, did not even deign to cast a look in pantomime's direction, expecting to find in its domain nothing of consequence for the literary and cultural history of the empire.

5. Even in the case of the seemingly factual inscriptions, there is no way of knowing to what extent the subjective element has exaggerated, if not the facts themselves, at least the importance of events, etc.

6. Very broadly on issues of methodology in dance studies, see Foster (1995).

7. Cf. Chapter 5§1, with note 16.

8. Cf. Foster (1995: 6), warning that in the evaluation of 'fragments of past bodies, a historian's own bodily experience and conceptions of body ... intervene'.

9. We shall see in the course of this book that many of these can be identified: Ovid, Aristaenetus, Plotinus, Libanius and Nonnus, to name but a few.

10. The notion of 'discrepant experiences' ('each with its particular agenda and pace of development, its own internal formations, its internal coherence and system of external relationships, all of them co-existing and interacting with others') belongs to Edward Said and the discourse of colonialism; see primarily E. Said (1993: 35-50; quote from 36).

11. See primarily Jauss (1970: 14).

1. Pantomime Dancing Through the Centuries

1. See Athenaeus, *Sophists at Dinner* 20d; Hieronymus, *Interpretation of Eusebius' Chronicle* (on the year 22 BC; *PL* 27, cols 553-4); Zosimus, *New History* 6.1; entries in the so-called 'Suda' dictionary of the tenth century AD, under *Athenodorus, pantomime dancing*, and *Pylades*. The sources for the career of Pylades and Bathyllus are conveniently listed in Bonaria (1955-6: 50-5); Bonaria (1959: 237-9 and 231, respectively); for the sources with a brief discussion, see Leppin (1992: 284-5 and 217-18, respectively).

2. To these one can add not only the enraptured reaction of the banqueters, who found themselves 'on fire' because of the performers' passion (cf. Chapter 5§2), but also the Syracusan's relaying of the 'plot' in advance, so that his audience would understand the mimed actions (cf. Chapter 3§3, on Augustine's reporting of performance practices in his native Carthage). On the 'Dionysus and Ariadne' show as a precursor of imperial pantomime, see Weinreih (1948: 131-5); cf. Jones (1991: 191).

3. *Galli* were the flamboyant, self-castrating priests of Cybele's cult.

4. See Weinreich (1948: 19), with references.

5. I.e. the verb for dancing coupled with the accusative of the role danced: 'he danced a *gallus*'; see Kokolakis (1976: 217-29).

6. Some references can be found in Weinreich (1948: 13 n. 11).

7. See Robert (1930: 115) on *I.Priene* 113, lines 65-7.

8. See Robert (1969: 241) on *IGR* 1.975 (= *IC* 4.222A).

9. See, most conveniently, the register compiled by Garton (1972: 231-65), especially on C. Asinius Olympus, Metrodorus, C. Pomponius, Volumnia Cytheris, and Dionysia; female mime dancing at the *Floralia* included nudity (Valerius Maximus, *Memorable Deeds and Sayings* 2.10.8).

10. Some ancient sources (albeit from the first century AD) in Wiseman (1985a: 27 n. 43) and Webb (2002a: 287 n. 17); of earlier date may be the *emboliaria* (dancer in entr'actes) Galeria Copiola, mentioned in Pliny the Elder, *Natural History* 7.158.

11. For dancers among Sulla's boon companions, for example, see Plutarch, *Life of Sulla* 2.2-3. Diodorus Siculus (*The Library of History* 31.26.7) posits a taste for banqueting and *akroamata* (i.e. predominantly entertainments consisting of song and dance; cf. texts in Robert 1930: 116), to Scipio Aemilianus' generation.

12. See Wiseman (1985a: 30-2 and 46) and cf. Webb (2002a: 292, with n. 44) on the early age of death of female performers.

13. See, e.g., Polybius, *Histories* 30.22.8-11 (apud Athenaeus, *Sophists at Dinner* 615a).

14. In Livy's account (*From the Foundation of Rome* 7.2.4), the Romans summoned professional entertainers (*ludiones*) from Etruria, who danced (*saltantes*) to the sounds of the flute and 'performed graceful movements in the Tuscan fashion'. Livy's additional comment that the imported *ludiones* danced 'without any song', i.e. without any verbal accompaniment, and 'without the gesture needed for the imitation of the content of songs' (*sine imitandorum carminum actu*) has been rightly understood by Jory (1981: 154) to indicate that Livy contrasts the situation in 364 BC with that of his own times. In this respect, Livy's negative qualifiers of his contemporary dancers could only mean that, already in the years 30-25 BC (the time of composition of books 6-10; see Oakley 1997: 109-10), the historian was aware of an imitative dance that interprets and imitates sung narrative in a manner very similar to later pantomime performances.

15. Consider, however, Livy's justified scepticism concerning the material of early Roman history.

16. On a chorus of satyr-like dancers in Scipio's triumphal procession into Rome (201 BC), see Appian, *The Punic Wars* 66.

17. Verbal similarities between this passage and Athenaeus, *Sophists at Dinner* 20d-e, suggest that the two authors may have derived their material from a common source, possibly Aristonicus himself; cf. Jory (1981: 150).

18. Both dancers were so successful in their time that they seem to have initiated the trend whereby successive generations of *pantomimi* took their name from a great master of the art, so that we can trace, for example, two pantomimes by the name of Bathyllus and no fewer than five by the name of Pylades (see Bonaria 1959). For this reason the names of several pantomimes mentioned in the text (e.g. Paris, Septentrio, Theocritus) are followed by numerals (I, II, etc), indicating their position with respect to the first VIP dancer with the same name.

19. See primarily Macrobius, *Saturnalia* 2.7.18; Hieronymus, *Interpretation of Eusebius' Chronicle* (on the year 22 BC; *PL* 27, cols 553-4).

20. The idea for the introduction of a full orchestra may have come to Bathyllus via his native Egypt for, as Kraemer (1931: 136) demonstrated, an orchestra 'composed, in varying combinations, of clarinet, harp, lute and drum' was an element firmly entrenched in the Egyptian dance traditions.

21. Alongside Bathyllus' Alexandrian origins, we must not forget that the local guild of the Egyptian 'Artists of Dionysus' seated at Ptolemais is the only association of this kind to include a dancer (*orchêstês*: some kind of proto-pantomime? a pyrrhic dancer? a dancer in choruses?) among its members in Hellenistic times, as can be inferred from a decree dating from 240 BC: see Le Guen (2001: vol. 1, no. 61, line 45); Csapo-Slater (1995: 248-9). Certainly around 30 BC, at the time of Antony's celebrated frolics with Cleopatra, Egypt was a paradise for dancers (if we believe Strabo's picture of all-day and all-night unrestrained, licentious dancing in Canobus, close to Alexandria, at the time of the public festivals: *Geography* 17.1.17); in much later periods Alexandria was often an exception in the empire-wide bans on pantomimes: see, e.g., Malalas, *Chronicle* 17.12.

22. See Introduction, n. 10.

23. On the Sebasteion and cultural memory, see primarily Alcock (2001), (2002).

24. On the early pantomime riots and measures against the dancers, see Jory (1984).

25. Clearly some form of mime and dancing carried on in the West way into the Middle Ages, as can be gauged from the constant fulminations of the Church against dancing mimes and all kinds of scenic entertainers (testimonia collected in Faral 1910: Appendix 3, 272-327).

26. Syrian text translated in English in Wright (1882: 18, 20 and 21 and 35 respectively).

27. On pantomime bans occasioned by rioting in the early Byzantine period, see Browning (1952) and Cameron (1976: 226-9).

28. Apparently, the livelihood of 'innumerable' artists at the time depended on those funds: see *Secret History* 26.8-10. Procopius' testimony, however, disagrees with parts of Justinian's legislation, where clear provision for theatrical entertainments is made (see Stephanis 1986: 22 on an edict of 536 AD).

29. Text and translation for both Canons in Nedungatt and Featherstone (1995). Athough 'lascivious bodily movements, gestures and songs are time and again prohibited, and public dancing and cross-dressing in particular are denounced as pagan customs well into late Byzantine times' (Puchner 2002: 313), when the twelfth-century ecclesiastical commentators Zonaras and Balsamon annotate the canons of the Trullan council (see Ralles and Potles 1852: 424-6 and 448-51), it is patently clear that they themselves have not personally experienced anything even remotely approaching the pantomime dancing of the early Byzantine centuries.

30. Clusters of identifiable Greek dances have been studied by Delavaud-Roux (1993, on armed dances), (1994, on pacific dances), (1995, on Dionysiac dances).

31. Fine examples of early Greek mask dancing are the animal-headed figures depicted as dancing to the music of lyre and flute along the selvage of the 'Great Goddess' Despoina's cult statue in the Arcadian city of Lycosura and bull-headed archaic figurines (dating from before 1200 BC) from Cypriot sanctuaries in dancing combinations; see Lada-Richards (1999: 330, with bibliography) and more widely on this material, see Lawler (1964: 52-5, 58-73).

32. From a dance historian's perspective not all forms of dancing are mimetic, but for Plato and Aristotle alike the whole activity of dancing was perceived as an imitative art. In Plato's *Laws* it is said to originate in the 'imitation (*mimêsis*) of spoken narrative by means of gestures (*schêmasin*)' (816a), while in Aristotle's *Poetics* it is qualified as an imitation of character (*êthê*), emotions (*pathê*) and actions (*praxeis*) by means of rhythm expressed in spatial forms, that is to say, rhythm translated into *schêmata*, visual bodily configurations (1447a 26-8).

33. Plutarch, *Life of Theseus* 21; Pollux, *Onomasticon* 4.101. Lucian (*Dance* 34), however, rightly denies any *direct* choreographic connection between the *geranos* and the pantomime of his day.

34. Longus' language here is so clearly evocative of the fully-fledged pantomime dancer's art (for he *par excellence* can expound his subjects 'vividly' in a manner that evokes them to his audience's eyes; cf. Chapters 3 and 6§2) that one wonders whether the author has actually in mind a real-life pantomime, to which he refers in what seems to be the sympathetically disposed upper-class man's way of verbalising such performances.

35. In this category of ancient sources, see, most importantly, Athenaeus, *Sophists at Dinner* 15c-e and 628d; Lucian, *Dance* 16.

36. See Boyancé (1937: 88-91); Lada-Richards (1999: 98-102); Hardie (2004: 19-29). Across mystic cults, dancing was the hallmark of the initiatory purification ritual called 'enthronement' (*thronôsis*): see, e.g., Dio Chrysostom, *Oration* 12.33; Plato, *Euthydemus* 277d-e (on Corybantic initiation) and the further references in Lada-Richards (1999: 101 on Dionysiac initiations; 248-9 on Eleusinian rites).

37. Cf. Aristides Quintilianus, *On Music* 3.25; scholion on Lycophron's *Alexandra* 212; John Chrysostom *PG* 62.387, on dances as defining the realm of pagan mysteries. The abundant references to dancing as part of the afterlife bliss anticipated by initiates in mystic cults is also an excellent indicator of the importance of dancing as part of mystic initiation rites: see, e.g., Plutarch, *Moral Essays* 1105b and fr. 178 Sandbach; *CIL* 3.686 (late funerary epigram, where the deceased initiate is invited to join in or lead the dance as a satyr); a funerary epigram from Tusculum, where the deceased girl dances as the leader of the group (Merkelbach 1971); among literary reflections, see, e.g., Aristophanes, *Frogs* 326-36, 354, 395-7.

38. See primarily Boyancé (1960-1) and further Lada-Richards (1999: 78-80).

39. On Dionysiac festivals centring on the re-enactment of Dionysiac myths by males dressed as satyrs and females dressed as maenads, see Seaford (1994: 272); on the mimetic/commemorative aspect of Dionysiac rites, see, e.g., Diodorus, *The Library of History* 4.3.3.

40. See Plutarch, *Moral Essays* 293c-d; on the motif of descent/ascent as initiatory, see Lada-Richards (1999: 53-5, 78-86).

41. In Euripides' *Bacchae*, to take just one example, the quintessence of the Dionysiac experience is dancing the mystic rites of the god (see, e.g., 20-1, 63, 114, 132-4, 184, 190, 195, 205, 207, 220, 323-4, 482, 511); see further Lada-Richards (1999: 100-2).

42. See Bérard and Bron (1989) and Lada-Richards (1999: 334-5).

43. See, e.g., Pollux, *Onomasticon* 4.100 on *baukismos* as 'a dainty type of dance that liquefies the body'; Hesychius locates *baukismos* (s.v) in the semantic field of effeminacy (*thryptesthai*) and voluptuousness (*trypherômata*).

44. See, e.g., Pollux, *Onomasticon* 4.101; cf. Lawler (1950).

45. See, e.g., Pollux, *Onomasticon* 4.99 and 4.101 on the *mothôn* as a dance that is vulgar and appropriate to sailors; cf. Athenaeus' much-quoted story of the vulgar dance by means of which Hippoclides 'danced away' his own marriage (*Sophists at Dinner* 628cd).

46. See Athenaeus, *Sophists at Dinner* 629d, 630a; Hesychius, s.v. *thermastris*; Pollux, *Onomasticon* 4.102; Eustathius, schol. *Odyssey* 8.376.

47. See Lawler (1939: esp. 499); cf. Lawler (1946).

48. Athenaeus, *Sophists at Dinner* 629d-30a, and Pollux, *Onomasticon* 4.99-105, provide plentiful examples.

49. There have been many attempts at broad synthetic reconstructions of the manifold dance languages of the Greek world; see, indicatively, Emmanuel (1896; methodologically suspect); Latte (1913); Lawler (1964, the culminating point of some fifty articles on Greek dancing); Prudhommeau (1965). For an extensive but unwieldy theoretical discussion of Greek dance performances, see Naerebout (1997); for anthropologically inspired work on the significance of dancing in Greek culture, see primarily Lonsdale (1993) and Calame (1997 [1977]).

2. Pantomime and Other Entertainments

1. On the close interaction of mime, pantomime, erotic handbooks and the novel in antiquity, see Mignogna (1997); Morales (2004: 71-7).

2. See, e.g., John Chrysostom, *PG* 51.212, 55.158, 56.99, 62.262, 541; cf. Firmicius Maternus, *Mathesis* 8.8.1 (*pantomimos aut mimologos*). The joint calumny of pantomimes and mimes was apparently a tactic followed by Aelius Aristides, whose accusations against pantomime dancing Libanius undertakes to answer in his speech *In Defence of the Dancers* (*Oration* 64; see 10-11); according to Libanius, Aristides had hoped to blacken pantomime more easily by packaging it together with a genre of an even lower reputation (11). On the mime/pantomime overlap, see also Molloy (1996: 84-5).

3. Think, e.g., of tavern dancers in the mould of [Virgil's] Syrian temptress Copa (see Henderson 2002), the sexually explicit 'dancing girls from Gadiz' in Martial's poems (see Fear 1991) or the castanet dancers entertaining at village fairs and weddings in Hellenistic and Roman Egypt (see Kraemer 1931).

4. Female stage-entertainers are variously termed in our sources as *scenicae* or *thymelicae* or (with greater emphasis on dancing) *emboliariae* (cf. Chapter 1§1), *choreutriae*, *orchêstrides*, *saltatrices*, even *pantomimae*; on issues of terminology, see Webb (1997) and (2002a), both pioneering pieces on female performers in later antiquity. Inscription *CIL* 6 (ii) 10128 betrays a most interesting conflation of the *embolia* tradition and pantomime dancing, with the female dancer Sophe described as 'of the group or school of Bathyllus': as Webb (2002a: 290) writes, within that school 'she was in charge of the *emboliariae*', who, judging by our scanty sources, could find themselves 'attached to a particular group or style of pantomimes' (ibid.: 287).

5. Consider, e.g., Seneca, *Natural Questions* 7.3 or (with reference to a much earlier period) Macrobius, *Saturnalia* 3.14.7.

6. See, e.g., Martial, *Epigrams* 5.78.27-8; *Priapea* 19; *Greek Anthology* 5.129; Juvenal, *Satire* 6.314-15, 321-2, O19 and 11.164 (with scholion on line 162); Alciphron, *Letters of Courtesans* 14.4 and 6. Arnobius seems to have his eyes fixed on pantomimes when vilifying the dancers who, 'raising their haunches and hips, float along with quivering loins' (*Against the Gentiles* 2.42). The gloss on 'cinaedi' in the *Corpus Glossariorum Latinorum* (5.654.7) attributes the quivering of the buttocks in public to 'dancers or pantomimes' (*saltatores vel pantomimi*); see Adams (1982: 194). And, as we shall see in Chapter 11§4, the pantomime's abominable 'double', the transgressive public speaker, is painted by the sources 'with a shimmy in his walk'.

7. See, e.g., *Greek Anthology* 9.567; terms denoting 'wateriness' (*hygros, hygromelês, exhygrainomenos, hygrotês, hygrôs*) belong to the semantics of pantomime dancing (Pollux, *Onomasticon* 4.96-8; Lucian, *Dance* 19 and 73).

8. See, e.g., Ovid, *Loves* 2.4.30, *Art of Love* 3.350; [Virgil], *Copa* 2-3. On the further connotations of 'softness', see Chapter 5§1.

9. On *lygisma* and its cognates in the semantic field of female dancing, see Lawler (1950: 70-1); in pantomime dancing: Lucian, *Dance* 77 (cf. Jones 1986: 73); Tatian, *Address to the Greeks* 22.7; Philostratus, *Life of Apollonius* 4.21; Pollux, *Onomasticon* 4.97-8 (*lygizein, lygismos, lygistikon* in a section pertinent to pantomime dancing); Gregory of Nazianzus, *Oration* 21.12 (*PG* 35.1093, quoted in Chapter 5 n. 32); as late as the eighth century AD, a deacon named Epiphanius accuses monasteries polluted by the iconoclastic movement of harbouring satanic songs and *orchêstika lygismata*: see Mansi (1767: 13.329).

10. Such a *magôidos*, i.e. an effeminate (*malakos*) dancer with a drum, cymbals and clappers, appears in *P.Hib.* 54, 11-12 (245 BC): see Perpillou-Thomas (1995: 229) and Westermann (1924: 140 with n. 4).

11. See Robert (1938: 8-10) and Hunter (2002: 196-7).

12. Infamously loved by Sulla in the first century BC and among his close entourage of 'mime singers and dancers' (*mimôidois kai orchêstais*) (Plutarch, *Life of Sulla* 2.3-4 and 36.1).

13. Antipater of Sidon, *Greek Anthology* 9.567 (late second century BC); see Garton (1972: 148) and Wiseman (1985a: 34-5, with n. 65).

14. See Xenophon, *Symposion* 2.1, 2.8, 2.11; in Artemidorus' *Interpretation of Dreams* 1.42, *orchêstai* and *thaumatopoioi* are grouped together as professionals 'unable to work without their hands'; in Dio Chrysostom's speeches, pantomimes and jugglers can be found on an ordinary day rubbing shoulders with each other in a city's hippodrome (see *Oration* 20.10). The fluidity of the dividing lines between the expertise of pantomimes and wonder-makers is perhaps reflected in the text of an imperial inscription found in Delphi (*F.Delphes* III (i), no. 469), honouring Neikon, *orchêstên kai thaumatopoion* (see Robert 1969: 222, who nevertheless considers Neikon a dancer of a lower rank). Cf. Nicoll (1931: 35-7).

15. On this passage of Gregory, see Lada-Richards (forthcoming, a). It is unfortunate that we do not have more information on puppet-showmen (cf. Xenophon, *Symposion* 4.55; Athenaeus, *Sophists at Dinner* 19e) in the ancient world: from Apuleius' *About the Universe* 351 we gather that they made their figures move in the tortuous way that was almost a hallmark of pantomime dancers; see Reich (1903: 669-75).

16. See Libanius, *Oration* 64.104: 'And when he has taken him on, the gymnastic trainer will twist him round into more numerous and more remarkable bends than a wrestler, bringing up both his feet over the back onto his head and in addition even forcing them back to project further past the face so that his heels approach his elbows. And when he has made the body into a circle, like some willow cane, he sets it in motion for running like a hoop, and it runs' (trans. Molloy 1996: 171). We get a very similar picture from John Chrysostom, who refers to the apprentice pantomime's struggle 'to arch his whole frame in the precise shape of a wheel and set it spinning on the ground' (*PG* 49.195).

17. See, e.g., Nonnus, *Dionysiaca* 19.155 and 274-80; Claudian, *Against Eutropius*

2.359-61 (elegant revolutions of the body; twisting the flanks into a boneless arch); Pollux, *Onomasticon* 4.105; Sidonius Apollinaris, *Poem* 23.270.

18. See, e.g., Homer, *Odyssey* 4.18-19; Xenophon, *Symposion* 2.11, 2.22, 7.3, *Anabasis* 6.1.5 and 9; Plato, *Euthydemus* 294e, where tumbling on swords or whirling around on a wheel are envisaged as the uppermost level of dancing prowess; on acrobats (with some pictures), see also Nicoll (1931: 35-7).

19. Cf. Jones (1991: 188). For equally breathtaking combinations of acrobatics with dance, see Claudian, *Panegyric on the Consulship of F. Manlius Theodorus* 320-4 and Philostratus, *Life of Apollonius* 2.28. On the difficulty in distinguishing genuine acrobats from dancers in pre-Roman Egypt, see Perpillou-Thomas (1995: 228).

20. The vast majority of *fabulae salticae* mentioned in Lucian's dialogue have a counterpart in classical tragedy (counting, of course, the fragments and the known titles). We should also note here an inscription (*CIL* 14.4254) from Tivoli (dating from 199 AD) set up in honour of L.Aurelius Apolaustus Memphius: his successful roles listed here are adaptations of tragedies by Euripides (*Heracles, Orestes, Trojan Women, Bacchae, Hippolytus*) and Sophocles (*Tympanistae*); see Jones (1986: 73 with n. 26); Csapo-Slater (1995: 382).

21. See primarily *F.Delphes*, III (i), no. 551 (lines 1-2); *F.Delphes*, III (ii) no. 105; *I.Ephesus* II.71; *SEG* 1.529 (from Apameia on the river Orontes); *I.Magnesia* 165; *IGR* 4.1272 (cf. *RÉG* 4 (1891) 174, no. 2); in a funerary epigram from the Pontic Heraclea the genre is referred to as 'rhythmical tragedy' (*enrythmos tragôidia*; see Sahin 1975: 294, line 15), while an inscription from Magnesia is unique in opting for the variant 'rhythmical tragic poetry' (*enrythmon | tragikên poiêsin*: *I.Magnesia* 192, lines 11-12, with Slater 1996: 199). In general, see Robert (1930), and cf. Athenaeus, *Sophists at Dinner* 20d (on pantomime as *tragikê orchêsis*) and *Greek Anthology* 9.248, 4. A most interesting insight into the enduring public perception of pantomime's affinity with tragedy comes from the sixth-century historian Procopius of Gaza, who refers disparagingly to the writers of pantomime libretti as *tragôidodidaskaloi*, 'tragedy teachers', and shudders at the thought that he himself might be associated with their kind: see *Secret History* 1.4, with Theocharidis (1940: 30).

22. See on this subject Kelly (1979) and E. Hall (2002: esp. 27-30), a fascinating discussion.

23. Suetonius, *Life of Caligula* 57.3; see Easterling 1997a: 218-21.

24. Augustine, *City of God* 7.26; cf. ibid. 18.10, on divine tales treated in the theatre in song and dance amid rounds of applause (*inter theatricos plausus cantantur atque saltantur*). The exact nature of the spectacles alluded to in this and other passages of Augustine's voluminous writings is impossible to determine, but they do give us an excellent idea of the close affinity between tragic and pantomime renditions of mythical material in late antiquity. Most importantly, such overlaps are a feature of the early imperial scene as well: see, for example, Dio Cassius, *Roman History* 59.29.6, where it is unclear whether 'to dance (*orchêsasthai*) and act (*hypokrinasthai*) a tragedy' refers to two separate shows or to 'an elaborate entertainment involving a combination of dance, song, and spoken dialogue' (E. Hall 2002: 28).

25. Lucian's narrative certainly captures the antagonism between the two genres when Lycinus, the pantomime lover, pronounces the *orchêstês* infinitely superior to his great rival, the tragic performer (see *Dance* 27-30, including the lengthiest extant description of a *tragôidos* in antiquity), and judges pantomime's *fabulae* as 'more varied' (*poikilôterai*) and 'more learned' (*polymathesterai*) than tragedy's own plots (*Dance* 31). However, Lycinus' scathing assessment notwithstanding, the real-life pantomime may not have been so self-assured. Anxious looks over the fence and into the pastures of his more prestigious siblings must have been a fact of his professional existence as well as part and parcel of his struggle for professional emancipation.

26. See E. Hall (1999a), (2002); Easterling and Miles (1999: 101-2); cf. Lada-Richards (2002: esp. 412-15).

27. See, however, the 'evidence ... for the writing of new dramas and the continued production of full plays in the period of the Roman empire', as presented concisely by Jones (1993: quote from 40).

28. Such may have been the case in fourth-century performances of Timotheus' dithyramb *Scylla*; see Hordern (2002: 250); on the increasing dramatisation and mimeticism of musical performance from the late fifth century onwards, see Csapo (2004).

29. *kai têi tou pantos kinêsei sômatos*: see Pausanias, *Description of Greece* 9.12.6.

30. This is how Artaud (1958: 38) encapsulated the distinction between 'Occidental' and 'Oriental' (especially Balinese) theatre.

31. In the perspective of hostile Christians, to be sure; see, e.g., Prudentius, *Crowns of Martyrdom* 10.221.

32. In Lucian alone, see *Dance* 80 (the tecnophagy of Cronus and Thyestes), 39 (stones transformed into human beings in the Deucalion myth), 41 (Cadmus' transformation into a snake), 48 (Callisto's transformation into a bear), 57 (general stipulation that the dancer should know all the plots revolving around transformation). Even in the fifth century AD, Sidonius Apollinaris (*Poem* 23.277-99) refers to pantomime subjects such as 'the feast of Thyestes' and the 'dismembered boy', Jove turned into a bull and Mars 'with a wild boar's form'. On the whole, Horace (*Art of Poetry* [*Letters* 2.3] 185-9) may well be protesting against the tragic stage's contamination by a pantomime aesthetics when stipulating that acts such as murder, cannibalism and metamorphosis should not be acted on the stage. On the other hand, as far as comparison with Greek tragedy goes, we must always take into account the fact that our surviving tragic plays may well be giving us the false impression of a genre considerably more 'refined' than Athenian tragedy really was. Sophocles, for example, did write plays on both cannibalism (*Thyestes*) and metamorphosis (*Tereus*) and we can only speculate today as to how such plots would have been handled on the classical Athenian stage.

33. Among the pantomime plots mentioned in Lucian's exposition, several appear to foreground even journeys or a hero's roaming over vast expanses, in heaven, earth or the domains below (see, e.g., *Dance* 40 and 46).

34. For the significance of this tale in the context of Lucian's dialogue and in the Western theatrical tradition, see Lada-Richards (forthcoming, b).

35. Tecmessa is the most likely candidate in *Ajax* 235-44 and 296-300. To be sure, Ajax does step, still mad, onto the stage when summoned by Athena (*Ajax* 91ff.), but, although he holds a heavy, blood-stained whip in hand, he only *speaks* of violence already accomplished (*Ajax* 94-100) or planned (*Ajax* 108-17).

36. The title of the pantomime described by Lucian's Lycinus may well have been *Aias Mainomenos*, *Ajax mad*; the 'madness of Ajax' is one of the staple pantomime topics mentioned in *Dance* 46.

37. For a fuller discussion of *Dance* 83-4 in relation to Sophocles' *Ajax*, see Lada-Richards (forthcoming, a).

38. Heracles' madness: compare Euripides' *Heracles Mad* with Macrobius, *Saturnalia* 2.7.16-17; Phaethon: compare Euripides' *Phaethon* (fragmentary) with Nonnus' *Dionysiaca* 30.108-16. See Lada-Richards (forthcoming, a).

39. For caveats to this proposition, see Lada-Richards (forthcoming, a).

40. Probably still referring to Telestes.

41. Aristocles apud Athenaeus, *Sophists at Dinner* 22a; cf. Pickard-Cambridge (1988: 251) and Wiles (1997: 119).

3. 'Technologies' of the Body

1. See, e.g., *PG* 51.212, on the necessity to keep mimes and pantomimes away from one's daughter's wedding celebrations; *PG* 55.158, against those who hire mimes and pantomimes for their banquets, turning thus their house into a theatre; *PG* 62.386, on the turpitude of bringing into one's house 'effeminates and pantomimes' (*malakous andras kai orchoumenous*) for a wedding banquet.

2. See Westermann (1924) and (1932). *P.Flor.* 74 (dated 181 AD), in particular, preserves a contract for the hire of two pantomimes with musicians and others for five days. On the subject of professional dancers in Roman Egypt we can look forward to the forthcoming work of Marjaana Vesterinen.

3. While giving examples of people who can carry on with their own occupation even in the midst of manifold distractions, Dio Chrysostom (*Oration* 20.9) mentions panto-mimes and dancing-masters, performing or teaching in the street, oblivious of those peddling or picking a fight around them.

4. Lucian's comments should undoubtedly be taken with a large pinch of salt, since they are clearly meant to flatter (cf. Chapter 12); it is, nevertheless, extremely plausible that levels of pantomime connoisseurship of the kind exposed in Plotinus (*Enneads* 4.4.33), for example, were highest in the traditional hot-seats of the art, such as the great urban centres of the East, Antioch and Alexandria.

5. 'There was a wooden mountain, constructed with sublime craftsmanship in the likeness of that famous mountain that Homer the bard celebrated in song, Mount Ida. It was planted with turf and live trees and on its very top it poured forth river water from a flowing fountain made by the engineer's hand. A handful of she-goats cropped the low grass...' (*Metamorphoses* 10.30). At the end of the performance, 'a chasm in the earth opened and swallowed up the wooden mountain' (*Metamorphoses* 10.34).

6. And, in any case, as we shall see below, the spectacle described by Apuleius deviates in many respects from what we might call, for want of a better term, the pantomime 'norm'.

7. See Pollux, *Onomasticon* 4.131 and 126; Vitruvius, *On Architecture* 5.6.8; more generally on these issues, see Bieber (1961: 75 and 180) and Beacham (1991: 169-82). For further consideration of pantomime scenery and stage-space, see Lada-Richards (forthcoming, a).

8. The best known example of a privately owned troupe is that of the pantomimes kept by the wealthy widow Ummidia Quadratilla, who also exhibited them at the theatre (presumably, for profit): see Pliny the Younger, *Letters* 7.24 (see further Chapter 8§1).

9. On the splendour of pantomime clothing, cf. Chapter 11, n. 46.

10. Not only does Fronto live at the height of pantomime's popularity, but he is also a teacher of Lucius Verus (Julius Capitolinus, *Verus* 2.5), the pantomime-mad co-em-peror of the mid-second century AD. If he did accompany his royal charge to the theatre, he may even have been tutored himself in the finer points of pantomime technique by a first class connoisseur, an assumption that would make his testimony supremely valuable for us today. In any case, Fronto and Verus do seem to be exchanging views on matters of excellence in pantomime dancing, as can be seen from one of Fronto's letters, where the orator argues that Pylades (III) is superior to his master (Pylades, II) and equal to Verus' own freedman, L. Aelius Aurelius Apolaustus Memphius (Fronto, *To the Emperor Verus*, I.2 [p. 111 van den Hout] ; dated 161 AD).

11. All the most interesting for us because Apuleius (born *c.* 120 AD) was an exact contemporary of Lucian.

12. See further Regine May's piece in Hall and Wyles (forthcoming).

13. Although female pantomimes were by no means unheard of; in the *Greek Anthology* only, see the epigrams for the dancing stars Rhodocleia (16.283), Helladia (16.284, 286, 287), and Libania (16.288). A pygmy female pantomime, specialising in the roles of Andromache and Helen, is the subject of *Latin Anthology*, I.1 (Shackleton Bailey) 305, while the twenty-sixth epistle in Aristaenetus' first book of *Letters* is addressed to the astoundingly versatile female pantomime Panarete.

14. The art of acting (*hypokrisis*), impersonating characters other than one's own, is foregrounded in Lucian's treatise as 'the chief preoccupation and aim of pantomime' (*Dance* 65).

15. But see below §2.

16. The most remarkable feature of the pantomime mask was its closed mouth, which Lucian explains thus: 'it does not have an open mouth like the others (i.e. the masks of comedy and tragedy), but a closed one, because the dancer has many people to do the shouting on his behalf' (*Dance* 29). The existence of a closed mouth is one of the foremost distinguishing traits of pantomime masks in art; see Jory (1996) and (2002).

17. Cf. Manilius, *Matters of Astronomy* 5.482a and 480b, on the pantomime who, single-bodied, assumes all the roles himself and, although one man, can represent a crowd (*turbam*).

18. Libanius (*Oration* 64.97) describes it as 'a straight rod of iron protruding from the sandal', capable of making 'enough noise'; cf. ibid. 95. On the *scabellum*, see Bélis (1988), a most learned piece.

19. According to Bélis (1988: 328), the *scabillarius* also functioned as a 'chef d'orchestre', giving the *tempo* to the group of the musicians. For *Collegia Scabillariorum*, associations of *scabillarii* in Roman inscriptions, see Bonaria (1955-6: nos 1255, 1257, 1258, 1260-3).

20. Libanius (*Oration* 64.96) speaks of 'wooden boards'; Jacob of Serugh, describing pantomime dancing from the banks of the Euphrates in the late fifth- and early sixth-century AD, speaks of a 'stone floor' (*Homily* 2, F4r[b], and *Homily* 4, F18r[b]; text in Moss 1935: 104 and 107) and a shoe 'circl[ing] on marble' (ibid., 107); a marble floor we also find in Claudian, *Against Eutropius* 2.360.

21. Most impressively, Aristides (apud Libanius, *Oration* 64.95) seems to have argued that the *scabellarii* are an inducement to *malakia* (effeminacy; cf. Chapter 5§1); against the din of the *scabellum*, cf. Arnobius, *Against the Gentiles* 2.42 (*scabillorum concrepationes*), 7.32 (*crepitus scabillorum*); Jacob of Serugh, *Homily* 2, F4r[a] (text in Moss 1935: 104).

22. Cf. especially the dancer's designation as 'an actor of rhythmic tragic movement', already discussed in Chapter 2.

23. So, for example, in an epigram by Leontius Scholasticus (*Greek Anthology* 16.287), the female pantomime Helladia is said to be responding to a soloist's new song about Hector.

24. See, e.g., Aristides apud Libanius (*Oration* 64.87-8), who nevertheless agrees that there is little musical precision in such songs (ibid. 88); cf. E. Hall (2002: 29) for the suggestion that pantomime songs must have been 'less difficult than the virtuosic libretti of the tragic singer'.

25. But cf. Aristides, apud Libanius, *Oration* 64.87-94.

26. Vocal talent must have been an essential component of a good performance in those plays whose plots revolved around an exquisite mythical singer, like Orpheus or Philomela or Cassandra (see E. Hall 2002: 29). The role of singing against the background of the pantomime's graceful movements is spotlighted in an epigram by Crinagoras (*Greek Anthology* 9.542), addressed to the (otherwise unknown) librettist and vocalist Philonides; cf. *Greek Anthology* 16.287.

27. Or, at least, figures not providing good opportunities for virtuoso dancing.

28. Cf. Lucian, *The Mistaken Critic* 19, where such a character's function is generically described as 'partnering the dancers', 'acting secondary parts for the dancers' (*hypokrinesthai tois orchêstais*).

29. It may well be that this is the meaning of 'he [i.e. the pantomime] will match the chorus-singers with his gestures', in Manilius, *Matters of Astronomy* 5.484.

30. On the necessity of close congruity between dance and song for the engendering of emotion, cf. the beautiful thoughts of Zeami (fifteenth century AD), founder of Noh, the classical dance drama of Japan: see Rimer and Masakazu (1984:77) and (ibid.: 76), on the optimal way of word-and-movement interaction. Among our pantomime sources, we can single out Apuleius, *Metamorphoses* 10.32, where Venus proceeds with 'delicate gestures' *in response to* the 'soft sound' of the flutes, and Aristaenetus, *Letter* 1.26, 12-13, where Panarete's somatic transformations are tied up with the harmonious tunes of the accompanying songs.

31. Cf. Plotinus, *Enneads* 4.4.33, on the performance's external elements, such as the piping and the singing, as changing in tandem with the moving body of the dancing star.

32. In Quintilian's time, *saltatio* can be primarily understood as pantomime dancing.

33. On the magnificent powers of expression that reside in the human hand, see primarily Quintilian, *Training* 11.3.85-7, where hands are credited with their own sublime language, 'almost as expressive as words'.

34. The use of *graphein* (to write) to designate the depictive function of mimetic dancing goes at least as far back as Xenophon (*Symposion* 7.5), while in Lucian's *Dance* 84 the casting of a dancer into a role is similarly expressed as *graphein*.

35. Pantomime literature is full of such conjunctions of contradictory terms; see, e.g., Cassiodorus, *Various Letters* 4.51.8: 'clamorous silence' (*silentium clamosum*); Nonnus, *Dionysiaca* 5.105: 'voiceless voice', 19.156: 'speaking silence', 19.200: 'silence which tells many a tale (*poikilomython*)'.

36. *linguosi digiti*, in Cassiodorus, *Various Letters* 4.51.8; cf. Nonnus, *Dionysiaca* 7.21; Anonymous, in *Latin Anthology*, I.1 [Shackleton Bailey] 100, 10. The dancer's fingers are mentioned (or their expertise praised) in Nonnus, *Dionysiaca* 19.157, 30.111; Leontius Scholasticus, *Greek Anthology* 16.283, 3-4. On well-formed fingers as a requisite of the would-be dancer, see Libanius, *Oration* 64.103.

37. Speaking hands or palms are a common theme in pantomime literature. See, e.g., Nonnus, *Dionysiaca* 5.106; Claudian, *Panegyric on the Consulship of F. Manlius Theodorus* 313; Cassiodorus, *Various Letters* 1.20; *IG* 14.2124, 1.

38. *verba manibus expedire*, in Novatian, *On the Spectacles* 6.4; cf. Anonymous, in *Latin Anthology*, I.1 [Shackleton Bailey] 100, 4, where the pantomime 'promises' to 'project words' (*prodere verba*) with 'skilful hand'.

39. For the pantomime's 'nods' (more generally, gestural signs, signifying gestures), cf. *Greek Anthology*, 9.505, 18; Nonnus, *Dionysiaca* 7.21 (having nods for words), 19.202.

40. It is perhaps for this reason that a third-century AD fragmentary curse tablet found in Syria and targeting a pantomime of the faction of the Blues named Hyperechius instructs the binding of all his body members: 'Bind his neck, his hands, his feet, bind, bind together his ... his sinews, his ... pulse, his ankles, his steps, the bottom of his feet ... his stomachs, his mind, his midriff' (translated text from Gager 1992: 53); see also Robert (1990: 38).

41. See, e.g., Apuleius, *Metamorphoses* 10.32: 'sometimes she would dance (*saltare*) with her eyes alone (*solis oculis*)'; Nonnus, *Dionysiaca* 5.107; a non-furtive look is a requirement for an aspiring dancer, according to Libanius, *Oration* 64.103.

42. Lycinus' exposition has turned the shape-shifting sea-god of *Odyssey* 4 into a dancer.

43. On the pantomime as another Proteus, cf. Libanius, *Oration* 64.117, and Aristaenetus, *Letters* 1.26, 11-12, where a female pantomime is hailed for her ability to slip into manifold shapes, like 'Proteus of Pharus'.

44. See Lada-Richards (forthcoming, a).

45. Pantomime is linked to painting and sculpture in Lucian, *Dance* 35 and the pantomime compared to a painter in Aristaenetus, *Letters* 1.26 (see further Chapter 6§2). The language of the plastic arts (such as 'image', 'picture', 'drawing', 'sketching', 'depicting') applied to pantomime is impressively active in Nonnus: see, most importantly, *Dionysiaca* 5.104-6, 19.201, 210, 216-17, 219. Cf. Lada-Richards (forthcoming, a).

46. Swiftness is also the foremost characteristic of pantomime dancing as refracted in Nonnus' *Dionysiaca*: in book 19, Bacchus' dancing contest (described in the characteristic language of pantomime dancing, especially at 19.200-26) is introduced as 'the contest of nimble feet' (19.139); cf. *Dionysiaca* 7.19, where the dancer moves 'in quick revolutions', and Pollux, *Onomasticon* 4.97, recording that the dancer can be called 'swift-footed'.

47. Cf. John Chrysostom who, despite the virulence of his anti-theatricality, can spare a gasp of admiration for the dancers floating on the *orchêstra*, 'using their limbs as if they were wings' (*PG* 49.195).

48. It cannot be stressed too strongly, however, that what Libanius allows us to glimpse in this passage is not necessarily the average fourth-century AD pantomime of flesh and blood: it is predominantly the dancer as he emerges from an admiring intellectual's pen, coated, as it were, repeatedly with the veneer of an educated man's literary and cultural armoury. See further Lada-Richards (forthcoming, a).

49. For pantomime's reliance on 'imaginary props', conjured up by the dancer's expressive and pictorial gestures and tremendously evocative, despite their lack of materiality, see Lada-Richards (forthcoming, a).

50. Zarrilli (1990: 133; cf. ibid. 132), drawing on practitioners of Eastern dance tradition, such as the Indian *kathakali* or the Japanese *Noh*. Midway between 'embodied' and intellectual performance memory stands Libanius' remark that the apprentice pantomime divides his time between practising and reflecting on what he has been practising: 'for even when he has stopped moving, he must preserve in his soul what has been achieved through his toil' (*Oration* 64.105). For the special importance of learning by means of the body in pantomime dancing, see Ruth Webb's piece in Hall and Wyles (forthcoming).

51. Bethe and Brazell (1990: 177 and 167 respectively).

52. The preliminary appearance of a person introducing the *fabula* to the spectators may also be inferred from Lucian's *Mistaken Critic* 19, where the author's opponent, a former 'second fiddle' to the dancers, is said to have been coming forward to the stage, ahead of anyone else in time, stupendously arrayed, in golden sandals and kingly dress, in order to announce the name of the danced drama or solicit the audience's goodwill. In later times, the notion of a herald brings to mind in the first place the Italian Renaissance practice of having plays 'introduced by a choric figure, the *festaivolo*, often in the character of an angel, who remained on the stage during the action of the play as a mediator between the beholder and the events portrayed' (see Baxandall 1988: 72). Most importantly, it has survived in the practices of eighteenth-century pioneering ballet forms, conceived as direct revivals of the ancient pantomime genre. In the programme notes accompanying such productions, the choreographer (ballet-master) would explain not just the story, but also the precise movements his dancers were about to use in order to express the action and concomitant emotions. So, for example, in the libretto for *The Loves of Mars and Venus* (1717), John Weaver, dancer, ballet-master and pioneering theoretician of the dance (see Postscript), both lists the emotions about to be portrayed and instructs the spectators in the signs that will externalise them: 'This last *Dance* being altogether of the *Pantomimic* kind; it is necessary that the Spectator should know some of the most particular Gestures made use of therein; and what Passions, or Affections, they discover; represent; or express' (text in Ralph 1985: 752). Weaver even proceeds to elucidate the exact relation between choreography and the expressed passions; see, e.g., Ralph (1985: 754): '*Jealousy* will appear by the Arms suspended, or a particular pointing the middle Finger to the Eye; by an irresolute Movement throughout the Scene, and a thoughtfulness of Countenance.'

53. Cf. *On Christian Doctrine* 2.3.4, where it is claimed that the 'pantomimes present certain signs to those in the know (*scientibus*), by means of the movements of all of their limbs': such signs are 'like some kind of visible words (*verba visibilia*)'. Somewhat milder seems the opinion expressed in Augustine's *On Order* 2.11.34, where the pantomime's gestures are said to be 'signs of things' for those 'watching attentively' (*bene spectantibus*).

54. Augustine's comments on pantomime, however, should be seen as inextricably interwoven with his belief in the man-made nature of all signs, which he understands not as naturally inherited but as culturally determined and hence requiring explanation.

55. See, most recently, J. Hall (2004), arguing that the hand gestures recommended in Quintilian's treatise did not form part of 'a complex and artificial system largely alien to the experience of most Romans' (152), but were very much in line with existing gestural practices and habits, all forming part of 'the Roman cultural heritage' (160).

56. It should be stressed, however, that Plotinus' argument forms part of his broader conception of the harmonious cosmic dance, and must be properly appreciated in this light.

57. See Anonymous, in *Latin Anthology*, I.1 [Shackleton Bailey] 100, line 9.

58. Cf. Libanius' memorable image (*Oration* 64.104) of the pantomime's hands and feet following the rest of the body as if they were made of wax.

59. Cf. Hieronymus, *Letter* 43.2, against the pantomime's multiple transitions from Hercules' robustness to Venus' softness to Cybele's quavers.

60. For this meaning of *sympaschein* as 'being affected in common, in correspondence with', see primarily Ps.-Aristotle, *Physiognomics* 805a6-8, 808b12-15.

61. From a negative perspective, see Hieronymus, *Against the Pelagians* 3.12.20-4.

62. See Lada-Richards (2003c: esp. 21-9) for a full discussion.

63. Account of the Countess De Boigne, quoted in Holmström (1967: 114).

64. Contemporary account; quoted in Holmström (1967: 118)

65. For the possibility that William Hamilton did perceive his wife's performances as linked with the idea of ancient pantomime dancing, see Lada-Richards (2003c: 28).

66. The phrase was memorably used by Fantham (1989), with respect to Roman mime.

67. Cf. Procopius, *Panegyric for the Emperor Anastasius* (*PG* 87[3].2815, 16), and Jacob of Serugh, *Homily* 2, on the pantomime as 'bound up upon his breast, in order that he may appear as a woman' (F4r[a]; text in Moss 1935: 104).

68. Cf. *Greek Anthology* 11.253; 16.289.

4. Pantomimes and their Body 'Politic'

1. In very general terms, see Desmond (1993-4), a pioneering article.

2. See Franko (1993) and Washabaugh (1996) respectively.

3. However, the relation of Wigman's dances to fascist Germany was deeply ambivalent and cannot be reduced to a simple formula of collaboration or opposition; see Manning (1993) for a masterful narrative.

4. For the early imperial period, see Jory (1984) and Slater (1994); for riots and theatrical claques in the later Byzantine period, see Browning (1952) and Cameron (1976: esp.193-229); for a sketch of the history of pantomime-related troubles in the first centuries AD, see Cameron (1976: 223-5); Jory (1984); Fantham (1996: 147-8).

5. In Tacitus (*Annals* 4.14.3), for example, we hear that Tiberius considered the dancers as 'fomenters of sedition against the state and of debauchery in private houses'; cf. Dio Cassius, *Roman History* 57.21.3, explaining that pantomimes were expelled from Rome and given no place in which to practise their art in 23 AD, because they 'dishonoured women and instigated partisan discord'.

6. Cf. the funerary inscription (*IG* 14.1683) for a pantomime (or perhaps mime) who boasts of having 'entertained senators, ladies, and kings' (line 5). In Philostratus (*Lives* 589) senators and equestrians are said to belong to the regular audience of pantomime displays.

7. As, e.g., in Pliny the Younger, *Letters* 7.24 (see Chapter 8§1); a wealthy senator, Valerius Asiaticus, kept a private company of pantomimes (*scaenici Asiaticani*) in Gaul (see Lavagne 1986).

8. Private performances for the delectation of élite audiences can also be inferred from Tacitus (*Annals* 1.77.4), where Tiberius is said to have forbidden pantomime performances outside the designated public stages; Augustus brought pantomimes as entertainers at his dinner parties (Suetonius, *The Deified Augustus* 74; Macrobius, *Saturnalia* 2.7.17 refers to Pylades' performance of 'Heracles mad' in Augustus' banqueting hall, shortly after having danced the same role in the theatre); a (travesty of a) dance performance to the accompaniment of flutes and the *scabellum* was given by Caligula to a summoned audience of three consulars (Suetonius, *Life of Caligula* 54.2; cf. Dio Cassius, *Roman History* 59.5).

9. Referring to pantomime's cognate genre, the equally popular mime, the exiled Ovid (*Sorrows* 2.502) brings to the Emperor's attention that 'most of the Senate' are spectators.

10. In Dio Cassius (*Roman History* 57.14.10) we read that Drusus was so friendly with the pantomimes that even the laws passed by Tiberius were not enough to discipline them; pantomimes together with the leaders of their factions (Suetonius, *Life of Tiberius* 37.2) went into exile for 14 years in 23 AD, immediately after Drusus' death.

11. Pliny the Elder, *Natural History* 7.184 refers to two equestrians caught by death while in the embrace of the beautiful pantomime Mysticus (I).

12. On the deliberate self-degradation of imperial élites, attracted by the 'peculiar glamour of infamous professions' (Edwards 1997: 85), see Levick (1983); Barton (1993); Edwards (1997). Restrictions on the public performance of the upper classes had been put in place at least since 38 BC for senators and 22 BC for knights. For the history of such legal measures, see Levick (1983).

13. The text of Tiberius' ban is preserved on a fragmentary inscription from Larinum (South Italy); see Levick (1983).

14. In fact, Jory (1981: 148) argues that the games of Marcellus in 23 BC (rather than 22 BC, the date given by the later chroniclers) were pantomime's official launch-pad. Dio (*Roman History* 55.10.11) refers again to 'knights in the orchestra' in his account of games held in 2 BC.

15. E.g., *CIL* 14.2113, recording the pantomime M. Aurelius Septentrio's admission to the ranks of the *juvenes* of Lanuvium (line 11; see Morel 1969), and an inscription from Leptis Magna in North Africa, where M. Septimius Aurelius Agrippa, freedman of Caracalla, boasts of having been 'received' (*receptus*) among the young men of Milan (see Guey 1952).

16. Maecenas and Bathyllus: see Tacitus, *Annals* 1.54.2. Gaius Caligula and Messalina were captivated by Mnester: Gaius used to kiss the pantomime in the theatre (Suetonius, *Life of Caligula* 55.1; cf. 36.1), while Messalina's passionate affair with Mnester (Dio Cassius, *Roman History* 60.22.4-5, 60.28.3) was a matter of common knowledge even among the enemies (ibid. 60.28.4). Trajan was enamoured of Pylades (II) (Dio Cassius, *Roman History* 68.10.2), while the empress Domitia was inflamed by Paris II (Suetonius, *Life of Domitian* 3.1).

17. Murdered on the emperor Domitian's orders in the middle of the street (Dio Cassius, *Roman History* 67.3.1), exemplifying the dark side of pantomimic superstardom.

18. 'Pelopea' and 'Philomela', most probably meant as titles of pantomime libretti, were among the most popular pantomime roles (e.g., Lucian, *Dance* 43; Apuleius, *Apology* 78; Sidonius Apollinaris, *Poem* 23.278), affording the dancer ample scope for erotic dancing.

19. See Suetonius, *The Deified Augustus* 45.4, on the scourging of the pantomime Hylas in the atrium of his own house, 'with everyone watching', upon the complaint of a praetor.

20. See Suetonius, *Life of Caligula* 11 and 54.1; Dio Cassius, *Roman History* 59.5.5.

21. In the eyes of others, such freedom was the mark of his 'enslavement' to pantomimes and stage folk: 'he was the slave of the dancers', Dio Cassius (*Roman History* 59.5.2) writes.

22. See Horace Walpole's letter to Horace Mann (dated 25 February 1742): Lewis (1955: 343), with Castle (1986: 3).

23. In Macrobius' version (*Saturnalia* 2.7.19), the pantomime offers his political advice more openly still: '*let* them busy themselves with our affairs'.

24. Gaius, for example, faced popular unrest because his wife's infatuation with the pantomime Mnester kept the dancer consistently off stage (Dio Cassius, *Roman History* 60.28.3).

25. To take just one example, Tiberius Iulius Apolaustus, a real sensation in the Hellenised East in the second half of the second century AD, was made a *bouleutês* (councillor) of Magnesia on the Maeander, Athens, Pergamum, Tralles, Laodicea, Miletus, Nicomedia, Nicaea, Caesarea, Nicopolis, Mytilene, Hierocaesarea, Magnesia on Mt Sipylon, Cyme, Thebes, Plataea, Chaeronea and Messene; he had statues erected in his honour at Ephesus, Athens, Pergamum, Magnesia, Laodicea, Miletus, Hierocae-saerea, Thyatira, Corinth, Nicopolis, Patras, Sardis, Messene, Nyssa, Cyme, Thebes and Plataea; see *F.Delphes*, III (i), no. 551, and Robert (1930).

26. Here pantomimes were usually free, as opposed to Rome, where they were usually slaves and freedmen.

27. See, e.g., *ILS* (II.i) 5186 (offering even the title of an augur), 5193, 5194, 5195; *I.Magnesia* 192; *F.Delphes*, III (i), no. 551; *F.Delphes*, III (ii), no. 105; on an inscription from Thyatira (*IGR* 4.1272; cf. *RÉG* 4 (1891) 174, no. 2), the Council honours Paris (III) from its own coffers (lines 3-4); for *proxenia*, see, e.g., *IC* 4.222A (= *IGR* 1.975), line 5 (from Gortyn); for *ateleia* as a reward for Olympic victors, see, e.g., Malalas, *Chronicle* 12.10 (*ou syneteloun ... asynteleis ... aleitourgêta*), with Roueché (1993: 3). See further Robert (1930); Guey (1952); for a translation of some of these texts, see Csapo-Slater (1995: 382).

28. The founder of the genre, the Cilician Pylades (I), was so wealthy by the end of his life that he was able to finance a festival in the capital itself in 2 BC (Dio Cassius, *Roman History* 55.10.11). Writing much later in the first century AD, Seneca refers to female pantomimes getting married with dowries of one million sesterces (*To Helvia, On Consolation* 12.6). A ceiling on pantomimes' salaries as a means of curbing their influence and power was felt necessary at several junctures, while by the sixth century AD pantomimes (no less than charioteers) 'were paid (monthly) salaries direct from public funds' (Cameron 1976: 220, on the evidence of Cassiodorus).

29. For the kinds of festivals in the Roman empire and their importance in urban life, see Price (1984); Spawforth (1989); Mitchell (1990); Roueché (1993: esp. 1-11); van Nijf (2001); in a regional context, see Wörrle (1988).

30. See, e.g., *I.Magnesia* 192 (with Slater 1996: 197-8); *I.Stratonicea*, II (i) 691; *CIL* 12.188: epitaph for the young Septentrio (II), who 'danced and pleased' (*saltavit et placuit*); Dio Cassius, *Roman History* 60.28.5. On the notion of 'being pleasing to', 'satisfying, entertaining the people' as a marker of a successful performance, see Robert (1930: 118).

31. See, e.g., *I.Priene* 113, 63ff. (cf. Chapter 1).

32. The inscription (first published by Wörrle 1988: 4-17; English trans. Mitchell 1990) is the record of the foundation by C. Iulius Demosthenes of a penteteric agonistic festival, and provides for the appearance (from the 19th to the 21st day of the festival) of 'hired performances (*paramisthômata*) that will include mime artists and spectacles (*akroamata*) and displays (*theamata*)'. To the same days are also assigned 'the other spectacles which please (*areskontôn*) the city', first and foremost among which Wörrle (1988: 253) rightly understands the public's 'most beloved' performers, the pantomimes. On the meaning of *akroama* in such contexts as 'spectacle' (private or paid-for by public benefactors, but in either case not of a competitive nature), see Robert (1989: 54); cf. Robert (1930: 116, texts) and Robert (1969: 684). For other explicit references to pantomime dancers as part of the manifold 'pleasures' (*terpseis*) and 'delights' (*athyr-mata*) of imperial festivals, see, e.g., Malalas, *Chronicle* 12.6 or Philo Judaeus, *Against Flaccus*, 85.

33. See *SIG*³ 850, referring to the 'usual course of action for men in public life', individuals who, 'in order to procure for themselves fame on the spot, spend their love of honour (*philotimian*) on shows and distributions and on founding competitions'.

Thus, an official decree from Calindoia (Macedonia) (*SEG* 35 [1985] no. 744; 1 AD) honours as an example for public emulation a local benefactor who provided 'spectacle and entertainment and merriment for the soul' (line 25) in the course of the many public dinners, feasts, and sacrifices he financed at his own expense as an *agonothetês*.

34. Text in Calder and Cormack (1962: no. 492b); see Robert (1930: 116) and Roueché (1993: 2).

35. *I.Stratonicea*, II (i) 691, lines 3-5; cf. *BCH* 5 (1881: 187). It cannot be stressed strongly enough, however, that such demagogic tactics could be equally sneered at by members of the intellectual élites (cf. Chapter 9§3) as 'uncultured and inartistic holds upon the people' (Plutarch, *Moral Essays* 802d), 'harlots' flatteries' (*hetairikais ... kolakeiais*), which can bestow upon the giver only an 'ephemeral and uncertain reputation' (821f), 'with nothing honourable or dignified in it' (823e).

36. Cf. Cicero, *On Moral Duties* 2.57-8; *On Behalf of Murena* 37-40; see, however, the very cautious discussion of Gruen (1992: 183-222).

37. See Menander Rhetor, *Division of Epideictic Speeches* 1.366, 1-367, 8, on the elements that 'add lustre and renown to a festive congregation'.

38. For the distinction, see, e.g., Robert (1982: 709-19); Spawforth (1989); Mitchell (1990); Roueché (1993: 2-5).

39. *IGR* 4.1272; cf. *RÉG* 4 (1891) 174, no. 2.

40. Ostensibly, because it was not deemed distinguished enough to be classed as a 'competitive' (*enagônios*) art (e.g., Lucian, *Dance* 32, wittily turning the argument of lack of prestige on its head), but in reality, as Slater (1994: 124, n. 26) notes, because 'pantomime competitions were known to be dangerous to social order'. In any case, Lucian's remark indicates that at the time of the dialogue's composition, *c.* 162-5 AD, pantomime is still not part of the competitive circus of the Greek East.

41. See Slater (1995) and especially (1996), on *I.Magnesia* 192; despite errors, Robert (1930) was the first to realise the significance of this inscription for the dating of pantomime competitions. And, as Jory (2002: 253) reminds us, the 'catalyst' for the decision to include pantomime into the festival programme in the East must have been Lucius Verus' enthusiasm for the genre and its artists (cf. Julius Capitolinus, *Verus* 8.6-11). In the West, the competitive element played a large part in the development of the genre (and its popularity) almost since its emergence as a separate form of entertainment: *ILS* 5197, from the Augustan period, hails Gaius Theorus as 'victor' against his antagonists in Rome, and there is every reason to believe that, from very early on, pantomime stage-shows took the form of competitions between individual performers, usually vying to outdo each other in the antagonistic performance of the same role (Jory 1984: 64-6). Pantomime contests (carrying a prize of 4000 drachmas for the winner) were at some point part of the programme of the *Sebasta*, the Greek-style games (instituted in honour of Augustus) at Naples (cf. Lucian, *Dance* 32), but precise dating remains hazardous.

42. According to Lucian, pantomime's thematic span does not go beyond the time of 'the Egyptian Cleopatra' (*Dance* 37).

5. Pantomimes and their Body Dangerous

1. See, most recently, Murray and Wilson (2004).

2. Cf. the seminal work of Lonsdale (1993) and Calame (1997).

3. For fascinating forays into these issues, see Edwards (1993) 98-136 and ead. (1997).

4. The entire section of *Saturnalia* 3.14.1-10 is eminently enlightening in this respect.

5. Crato's language is remarkably close to that of the Church Fathers, for whom the play-goer leaves the theatre having received a million wounds (*myria traumata labôn*), from which he actually derives pleasure; see primarily John Chrysostom, *PG* 56.267,

59.333. Like Chrysostom's capricious flock, Lycinus praises his own disease (*Dance* 6), greedy to imbibe an even bigger draught of poison.

6. On the infectious madness of pantomime spectacles, 'maddening' the viewer 'with dancing', see Jacob of Serugh, *Homily* 5 (F 22v[b]; text in Moss 1935: 112); cf. Tertullian, *On the Spectacles* 15-16.

7. John Chrysostom's pronouncement 'where there is dancing, there is the devil' (*PG* 58.491) encapsulates the attitude of the Church towards pantomime and all cognate spectacles.

8. In Tatian's view (*Address to the Greeks* 22.1), 'such a man' is an 'actor of murders, a demonstrator of adultery, a treasure-trove of madness, an educator of sexual perverts'; although Tatian condemns all spectacles, his eye is fixed on pantomime in this passage.

9. Theatre-goers are bound to return to their bedchamber even 'more heavily corrupted' (*corruptiores*) than before (Lactantius, *Divine Institutes* 6.20.31), women especially bearing the brunt of theatre's defiling power (see, e.g., Cyprian, *To Donatus* 8). In Chrysostom's homilies, mimes and pantomimes are firmly interlocked as discourses 'full of lawlessness, monstrous distortions, shameful deeds', adept at fashioning their viewers into adulterers and lawbreakers (see, e.g., *PG* 57.426-7).

10. This is not to say, of course, that Christians do not have additional reasons for condemning pantomimes, such as the perpetuation of idolatry and paganism; the public's exposure to shameful stories concerning the divine; the ignominy of exchanging one's god-fashioned self for a multiplicity of alien masks. See, e.g., Jacob of Serugh, *Homily* 3, F10r[a] (text in Moss 1935: 106), on pantomime as 'a sport which introduces paganism by means of lying stories'; Tertullian, *On the Spectacles* 15, 23, and *passim*; Arnobius, *Against the Gentiles* 4.36; Hieronymus, *Letter* 43.2.

11. The notion of the spectator's utter ruin, defilement, perdition, tolls like a bell throughout Libanius' speech; see, e.g., *Oration* 64.31, 57, 59, 60, 61, 64, 70, 82.

12. See Lada-Richards (2003b: especially 46-54, with bibliography).

13. *Poems* 2.2.8, 93-4 (*PG* 37.1583), where pantomimes are said to be 'men, women, effeminate males, | frankly speaking, neither male nor female'.

14. Gregory of Nazianzus, *Poems* 2.2.8, 95-7 (*PG* 37.1583).

15. See, e.g., Cyprian, *To Donatus* 8 (*enervati corporis*); Lactantius, *Divine Institutes* 6.20.29 (*enervata corpora*); Minucius Felix, *Octavius*, 37.12 (*enervis histrio*). Crucially, the connotations are also sexual, since *nervus*, literally 'sinew', 'tendon', is Latin slang for 'penis', so that *enervare* can also mean 'castrate'; see Adams (1982: 38). In Greek, cf. Libanius' rebuttal of Aristides' accusation that pantomime songs effeminate the soul: 'nor does each theatre-goer who listens [i.e. to the songs] sit there deprived of his manhood (*ekneneurismenos kathêtai*)' (*Oration* 64.92).

16. In the Greek sources, this idea is mostly expressed with compounds of the verb *klaô*, i.e. 'break' or 'break off'. So, for example, in Crato's view, the pantomime is a man 'breaking himself up (*kataklômenôi*) to no avail' (*Dance* 5); for Tatian (*Address to the Greeks* 22.7), he is 'in all kinds of ways broken into two' (*pantoiôs diaklômenon*), while for Gregory of Nazianzus, pantomimes 'break up their nature in tandem with the bending of their limbs' (*melôn lygismois synkataklôntes physin*) (*Poems* 2.2.8, 92: *PG* 37.1583). Cf. Libanius, *Oration* 64.60; Procopius of Gaza, *Panegyric for the Emperor Anastasius* (*PG* 87[3].2815, 16). In Latin writings, *frangere*, 'to break into pieces', 'shatter', is by far the commonest occurrence. See, e.g., Cyprian (*To Donatus* 8), on the most successful dancer being the one who goes into greater lengths in order to 'fragment the man in him into a woman' (*quisque virum in feminam magis fregerit*) (cf. Chapter 10§1); Novatian, *On the Spectacles* 6.6, on the pantomime as a 'man fragmented (*fractus*) with respect to all his limbs'; Hieronymus, *Letter* 43.2, 79.9 (the addressee is warned to shun a *histrio fractus in feminam*); cf. Cyprian, *Letter* 2.2.1, on the pantomime instructor teaching 'in what way the male will be broken up (*frangatur*) into a woman'. We also find the notion of the pantomime as 'twisting' (*distorquens*), 'torturing' his body in unnatural contortions: see, e.g., Novatian, *On the Spectacles* 3.2 ('distorting his body with obscene movements'). Extremely telling for the pantomime's perceived movement vocabulary is also the verb *sinuare*, i.e. 'bend', 'wind', 'move in sinuous curves': see, e.g., *sinuare gestus*, in Ambrosius, *Letters* 1.58.5 (*PL* 16.1179).

17. On *mollitia* as a marker of effeminacy in Roman socio-cultural discourses, see especially Edwards (1993: 63-97 and *passim*).

18. For Ambrosius, for example, the songs 'soften up the mind (*mentem emolliant*) for love' (*PL* 14.157); Aristides (apud Libanius, *Oration* 64.87) condemns pantomime songs as 'of softer texture and harmful with respect to masculinity', and just stops short of accusing the noise produced by the *scabellarii* as capable of instigating softness (ibid., 95).

19. Cf. Hieronymus, *Against the Pelagians* 3.12.24; Ambrosius, *Letters* 1.58.5 (*PL* 16.1179); John Chrysostom, *PG* 57.427 ('youths softening themselves up', *malakizomenoi*) and 58.489; Maximus of Turin, *PL* 57.257. For John Chrysostom (*PG* 59.120), even listening to casual talk about dancers is bound to make someone 'soft' (*malattesthai*).

20. Most interestingly, John Chrysostom uses the simple adjective *malakos*, 'soft', as a shorthand for pantomimes: see, e.g., *PG* 51.211, 62.386.

21. See Corbeill (1996: 137). On the association, see, e.g., Lucian, *On Salaried Posts in Great Houses* 27 and *RE*, s.v. *kinaidos*, cols. 259-61. Cf. the suggestion that the pantomime has been indoctrinated into sexual passivity in order to succeed in his profession (Tertullian, *On the Spectacles* 17). In the broader perspective of imperial and late antique *theatrophobia*, pantomimes (just as much as actors in general: see Edwards 1993, 1997) are *de facto* available 'on the sex market', as prostitutes, *pornoi*: see Aristides, apud Libanius, *Oration* 64.38, 39, 43 (and Libanius' rebuttal, ibid. 40-9).

22. For this use of *mentire* ('counterfeit') in relation to female imitation in pantomime dancing, cf. Lactantius, *Divine Institutes* 6.20.29.

23. See primarily Wüst (1949: cols. 847-9, heavily based on Lucian and Libanius) and Kokolakis (1959: 51-4). Female roles, such as 'the birth-pangs of Leto' (Lucian, *Dance* 38), seem to have required a realistic re-enactment of the female body's gender-specific experiences and motions (cf. Chapter 2§1).

24. Choricius of Gaza, *Oration* 21.1 (p. 248 Foerster-Richsteig).

25. Jacob of Serugh (*Homily* 5, F21v[a] and 22v[b]; text in Moss 1935); cf. Arnobius, *Against the Gentiles* 4.35, on Jupiter's deceptive adulteries enacted on the pantomime stage and on Venus represented in love by means of dancing (*amans saltatur Venus*); Sidonius Apollinaris (*Poem* 23.281-97) talks of Zeus and Europa, Danae, Leda and Ganymede (identical list in Arnobius, *Against the Gentiles* 7.33), as well as Mars and Venus, and Perseus and Andromeda.

26. *poikilê phlox hêdonôn exaptetai*: Gregory of Nazianzus, *Poems* 2.2.8, 107 (*PG* 37.1584); *scintillas libidinum conflabellant*: Tertullian (*On the Spectacles* 25); for Novatian (*On the Spectacles* 6.6), pantomimes are the dancing ground of 'ancient fabled lusts', more precisely 'the fable of Greek lust' (ibid. 3.2).

27. Prudentius (*Crowns of Martyrdom* 10.221) seems to imply that the sexual act itself was performed on the stage, an allegation with which we could compare the scandal created by Nijinsky's final pose in *L'après-midi d'un faune*, interpreted by some critics as the public performance of an indecent sexual act.

28. Procopius of Gaza, *Panegyric for the Emperor Anastasius* (*PG* 87[3].2815, 16); cf. Aristides, *apud* Libanius, *Oration* 64.59; Lactantius, *Divine Institutes* 6.20.30-1 (extending also to the mime*)*.

29. On pantomime songs as 'feminising' (*thêlynonta*) the 'tenor of one's heart' (*kardias tonon*), see Gregory of Nazianzus, *Poems* 2.2.8, 100-1 (*PG* 37.1584).

30. In the context of Ovid's poetry, this is the flame for a girl.

31. The coupling of sexual arousal with perverse sexual passivity is frequent in Christian calumniations of pantomime dancing; see, e.g., Tatian, *Address to the Greeks*, where the pantomime is a demonstrator of adultery (22.15) no less than a teacher of sodomitic pleasures (*kinaidôn paideutên*) (22.12).

32. See Novatian (*On the Spectacles* 6.6), lambasting the pantomime, who frustrates the distinction between male and female, as he does not fully conform with either gender (*nescio quem nec virum nec feminam*); cf. Gregory of Nazianzus, *Oration* 21.12 (*PG* 35.1093), where the pantomime experience is boiled down to the performer's 'triumphal dancing over the spectators with manifold and sexually ambiguous bends and twists (*pantoiois kai androgynois lygismasi)*'.

33. Gregory of Nazianzus, *Poems* 2.2.8, 99 and 98 (*PG* 37.1583-4).

34. See Orgel (1996: 10-30; quote from 29). For cross-cultural comparisons between the gender anxieties haunting the anti-stage polemic of Renaissance England and the polemical discourses against ancient pantomime, see Lada-Richards (2003a: 66-70).

35. For *scopophilia* in ancient erotic narratives, see Morales (2004).

36. See Martial, *Epigrams* 11.13; cf. Jory (1996: 10), on the telling 'Cupido' as a pantomime's name on a medallion from Lyon.

37. Quote from Flaubert (1991: 101-2), a masterful reworking of the biblical episode.

38. For a similar reading of the dynamics between viewer and viewed in pantomime and other dance spectacles condemned by the Church Fathers, see Webb (1997: especially 131-5), a fascinating paper.

39. Cf. Philostratus, *Life of Apollonius* 4.2, on theatre spectators in Ephesus as 'overcome' (*hêttêmenoi*) by pantomime dancers.

40. Simultaneously, however, as we shall see in Chapter 9, élite discourses carefully *constructed* the pantomime's body as lying at the antipodes of manly, respectable deportment.

41. Jules Janin, *Journal des Débats*, March 2, 1840, quoted in Guest (1980: 21). In Rome a pantomime dancer can boast none of the warlike, social or political qualities which are thought to circumscribe the terrain of Roman *virtus*.

6. Emancipating Pantomime

1. Exemplified in the text by Crato.

2. Actors were, of course, perceived as professional artists, especially in view of their belonging to the 'umbrella' performance association of the 'artists (*technitae*) of Dionysus'; dancers, however, were especially vulnerable to the charge of amateurism and, in any case, Lucian's text is the first theoretical exposition of the difficulties, requirements and merits of the actor's art in the Western theatrical tradition.

3. For a very brief discussion, see Postscript.

4. We are not in a position to know whether the authors of all those treatises on dicing, swimming, facial cosmetics, dinner-party manuals, etc., mentioned by Ovid in *Sorrows* 2.471-90, undertook the challenge of legitimising such trifling pastimes.

5. See Zeitlin (2001: 218) and Maffei (1991). Cf. Philostratus the Younger, *Images*, Proem 6, aligning painting with poetry, their kinship being based on their common reliance on *phantasia* (imagination).

6. pp. 261, 13-14 and 268, 30-269, 26 (Kayser). On Philostratus' treatise, see now König (2005: esp. ch. 7).

7. Consider, e.g., Quintilian, *Training* 1.10-11 or Messalla's invocation of grammar and music, mathematics and legal studies no less than 'the subtlety of dialectic [argument and analysis], the practical teachings of ethics, and the changes and causes of natural phenomena' (Tacitus, *Dialogue* 30.4) in his bid to advertise rhetoric as the quintessence of the dignified arts.

8. On the immense social value of *paideia*, see e.g., Morgan (1998), passim. The role of education as a basis for vertical distinctions in society remains unchanged in the centuries that separate Lucian from Libanius. Cf. Lucian's *Dream* 11 and 13. More specifically on the matter of the genre's 'learning', Lucian is not a solitary voice. Polyhymnia, the Muse of pantomime (cf. *Dance* 36), can be referred to as 'full of wisdom', *pansophos* (*Greek Anthology* 9.504, 7), and 'erudite' (*docta*, in Dracontius [fifth century

AD], *Romulea* 10 [Medea] 17). In Libanius (*Oration* 64.112) pantomime is said to provide *didachên*, instruction, in the deeds of old. Cf. *IG* 14.2124, 4, where a pantomime dancer is said to have 'adorned' (*kosmêsas*) the entire stage 'with multifarious lessons (*didachais*)'. Pantomime, especially as performed by its great practitioners and in the urban centres, in front of more demanding audiences steeped in theatrical tradition, must have had an unmistakable degree of polish and sophistication. Even the lowly genre of the mime could many a time exhibit the features of 'sophisticated entertainment' (see Wiseman 1985a: 30) and consequently be accorded its share in *doctrina*, on account of some of its exceptionally gifted practitioners (see McKeown 1979: 72, with references to Aulus Gellius and Seneca).

9. Lucian himself uses it again in his *Portraits* (see especially *Portraits* 16).

10. On polymathy as an essential attribute of the Second Sophistic, see Chapter 7.

11. Nor are they unexpected, of course, as in the Greek cultural tradition dance is a constituent part of *mousikê*, itself under the protection of the Muses, daughters of Zeus and Mnemosyne (Hesiod, *Theogony* 54-71). On Polyhymnia, in particular, as the pantomime Muse, see the sources assembled in Jory (1996: 12, n. 34).

12. Morgan (1998: 251); cf. Kaster (1988) and Cribiore (2001).

13. See, e.g., Pliny the Younger, *Letters* 2.3.3 and Seneca the Elder, *Legal Disputations* 1, Preface 18.

14. On the other hand, there may also be a great deal of 'formulaic', so to speak, material embedded in such comments: in Lucian's *Dream*, for example, it is *Paideia* herself who promises her would-be pupil that 'no past event nor anything that is now meant to happen will escape your notice, but with my aid you will even foresee the future' (*Dream*, 10).

15. Interestingly, Jory (2001: 18) sees a possible 'association with the Muses' reflected in the 'scrolls which appear on a number of appliqué medallions depicting pantomime dancers which have been discovered in the Rhone valley and can be dated to the second century AD'.

16. Cf. Livy's famous formulation in the preface of his Roman history: 'This in particular is healthy and profitable in the knowledge of history, to behold specimens of every sort of example set forth in a conspicuous monument' (*From the Foundation of Rome*, Preface 10; trans. Feldherr 1998: 1); see Feldherr, ibid., 1-12.

17. Of course, we should not forget that, to a very large extent, the preservation and transmission of cultural memory were quintessential functions of dancing in ancient societies: dance is a crucial means in the process of educating and acculturating the young, precisely because of its potential to transmit from one generation to the next the lore of tribal knowledge and the community's key moral, ethical, and religious values (hence the special role of dancing in initiation ceremonies). For the Greek world, see primarily Jeanmaire (1939) and Calame (1997).

18. The association of dancing with rhetoric as an emancipating technique is, from early on, a fixture in European treatises in support of the dance. See, e.g., Arbeau (1967 [1588]: 16), on dancing as 'a kind of mute rhetoric by which the orator, without uttering a word, can make himself understood by his movements and persuade the spectators that he is gallant and worthy to be acclaimed, admired, and loved'. The frequency of the association thickens in the eighteenth century.

19. Cf. Aristaenetus, *Letters* 1.26, where the encomiast wonders whether to address the pantomime as an 'orator' (*rhêtora*, line 7), on the basis that she 'brings speeches to light' (8-9).

20. On *saphêneia*, clarity, as an indispensable ingredient of the pantomime's art, see Lucian, *Dance* 36; on the dancer's *saphêneia* as bypassing the need of verbal mediation, see *Dance* 62, 63, 64. For *saphêneia* (coupled with 'vividness', *enargeia*) in rhetorical theory, see, e.g., Quintilian, *Training* 8.3.62; Hermogenes, *Preliminary Exercises* 10, 'On description' (*RG* 2: p. 16, 32-4); Anonymous, *Art of Rhetoric* (*RG* 1: p. 439, 10-11); Aelius Theon, *Preliminary Exercises* 11, 'On Description' (*RG* 2: p. 119, 27-9).

21. For declamation as a rhetorical genre in the fold of sophistic performances, see Chapters 9§1 and 11.

22. In *Dance* 67 Lycinus stipulates that a pantomime must acquire the mode of operation of the cuttlefish, 'clinging close' to his subject-matter and 'dwelling together with' (*synoikeioun*), i.e. conforming himself to, all the characters in his plots.

23. The claim is merely attributed to someone hazarding extravagant statements.

24. Once purged of its exaggerated claims, Lycinus' bid for an harmonious coexistence of philosophy and dancing is not as preposterous as it might first appear. Not only have philosophers and aestheticians throughout the centuries been systematically concerned with dancing, but scholars have also brought a wide range of philosophical perspectives to bear on their analysis of movement and form in dance. As Sheets-Johnstone (1984: 124) puts it, there is scope for showing 'how we can clarify and deepen our understanding of dance through philosophical inquiry in general'. As far as individual dancers are concerned, the case of Isadora Duncan springs to mind. She was enraptured by Nietzsche's *Zaratustra* (in her own words, 'the seduction of Nietzsche's philosophy ravished my being'), believed she found inspiration for 'movements of pure beauty' in Kant's *Critique of Pure Reason*, and proclaimed as her only dance masters 'Jean Jacques Rousseau (*Émile*), Walt Whitman, and Nietzsche' (see Duncan 1996 [1928] 104, 103 and 62 respectively).

25. It is, however, very doubtful that painting and sculpture could have carried unequivocal authorising power (consider, e.g., Plutarch, *Life of Pericles* 2.1; Seneca, *Letter* 88.18 or Valerius Maximus, *Memorable Deeds and Sayings* 8.14.6). Most interestingly with respect to Lycinus' attitude in *Dance* 35, one should consider Lucian's own *Dream*, inscribing a fully-fledged intellectual denigration of painting's sister art, sculpture, as an entirely brainless and illiberal trade. For an intermediate attitude (*just* consenting to affix sculpture and painting to the list of the solemn and reasoned as opposed to the contemptible, mechanical and base arts), see Galen, *Exhortation to Study the Arts* 14, 39.

26. One is tempted to compare Lucian's *Portraits* 3, where the same kind of compliment is paid to the encomiast's subject, Panthea (mistress of Lucius Verus, the co-emperor). With respect to pantomime, we hear in Libanius (*Oration* 64.116) that even a consummate sculptor would 'yield the first place to the dancers' in a contest of sculptural beauty. Painterly qualities were deemed indispensable in the eighteenth-century 'action ballet', inspired by Noverre's acquaintance with writings on ancient pantomime, in particular Lucian's dialogue (cf. Postscript); see Noverre (1930: 9, and passim); for the eighteenth century's pictorialism in dance, see Lada-Richards (2004b).

27. The cognate verb *diagignôskein* occurs in the context of literary criticism; see, e.g., Philodemus, *On Poems* 1, 193.

28. Noverre (1930: 36) is interesting reading here in comparison to Lucian: 'The *maître de ballet* who ignores the study of music will ill-phrase the melodies and understand neither their spirit nor their character. [...] The ability to select good music is as essential a part of dancing as the choice of words and the art of devising happy phrases is to eloquence'.

29. Such were perhaps the talents of the pantomime honoured by *I.Magnesia* 192, who is said to have excelled in 'tragic rhythmic *poetry*', as opposed to the standard tragic rhythmic 'movement' (*kinêsis*) of similar inscriptions (Chapter 2§2); see Slater (1996: 199), who suggests that the pantomime in question may have orchestrated the music for the songs of the libretto, 'usually the work of a *musicarius* (*ILS* 5252, 5239)'.

30. See Hilgard (1901: 170, lines 8-9).

31. See Sextus Empiricus, *Against the Grammarians* I. 79, the opinion being attributed to Crates of Mallos; ibid., 248, where 'subordinating grammar to literary criticism' is attributed to Crates' pupil, Tauriscus. See further Asmis (1995: 162).

32. Unlikely, but not impossible, if we compare the erudition of one Lucius Crassicius, about whom Suetonius (*On Teachers of Grammar and Rhetoric* 18) records that he was initially an assistant to 'the writers of mimes', then took up the teaching profession, published a famously learned commentary on one of the most sophisticated Hellenistic poems, and finally, after having taught 'many noble students', turned his hand to philosophy (see Wiseman 1985b). No less than the mime genre, which was often targeted to a more cultured, refined public, pantomime may well have attracted some very able minds.

33. On the debate on whether or not such euphonic critics (sometimes simply labelled *hoi kritikoi*) belonged to a self-conscious group or even 'school', see, e.g., Porter (1995); Janko (2000: 120-8).

34. See, e.g., the praise of VIP pantomime Tiberius Iulius Apolaustus for his 'orderly way of life' (*tên tou biou kosmion anastrophên*) alongside his excellence in his *technê* (*F.Delphes* III (i) no. 551, lines 29-30). Possible variants of this formulation include: 'on account of his piety and the modesty of his character'; 'on account of the discreetness of his character'; 'on account of his modesty of character and goodness' (texts in Robert 1930). On a Latin inscription found in Libya, the dead pantomime Vincentius is said to have been 'upright, virtuous... blameless in his dealings with everyone and temperate' (*probus, bonus....* | *per omnis innocens et continens*) (text in Bayet 1967: 441, lines 4-5). Highlighting moral decency becomes vital in the commemorative self-definition of the equally despised mimes (see, e.g., Robert 1969: 681 on a mime from Nicomedia). More generally, it is important to note that in the self-presentation of the 'Artists of Dionysus', the professional guilds of all those involved in theatrical performances from the Hellenistic times onwards, *eusebeia* (piety) played a cardinal role, taking precedence even over professional skill 'in inscriptions recording their activities and praising their virtues' (Lightfoot 2002: 217 and *passim*).

35. For a close examination of all aspects of this paragraph, especially the function of the mirror symbol in aligning pantomime with the prestige of moralising discourse, see Lada-Richards 2005.

36. See primarily Bartsch (2000) and, in a broader cultural context, McCarty (1989); Frontisi-Ducroux and Vernant (1997).

37. See Diogenes Laertius, *Lives and Opinions of Eminent Philosophers* 2.33.

38. For Socrates' admonition, see also Plutarch, *Moral Essays* 141d; Apuleius, *Apology* 15; for Apuleius' defence of the mirror in the philosopher's hands, see *Apology* 13-16.

39. See, e.g., Plato, *Alcibiades* I (esp. 133b); Plutarch, *Moral Essays* 85a-b (good men of the present and the past), *Moral Essays* 14a (advice to look at the life of one's father as at a mirror); Seneca, *On Clemency* 1.1 (Seneca's own treatise on mercy hoping to reveal, as a mirror does, Nero to himself). On Plutarch and mirrors, see Duff (1999: 31-2).

40. Amid a vast literature, see most helpfully (for the Roman world) Mayer (1991); for Plutarch's use of *exempla* in his *Lives*, see Duff (1999: passim).

41. See further Lada-Richards (2005).

42. Of course, Lycinus' line of defence has an excellent Platonic pedigree, insofar as Plato in the *Laws* (book 2) argues for the key role of dancing in the inculcation of moral uprightness in the young.

43. Lycinus' perspective in *Dance* 71 is remarkably similar to that of Solon's Scythian guest, Anacharsis, who claims to be unable to understand what pleasure there can be in watching men striking and pummelling each other, covered in blood and dust (see Lucian, *Anacharsis*, esp. 11).

44. See van Nijf (1999), (2001), (2003), (2004); König (2005).

45. See, however, König's (2005: 51) cautionary note that 'the inculcation of the rhetorical, literary and musical skills which were seen as central to civilized elite identity' was 'never widespread enough or formalized enough to be viewed as the main function of *gymnasion* education, or as the main reason for its prestige', the central place being 'occupied by a combination of athletic and military exercises'.

46. See, e.g., *Dance* 72: 'How then is dancing not a thing full of harmony, sharpening the soul on the one hand while exercising the body on the other.'

47. Some kind of overlap between pantomime and wrestling is indicated by the elusive terms *orchêstopalê* and *orchêstopalarios*, occurring on a handful of inscriptions (see Slater 1990; Stephanis 1988: nos 99, 257, 2471).

48. See *Dance* 78: 'pantomime is not free from competitive gesticulation (*tês enagôniou cheironomias*), but participates in the athletic accomplishments of Hermes and Pollux and Heracles'.

49. See, e.g., Xenophon, *Symposion* 2.19. Plotinus, *Enneads* 5.9.11, directly coupling *orchêsis* and *cheironomia*; see further Sittl (1890: 242 n. 2).

50. See, e.g., the funerary epigram for the pantomime Crispus (Sahin 1975: 294, line 16); cf. Juvenal, *Satire* 6.63; Aristaenetus, *Letters* 1.26.18 (every spectator attempts to become a *cheironomos*). See also Hesychius, s.v. *cheironomos*.

51. For *cheironomia* in the *palaestrae*, see, e.g., Plutarch, *Moral Essays* 747a-b; Dio Chrysostom, *Oration* 32.20.

52. *Kinêsis* (movement), *charis* (grace), *morphê* (beauty), *eurhythmia* (good sense of rhythm), *syntonia* (intensity of exertion), *eutonia* (vigour) apply to both athletics and pantomime dancing; see Robert (1990: 497-506).

53. Philostratus (*Lives* 525) ascribes this comment to the sophist Dionysius of Miletus, allegedly pronounced when he heard his younger rival Polemo declaim.

54. See, e.g., Plato, *Meno* 80a-b; Lucian, *Nigrinus* 35; Apuleius, *Metamorphoses* 3.22.

55. Ubiquitously presented as the standard response to pantomime performances: see, e.g., Choricius, *Oration* 21.1; *Greek Anthology* 7.563, 4. *Thelxiphrôn*, i.e. 'enthralling', is almost a fixture in descriptions of pantomimic gestures (see, e.g., *Greek Anthology* 9.505, 17).

56. See, e.g., Galen, *On the Usefulness of the Parts of the Body* 3.1 (*ekplêttein* and *kêlein* versus *didaskein*); Eratosthenes (apud Strabo, *Geography* 1.1.10, pitting *psychagôgia*, as the aim of poetry, against instruction, *didaskalia*); Sextus Empiricus, *Against the Grammarians* I.297 (truth versus *psychagôgia*/fiction [*pseudos*] in a prose vs. poetry polarity); see further Janko (2000: 147-8). The polarity's inflexibility can best be gauged from Polybius, *Histories* 2.56.11-12, where tragedy's *ekplêxis* and *psychagôgia* are diametrically opposed to history's aim of 'instructing' (*didaxai*) and 'persuading' 'the lovers of knowledge' for their own benefit. Lycinus' pantomime, by contrast, lays claim to all these functions simultaneously.

57. Consider, e.g., Aristophanes, *Acharnians* 658, *Frogs* 687, and the famous 'Aeschylean' bon mot in *Frogs* 1055 that poets are to adults what teachers are to children (cf. *Frogs* 1008-10).

58. Poetry and dance are memorably combined in Plutarch's modification of Simonides' famous saying about poetry and painting: the correct thing, Plutarch argues (in the voice of the philosopher Ammonius), would be to call dancing 'silent poetry' and poetry 'articulate dancing' (*Moral Essays* 748a). In the specific case of pantomime dancing, an *orchêstês* could many a time attract vocabulary associated with poetic composition. In Nonnus, for example, the pantomime is said to 'weave' (*hyphainein*) his figures, just as a poet weaves his songs (*Dionysiaca* 19.202, 263); cf. Montiglio (1999:269 and 274).

59. Homer's text in *Odyssey* 4.220-1 runs thus: 'and immediately into the wine from which they drank she put a drug | grief-removing and assuaging anger and inducing forgetfulness of every sorrow (*kakôn epilêthon hapantôn*)'; Lucian substitutes *lêthedanon* for Homer's *kakôn epilêthon hapantôn*.

60. *Odyssey* 4, however, is not the sole intertext of *Dance* 79. Lycinus' theatre-goer who, while in the throes of grief, departs with a lighter heart, takes us straight into *Theogony* 98-103, Hesiod's famous assertion that the Muse-inspired poet makes a man forget his 'grave thoughts' and 'griefs'.

61. The claim on pantomime's behalf is much more elaborately made in Libanius, *Oration* 64.115.

62. The classic passage here is Gorgias, *Encomion of Helen* 14.

197

63. Interestingly, a diametrically opposite 'legitimising' tactic is adopted in Lucian's spoof *On the Parasite*. There Simon sets out to prove that Parasitic surpasses all the other arts put together by arguing for its complete and utter self-reliance: it is the best because it, alone, needs no other art (*Parasite* 21).

64. Mirrors are the greatest culprits here, emblematic, as they are, of the female world and femininity itself.

65. For a full discussion, see Lada-Richards (forthcoming, b).

7. Lucian's *On the Dance* or The Sophist's Pantomime

1. The literature on the Second Sophistic has been growing apace in the last few decades; very selectively, see the landmark studies and/or collections of Boulanger (1923a); Bowersock (1969) and (1974); Reardon (1971); Bowie (1974) and (1982); Russell (1983); G. Anderson (1989); Gleason (1995); Swain (1996); Schmitz (1997) and (1999); Korenjak (2000); Goldhill (2001); Whitmarsh (2001); for an insightful recent overview of the phenomenon, see Whitmarsh (2005).

2. Cf. Borg (2004a), demonstrating that in depictions of *pepaideumenoi* on Roman sarcophagi of the first centuries AD the all-encompassing nature of the dead man's *paideia* is frequently highlighted by iconographic means, for example, by the suggestive portrayal of the nine Muses next to his own figure.

3. For the social correlatives of *paideia* in this period, see primarily Whitmarsh (2001: 90-130) and summarily Whitmarsh (2005: 13-15).

4. See Isocrates, *Oration* 4.50, asserting that Athens has caused the 'name of Greeks' (*to tôn Hellênôn onoma*) to designate 'those who share our education', rather than simply those whose *genos*, descent, is Greek. In Philostratus' *Lives of the Sophists*, terms of Greekness, such as *hoi Hellênes, to Hellênikon* and similar appellations, designate the *pepaideumenoi*, usually a sophist's own followers; see for references Whitmarsh (2005: 14, n. 35).

5. See Whitmarsh (2001: 27): ' "becoming Greek" meant constructing one's own self-representation through and against the canonical past'.

6. On memory of the past as 'sedimented, or amassed, in the body', see Connerton (1989: 72).

7. See the translated Syrian text in Wright (1882: 35, ch. 46). Cf. Vesterinen (2003: 50): 'Dance can teach the alphabet and further transmit the good, wholesome Greek stories to the audience. Thus the dancer's body serves as a Hellenizing instrument.'

8. Such as, for example, cities on the remote Eastern fringes of the vast Roman administrative province of Asia (roughly equivalent to part of modern Turkey).

9. Cf. Yegül (2000: 148), who notes that 'under the empire even the remote mountain towns of Pisidia and Lycia claimed glorious bonds with glorious founders and old Greece'.

10. See primarily Spawforth and Walker (1985), who argue (ibid.: 81) that 'the league's fastest period of growth ... fell in the years immediately after its foundation'.

11. Woolf (1994: 134); cf. Spawforth and Walker (1985: 82).

12. See Robert (1987: 96ff.), on the genealogies constructed to connect cities in Asia Minor to Argos on the Greek mainland via clever manipulations of Perseus' legends. Genealogists, who also had to beaver away at historical sources, would have had, according to Robert (ibid.: 128), a particularly heavy load in the wake of Hadrian's institution of the Panhellenion. On the manifold challenges involved in the genealogist's task (e.g., the need to tap the hidden corners of obscure mythological traditions in search of useful local variants of panhellenic myths), see Curty (1995: 242-53).

13. *Dance* 34: 'Besides, I expect you to understand and bear in mind this as well, that my present topic is not to offer a genealogical account of the entire phenomenon of dancing ... '

14. See *Dance* 7, a side-reference to those who compose 'the truest genealogies of dancing' (*talêthestata orchêseôs peri genealogountes*); cf. *Dance* 33.

15. Cf. Alcock (2001: 331), on civic genealogies as exemplifying a type of 'promotion by pedigree'.

16. So, for example, the Phrygian city of Cibyra boasts of its inclusion *eis tous Panhellênas* on account of its Greek stock (*dia te to genos Hellênikon on*): *IG* 14.829, lines 10 and 6 (text conveniently in Curty 1995: 204).

17. Interestingly, the Syriac homilist Jacob of Serugh (*Homily* 5, F 21v[b]) also posits 'the beginning of the story of the dancing of the Greeks' in cosmogonic myths: 'They say that the grandfather of their gods was devouring his sons; and as a dragon (swallows) a serpent, so he (sc. Cronus) was swallowing the child of his belly' (English text in Moss 1935: 109-10).

18. These include tragic and comic dancing on the Athenian stage (*Dance* 26).

19. Nevertheless, we must point out that non-Greek places too feature in Lycinus' discussion: India (*Dance* 17), Ethiopia (*Dance* 18), Egypt (*Dance* 19, 59), Italy (*Dance* 55; cf. 20, referring specifically to the *orchêsis* of the Romans), Phoenicia (*Dance* 58): one of Lycinus' ways of proving the respectability of dancing is to impress upon his interlocutor that dancing is a universal practice, knowing no geographical or cultural boundaries.

20. On civic kinship ties, see Curty (1995: esp. 259-63 and passim).

21. Some cities applying for admission thought it safer to claim for themselves Greek origin on the basis of affiliation to more than one cities of mainland Greece. Thus, Phrygian Synnada in Asia Minor claimed to have been founded jointly by Athens and Sparta (Spawforth and Walker 1986: 89), while Cibyra claimed to be a colony of Sparta and *syngenis* (a relative) of Athens (Curty 1995: 204).

22. For the imperial period, cf. Swain (1996: 411) on the great importance of 'tales and deeds of purely local relevance'.

23. Text with French translation in Curty (1995: 13-14) and Robert (1987: 78-80); line 19 of the inscription praises Antiochus' 'perfection in culture' (*tan en paideiai teleiotata*).

24. Starting from premises different from mine, Garelli-François (2004: 117) sees the geographical layout of Lucian's text (*Dance* 38-60) as 'the inversion ... of the Roman territorial conquest, turned into a Greek mythological and cultural conquest' (my translation).

25. See further Alcock (2001: 329), on the Greeks' fascination with their own past in the early imperial period as taking on 'a variety of manifestations, ranging from ... sophistic displays on antique topics, to the use of a pure form of Attic Greek based on classical models, to the giving of hallowed names such as Achilles or Theseus, to the employment of archaic systems of dating or measurement, to the use of old-fashioned styles in inscriptions, to the writing of "guidebooks" (such as Pausanias' *Description of Greece*) which lingered on antiquities, while frequently disregarding more recent monuments'.

8. Pantomime, the Intellectual's Equal?

1. Albeit with some qualifications, as we shall see in Chapter 11.

2. For this notion, see Powell (1969: 245), on the life of nations.

3. For the distinction, see Bourdieu (1984: 483).

4. Such distinctions, however, cannot be hard and fast. For what can we say when a political *and* intellectual player, like Maecenas, becomes enamoured of pantomimes? Or when Horace, Varius and Virgil have great fun at a party which includes lowbrow entertainment, such as 'the dance of the shepherd Cyclops' (see Horace, *Satires* I.5.62-4)? Some were clearly able and willing to appreciate pantomime's own brand of culture and sophistication – such as it was and for what it was. On the intellectual élite's interest in pantomime's cognate genre, the mime, see McKeown's (1979) seminal article.

5. For this notion, albeit in a different context, see B. Anderson (1983: 6).

6. See Bakhtin (1984: 471).

7. The distinction between 'high' and 'popular' culture, as experienced in real life and as presented by élite texts in the post-classical world, is of paramount importance, as the two pictures do not necessarily coincide. As Hunter (2003: 479) warns, 'the opposition itself is, in part at least, the creation of the élite texts themselves'.

8. On 'the gap between the educated and the non-educated' as being 'far more explicit than before' in the period of the Second Sophistic, see Swain (1996: 33). According to Dio Chrysostom, it was the sophists in particular who were 'arrogant' and thought they knew more than other people (*Oration* 6.21). On the pivotal role of *paideia* in constructing or consolidating socio-cultural differences in the same period, see Whitmarsh (2001: 90-130) and, from a variety of different angles, Connolly (2001a) and (2003). More generally, on *paideia* in the first centuries AD in the Eastern part of the empire, see (very selectively) Bowie (1974); G. Anderson (1989); Flinterman (1995); Whitmarsh (1998); for Lucian's own *paideia*, see Bompaire (1958).

9. See Aulus Gellius, *Attic Nights*, Preface 19-20 and cf. Aristophanes, *Frogs* 354ff. On the late antique perception of literary culture as a mystery, accessed by initiation, see Kaster (1988: 16 with n. 7).

10. Judging by the way they are fashioned in both Greek and Roman texts, the idiolects of the *pepaideumenos* and the ordinary man seem as unlikely to meet in their ways of appreciating art as in their ways of enjoying a banquet. For a sweeping and striking look over the areas where the foolish many and the sensible, educated few behave differently, see Dio Chrysostom, *Oration* 32.53-5 (extending over manner of eating, walking, playing, attending the theatre and the games). Similar 'distancing' acts, however, are also performed on the part of the ignorant (see, e.g., Pliny the Younger, *Letters* 9.17.3; Petronius, *Satyricon* 53; Dio Chrysostom, *Oration* 32.7; Lucian, *Dream* 7-8): although in such cases the voice of the 'many' is filtered through the very same élite mentality and texts they purport to repudiate, traces of an 'inverse' intellectual snobbery are patently clear.

11. Libanius' correspondence too offers excellent insights into parents' anxieties over the destructive influence the theatre may have on their youngsters' progress; see, e.g., *Letter* 373.

12. Basil of Caesarea, *PG* 29.80; cf. Cyprian, *To Donatus* 8; Novatian, *On the Spectacles* 6.2.

13. For the Second Sophistic's linguistic link to the classical past, see, among a rapidly growing bibliography, Swain (1996: 17-64); Schmitz (1997: 67-96). For literate education in the wider spectrum of the Hellenistic and Roman worlds, see Morgan (1998).

14. See, however, Horrocks (1997: 81), on the lack of 'consensus as to which "classical" authors could legitimately be appealed to'.

15. See, most notably, Galen, who, motivated by professional anxiety over athleticism's encroachment on his own medical practice, considers the soul of any young man who engages in one of the arts mastered 'through corporeal effort' 'brutish and bestial' (*Exhortation to Study the Arts*, 14.39); cf. *Exhortation* 11.27, on athletes as 'unable to perceive anything with any accuracy and mindless like the irrational animals'.

16. A most impressive passage in this vein is Seneca's letter to his friend Lucilius, advising him to return quickly 'from the body to the mind', since excessive labouring over physical exercises 'drains the brain and renders it ill-adapted for mental effort and the more severe studies' (see *Letter* 15.2-5; cf. Gleason 1995: 111). Cf. Seneca, *Letter* 80.2 and Quintilian, *Training* 1.11.15). For the Christian tradition, fundamentally hostile to the body, see, e.g., Basil of Caesarea, *To Young Men, on How they Might Derive Profit from Pagan Literature* 16 and 12. On Seneca and Galen's attitudes to athleticism, see now König (2005).

17. On the notion of 'mental gymnastics' or 'gymnastics of the soul' as a metaphor for literate educational practices in antiquity, see primarily Cribiore (2001) passim. The metaphor goes back to Plato, *Republic* 498b.

18. Text on a second-century AD ostrakon from Oxyrhynchus: see Henrichs (1967: 45-6).

19. See *Dance* 6 on pantomime as 'exercising' the soul of its viewers by means of 'the most beautiful sights'.

20. Hunter (2002: 190-1); only Menander succeeded in crossing the threshold from drama to literature and hence became 'fully appropriated into élite *literary* culture' (see Hunter 2002: 194). See further, Chapter 9§3.

21. Habinek (1998: 107), on the other hand, attaches greater importance to the reciting poet's invocation of a *performance* medium in order to publicise his work to a group of carefully targeted and potentially influential listeners.

22. See, e.g., Bowie (1974) and (1991: esp. 198-9).

23. Cf. Horrocks (1997: 81); Whitmarsh (2001: 272), on Attic Greek as 'the *lingua franca* of the educated elites, the common cultural store which bound them together and excluded the lower classes'.

24. See E. Hall's fascinating paper (1999b): quotes from 336 and 337.

25. See Webb (2001: 307), on the engagement with 'the narrative content of epic and tragedy' required by the *progymnasmata*: 'This kind of knowledge would not necessarily have been the exclusive preserve of the educated elite since this mythological *koinê* was still represented on the stage and in the visual arts.'

9. A 'Margin of Mess'

1. Thus, inevitably, here, the majority of my sources come from the Latin-speaking part of the empire.

2. Cf. the way Philostratus introduces the preoccupations of the period he names 'the Second' Sophistic: *Lives* 481.

3. Bibliography on sophistic declamations in the East of the empire is substantial; see, most importantly, Reardon (1971: 104-13); Russell (1983); G. Anderson (1989: 89-99); Schmitz (1997: especially 110-27); rich material can now be found in Whitmarsh (2005), with up-to-date bibliography. On declamatory themes from myth and especially history (predominantly related to the period from the Persian wars to Alexander the Great), see, e.g., Kennedy (1974: 19-20); Bowie (1974: 170-3); Swain (1996: 93-7); Schmitz (1999). Exceptionally, Swain (ibid.: 93, n. 72) comments on the common elements between pantomime and performance rhetoric with respect to their shared mythological and historical themes.

4. See Hermogenes, *Preliminary Exercises* 9, 'On Characterisation'; Aelius Theon, *Preliminary Exercises* 10, 'On Personification'; ancient texts can be found in the second volume of Spengel, *RG* (pp. 15-16 and 115-18 respectively), translations in Kennedy (2003).

5. See Russell (1983: 82): 'These men were actors: one day Persian kings ... the next day solemn Spartans, misanthropic peasants or crippled veterans', and cf. Pernot (2000: 200). Reardon (1971: 107 and n. 32), for whom the *meletai* (declamations) were 'real theatrical pieces' ('véritables pièces de théâtre'), sees the sophists renowned, as actors are, for their impersonation of particular favourite roles. On the theatricality of sophistic performance, see further Chapter 11, especially §3-4.

6. Cf. Russell (1983: 14). On the same phenomenon in the preliminary rhetorical exercises of 'characterisation', cf. Cribiore (2001: 228).

7. Cf. Russell (1983: 83).

8. See, e.g., Webb (2001), on myth in the *progymnasmata*.

9. On the severe mental toil such exercises required, see, e.g, Cribiore (2001: 228-9).

10. See the fascinating insights of Morgan (1998) and Cribiore (2001).

11. Among a vast number of interesting passages, see, indicatively, the caveats in Quintilian, *Training* 1.11.3, 11.3.181, 184; Cicero, *Orator* 18.59.

12. Cf. Richlin (1997: 100) and Gleason (1995: 116): 'The trick is to learn from actors without seeming to have done so.' On the uneasy boundary between oratory and the stage, see further Gleason (1995), especially ch. 5; Connolly (1998); Gunderson (1998) and (2000: especially ch. 4).

13. As exemplified in the attitude of Lucius Torquatus in Aulus Gellius' narrativised discussion (see below) of rhetorical boundaries (*Attic Nights* 1.5); cf. Quintilian, *Training* 1.11.16.

14. Cf. the demarcation of the orator's ground in the anonymous *Rhetoric for Herennius* (3.26) as lying between the elegance (*venustas*) of actors and the baseness (*turpitudo*) of day labourers. On the delicate balancing act, as negotiated by segments of the performing élite, see Chapter 11.

15. Cf. Cicero, *On the Orator* 3.220, quoted by Quintilian himself in *Training* 1.11.18. Among the many discussions of this passage, see Gleason (1995: 116-17). On *cheironomia* and dancing, cf. Lucian, *Dance* 78 and Chapter 6§4.

16. Even so, in Chapter 11 we shall meet a special VIP league of élite declaimers of the first centuries AD, especially in the Eastern half of the empire, who *did* 'cross over' into the realm of the theatrical, mostly to their advantage.

17. On the notions of 'dissolution' and 'softness' in association with hostile constructions of pantomime dancing, see Chapter 5§1.

18. Aulus Gellius, *Attic Nights* 1.5.2; Cicero, *Brutus* 303.

19. For the uncertainty of the equation *saltatrix* : female dancer/pantomime, see Webb (2002a: esp. 284-7), although Dionysia's period of fame (*c.* 76-62 BC; see Garton 1972: 249) antedates the formal emergence of the pantomime genre in Rome (see Chapter 1). Among the many discussions of Aulus Gellius' story, see Edwards (1993: 97) and Gunderson (2000: 127-32). In Valerius Maximus' version (*Memorable Deeds and Sayings* 8.10.2), Hortensius is said to have laboured more on the grace of bodily movement than verbal eloquence itself, to the extent that people were more attracted by the sight of him than what he had to say, while actors of Aesopus' and Roscius' standing adapted his forensic gestures to their own stage action.

20. On this much discussed Senecan passage, see (very selectively) Edwards (1993: 82); Gleason (1995: 109); Corbeill (1997: 115).

21. See, e.g., Quintilian, *Training* 11.3.89, legislating that 'the orator must be as far removed from the dancer as possible (*abesse ... plurimum a saltatore debet orator*)' and that the type of gestures appropriate to stage-mimicry must be 'kept at the farthest distance in pleading' (*Training* 11.3.88).

22. The requirement that the orator's (and every real man's) neck be straight is ubiquitous in Greek and Latin sources; on the orator, see, e.g., Quintilian, *Training* 11.3.82.

23. Even the rhetorical models of the good speaker can be conveyed in bodily terms: see, e.g., Lucian's comparison of good speeches to well-sculpted bodies, 'compressed and full of sinews and hard, their contours hewn with exact precision' (*Professor* 9).

24. Seneca, *Letter* 114.1; cf. Quintilian, *Training*11.1.30.

25. See, e.g., Tacitus, *Dialogue* 39.2; Seneca, *Letter* 114.1; Seneca the Elder, *Advisory Speeches* 7.12, 2.23. On the connotations of effeminacy accompanying the words 'broken'/'break' (*fractus, infractus, frangere*; Greek *keklasmenos*) in ancient rhetorical criticism, see Gleason (1995: 112).

26. See, e.g., Seneca the Elder, *Legal Disputations* 2, Preface 1.

27. See, e.g., Seneca, *Letter* 114.4; Anonymous, *Rhetoric for Herennius* 4.11.16.

28. See, e.g., Quintilian, *Training* 4.2.39, on orators who 'behave wantonly' (*lasciviunt*) in theme, words, composition and corporeal mannerisms alike; cf. Seneca, *Letter* 114.2, on the 'wantonness' (*lascivia*) of public orations. In Quintilian (*Training* 2.5.10) bad speeches can be full of 'lascivious, effeminate' expressions.

29. See, e.g., Anonymous, *Rhetoric for Herennius* 4.11.16, on the style that is 'without sinews and joints' (*sine nervis et articulis*), 'flowing hither and thither' (*fluctuat huc et illuc*), and unable to proceed with sufficient virility.

30. However, the disquieting partnership of pantomimic and rhetorical style antedates pantomime's meteoric rise. For example, some of the pantomime's most frequently lambasted bodily sins are matched by Cicero's perceived offences of style – according to his detractors, Cicero was 'loose and sinewless' (*solutum et enervem*, a criticism attributed to Calvus) or, in Brutus' words, 'broken and loose in the loins' (*fractum atque elumbem*) (Tacitus, *Dialogue* 18.4-5). Cf. Richlin (1997: 107). In Quintilian's version (*Training* 12.10.12), contemporary criticism saw Cicero as 'broken (*fractum*) in his composition' and 'almost ... softer (*molliorem*) than a man'.

31. Cf. Tacitus, *Dialogue* 26.2-3, quoted above.

32. According to Joy Connolly's influential work (cf. Chapter 11, esp. §3), Greek-speaking sophists 'reclaim the theatrical aspects of rhetoric which Roman rhetoricians are so eager to disavow and demonize': see Connolly (2001a: 92).

33. See Gunderson (2000: 133), who understands the orator's body as 'set against other, unauthorized bodies'. The orator achieves 'self-recognition in contradistinction to a constitutive outside, the actor. The actor inhabits the illegitimate body the handbook discovers for its student', so that 'Without the theatrical, there would be no boundary by which to compass the authorized delivery.'

34. For a similar discussion of performative patterns of the post-classical world on both sides of the Mediterranean basin, see Lada-Richards (2004a: 66-72), where some of the ideas contained in this section were first aired.

35. A glimpse of the variety of performances on offer can be gained from, e.g., Athenaeus, *Sophists at Dinner*19a-20b (jugglers, conjurers, marionette-players), 620b-21c; Plutarch, *Life of Lycurgus* 19.2 (jugglers swallowing swords on the stage), *Moral Essays* 673b, 711b-13f; Dio Chrysostom, *Oration* 8.9, 27.5; Manilius, *Matters of Astronomy* 5.438ff.; Petronius, *Satyricon* 53; Apuleius, *Metamorphoses* 1.4 (acrobats and street performers); Sidonius Apollinaris, *Poem* 23.300-3 (female players of the *kithara*, flute-players, mimes, rope-dancers, clowns); Arnobius, *Against the Gentiles* 2.38 (pantomimes, mimes, actors, singers, trumpeters, flute- and reed-players, those who jump from one horse's back to another's [*desultores*], walkers on stilts, rope-dancers, jugglers); John Chrysostom, *PG* 49.195 (pantomimes, jugglers, rope-dancers, performers of acrobatics with the aid of a long pole); cf. Nicoll (1931: 84-5) and Jones (1991: 185-98), where some of these passages are discussed. For pantomime's possible cross-pollination with such lowbrow entertainments, cf. Chapter 2§1.

36. As can be seen most dramatically in the contest between rhetoric and poetry 'staged' in Tacitus' *Dialogue*.

37. See Bourdieu (1984: 56): 'Tastes (i.e. manifested preferences) are the practical affirmation of an inevitable difference. It is no accident that, when they have to be justified, they are asserted purely negatively, by the refusal of other tastes. In matters of taste, more than anywhere else, all determination is negation; and tastes are perhaps first and foremost distastes, disgust provoked by horror or visceral intolerance ('sick-making') of the tastes of others.'

38. Plutarch, *Moral Essays* 712e, on a type of mime called *paignion*, on which see Davidson (2000).

39. See Bourdieu (1984: 61); cf. Levine (1988: 234) on twentieth-century American culture: 'The cultural fare that was actively and regularly shared by all segments of the population belonged *ipso facto* to the lower rungs of the cultural hierarchy.'

40. See Horace, *Art of Poetry* (*Letters* 2.3) 185-8; the stories spurned by Horace here are among the pantomime subjects mentioned by Lucian (*Dance* 40, 41, 43). Cf. Chapter 2§2.

41. Cf. Seneca, *Letter* 29.12, where the crowd's cheering and clapping are sneeringly dismissed as *pantomimica ornamenta*, i.e. trappings of distinction that befit only pantomime dancers; for the paradigmatic value of such applause, cf. Claudian, *Against Eutropius* 2.402-5.

42. On Aristides' concomitant twinning of transgressive élite orators with pantomime dancers, see Chapter 11§4.

43. As opposed to that portion of the soul that is animalistic and grass-fed and can neither understand nor respond to reason; see Plutarch, *Moral Essays* 713b-c.

44. Meaning, waste away their strength almost to the point of death.

45. See Juvenal, *Satire* 11.162-82; Pliny the Younger, *Letters* 9.17, discussed briefly by Hunter (2002: 195-6). Cf. Pliny the Younger, *Letters* 1.15.2-3, where a modest dinner with a comic play or a reader or a singer is considered as far superior to a lavish dinner with Spanish dancing girls, and Pliny, *Letters* 3.1.9, where the performance of comedy between dinner courses is said to add to the pleasures of the table 'a seasoning of letters'. In *Letters* 9.6, Pliny takes care to distance himself and his literary work from the idleness of the crowds watching the races, and feels proud that their pleasure (*voluptas*) is not identical to his (esp. 3-4). For the Republican period, see, e.g., Cicero, *Letters to his Friends* 205.2 (annoyance at having to sit through mimes, without having anyone to share a laugh with '*docte*', in a sophisticated way).

46. See Horace, *Letters* 2.1.182-207 and cf. Habinek (1998: 98). On the nature of Terence's equally famous pitting of rope-dancers, boxers and gladiators against his own drama's intellectual superiority, see Lada-Richards 2004a.

47. Menander, in particular, was the author who made the most spectacular leap from a downgraded performative world to that of the upper-class dinner party and of élite reading culture. As Hunter (2002: 194) writes, 'Menander had been fully appropriated into élite *literary* culture; drama has become literature'. See, in particular, Plutarch, *Moral Essays* 712b-d, and 854a-c, where it is claimed that a play of Menander is fully worth the *pepaideumenos*' visit to the theatre. To quote Hunter (2000: 272) again, Menander stands for the poet 'of civilised (i.e. élite) good order'.

48. On derivative (and spurned) dramatic forms, such as varieties of para-tragedy (*hilarôidia*) and para-comedy (*magôidia*), 'perceived as a "perversion" of classical drama' (Hunter 2002: 197), see, e.g., Athenaeus, *Sophists at Dinner* 621c-d (with Hunter 1995: 162 and Hunter 2002: 196-7) and Strabo, *Geography* 14.1.41 (with Hunter 2002: 196). From an élite perspective, the performances of *hilarôidoi*, *simôidoi*, *magôidoi* and *lysiôidoi* (the precise meaning of each term is uncertain; cf. Chapter 2§1) were 'seen as debasements of "high", educative texts' (Hunter 2002: 196). At the heart of the élite attitude lies the perception that 'parodic and parasitic forms such as "mimes" and farces which exploited material drawn from "higher" genres such as tragedy and New Comedy confused the proper *order* of things' (Hunter 2000: 275).

10. Dancing on the Brink

1. See Chapter 9.

2. The case of Diaghilev's 'Ballets Russes' is certainly a telling example; see very briefly Lada-Richards (2003a: 25).

3. Lucan wrote 14 pantomime libretti (*salticae fabulae*), according to the so-called 'Vacca' life. For Statius, see Juvenal, *Satire* 7.86-7.

4. Ovid, who tells us that top rates are commanded by the composers of obscene mimes, reminds Augustus that his own poems 'have often been danced in public' (*et mea sunt populo saltata poemata saepe*), and have beguiled Augustus' eyes (*Sorrows* 2.509-14 and 519-20). We would have been justified in thinking that Ovid himself wrote pantomime libretti, but in *Sorrows* 5.7b.25-8, all the while testifying once again to the pantomimic dancing of his verses (*carmina ... saltari nostra*) to wild applause and in packed theatres (*pleno ... theatro*), Ovid claims never to have written anything for the (popular) stage (*nil equidem feci ... theatris*). This probably means that Ovid's poems lent themselves to easy adaptation (by professional librettists?) for the pantomime stage, just as we know Virgil's poems did (see Suetonius, *Life of Nero* 54, on the emperor's vow to dance publicly 'Virgil's Turnus'; cf. Macrobius, *Saturnalia*, 5.17.5, on the endless pantomimic adaptations of the Dido and Aeneas episode). Which particular parts of Ovid's verses were reworked for the pantomime stage we cannot know for sure (see Luck 1977:

307), but the *Heroides* with their heavily erotic material are prime suspects (Luck 1977: 307 and 153; cf. Owen 1924: 271), while, of course, the mythological substratum of his *Metamorphoses* coincides very neatly with the range of material described in *On the Dance*.

5. Thus Seneca the Elder (*Advisory Speeches* 2.19), on the shadowy figure of Silo, introduced as a composer of pantomime libretti (*qui pantomimis fabulas scripsit*). Crinagoras (*Greek Anthology* 9.542) mentions with admiration a composer of libretti called Philonides. Even a high dignitary could be writing songs for pantomime dancers: see Libanius, *Oration* 33.3, on Tisamenus, governor of Syria (needless to say, such a preoccupation is a godsend to his enemies). Similar is the situation with respect to mime composition: mimographers could be men of learning (cf. Suetonius' story regarding L. Crassicius; see Chapter 6 n. 32) and/or high rank, like the knight D. Laberius (see Wiseman 1985a: 187), but their compositions were performed by actors belonging to a different social class.

6. Some kind of prostitution is implied in Juvenal's *Satire* 7.87, where it is claimed that Statius will starve 'unless he sells' his 'untouched *Agave*' (*intactam Agaven*) to VIP pantomime Paris: here *intactam* means both 'previously unperformed' but also sexually pure, 'virginal'. See Courtney (1980: 360) and Braund (1988: 60).

7. See Jory (1996: 10) and cf. Jory's contribution in Hall and Wyles (forthcoming).

8. So Cassius Severus in Seneca the Elder, *Legal Disputations* 3, Preface 10.

9. Ambivalent social positioning was the hallmark of pantomime's sibling art, the mime. Although the genre was extremely fashionable and its performers could reach the heights of success, an association with mime actors and (especially) actresses/dancers was a trusted weapon for the defamation of an enemy, as Cicero's campaign against Verres, Catiline, Clodius and Antony could testify (see Sutton 1984). John Chrysostom has both mimes and pantomimes in mind when he protests that the crowds welcome such people into the city 'like ambassadors or generals', but allow their real *infamia* to shine through when they do not tolerate being seen walking next to them in everyday life (*PG* 57.425).

10. This appears all the more interesting, once we take into account the 'real' Lucian's possible experiences: brought up in Syria, a pantomime's paradise, to parents outside the intellectual élite (see Chapter 12), Lucian must have come into contact with the art early on in his youth. Indeed, he must have come across a pantomime version even more fleshly, carnal, exotic and salacious than the one performed in the great urban centres of the Hellenised Asia Minor or in Rome, and may well have experienced at first hand (and liked?) the libidinous chemistry of a performance.

11. See Dio Chrysostom, *Oration* 32.55; cf. Aristaenetus, *Letters* 1.26, 13-18; in a similar vein, Libanius enthuses that a pantomime's leaps can spur the lazy and the elderly to imitation, overcoming both laziness and age (*Oration* 64.117). In any case, one wonders whether Lycinus' depiction of an audience as leaping and shouting and flinging their garments about (*Dance* 83) at a performance of 'Ajax mad' gone awry gives a more accurate impression of the nature of pantomime theatre-response than other sections of the dialogue.

12. In modern psychological terms, what Tatian, Aristaenetus and others describe with respect to pantomime viewing is the condition often referred to as 'motor mimicry', a 'primitive' form of empathy, whereby the observer of an action carried out, or a corporeal position adopted by another person, responds, almost by reflex, as if he were physically *in* the other's place: 'When we see a stroke aimed, and just ready to fall upon the leg or arm of another person, we naturally shrink and draw back on our leg or our own arm' (Adam Smith, *The Theory of Moral Sentiments*, quoted in Bavelas et al., 1987: 317). For Greek examples, cf. Plato, *Charmides* 169c; Homer, *Iliad* 4.148-50. The Greek term denoting the viewer's emotional response as entirely *congruent* with the observed agent's feelings and condition is *sympatheia* (see further Lada-Richards 1993).

13. See especially *Dance* 63-4, and the explicit statement in *Dance* 62 that the

205

pantomime's subject-matter becomes manifest 'without the need of any interpreter' (*mêdenos exêgêtou deomenon*).

14. Cf. Athenaeus' assertion (*Sophists at Dinner* 20d) that the dancing of Apolaustus Memphius expressed the tenets of Pythagorean philosophy far better than any words could (cf. Chapter 6§2 and Chapter 11§2).

15. Non-verbal erotic summoning linked with dancing can be found, e.g., in Apuleius' *Metamorphoses* 10.32, a most evocative description of Venus' silent promises to Paris in a quasi-pantomime rendition of the 'Judgement of Paris' legend (cf. Chapter 3§2).

16. The same monkey story in two different guises is told in *The Dead Come Back to Life* 36 and *Apology* 5.

17. Cf. Zeitlin (2001: 230), on the 'metaliterary atmosphere' of this dialogue's companion piece entitled *In Defence of the Portraits*.

18. Panthea was the sophisticated courtesan from Smyrna, mistress of Lucius Verus.

19. Crato, for example, expects to hear from Lycinus *lêron tina*, a load of rubbish (*Dance* 6).

20. See Pease (1926); Burgess (1987: 157-66); Pernot (1993: 532-46).

21. Think, e.g., of pantomime as the spectacle that brings together instrumental music, song and dance (*Dance* 68); the emphasis on rhythm and harmony (6, 81, 72); the importance of the dancer's hands as a communicative channel independent of speech (63); the primacy of somatic transformation as well as overall versatility (67), turning the dancer into the human analogue of the legendary Proteus (19); the single dancer's dancing of all of the libretto's roles, male and female (63, 67), at the drop of a mask (66); the sheer beauty of the dancer's attire and mask, which, in contrast to spoken drama, has its mouth closed (29); the beauty of the singers' voices (63); the importance of clarity (*saphêneia*) (36, 62) in the dancer's gestures; the importance of impersonation and acting (*hypokrisis*) in the dancer's art (65), conceived as a display of *êthos* and *pathos* (35, 67), as well as the mimetic demonstration of the plot (62, 67); pantomime's mythical repertoire and its affinity with tragedy (31); pantomime's favourite topics (37-61), including the emphasis on love and transformation in its plots; pantomime's affinity with athletic exercises (71) and its links with the plastic arts (35); the difficulty of pantomime training (35) and the demands on the physical build of the dancer (75, 77-8); the antiquity of pantomime and its gradual progression to the kind of entertainment it was in Lucian's time (7, 34). Even Crato's prejudices against the genre, are, as we saw in Chapter 5, good reflections of anti-pantomime mentality as expressed in other sources.

22. A common encomiastic tactic; see, e.g., Aelius Theon, *Preliminary Exercises* 8, 'On encomium and invective' (*RG* 2: p. 112, 8-10); Menander Rhetor, *Division of Epideictic Speeches* 1.356, 19-20 and 2.370,30-2.371,3.

23. It is highly conceivable that Lucian's intended audience was the city of Syrian Antioch (elegantly complimented on its perspicaciousness on pantomime matters in *Dance* 76) at the height of pantomime's popularity in the region, officially sanctioned by the *pantomania* of the co-emperor, Lucius Verus, resident at the time in Antioch itself (see further Chapter 12§2); possible addressees of a more select kind would have been the court of Lucius Verus, although there is no precise evidence for Lucian's direct association with Verus' intimate milieu.

11. Who is Afraid of Pantomime Dancers?

1. The question of how to distinguish between 'sophists', 'philosophers', and 'orators' was notoriously murky ground in the first centuries AD (see, e.g., Stanton 1973). Although terminological distinctions have no bearing on my argument here, I use the term 'sophist' primarily in order to refer to the mega-stars in the élite performance circus, those public lecturers blessed with fame, money, honours and students.

2. *Oration* 8.9 (on the motley crowds at the *panêgyris* for the Isthmian games); cf.

Oration 12.5 (on orators, writers of verse and prose and sophists at the Olympic festival); *Oration* 27.5 (on the great national *panêgyreis*, where one can find tradespeople and displayers of their arts and crafts alongside reciters of epic and tragic poetry or prose); cf. *Oration* 20.10 (on the medley of flute-players, dancers, jugglers, singers and story-tellers in the Hippodrome). On festive assemblies in the imperial East, see van Nijf (1997: ch. 3).

3. And an exact contemporary of Galen, Lucian and Aelius Aristides, active primarily in the East. See Sandy (1997); Harrison (2000: 1-10).

4. Philostratus' *Lives of the Sophists* is full of examples of fabulous rewards reaped by sophists on account of their talent. For wonderful satire of worldly success via sophistry as a profession, see Lucian, *Dream*, esp. 11-13: interestingly, the trappings of the sophist's success (being the object of everyone's envy, being honoured by those prominent in ancestry and wealth, etc.) would also have applied to VIP dancers.

5. On sophistic rivalries, see, e.g., Bowersock (1969: 89-100) and G. Anderson (1989: 90-2), drawing upon Philostratus' *Lives*. More fundamentally on the agonistic nature of the Second Sophistic, see Gleason (1995); Whitmarsh (2001).

6. On the competitive element entrenched in the genre from its earliest days, see Chapters 1§1 and 4 §1 and §2; the flip-side of one dancer's spectacular success was his antagonist's humiliation.

7. The 'zero-sum' *êthos* does not escape Lucian's satirical eye. Boasting of his success, the teacher of new-fangled rhetoric positions himself with regard to his rivals: 'the fullness of my voice eclipses theirs just as much as the sound of a trumpet drowns that of flutes and the buzz of cicadas prevails over bees and choruses overshadow their leaders' (*Professor* 13).

8. Sophists would often perform in theatres, the pantomime's kingdom, and pantomimes in *odeia*, smaller buildings more congenial to activities such as poetic recitations; on the sophist's venues, see Russell (1983: 75-7); G. Anderson (1989: 90-2); Korenjak (2000: 27-33).

9. Dio Chrysostom (*Oration* 32.22 and passim) refers in vivid colours to the intimidating tumult, derisory laughter, anger, hissing and scoffing of crowds listening to oratorical displays, while Philostratus records several stories of sophistic failure; note, e.g., Philagrus' humiliation by Herodes' pupils in the theatre of Agrippa in Athens (*Lives* 579) and Heraclides' breaking down, in mid-speech, in front of the emperor Severus (*Lives* 614).

10. The haughty (and often pretend) literary connoisseur, whose dearest ambition is to 'dissect' each speaker anatomically, is a fixture in the writings of this period; see, e.g., Lucian's satirical advice on how to criticise the speaker most effectively (*Professor* 22), and cf. Plutarch's attempt at dissuading young men from the habit of scrutinising all of the speaker's little slips, his every word and action (*Moral Essays* 45e).

11. As Libanius (*Oration* 64.57) puts it, pantomime viewers scrutinise the position of the dancer's feet, the pathways traced by his hands, the harmony of his gestures, and the general elegance of the entire performance.

12. From the *Humorist's Magazine* (n. d.), quoted in West (1991: 9).

13. Yet whereas the pleasure a pantomime connoisseur derives from examining the dancer's mobile architecture is devoid of personal gain, the listener who puts the speaker on the grid in the course of a sophistic declamation does so in order to turn the limelight on himself. As becomes obvious many a time in the writers of this period, it is only through the vivisection of his victim that the listener succeeds in staging his own rival performance.

14. See, e.g., Apuleius, *Flowery Excerpts* 9.5. On sophistic performances as 'crises', see Schmitz (1999: 81).

15. Most interestingly, Lucian compares the perils of oratorical fame (albeit the fame gained via the traditional route of 'manly' and erudite rhetoric) to the perils of rope-dancing: like the rope-dancer, the élite declaimer must not make the slightest faux-pas or set a foot out of the prescribed line or let his body-weight sway more than necessary on either side (*Professor* 9).

16. In Lucian's work, cf. *Heracles* 7, where an audience's power over the public lecturer is compared to a large jury's power over the defendant in a court of justice.

17. That is, of course, allowing for some degree of rhetorical exaggeration.

18. This may well have been L. Aurelius Apolaustus V Memphius (senior), whom Verus brought with him from Syria to Rome. See Julius Capitolinus, *Verus* 8.10-11 and Leppin (1992: 208).

19. For the notion of 'deep play', see Geertz's celebrated anthropological piece entitled 'Deep Play: Notes on the Balinese Cockfight' in Geertz 1973.

20. A couple of examples will suffice here, though the matter requires a more detailed investigation. Sophists and pantomimes alike aimed to cast a spell upon their viewers. In the case of pantomimes, we saw (Chapter 6§5) Lycinus' insistence on the genre's power as a *thelktêrion*; sophists, however, were masters of auditory *thelxis*, attracting, as pantomimes did, comparisons to mythical enchanters (e.g., Philostratus, *Lives* 520, on Scopelian as Orpheus or Thamyris). If a pantomime could 'transport' his viewer vicariously into the very centre of the action, enabling him to visualise persons, places and events (e.g., Libanius, *Oration* 64.116; Manilius, *Matters of Astronomy* 5.484-5), the sophist also liked to boast of similar powers (e.g., Apuleius, *Flowery Excerpts* 18.6-8). Most importantly, the techniques of pantomime and sophist converged on the issue of their versatility. In the dancer's case, audiences were mesmerised by his 'protean' somatic flexibility, their admiration proportionate to the number and variety of characters he was required to impersonate within a single story. In the case of the sophist, it was literary and stylistic versatility that mattered (cf. Apuleius' boasting in *Flowery Excerpts* 9.27-9, 20.6) but also, crucially, the variety of tone, expression and bodily deportment accompanying the impersonation of the characters who peopled his many declamations. Interestingly, Dionysius of Halicarnassus compares the élite orator to Proteus, 'who could effortlessly assume all shapes' (*Demosthenes* 8; cf. *Dance* 19, comparing the pantomime to Proteus). And Choricius in the sixth century AD transfers implicitly the pantomime's versatility to the sophist's tongue, which, like the dancer's body, is 'ductile and easily turned wherever one may wish (*euagôgon kai rhadiôs, hopoi an bouloito, strephomenê*)' (*Oration* 34.5, p. 384 Foerster-Richtsteig).

21. Cf. Lucian, *On the Hall* 19, where the 'delight of the eyes' is pronounced 'invincible' (*amachon*) and what one sees is said to be far more effective than what one hears (ibid. 20).

22. Interestingly, on the Christian side of élite discourses, John Chrysostom (*PG* 59.25) singles out as a matter of especial pride the fact that a priest officiates without any need of musical instruments, without tapping rigorously the *orchêstra* with his foot, without a mask and without a golden dress. In other words, the Christian preacher dares to do what the pagan declaimer looks upon with trepidation: he dissociates his performance from the theatrical and pantomimic shows.

23. So, for example, Aper in Tacitus' *Dialogue* 7.3-4 conveniently forgets that orators do not have the monopoly of fame and glory in the Roman city – in fact, it is much more likely that the 'first names children are taught to utter' (7.4) were the names of dancing idols rather than those of practising orators.

24. Where one could practise rhetoric in front of a discerning (even if sometimes hostile) audience (see, e.g., Pliny the Younger, *Letters* 7.17.12).

25. While, of course, as Connolly (2001a: 86) remarks, such 'rhetoric of effortlessness' was itself 'simply another part of the sophists' self-stylization'. On the necessary mannerism of the faint, sweet and tender smile, see Lucian, *Professor* 12.

26. On Lucian's use of *hypokrisis* as a connecting tissue between *meletai* (declamations) and pantomimes, see Chapters 6§2 and 9§1.

27. As Connolly (2001a: 86) rightly observes, opportunities for intensely mimetic acting would have been abundant in the sophists' declamations, as they were regularly called upon to re-enact physically 'the agonies of individuals on the point of crisis or death, wailing over dead children, or crying out desperately to their audience to fight the Persians or resist Philip'. For Plutarch (*Moral Essays* 42a), 'theatrical subject-matter' (*tôn pragmatôn ta dramatika*) is the prerogative of sophistic speeches.

28. Scopelian, for example, treated himself to 'pitch [for depilation] and professional hair-removers', while Alexander 'Clay-Plato' had a worldwide reputation for 'fashioning his hair and polishing his teeth and filing his nails and always smelling of perfume' (Philostratus, *Lives* 536 and 571). On the effeminacy connoted by male depilation and, in general, beautification, see Clement of Alexandria, *Tutor* 3, ch. 3. On the 'monstrosity'/gender-indeterminacy of a depilated man, see Epictetus, *Discourses* 3.1.28. For a satire of sophistry's effeminate elegance, cf. Lucian, *Doubly Accused* 31.

29. According to Lucian's caricatural Professor of sophistic-style rhetoric, a shameless sing-song delivery and an effeminate gait are occasionally 'sufficient in themselves' for safeguarding the aspiring superstar's success (*Professor* 15). As Branham (1989: 35) puts it, 'Rhetoric is branded as a licentious vamp, happily vulgarized to fit the fashions of the time.'

30. See, e.g., Lucian, *Demonax* 12, with Gleason (1995: 135).

31. Philostratus, *Lives* 513: Dionysius had been delivering his declamations 'in a sing-song style'; cf. ibid. 589, on Hadrian's seductive rhythms, both in prose and when he sang in recitative.

32. On audience demand for and oratorical delivery of the 'singing style', see primarily Dio Chrysostom, *Oration* 32.68: 'For, as they [i.e. élite declaimers] see your earnest interest in sung orations and your yearning for them, all declaimers now sing (*pantes aidousi*), the orators as well as the sophists, and all speeches are rounded off with song'; cf. Dio, ibid. 10; Lucian, *Professor* 15 (on the orator's need of a 'shameless singing delivery') and 19 (advice to the orator to turn everything into song).

33. It comes as no surprise, then, that the *pepaideumenos*' transition from traditional philosophy to display-performance in sophistic style could be expressed in contemporary sources in terms of a complete revamping or, better say, a full-scale 'theatricalisation', of austere personal habits; see, e.g., Philostratus, *Lives* 567, on Aristocles of Pergamon.

34. And, in any case, such constructions of one's opponents pre-date the rise of both sophists and pantomime dancers. See, e.g., the Ciceronian corpus of invective (cf. Chapter 9§2) or Dionysius of Halicarnassus' literary criticism, where the kind of rhetoric the author dislikes is dismissed as 'intolerable with respect to its histrionic shamelessness, ill-bred and with no share in philosophy or any other branch of liberal education' (*On the Ancient Orators* 1).

35. Dio Chrysostom, for one, acknowledges the existence of decent, i.e. non-showy, sophists, to whom men ought to offer 'libations and incense' (*Oration* 35.10).

36. Cf. Gleason (1995: 76), speaking of imperial élites in general: 'While some men aspired to the sort of *chic* that could "carry off" elegant grooming habits that normally invited accusations of effeminacy, others feared mockery so greatly that they submitted their flabby breasts to correction by the surgeon's knife.'

37. The famous Isaeus, for example, is thought by Philostratus (*Lives* 513) to have found his 'winning' style only after having abandoned the ostentatiousness and theatricality that were the hallmark of some of his peers.

38. See e.g., his *Oration* 4.35, where Dio claims that 'nothing differentiates a sophist from a licentious eunuch'; the true education, on the other hand, which Dio himself (like Diogenes in the speech) possesses and imparts, is semantically interchangeable with true manhood (4.31). On Dio's virile self-definition through rhetorical performance, see Whitmarsh (2001: 186-200).

39. Schmitz (1999: 75); cf. Whitmarsh (2001: 256).

40. Both Gleason and Connolly pose the question. Connolly (2001a: 90-1) asks: 'Why did the sophists take such risks? ... why did some men adopt mannerisms of self-presentation that served as stylized signifiers of the feminine and the non-élite in both their performances and their daily lives?' Cf. Gleason (1995: 161): 'When we savor the intensity of critical contempt that the "effeminate" style provoked, we may well wonder why so many dared to adopt it.' Gleason (1995: 162) never gives a full answer apart from stating that 'There was something manly, after all, about taking risks – even the risk of being called effeminate'. For Connolly's position, see next note.

41. At this point I part company with Connolly's argument (2001a; cf. 2001b). Although I am perfectly happy to understand the sophists' prominent 'classicism' as 'capable of expressing a resistant relation to dominant influences in politics and culture' (2001a: 94), I believe that the double sin of theatricality and effeminacy has much more to do with the frictive negotiations between élite and popular performance culture than between Greek cultural identity and Roman political power in the Eastern part of the empire. Much more than 'shoot[ing] a politically edged glance at the deepest anxieties of Roman rhetoric' (Connolly 2001a: 92), transgressive sophists were shooting anxious glances at their theatrical rivals in the entertainment circuit of imperial Greece.

42. For example, it would not be implausible to argue that the high-pitched sing-song mannerisms adopted by some sophists were intended to rival the sheer variety of tone and register displayed by the virtuosi tragic singers, the professional *tragôidoi* (on whom, see E. Hall 2002). Singing was also an indispensable part of mime and panto-mime performances throughout antiquity.

43. Possibly alongside its cognate genre, the mime.

44. Lycinus' tale of the barbarian who, though unable to understand the accompa-nying songs, 'understood every single bit' of a gifted pantomime's performance in Nero's court (*Dance* 64; cf. Postscript), is cast in the same mould as Philostratus' stories.

45. See, e.g., Philostratus, *Lives* 572 (exquisite costume), 587 (very expensive clothes and precious gems); from a hostile point of view, see Epictetus, *Discourses* 3.1.1, 3.23.35 (a fancy cloak or dainty mantle); in a satirical vein, see Lucian, *Professor* 15 (on the need for a flowery or white dress, allowing the body to 'show through'), 16, 17; *Dream* 11 (splendid dress worn by the sophistically inclined 'Lady-Education'), 16; *Doubly Accused* 31. More generally, against the practice of wearing 'a womanish and luxurious dress' when declaiming, see Quintilian, *Training* 8, Preface 20.

46. On the dancer's dress, see, e.g., Lucian, *Dance* 2 (soft dresses), 63 (silk vest-ments); Libanius, *Oration* 64.52 (ankle-length tunics embroidered with gold). As Jory (1996: 5) sums it up, our literary evidence points to 'flimsy, sometimes diaphanous, robes of silk that were occasionally embroidered with gold, that were decorated with fringes, and that reached down to the ankles'. Material evidence corroborates such insights. See again Jory (1996: 19): 'The costumes ... share a number of common features, some representations seeming to indicate transparent, or at the minimum delicate, fabrics, and others clearly showing quilting or rich embroidery on heavier and more voluminous material.' On similar dress codes adopted by clearly eroticised low-brow female dancers, see Fear (1991); cf. Webb (2002a: 286), on *orchêstrides* (female dancers/pantomimes) in long, see-through robes represented in Coptic textiles. On splendid dresses (scarlet, damask, crimson, purple) in pantomime's cognate pyrrhic dancing, see e.g., Fronto, *Letters* 1.5.4 (p. 9 van den Hout).

47. This is Gunderson's (2000: 155) felicitous translation of the Greek, capturing brilliantly the idea of a 'sexualized step', as he puts it. The bad orator's 'mincing walk is the gait of a *cinaedus*, as the Romans might call him. Such a man shakes his genitals and buttocks, drawing attention to them, attracting desire, promising pleasure' (Gun-derson, ibid.).

48. Lucian may well be glancing at the throngs of disciples and admirers gathering round (and following in their travels) the most flamboyant sophists; see, e.g., Philostra-tus, *Lives* 520 (Scopelian followed to Ionia by a 'brilliant crop of youths', enamoured with his wisdom), 562 (Herodes, followed to Athens by youths hanging on his lips for love of his words), 587 (Hadrian, escorted by all lovers of Hellenic culture); cf. Dio Chrysostom, *Oration* 4.14, 4.35, 35.8-9 (scoffingly, on sophists surrounded by young men leaping as the bacchants leap around Dionysus). In Lucian's own *Doubly Accused* 31, Rhetoric is cast in the role of the female 'beloved' indulging her 'meretricious habits' (Branham 1989: 35), i.e. serenaded by drunken lovers and answering back their calls in a wanton disposition. In Lucian's *Nigrinus* too, we are treated to an almost openly erotic (cf. Whitmarsh 2001: 275-6) reconstruction of the virtuoso rhetorician, whose speech and overall demeanour have been adoringly retained in the deeply 'wounded' listener's heart (cf. the 'innumerable wounds' gratefully received by pantomime and mime lovers in the homilies of John Chrysostom, e.g., *PG* 56.267; 59.333). About the pantomime, correspondingly, hang *cinaedi*, i.e. licentious feminised men (see Lucian, *The Ignorant Book Collector* 22). On the sheer size of some pantomime retinues, cf. Pliny the Elder, *Natural History* 29.5.9; on knights and senators thronging round pantomimes in Rome, see Tacitus, *Annals* 1.77.4 (cf. Chapter 4§1).

49. Interestingly, *areskein* ('to please', cf. 34.51) is a term that also describes the pantomime's relation to his public in inscriptions (cf. Chapter 4, nn. 30, 32).

50. See, e.g., *Oration* 34.2 (willing sin), 3 (willing licentiousness; cf. 51), 6 (willing exchange of better for worse), 9, 11 (willingly transgress, *hekontes ekbainein*), 49 (willingly offend), 50 (willingly sin for the sake of *psychagôgein*; cf. *psychagôgia* on pantomime inscriptions: Chapter 4, n. 31). On Aristides' *Oration* 34, see Boulanger (1923a: 265-70) and note especially the argument that, all the while he pours scorn on his adversaries, Aristides is fully conscious of the danger they pose because of their widespread popularity (ibid.: 265).

51. Cf. Connolly (2003: 312): 'Even the most problematic areas of the profession – elegant and refined personal style, and expertise in acting – could be represented as the products of physical endurance.' On the repeated stressing of manliness in Philostratus' *Lives*, see Whitmarsh (2001: 188-9); on the 'contradiction and unease in the ideology of rhetorical performance', see further Gleason (1995), who sums up the sophist's balancing act as 'the challenge embodied by the practitioners of "depilated" rhetoric' (129).

52. On Polemo, see primarily Gleason (1995).

53. See *Oration* 34.23. *Exorcheisthai* literally means to burlesque or vulgarise through mimetic dancing what is supposed to be kept secret. As Lycinus explains in *Dance* 15, because rhythm and dance played a pivotal role in initiation ceremonies into mystic cults (see further Lada-Richards 1999: 99-102; Hardie 2004), 'those who speak openly of the mysteries in conversation are widely said to be dancing them out (*exorcheisthai*)'. In the case of Aristides' speech, *exorcheisthai* refers to the burlesquing of the mysteries of rhetoric (on which, see Korenjak, 2000: 214-19); cf. Epictetus, *Discourses* 3.21.13. Gleason (1995: 124), who discusses *Oration* 34, comes closest to my main contention in this chapter when writing: 'We may suspect that blurring the boundaries between rhetoric and popular entertainment was a type of "burlesque" that particularly ruffled Aristides.'

12. Controlling Theatre in the Imperial East

1. See Whitmarsh (2005: 47 and 27 respectively). Although, as we shall see in this chapter, there is a real gulf separating what we might call a 'hard core' sophistic mentality from Lucian's perspective, the affinities between the principles of epideictic (display) oratory and Lucian's work are undeniable. In the first place, like a globe-trotting intellectual, Lucian did embark on the customary 'grand tour' of urban centres that was the hallmark of sophistic activity in the first centuries AD, and got as far west as Gaul. Secondly, despite the fact that his literary output does not fall neatly into the kind of display-performances that Philostratus' 'sophists' were accustomed to give (cf. Chapter 11), he himself is saturated with the same 'brand' of Greekness that forms the backbone of sophistic education, namely the literature and culture of pre-Roman Greece, expressed in Attic style. Thirdly, despite his unforgiving satire of the showiness, pretentiousness and emptiness of contemporary display-orators, there is no doubt that his supreme cultural influences must be located in the broader milieu of the élite agonistic rhetorical performances of the second century AD (cf. Bompaire 1958: 153). Even as a composer of literary dialogues, an activity which he (in the persona of 'The Syrian') claims to have started as a substitute for his speech-making career (*Doubly Accused* 32), Lucian did not leave the mentality of a display-orator behind: in his hands, the austere dialogic form was fashioned in such a way as to become attractive to the public (*Doubly Accused* 34). See MacLeod (1991: 3) on Lucian's continued travels (mainly in Greece and Ionia) and public readings of his work until late in his life, that is to say, after his 'eminently rhetorical disavowal of rhetoric' (Whitmarsh 2001: 263).

2. See primarily Branham (1989), a path-breaking publication; Whitmarsh (2001: 247-94); Goldhill (2002: 60-107); cf. S. Saïd (1993); Dubel (1994).

3. Branham (1989: 13) refers to 'a repertoire of over 170 characters'.

4. As S. Saïd (1993: 263) writes, 'Certainly the distance between Lycinos and Loukianos is slim, but it does nonetheless exist' (my translation).

5. The only tangible 'reality' (his name and a lock of hair) with respect to Lucian's own self is safely put away (or so a narrator self-styled as Assyrian tells us) inside a casket kept in the temple of the Syrian Goddess in the holy Syrian city of Hierapolis (*On the Syrian Goddess* 60).

6. On declamations as 'theatre' and élite declaimers as 'actors', see Chapters 9§1 and 11§3-4.

7. Cf. Branham (1989: 5), on Lucian 'entering into a gallery of roles', offering thus 'a series of rhetorical experiments'.

8. See, most strikingly, Lucian, *Professor* 17 (cf. *Word-flaunter* 14), where 'handiwise' (*cheirisophon*; cf. *Dance* 69) is one of the ridiculous and pompous coinages the aspiring orator is urged to use in order to astound the gaping crowds. Cf. also the scorn for an opponent's involvement in pantomime performances (*The Mistaken Critic* 19); the side-swipe at the 'dancing-master' in rich Roman houses (*On Salaried Posts in Great Houses* 27); the sneer at those – collectively branded as effeminates – who hang around pantomime stars (*The Ignorant Book Collector* 22). The ironical compliment paid to the book collector as 'supremely wise and consummate in learning (*akron en paideiai*)' (*Book Collector* 26) sounds remarkably close to the praise of the pantomimic art as 'reaching the summit of all learning (*pasês paideuseôs es to akrotaton aphiknoumenês*)'(*Dance* 35).

9. It was annexed by Rome in *c.* 72 AD.

10. In *Doubly Accused* 27, Lucian has 'Rhetoric' complain that she found him/The Syrian wandering about in Ionia, a young lad 'still barbarian in speech' (*barbaron eti tên phônên*); for the controversy over the exact meaning of 'barbarian' tongue here, see Lightfoot (2003: 205 and n. 554), with earlier bibliography.

11. Lucian himself is proud of the 'Attic grace' of his prose and its 'conformity to the classical canon' (*Zeuxis* 2); on his touchiness on linguistic matters, see Swain (1996: ch. 9).

12. Yet not so odd as to not exemplify the culture of the Second Sophistic within which he lived and breathed.

13. Swain (1996: 303) is right in stressing the significance of the fact that 'Lucian ... came from a cultural environment that was very different from that of an Aelius Aristides', as well as in suspecting that 'he was not fully accepted by the Greek elite' (ibid.: 311).

14. The personified Rhetoric's distinction between 'The Syrian'/Lucian, branded as 'poor and of humble origin', and other seekers of education in Ionia, designated as 'rich and good-looking and of brilliant ancestry' (*Doubly Accused* 27), speaks volumes about the gulf which must have separated the foreign outsider from the nobility of pedigree and money which nourished the most luminous stars of the Second Sophistic.

15. Cf. Lucian's own expression *entos tês kinklidos*, roughly equivalent to 'within the pale', used of the rich Roman household in *On Salaried Posts* 21.

16. It is undoubtedly significant that Rhetoric considers the registration of a Syrian among her 'own clansmen' as an irregularity, as suggested by the use of the verb *para-graphô*.

17. See Lucian, *Doubly Accused*, where the most probable 'mask' for Lucian is the figure of a Syrian, who refers to himself and his practices as 'barbarian' (27 and 34); *The Dead Come Back to Life* 19 (Syrian; of barbarian descent; barbarian in language); *On the Syrian Goddess* 1 ('I write these things being myself Assyrian'); *The Ignorant Book Collector* 19 ('I too am a Syrian'). Most importantly, in *Scythian* 9 an explicit parallel is drawn between the narrator's/Lucian's own position vis-à-vis Hellenic culture and that of the legendary Scythian Anacharsis, 'also a barbarian' (*barbaros … kakeinos*), who visited Greece in the sixth century BC 'out of a longing for Greek culture' (*Scythian* 1). The dismissive characterisation of the land beyond the Euphrates as *hyperorios*, i.e. 'beyond the pale', in *Doubly Accused* 14 is highly indicative of Lucian's own sense of cultural marginalisation (cf. Swain 1996: 307). Cf. *Doubly Accused* 27 and *Scythian* 3, with respect to the dominant culture's derisive scrutiny of the newcomer's external appearance.

18. Although Lucian's anomalous positioning with respect to Greek cultural orthodoxies has been fully taken on board by readers of other treatises (see, e.g., Elsner 2001 and Lightfoot 2003, for *On the Syrian Goddess*; Branham 1989: 82-14 and König 2005: 80-96, for *Anacharsis*; Swain 1996 and Whitmarsh 2001 on Lucian in general), it has never been brought to bear on scholarly readings of pantomime's emancipation in *On the Dance*.

19. The mainstream sophistic disdain of pantomime as newfangled nonsense, unrelated to prior dance-vocabularies of the Greek world, can be gauged from Aristides' anti-pantomime treatise, insofar as it can be reconstructed from Libanius' *Oration* 64 (see 19 and 23). It is perhaps in answer to such criticisms that Lucian, as we have already seen in Chapter 7, took the trouble to invest the genre with a noble pedigree by rooting it firmly into the age-old dance traditions of Greek and Hellenised lands.

20. In modern scholarship, cf. Bompaire (1958: 356), who deems an encomium of pantomime 'opposed to the Hellenic tradition', and joins the line of those early scholars who excised the dialogue from the list of genuine Lucianic works. Given the nature of the arguments pronounced against Lucianic authorship in the late nineteenth and early twentieth centuries, no one is seriously worried about the authenticity of the dialogue today, especially after Robertson's essay (1913) cleared the air in a more or less decisive way. Cf. Jones (1986: 69, n. 3) and G. Anderson (1977: 275): 'There has never been any single cogent argument for denying the authenticity of *De Saltatione*, generally ascribed to Lucian.'

21. Cf. Branham (1997: 251), on Lucian's invaluable combination of 'an outsider's perspective with an insider's knowledge'.

22. Cf. Swain (1996: 312), on Lucian's 'relative isolation' inside the sophistic circles as capable of explaining 'why Lucian does stand as a critical commentator on the culture of his contemporaries, observing its strengths and weaknesses, praising its good points and merits, and relentlessly probing its vanities and pretensions'.

23. For Lucian's dialogue as a response to Aristides' *Against the Pantomimes*, see Mesk (1908). Given the absence of even a shred of independent evidence, Boulanger (1923b) is rightly cautious, although, rightly again, he does see how the *katêgoria* (indictment) issued after 'a long preparation' mentioned in *Dance* 1 might well have been Aristides' impassioned tirade. On this issue, see also Molloy (1996: 87-9).

24. Needless to say, even those of us who are committed J.K.Rowling fans would not go that far in earnest!

25. See Robertson (1913; written in Antioch, between 162 and 165 AD); Robert (1930: 121-2); Jones (1986: 68) favours the years 163 (Verus' arrival at Antioch) and 164 (estimated time of Lucian's return to mainland Greece).

26. In the late second century AD, internationally famous pantomimes could be admitted to the worldwide Guild of the Artists of Dionysus (see Jory 1970: especially 238-40) and hold offices in it, especially as priests.

27. My thoughts on this point owe much to Bakhtin (1981: 358-66).

28. Pylades (I), for example, was said to have written a treatise on dancing (Athenaeus, *Sophists at Dinner* 20e).

29. See Bourdieu (1993: 164), on agents occupying 'a dominated position in the dominant class', being 'owners of a dominated form of power at the interior of the sphere of power'.

Postscript

1. Dubos (1748: 173), rendering Cassiodorus, *Various Letters* 1.20.

2. Providing the interlude between an opera's or a play's acts, or being staged as an afterpiece entertainment.

3. The concept of ballet as a picture returns with obsessive frequency in eighteenth-century writings on dance, especially the treatises of Weaver, Gallini, de Cahusac and Noverre, the last two owing a lot to Diderot's pictorial conception of dramatic art.

4. See de Pure (1972 [1668]); Ménestrier (1984 [1682]); Calliachius (1718 [1713]); Ferrarius (1718 [1714]); Bonnet (1969 [1723]); Dubos (1748).

5. See de Cahusac (2004 [1754]); Noverre (1930 [1760, 1803]); Weaver's most pertinent treatises are: *An Essay Towards an History of Dancing* (1712); *Anatomical and Mechanical Lectures upon Dancing* (1721) and *The History of the Mimes and Pantomimes, with An Historical Account of several Performers in Dancing, living in the Time of the Roman Emperors* (1728). They are all reproduced in fascimile in Ralph (1985), whence all my quotations are taken.

6. The lack of an imitative element in theatrical dancing is also deplored in eighteenth-century histories of the stage; see especially Gildon (1970: 154).

7. See, e.g., Gallini (1772: 39); Weaver (in Ralph 1985: 590).

8. Contemporary document, quoted in Guest (1996: 107).

9. See Gallini (1772: 267 and 262 respectively).

10. The list even includes non-mainstream sources, such as the letters of Aristaenetus, the writings of Cassiodorus (very widely quoted), Sidonius Apollinaris (poem 23 translated whole in Dubos 1748: 205), Manilius, Nonnus, etc.

11. See, e.g., Calliachius (1718: 752-3); Ferrarius (1718: 687); Dubos (1748: 207); Weaver (in Ralph 1985: 638 and 708); de Cahusac (2004: 116-18, imaginatively embellished); Gallini (1772: 253-4, substantially modified); among acting manuals, see, e.g., Siddons (1822: 207-8).

12. See, e.g., Vossius (1673: 65); Ménestrier (1984: 172-3 and 42); Calliachius (1718: 754-5); Ferrarius (1718: 688); Dubos (1748: 218-19); de Cahusac (2004: 96-8, imaginatively embellished); Gallini (1772: 255-8); Weaver (in Ralph, 1985: 607-12 and 691, with Ralph's remark at 610 that 'Lucian's report of this incident [i.e. Demetrius' conversion] is among the most important in the literature of dance apology'). Lucian's twin anecdotes also made it into stage-history (see, e.g., Betterton 1741: 38 and 70-1) and acting manuals, such as Gildon (1970: 25, 49-50); Austin (1806: 261) and Siddons (1822: 237).

13. See Diderot 1965 [1751]: 52-3; Diderot does actually quote from Lucian the praise Demetrius accorded to the pantomime in the Second of his *Entretiens sur le Fils Naturel* of 1757 (text in Versini 1996: 1144).

14. In Gildon's seminal treatise on the stage, the 'barbarian of Pontus' anecdote corroborates the contention that 'by Action and Gesture ... we make our Thoughts and Passions intelligible to all Nations and Tongues' (1970: 50); cf. O'Brien (2004: 88).

15. Cf. Lucian, *Dance* 67, a section Weaver (in Ralph 1985: 700) quotes in translation.

16. Text in Versini (1996: 1143). On Diderot's fascination with expressive pantomime, see primarily (among a large bibliography) Josephs (1969); Goodden (1986) and (2001); Roach (1993: 117-59).

17. Noverre (1930: 99) explicitly disjoined the concept of ancient pantomime, 'the noble pantomime', from 'that low and trivial form of expression which Italian players have introduced into France, and which bad taste would appear to have accepted'.

18. The great Louis Dupré, dancing legend of the Paris Opéra, as Mars, and the beautiful dancer and actress Hester Stanlow, as Venus; Weaver himself danced the role of Vulcan.

19. See Weaver, in Ralph (1985: 767 and 841 respectively).

20. See in general Avery (1934).

21. See Winter (1974: 61): 'Weaver's practical realizations were far in advance of anything his contemporaries attempted, although they reflected his period's theoretical treatises which were occupied with discussion of Greek and Roman pantomime.'

22. On Servandoni's spectacles, see Bergman (1960: 72).

23. In his *Lettere di Gasparo Angiolini a Monsieur Noverre sopra i balli pantomimi*, quoted in B.A. Brown (1991: 152), in translation.

24. On Hilverding, see B.A. Brown (1991: esp.143-93); Winter (1974: esp. 92-9). According to Winter (1974: 95), Hilverding's choreography was 'a century in advance of its time' with respect to the rendering of emotion by means of the entire moving body.

25. Angiolini, *Lettere* (above, n. 23), as quoted in B.A. Brown (1991: 285), in translation.

26. The ballet premiered on 17 October 1761 and is considered a 'landmark in the history of theatrical dance' (B.A. Brown 1991: 282).

27. 'un Ballet Pantomime dans le goût des Anciens', fol. a2 of the ballet's accompanying programme; reproduced in Engländer (1966: 24).

28. See the last page of Angiolini's *Dissertation*, as reproduced in Engländer (1966: 28).

29. Noverre notoriously neglected to acknowledge any of his predecessors in either the theory or the practice of ancient pantomime's revival, a failure acrimoniously pointed out to him by Angiolini in the course of their long dispute (see Carones 1987).

30. Noverre and de Cahusac mostly use the terms 'ballet en action' and 'ballet d'action', i.e. 'action ballet'; another contemporary term was 'heroic ballet'.

31. Guest (1996: 76), with quotation from a contemporary document at 77.

32. See Guest (1996: 101), quoting from an early nineteenth-century document.

33. See, e.g., Noverre (1930: 26): 'if steps be not guided by the dancers' brains, they will always go astray, and their execution will be mechanical'; cf. ibid., 28, 29, 105, 108; Gallini (1772: 65, 96-7, 260).

34. Weaver, in Ralph (1985: 403); cf. Crato's accusations in Lucian, *Dance* 2-3.

35. Weaver, in Ralph (1985: 595); cf. Ménestrier (1984: 171); Noverre (1930: 32).

36. See, e.g., Weaver, in Ralph (1985: 618, 632-3, 688, 697); Ménestrier (1984: 171-3); de Cahusac (2004: 100).

37. In the pages that follow, Noverre adds geometry, painting, anatomy and music to the ballet-master's necessary accomplishments.

38. See Gildon (1970: 138-9), borrowing from Lucian, *Dance* 35 and 74.

39. For oblique refractions of pantomime dancing in the late eighteenth and early nineteenth century, see Lada-Richards (2003c), on the mimoplastic art of Emma Hamilton and the pantomime-like poses of equestrian sensation Andrew Ducrow. On the afterlife of pantomime, see further Hall, in Hall and Wyles (forthcoming).

Bibliography

Adams, J.N. (1982), *The Latin Sexual Vocabulary* (Duckworth).

Alcock, S. (1997), 'The Heroic Past in a Hellenistic Present', in P. Cartledge, P. Garnsey and E. Gruen (eds), *Hellenistic Constructs: Essays in Culture, History and Historiography* (University of California Press) 20-34.

—— (2001), 'The Reconfiguration of Memory in the Eastern Roman Empire', in S. Alcock et al. (eds), *Empires: Perspectives from Archaeology and History* (Cambridge University Press) 323-50.

—— (2002), *Archaeologies of the Greek Past: Landscape, Monuments, and Memories* (Cambridge University Press).

Anderson, B. (1983), *Imagined Communities: Reflections on the Origin and Spread of Nationalism* (Verso).

Anderson, G. (1977), 'Lucian and the Authorship of *De Saltatione*', *GRBS* 18: 275-86.

—— (1989), 'The *Pepaideumenos* in Action: Sophists and their Outlook in the Early Roman Empire', *ANRW* ii. 33.1: 79-208.

Arbeau, T. (1967), *Orchesography* (trans. M.S. Evans; French original 1588) (Dover Publications).

Artaud, A. (1958), *The Theater and its Double* (trans. M.C. Richards; French original 1938) (Grove Press).

Asmis, E. (1995), 'Philodemus on Censorship, Moral Utility, and Formalism in Poetry', in D. Obbink (ed.), *Philodemus and Poetry: Poetic Theory and Practice in Lucretius, Philodemus, and Horace* (Oxford University Press) 148-77.

Austin, G. (1806), *Chironomia: or a Treatise on Rhetorical Delivery* (T. Cadell and W. Davies).

Avery, E.L. (1934), 'Dancing and Pantomime on the English Stage, 1700-1737', *Studies in Philology* 31: 417-52.

Babcock, B.A. (1978), 'Introduction', in ead.(ed.), *The Reversible World: Symbolic Inversion in Art and Society* (Cornell University Press) 13-36.

Bacon, H.H. (1995), 'The Chorus in Greek Life and Drama', *Arion* 3.1: 6-24.

Bailey, P. (1994), 'Conspiracies of Meaning: Music-Hall and the Knowingness of Popular Culture', *P&P* 144: 138-70.

Bakhtin, M.M. (1981), *The Dialogic Imagination: Four Essays* (ed. M. Holquist; trans. C. Emerson and M. Holquist) (University of Texas Press).

—— (1984), *Rabelais and his World* (trans. H. Iswolsky; first published 1965) (Bloomington).

Barthes, R. (1975), *S/Z* (trans. R. Miller) (Jonathan Cape).

Barton, C.A. (1993), *The Sorrows of the Ancient Romans: the Gladiator and the Monster* (Princeton University Press).

Bartsch, S. (2000), 'The Philosopher as Narcissus: Vision, Sexuality, and Self-Knowledge in Classical Antiquity', in R.S. Nelson (ed.), *Visuality Before and Beyond the Renaissance: Seeing as Others Saw* (Cambridge University Press) 70-97.

Bavelas, J.B., Black, A., Lemery, C.R., and Mullett, J. (1987), 'Motor Mimicry as Primitive Empathy', in N. Eisenberg and J. Strayer (eds), *Empathy and its Development* (Cambridge University Press) 317-38.

Baxandall, M. (1988), *Painting and Experience in Fifteenth-Century Italy* (2nd edn; Clarendon Press).

217

Bayet, J. (1967), 'Les vertus du pantomime Vincentius', in J. Bayet, *Mélanges de littérature latine* (Edizioni di storia e letteratura) 439-60.

Beacham, R.C. (1991), *The Roman Theatre and Its Audience* (Routledge).

—— (1999), *Spectacle Entertainments of Early Imperial Rome* (Yale University Press).

Bélis, A. (1988), '*Kroupezai, Scabellum*', *BCH* 112: 323-39.

Bérard, C. and Bron, C. (1989), 'Satyric Revels', in C. Bérard et al. (eds), *A City of Images: Iconography and Society in Ancient Greece* (trans. D. Lyons; French original 1984) (Princeton University Press) 131-50.

Bergman, G.M. (1960), 'La grande mode des pantomimes à Paris vers 1740 et les spectacles d'optique de Servandoni', *Theatre Research* 2: 71-81.

Bethe, M. and Brazell, K. (1990), 'The practice of Noh Theatre', in Schechner and Appel (eds), 167-93.

Betterton, T. (1741), *The History of the English Stage, from the Restauration to the Present Time* (E. Curll).

Bieber, M. (1961), *The History of the Greek and Roman Theater* (Princeton University Press).

Birkhan, H. (1989), 'Popular and Elite Culture Interlacing in the Middle Ages', *History of European Ideas* 10.1: 1-11.

Bloom, A. (1988), *The Closing of the American Mind: How Higher Education has Failed Democracy and Impoverished the Souls of Today's Students* (Penguin).

Bompaire, J. (1958), *Lucien écrivain: imitation et création* (de Boccard).

Bonaria, M. (1955-6), *Mimorum Romanorum Fragmenta* (Istituto di Filologia Classica).

—— (1959), 'Dinastie di Pantomimi Latini', *Maia* 11: 224-42.

Bonnet, J. (1969), *Histoire générale de la danse sacrée et profane* (Slatkine Reprints; first published 1723).

Borg, B.E. (ed) (2004), *Paideia: The World of the Second Sophistic* (de Gruyter).

—— (2004a), 'Glamorous Intellectuals: Portraits of *Pepaideumenoi* in the Second and Third Centuries AD', in Borg (ed), 157-78.

Boulanger, A. (1923a), *Aelius Aristide et la Sophistique dans la province d'Asie au IIe siècle de notre ère* (de Boccard).

—— (1923b), 'Lucien et Aelius Aristide', *Revue de Philologie* 47: 144-51.

Bourdieu, P. (1984), *Distinction: A Social Critique of the Judgement of Taste* (trans. R. Nice; French original 1979) (Routledge and Kegan Paul).

—— (1990), *In Other Words: Essays Towards a Reflexive Sociology* (trans. M. Adamson; French original 1987) (Polity Press).

—— (1993), *The Field of Cultural Production: Essays on Art and Literature*, edited and introduced by R. Johnson (Polity Press).

Bowersock, G.W. (1969), *Greek Sophists in the Roman Empire* (Clarendon Press).

—— (ed) (1974), *Approaches to the Second Sophistic* (American Philological Association).

Bowie, E. (1974), 'Greeks and Their Past in the Second Sophistic', in M. Finley (ed.), *Studies in Ancient Society* (Routledge) 166-209 (first published in *P&P* 46 [1970] 3-41).

—— (1982), 'The Importance of Sophists', *YCS* 27: 29-59.

—— (1991), 'Hellenes and Hellenism in Writers of the Early Second Sophistic', in S. Said (ed.), '*HELLENISMOS: Quelques jalons pour une histoire de l'identité grecque: Actes du Colloque de Strasbourg, 25-27 Octobre 1989* (Brill) 183-204.

—— (1996), 'Past and Present in Pausanias', in J. Bingen (ed.), *Pausanias Historien* (Fondation Hardt) 207-39.

Boyancé, P. (1937), *Le culte des Muses chez les philosophes grecs* (de Boccard).

—— (1960-1), 'L'antre dans les mystères de Dionysos', *Atti della Pontificia Accademia Romana di Archeologia* (3rd series, Rendiconti) 33: 107-27.

Branham, R.B. (1989), *Unruly Eloquence: Lucian and the Comedy of Traditions* (Harvard University Press).

——— (1997), 'Lucian', in W.W. Briggs (ed.), *Dictionary of Literary Biography,* vol. 176: *Ancient Greek Authors* (Gale Research).

Braund, D. and Wilkins, J. (eds) (2000), *Athenaeus and His World: Reading Greek Culture in the Roman Empire* (University of Exeter Press).

Braund, S.M. (1988), *Beyond Anger: A Study of Juvenal's Third Book of Satires* (Cambridge University Press).

Brecht, B. (1964), *Brecht on Theatre: The Development of an Aesthetic* (ed. and trans. J. Willett) (Methuen).

Brooks, P. (1993), *Body Work: Objects of Desire in Modern Narrative* (Harvard University Press).

Brown, B.A. (1991), *Gluck and the French Theatre in Vienna* (Clarendon Press).

Brown, P.R.L. (1988), *The Body and Society: Men, Women, and Sexual Renunciation in Early Christianity* (Columbia University Press).

Browning, R. (1952), 'The Riot of AD 387 in Antioch: The Role of the Theatrical Claques in the Later Empire', *JRS* 42: 13-20.

Bryson, N. (1983), *Vision and Painting: The Logic of the Gaze* (Macmillan Press).

Burgess, T.C. (1987), *Epideictic Literature* (University of Chicago Press).

Burian, P. (1997), 'Myth into *Muthos*: The Shaping of Tragic Plot', in Easterling (ed.), 178-210.

Calame, C. (1997), *Choruses of Young Women in Ancient Greece* (trans. D. Collins and J. Orion; first published 1977) (Rowman and Littlefield).

Calder, W.M. and Cormack, J.M.R. (1962), *Monumenta Asiae Minoris Antiqua,* vol. 8: *Monuments from Lycaonia, The Pisido-Phrygian Borderland, Aphrodisias* (Manchester University Press).

Calliachius, N. (1718), *De Ludis Scenicis Mimorum et Pantomimorum* (first published 1713); reprinted in de Sallengre, vol. 2: 715-67.

Cameron, A. (1976), *Circus Factions. Blues and Greens at Rome and Byzantium* (Clarendon Press).

Carones, L. (1987), 'Noverre and Angiolini: Polemical Letters', *Dance Research* 5.1: 42-54.

Castle, T. (1986), *Masquerade and Civilization: The Carnivalesque in Eighteenth-Century English Culture and Fiction* (Stanford University Press).

Chartier, R. (1984), 'Culture as Appropriation: Popular Cultural Uses in Early Modern France', in S.L. Kaplan (ed.), *Understanding Popular Culture: Europe from the Middle Ages to the Nineteenth Century* (Mouton) 229-53.

Cibber, C. (1968), *An Apology for the Life of Colley Cibber, With an Historical View of the Stage during his own Time* (edited with an Introduction by B.R.S. Fone; first published 1740) (University of Michigan Press).

Cohen, S.J. (1960), 'Theory and Practice of Theatrical Dancing in England in the Restoration and Early Eighteenth Century, part ii: John Weaver', *Bulletin of the New York Public Library* 64: 41-54.

Connerton, P. (1989), *How Societies Remember* (Cambridge University Press).

Connolly, J. (1998), 'Mastering Corruption: Constructions of Identity in Roman Oratory', in S.R. Joshel and S. Murnaghan (eds), *Women and Slaves in Greco-Roman Culture: Differential Equations* (Routledge) 130-51.

——— (2001a), 'Reclaiming the Theatrical in the Second Sophistic', *Helios* 28, 1: 75-96.

——— (2001b), 'Problems of the Past in Imperial Greek Education', in Too (ed.), 339-72.

——— (2003) 'Like the Labors of Heracles: *Andreia* and *Paideia* in Greek Culture under Rome', in Rosen and Sluiter (eds), 287-317.

Corbeill, A. (1996), *Controlling Laughter: Political Humor in the Late Roman Republic* (Princeton University Press).

——— (1997), 'Dining Deviants in Roman Political Invective', in Hallett and Skinner (eds), 99-128.

Courtney, E. (1980), *A Commentary on the Satires of Juvenal* (Athlone Press).

Cribiore, R. (2001), *Gymnastics of the Mind: Greek Education in Hellenistic and Roman Egypt* (Princeton University Press).

Csapo, E. (2004), 'The Politics of the New Music', in Murray and Wilson (eds), 207-48.

—— and Slater, W.J. (1995), *The Context of Ancient Drama* (University of Michigan Press).

Curty, O. (1995), *Les parentés légendaires entre cités grecques* (Librairie Droz).

Davidson, J. (2000), '*Gnesippus Paigniagraphos*: The Comic Poets and the Erotic Mime', in Braund and Wilkins (eds), 41-64.

Davies, P.V. (1969), *The Saturnalia [of] Macrobius: translated with an introduction and notes* (Columbia University Press).

de Cahusac, L. (2004), *La danse ancienne et moderne ou traité historique de la danse* (ed. N. Lecomte, L. Naudeix, J.-N.Laurenti; first published 1754) (Éditions Desjonquères).

Delavaud-Roux, M.-H. (1993), *Les danses armées en Grèce antique* (Publications de l'Université de Provence).

—— (1994), *Les danses pacifiques en Grèce antique* (Publications de l'Université de Provence).

—— (1995), *Les danses dionysiaques en Grèce antique* (Publications de l'Université de Provence).

de Mille, A. (1992), *Martha: The Life and Work of Martha Graham* (Hutchinson).

de Pure, M. (1972), *Idée des spectacles anciens et nouveaux* (Minkoff Reprint; first published 1668).

de Sallengre, A.H. (1718), *Novus Thesaurus Antiquitatum Romanarum* (H. du Sauzet).

Desmond, J.C. (1993-4), 'Embodying Difference: Issues in Dance and Cultural Studies', *Cultural Critique* 26: 33-63.

Dickie, M. W. (1993), 'Palaestrités/ 'Palaestrita': Callisthenics in the Greek and Roman Gymnasium', *Nikephoros* 6:105-51.

—— (2001), 'Mimes, Thaumaturgy, and the Theatre', *CQ* 51.2: 599-603.

Diderot, D. (1965), 'Lettre sur les sourds et muets' (1751), ed. P.H. Meyer, *Diderot Studies* 7: 37-91.

Dodds, E.R. (1951), *The Greeks and the Irrational* (University of California Press).

Dubel, S. (1994), 'Dialogue et autoportrait: les masques de Lucien', in A. Billault (ed.), *Lucien de Samosate* (de Boccard) 19-26.

Dubos, Abbé (1748), *Critical Reflections on Poetry, Painting and Music, with An Inquiry into the Rise and Progress of the Theatrical Entertainments of the Ancients* (trans. T. Nugent from the 5th edn, revised, corrected and enlarged by the author), 3 vols (John Nourse) (first published 1719; vol. 3 first published 1733).

Duff, T. (1999), *Plutarch's Lives: Exploring Virtue and Vice* (Clarendon Press).

Duncan, I. (1996), *My Life* (Victor Collancz; first edn.1928).

Dupont, F. (1997), '*Recitatio* and the Reorganization of the Space of Public Discourse', in T. Habinek and A. Schiesaro (eds), *The Roman Cultural Revolution* (Cambridge University Press) 44-59.

Easterling, P. (ed.) (1997), *The Cambridge Companion to Greek Tragedy* (Cambridge University Press).

—— (1997a), 'From Repertoire to Canon', in Easterling (ed), 211-27.

—— and E. Hall (eds) (2002), *Greek and Roman Actors: Aspects of an Ancient Profession* (Cambridge University Press).

—— and R. Miles (1999), 'Dramatic Identities: Tragedy in Late Antiquity', in R. Miles (ed), *Constructing Identities in Late Antiquity* (Routledge) 95-111.

Edwards, C. (1993), *The Politics of Immorality in Ancient Rome* (Cambridge University Press).

—— (1997), 'Unspeakable Professions: Public Performance and Prostitution in Ancient Rome', in Hallett and Skinner (eds), 66-95.

—— (2000), *Suetonius: Lives of the Caesars. Translated with an Introduction and Notes* (Oxford University Press).

Elsner, J. (1992), 'Pausanias: A Greek Pilgrim in the Roman World', *P&P* 135: 3-29.
—— (2001), 'Describing Self in the Language of Other: Pseudo (?) Lucian at the Temple of Hierapolis', in Goldhill (ed.), 123-53.
Emmanuel, M. (1896), *La danse grecque antique d'après les monuments figurés* (Hachette).
Engländer, R. (ed.) (1966), *Christoph Willibald Gluck: Don Juan/Semiramis: Ballet Pantomimes von Gasparo Angiolini* (Bärenreiter Kassel).
Fantham, E. (1989), 'Mime: the Missing Link in Roman Literary History', *Classical World* 82: 153-66.
—— (1996), *Roman Literary Culture: From Cicero to Apuleius* (Johns Hopkins University Press).
—— (2002), 'Orator and/et Actor', in Easterling and Hall (eds), 362-76.
Faral, E. (1910), *Les jongleurs en France au Moyen Age* (Librairie Honoré Champion).
Fear, A.T. (1991), 'The Dancing Girls of Gadiz', *G&R* 38: 75-9.
Feldherr, A. (1998), *Spectacle and Society in Livy's History* (California University Press).
Ferrarius, O. (1718), *De Pantomimis et Mimis Dissertatio* (first published 1714), reprinted in de Sallengre, vol. 2: 685-97.
Fish, S.E. (1976), 'Interpreting the *Variorum*', *Critical Inquiry* 2.3: 465-85.
Flaubert, G. (1991), 'Herodias', in *Three Tales* (trans. A.J. Krailsheimer) (Oxford University Press).
Flinterman, J.-J. (1995), *Power, Paideia and Pythagoreanism: Greek Identity, Conceptions of the Relationship between Philosophers and Monarchs and Political Ideas in Philostratus' Life of Apollonius* (Gieben).
Foster, S.L. (1995), 'Choreographing History', in ead. (ed.), *Choreographing History* (Indiana University Press) 3-21.
—— (1996a), *Choreography and Narrative: Ballet's Staging of Story and Desire* (Indiana University Press).
—— (1996b), 'Pygmalion's No-Body and the Body of Dance', in E. Diamond (ed.), *Performance and Cultural Politics* (Routledge) 131-54.
Foucault, M. (1977), *Language, Counter-Memory, Practice: Selected Essays and Interviews* (trans. D.F. Bouchard and S. Simon) (Blackwell).
Franklin, J.L. (1987), 'Pantomimists at Pompeii: Actius Anicetus and his Troupe', *AJP* 108: 95-107.
Franko, M (1993), *Dance as Text: Ideologies of the Baroque Body* (Cambridge University Press).
Friedländer, L. (1908), *Roman Life and Manners under the Early Empire*, vol. 2 (trans. of the 7th edn of *Sittengeschichte Roms*, by J.H. Freese and L.A. Magnus) (George Routledge and E.P. Dutton).
Frontisi-Ducroux, F. and Vernant, J.P. (1997), *Dans l'oeil du miroir* (Éditions Odile Jacob).
Gager, J.G. (1992), *Curse Tablets and Binding Spells from the Ancient World* (Oxford University Press).
Gallini, G.A (1772), *A Treatise on the Art of Dancing* (printed for the author).
Garelli-François, M-H. (2004), 'La pantomime antique ou les mythes revisités: le répertoire de Lucien (*Danse*, 38-60), *Dioniso* 3: 108-19.
Garton, C. (1972), *Personal Aspects of the Roman Theatre* (Hakkert).
Geertz, C. (1973), *The Interpretation of Cultures: Selected Essays* (HarperCollins).
Gildon, C. (1970), *The Life of Mr. Thomas Betterton, the Late Eminent Tragedian* (Frank Cass & Co; first published 1710)
Gleason, M.W. (1995), *Making Men: Sophists and Self-Presentation in Ancient Rome* (Princeton University Press).
Goethe, J.W. (1982), *Italian Journey 1786-1788* (trans. W.H. Auden and E. Mayer) (Penguin).

Goldhill, S. (ed.) (2001), *Being Greek under Rome: Cultural Identity, the Second Sophistic, and the Development of Empire* (Cambridge University Press).

—— (2002), *Who Needs Greek? Contests in the Cultural History of Hellenism* (Cambridge University Press).

Goodden, A. (1986), *Actio and Persuasion: Dramatic Performance in Eighteenth-Century France* (Clarendon Press).

—— (2001), *Diderot and the Body* (Legenda: European Humanities Research Centre, University of Oxford).

Greenblatt, S. (1994), 'Invisible Bullets: Renaissance Authority and its Subversion, Henry IV and Henry V', in J. Dollimore and A. Sinfield (eds), *Political Shakespeare: Essays in Cultural Materialism* (Manchester University Press; 2nd edn) 18-47.

Grotowski, J. (1968), *Towards a Poor Theatre* (Simon and Schuster).

Gruen, E.S. (1992), *Culture and National Identity in Republican Rome* (Cornell University Press).

Guest, I. (1980), *The Romantic Ballet in Paris* (2nd rev. edn.) (Dance Books).

—— (1996), *The Ballet of the Enlightenment: The Establishment of the Ballet d'Action in France, 1770-1793* (Dance Books).

Guey, J. (1952), 'Un pantomime de l'Empereur Caracalla citoyen de Leptis Magna', *Revue Africaine* 96: 44-60.

Gunderson, E. (1998), 'Discovering the Body in Roman Oratory' in M. Wyke (ed), *Parchments of Gender: Deciphering the Bodies of Antiquity* (Clarendon Press) 169-89.

—— (2000), *Staging Masculinity: The Rhetoric of Performance in the Roman World* (University of Michigan Press).

Habinek, T.N. (1998), *The Politics of Latin Literature: Writing, Identity, and Empire in Ancient Rome* (Princeton University Press).

Hall, E. (1999a), 'Actor's Song in Tragedy', in S. Goldhill and R. Osborne (eds), *Performance Culture and Athenian Democracy* (Cambridge University Press) 96-122.

——(1999b), 'Classical Mythology in the Victorian Popular Theatre', in *IJCT* 5.3: 336-66.

—— (2002), 'The Singing Actors of Antiquity', in Easterling and Hall (eds), 3-38.

—— and Wyles, R.(eds) (forthcoming), *New Directions in Ancient Pantomime* (Oxford University Press).

Hall, J. (2004), 'Cicero and Quintilian on the Oratorical Use of Hand Gestures', *CQ* 54.1: 143-60.

Hallett, J.P. and Skinner, M.B. (eds) (1997), *Roman Sexualities* (Princeton University Press).

Hansen, M. (1991), *Babel and Babylon: Spectatorship in American Silent Film* (Harvard University Press).

Hardie, A. (2004), 'Muses and Mysteries', in Murray and Wilson (eds), 11-37.

Harrison, S.J. (2000), *Apuleius: A Latin Sophist* (Clarendon Press).

—— (ed.) (2001), *Apuleius: Rhetorical Works*. Translated and annotated by S. Harrison, J. Hilton, and V. Hunink (Oxford University Press).

Hazlitt, W. (1930-4), *The Complete Works of William Hazlitt*, ed. P.P. Howe (J.M. Dent).

Hedgcock, F.A. (1911), *David Garrick: A Cosmopolitan Actor and his French Friends* (Stanley Paul and Co).

Henderson, J. (2002), 'Corny Copa, the Motel Muse', in E. Spentzou and D. Fowler (eds), *Cultivating the Muse: Struggles for Power and Inspiration in Classical Literature* (Oxford University Press) 253-78.

Henrichs, A. (1967) 'Zwei Fragmente über die Erziehung', *ZPE* 1: 45-53.

Hilgard, A. (ed.) (1901), *Scholia in Dionysii Thracis Artem Grammaticam* (Teubner).

Hobsbawm, E.J. (1972), 'The Social Function of the Past: Some Questions', *P&P* 55: 2-17.

Holmström, K.G. (1967), *Monodrama, Attitudes, Tableaux Vivants: Studies on some Trends of Theatrical Fashion 1770-1815* (Almqvist and Wiksell).

Hordern, J.H. (2002), *The Fragments of Timotheus of Miletus* (Oxford University Press).

Bibliography

Horrocks, G. (1997), *Greek: A History of the Language and its Speakers* (Longman).

Hunter, R.L. (1995) 'Plautus and Herodas', in L. Benz et al. (eds), *Plautus und die Tradition des Stegreifspiels* (Gunter Narr Verlag) 155-69.

———— (2000), 'The Politics of Plutarch's *Comparison of Aristophanes and Menander*', in S. Gödde and T. Heinze (eds), *Skenika: Beiträge zum antiken Theater und seiner Rezeption* (Wissenschaftliche Buchgesellschaft) 267-76.

———— (2002), ' "Acting Down": The Ideology of Hellenistic Performance', in Easterling and Hall (eds), 189-206.

———— (2003), 'Literature and its Contexts', in A. Erskine (ed), *A Companion to the Hellenistic World* (Blackwell) 477-93.

Janko, R. (2000), *Philodemus, On Poems: Book 1* (ed. with Introduction, Translation, and Commentary) (Oxford University Press).

Jauss, H.R.(1970), 'Literary History as a Challenge to Literary Theory' (trans. E. Benzinger), *New Literary History* 2.1: 7-37.

Jeanmaire, H. (1939), *Couroi et Courètes: Essai sur l'éducation spartiate et sur les rites d'adolescence dans l'antiquité hellénique* (Bibliothèque Universitaire de Lille).

Jenkins, I. and Sloan, K. (1996), *Vases and Volcanoes: Sir William Hamilton and his Collection* (British Museum Press).

Jones, C.P. (1986), *Culture and Society in Lucian* (Harvard University Press).

———— (1991), 'Dinner Theater', in W.J. Slater (ed.), *Dining in a Classical Context* (University of Michigan Press) 185-98.

———— (1993), 'Greek Drama in the Roman Empire', in R. Scodel (ed.), *Theater and Society in the Classical World* (University of Michigan Press) 39-52.

Jory, J. (1970), 'Associations of Actors in Rome', *Hermes* 98: 224-53.

———— (1981), 'The Literary Evidence for the Beginnings of Imperial Pantomime', *BICS* 28: 147-61.

———— (1984), 'The Early Pantomime Riots', in A. Moffat (ed.), *Maistor: Classical, Byzantine and Renaissance Studies for Robert Browning* (Australian Association for Byzantine Studies) 57-66.

———— (1995), '*Ars Ludicra* and the *Ludus Talarius*', in A. Griffiths (ed.), *Stage Directions: Essays in Ancient Drama in Honour of E.W. Handley* (*BICS* Suppl. 66) 139-52.

———— (1996), 'The Drama of the Dance: Prolegomena to an Iconography of Imperial Pantomime', in W.J. Slater (ed.), *Roman Theater and Society* (E. Togo Salmon Papers I) (University of Michigan Press) 1-27.

———— (2001), 'Some Cases of Mistaken Identity? Pantomime Masks and their Context', *BICS* 45: 1-20.

———— (2002), 'The Masks on the Propylon of the Sebasteion at Aphrodisias', in Easterling and Hall (eds), 238-53.

Josephs, H. (1969), *Diderot's Dialogue of Language and Gesture: Le Neveu de Rameau* (Ohio State University Press).

Kaster, R.A. (1988), *Guardians of Language: The Grammarian and Society in Late Antiquity* (Berkeley, Los Angeles and London).

Kelly, H.A. (1979), 'Tragedy and the Performance of Tragedy in Late Roman Antiquity', *Traditio* 35: 21-44.

Kennedy, G.A. (1974), 'The Sophists as Declaimers', in Bowersock (ed.), 17-22.

———— (2003) *Progymnasmata: Greek Textbooks of Prose Composition and Rhetoric. Translated with Introductions and Notes* (Society of Biblical Literature).

Kernodle, G.R. (1957), 'Symbolic Action in the Greek Choral Odes?', *Classical Journal* 53: 1-6.

Kokolakis, M. (1959), 'Pantomimus and the Treatise *Peri Orchêseôs* (*De Saltatione*)', *Platon* 11: 3-56.

———— (1976), *Philologika Meletêmata* (Athens; no publisher data).

König, J. (2005), *Athletics and Literature in the Roman Empire* (Cambridge University Press).

Bibliography

Korenjak, M. (2000), *Publikum und Redner: ihre Interaktion in der sophistischen Rhetorik der Kaiserzeit* (Beck).

Kraemer, C. (1931), 'A Greek Element in Egyptian Dancing', *AJA* 35: 125-38.

Kramer, L. (1990), 'Culture and Musical Hermeneutics: The Salome Complex', *Cambridge Opera Journal* 2: 269-94.

Lada-Richards, I. (1993), ' "Empathic Understanding": Emotion and Cognition in Classical Dramatic Audience-Response', *PCPS* 39: 94-140.

———— (1999), *Initiating Dionysus: Ritual and Theatre in Aristophanes'* Frogs (Clarendon Press).

———— (2002), 'The Subjectivity of Greek Performance', in Easterling and Hall (eds), 395-418.

———— (2003a), ' "A Worthless Feminine Thing?" Lucian and the "Optic Intoxication" of Pantomime Dancing', *Helios* 30.1: 21-75.

———— (2003b), ' "Within the Compasse of a Lye ...": Signs of Anti-theatricality on the Greek Stage?', *Nottingham Classical Literature Studies* 7: 21-56.

———— (2003c), ' "Mobile Statuary": Refractions of Pantomime Dancing from Callistratus to Emma Hamilton and Andrew Ducrow', *IJCT* 10.1: 3-37.

———— (2004a), 'Authorial Voice and Theatrical Self-Definition in Terence and Beyond: The *Hecyra* Prologues in Ancient and Modern Contexts', *G&R* 51.1: 55-82.

———— (2004b), '*Mythôn Eikôn*: Pantomime Dancing and the Figurative Arts in Imperial and Late Antiquity', *Arion* 2.2: 17-46.

———— (2005), ' "In the Mirror of the Dance": A Lucianic Metaphor in its Performative and Ethical Contexts', *Mnemosyne* 58. 3: 335-57.

———— (forthcoming, a), 'Tragedy into Dance: Reflections on the "Gestural" Space of Pantomime Dancing', in *Rethymnon Classical Studies*

———— (forthcoming, b), 'Becoming Mad on Stage: Lucian on the Perils of Acting and Spectating', *BICS* 49 (2006).

Latte, K. (1913), *De Saltationibus Graecorum: Capita Quinque* (Alfred Töpelmann).

Lavagne, H. (1986), 'Rome et les associations dionysiaques en Gaule (Vienne et Nîmes)', in *L'association dionysiaque dans les sociétés anciennes* (École Française de Rome) 129-48.

Lawler, L.B. (1939), 'The Dance of the Owl and Its Significance in the History of Greek Religion and the Drama', *TAPA* 70: 482-502.

———— (1946), '*Orchêsis Phobera*', *AJP* 67: 67-70.

———— (1950), 'Ladles, Tubs, and the Greek Dance', *AJP* 71: 70-2.

———— (1964), *The Dance in Ancient Greece* (Adam and Charles Black).

Le Guen, B. (2001), *Les associations de technites dionysiaques à l'époque hellénistique* (2 vols) (de Boccard).

Leppin, H. (1992), *Histrionen: Untersuchungen zur sozialen Stellung von Bühnenkünstlern im Westen des Römischen Reiches zur Zeit der Republik und des Principats* (Habelt).

Levick, B. (1983), 'The *Senatus Consultum* from Larinum', *JRS* 73: 97-115.

Levin, D.M.(1990), 'Postmodernism in Dance: Dance, Discourse, Democracy', in H.J. Silverman (ed.), *Postmodernism – Philosophy and the Arts* (Routledge) 207-33.

Levine, L.W. (1988), *Highbrow/Lowbrow: The Emergence of Cultural Hierarchy in America* (Harvard University Press).

Lewis, W.S. (ed.) (1955), *The Yale Edition of Horace Walpole's Correspondence*, vol. 17.1 (Clarendon Press and Yale University Press).

Lightfoot, J.L. (2000), 'Romanized Greeks and Hellenized Romans: Later Greek Literature', in O. Taplin (ed.), *Literature in the Greek and Roman Worlds: a New Perspective* (Oxford University Press) 257-84.

———— (2002), 'Nothing to Do with the *Technitai* of Dionysus?', in Easterling and Hall (eds), 209-24.

———— (2003), *Lucian, On the Syrian Goddess*, ed. with Introduction, Translation, and Commentary (Oxford University Press).

Lonsdale, S.H. (1993), *Dance and Ritual Play in Greek Religion* (Johns Hopkins University Press).

Loraux, N. (1981), 'Le lit, la guerre', *L'Homme* 21.1: 37-67.

Luck, G. (1977), *P. Ovidius Naso: Tristia, II: Kommentar* (Winter).

Macintosh, F. (2000), 'The Performer in Performance', in E. Hall, F. Macintosh and O. Taplin (eds), *Medea in Performance 1500-2000* (Legenda: European Humanities Research Centre of the University of Oxford) 1-31.

MacLeod, M.D. (1991), *Lucian: A Selection,* ed. with Introduction, Translation and Commentary (Aris and Phillips).

Maffei, S. (1991), 'La *Sophia* del pittore e del poeta nel Proemio delle *Imagines* di Filostrato Maggiore', *Annali della Scuola Normale Superiore di Pisa, Classe di Lettere e Filosofia* 21: 591-621.

Manning, S.A. (1993), *Ecstasy and the Demon: Feminism and Nationalism in the Dances of Mary Wigman* (University of California Press).

Mansi, J.D. *Sacrorum Conciliorum nova et amplissima collectio* (Florence 1767; no publisher data).

Masterson, M. (2004), 'Status, Play, and Pleasure in the *De Architectura* of Vitruvius', *AJP* 125: 387-416.

Mayer, R.G. (1991), 'Roman Historical *Exempla* in Seneca', in P. Grimal (ed.), *Sénèque et la Prose Latine* (Fondation Hardt) 141-69.

McCarty, W. (1989), 'The Shape of the Mirror: Metaphorical Catoptrics in Classical Literature', *Arethusa* 22: 161-95.

McKeown, J.C. (1979), 'Augustan Elegy and Mime', *PCPS* n.s. 25: 71-84.

Ménestrier, C.-F. (1984), *Des ballets anciens et modernes selon les règles du théâtre* (Minkoff; first published 1682).

Merkelbach, R. (1971), 'Dionysisches Grabepigramm aus Tusculum', *ZPE* 7: 280.

Mesk, J. (1908), 'Des Aelius Aristides verlorene Rede gegen die Tänzer', *Wiener Studien* 30: 59-74.

Mignogna, E. (1997), 'Leukippe in Tauride (Ach. Tat. 3, 15-22): mimo e "pantomimo" tra tragedia e romanzo', *Materiali e Discussioni per l'analisi dei testi classici* 38: 225-36.

Mitchell, S. (1990), 'Festivals, Games, and Civic Life in Roman Asia Minor', *JRS* 80: 183-93.

Molloy, M.E. (1996), *Libanius and the Dancers* (Olms-Weidmann).

Montiglio, S. (1999), 'Paroles dansées en silence: l'action signifiante de la pantomime et le moi du danseur', *Phoenix* 53: 263-80.

Morales, H. (2004), *Vision and Narrative in Achilles Tatius' Leucippe and Clitophon* (Cambridge University Press).

Morel, J.-P. (1969), '*Pantomimus allectus inter iuvenes*', in J. Bibauw (ed.), *Hommages à Marcel Renard: Collection Latomus* 102: 525-35.

Morgan, T. (1998), *Literate Education in the Hellenistic and Roman Worlds* (Cambridge University Press).

Moss, C. (1935), 'Jacob of Serugh's Homilies on the Spectacles of the Theatre', *Le Muséon* 48: 87-112.

Mulvey, L. (1975), 'Visual Pleasure and Narrative Cinema', *Screen* 16.3: 6-18.

Murray, P. 'The Muses and their Arts', in Murray and Wilson (eds), 365-89.

Murray, P. and Wilson, P. J. (eds) (2004), *Music and the Muses: The Culture of 'Mousikê' in the Classical Athenian City* (Oxford University Press).

Naerebout, F.G. (1997), *Attractive Performances* (J.C. Gieben).

Nedungatt, G. and Featherstone, M. (eds) (1995), *The Council in Trullo Revisited* (Pontificio Istituto Orientale, Roma).

Nicoll, A. (1931), *Masks, Mimes and Miracles: Studies in the Popular Theatre* (George Harrap).

Bibliography

Nilsson, M.P. (1957), *The Dionysiac Mysteries of the Hellenistic and Roman Age* (Gleerup).

Noverre, J.G. (1930), *Letters on Dancing and Ballets* (trans. by C.W. Beaumont from the rev. and enlarged edn: St Petersburg 1803) (Beaumont).

Oakley, S.P. (1997), *A Commentary on Livy, books vi-x,* vol. 1 (Clarendon Press).

O'Brien, J. (2004), *Harlequin Britain: Pantomime and Entertainment, 1690-1760* (Johns Hopkins University Press).

Orgel, S. (1996), *Impersonations: The Performance of Gender in Shakespeare's England* (Cambridge University Press).

Owen, S.G. (1924), *P. Ovidi Nasonis* Tristium: *Liber Secundus* (Clarendon Press).

Pasquato, O. (1976), *Gli Spettacoli in S. Giovanni Crisostomo* (Pontificium Institutum Orientalium Studiorum).

Pavis, P. (1980), *Dictionnaire du théâtre: termes et concepts de l'analyse théâtrale* (Éditions sociales).

Pease, A.S. (1926), 'Things without Honor', *CPh* 21: 27-42.

Pernot, L. (1993), *La rhétorique de l'éloge dans le monde gréco-romain* (2 vols) (Institut d'Études Augustiniennes).

—— (2000), *La rhetorique dans l'antiquité* (Librairie Générale Française).

Perpillou-Thomas, F. (1995), 'Artistes et athlètes dans les papyrus Grecs d'Égypte', *ZPE* 108: 225-51.

Pickard-Cambridge (1988), *The Dramatic Festivals of Athens.* 2nd edn, rev. John Gould and D.M. Lewis (Clarendon Press).

Porter, J.I. (1995), '*Hoi kritikoi*: A Reassessment', in J.G.J. Abbenes, S.R. Slings, I. Sluiter (eds), *Greek Literary Theory after Aristotle: A Collection of Papers in Honour of D. M. Schenkeveld* (Vrije University Press) 82-109.

Powell, E. (1969), *Freedom and Reality* (Batsford).

Prevots, N. (1998), *Dance for Export: Cultural Diplomacy and the Cold War* (Wesleyan University Press).

Price, S.R.F. (1984), *Rituals and Power: The Roman Imperial Cult in Asia Minor* (Cambridge University Press).

Prudhommeau, G. (1965), *La danse grecque antique,* vol. 1 (Éditions du Centre national de la recherche scientifique).

Puchner, W. (2002), 'Acting in the Byzantine Theatre: Evidence and Problems', in Easterling and Hall (eds), 304-24.

Ralles, G.A. and Potles, M. (1852), *Syntagma tôn Theiôn kai Hierôn Kanonôn,* vol. 2 (Chartophylax).

Ralph, R. (1985), *The Life and Works of John Weaver* (Dance Books).

Reardon, B.P. (1971), *Courants littéraires grecs des IIe et IIIe siècles après J.-C.* (Les Belles Lettres).

—— (ed.) (1989), *Collected Ancient Greek Novels* (University of California Press).

Reich, H. (1903), *Der Mimus* (Weidmann).

Reynolds, D. (2002), 'A Technique for Power: Reconfiguring Economies of Energy in Martha Graham's Early Work', *Dance Research* 20. 1: 3-32.

Richlin, A. (1997), 'Gender and Rhetoric: Producing Manhood in the Schools', in W.J. Dominik (ed.), *Roman Eloquence: Rhetoric in Society and Literature* (Routledge) 90-110.

Rimer, J.T. and Masakazu, Y. (1984), *On the Art of the Nô Drama: The Major Treatises of Zeami* (Princeton University Press).

Roach, J.R (1993), *The Player's Passion: Studies in the Science of Acting* (University of Michigan Press).

Robert, L. (1930), 'Pantomimen im griechischen Orient', *Hermes* 65: 106-22 (repr. in Robert 1969: 654-70).

—— (1936), 'Archaiologos', *RÉG* 49: 235-54 (repr. in Robert 1969: 671-90).

—— (1938), *Études épigraphiques et philologiques* (Champion).

Bibliography

—— (1969), *Opera Minora Selecta* 1 (Hakkert).

—— (1982), *Opera Minora Selecta* 6 (Hakkert)

—— (1987), *Documents d'Asie Mineure* (École Francaise d'Athenes).

—— (1989), *Opera Minora Selecta* 5 (Hakkert).

—— (1990), *Opera Minora Selecta* 7 (Hakkert).

Robertson, D.S. (1913), 'The Authenticity and Date of Lucian *De Saltatione*', in E.C. Quiggin (ed.), *Essays and Studies Presented to William Ridgeway* (Cambridge University Press) 180-5.

Rosen, R.M. and Sluiter, I. (eds) (2003), *Andreia: Studies in Manliness and Courage in Classical Antiquity* (Brill).

Rotolo, V. (1957), *Il Pantomimo: Studi e Testi* (Presso L'Accademia).

Roueché, C. (1993), *Performers and Partisans at Aphrodisias in the Roman and Late Roman Periods* (Society for the Promotion of Roman Studies).

Rudd, N. (1991), *Juvenal: The Satires* (Oxford University Press).

Russell, D.A. (1983), *Greek Declamation* (Cambridge University Press).

Sahin, S. (1975), 'Das Grabmal des Pantomimen Krispos in Herakleia Pontike', *ZPE* 18: 293-7.

Said, E.W. (1993), *Culture and Imperialism* (Chatto and Windus).

Said, S. (1993), 'Le "Je" de Lucien', in M-F. Baslez, P. Hoffmann and L. Pernot (eds), *L'invention de l'autobiographie d'Hésiode à Saint Augustine* (Presses de l'École Normale Supérieure) 253-70.

Sandy, G. (1997), *The Greek World of Apuleius: Apuleius and the Second Sophistic* (*Mnemosyne*, Suppl. 174; Brill).

Schechner, R. and Appel, W. (eds) (1990), *By Means of Performance: Intercultural Studies of Theatre and Ritual* (Cambridge University Press).

Schmitz, T. (1997), *Bildung und Macht. Zur sozialen und politischen Funktion der zweiten Sophistik in der griechischen Welt der Kaiserzeit* (Beck).

—— (1999), 'Performing History in the Second Sophistic', in M. Zimmermann (ed.), *Geschichts-schreibung und Politischer Wandel im 3. Jh. n. Chr.* (Franz Steiner) 71-92.

Seaford, R. (1994) *Reciprocity and Ritual: Homer and Tragedy in the Developing City-State* (Clarendon Press).

Sheets-Johnstone, M. (1979), *The Phenomenology of Dance* (Dance Books; 2nd edn).

—— (1984), 'Phenomenology as a Way of Illuminating Dance', in ead. (ed.), *Illuminating Dance: Philosophical Explorations* (Bucknell University Press) 124-45.

Siddons, H. (1822), *Practical Illustrations of Rhetorical Gesture and Action; Adapted to the English Drama from a Work on the Subject by M. Engel* (Sherwood, Neely and Jones).

Sittl, K. (1890), *Die Gebärden der Griechen und Römer* (Teubner).

Slater, W.J. (1990), 'Orchestopala', *ZPE* 84: 215-20.

—— (1993), 'Three Problems in the History of Drama', *Phoenix* 47: 189-212.

—— (1994), 'Pantomime Riots', *Classical Antiquity* 13: 120-44.

—— (1995), 'The Pantomime Tiberius Iulius Apolaustus', *GRBS* 36: 263-92.

—— (1996), 'Inschriften von Magnesia 192 Revisited', *GRBS* 37: 195-204.

Spawforth, A.J.(1989), 'Agonistic Festivals in Roman Greece', in A. Cameron and S. Walker (eds), *The Greek Renaissance in the Roman Empire. BICS*, Suppl. 55: 193-7.

—— and Walker, S. (1985), 'The World of the Panhellenion, 1: Athens and Eleusis', *JRS* 75: 78-104.

—— (1986), 'The World of the Panhellenion, II: Three Dorian Cities', *JRS* 76: 88-105.

Stallybrass, P. and White, A. (1986), *The Politics and Poetics of Transgression* (Methuen).

Stanton, G.R. (1973), 'Sophists and Philosophers: Problems of Classification', *AJP* 94: 350-64.

Stephanis, I.E. (1986), *Chorikiou Sophistou Gazês Synêgoria Mimôn* (introduction, text, translation, commentary) (Paratêrêtês).

—— (1988), *Dionysiakoi Technitai* (Crete University Press).

Straub, K. (1992), *Sexual Suspects: Eighteenth-Century Players and Sexual Ideology* (Princeton University Press).

Sutton, D.F. (1984), 'Cicero on Minor Dramatic Forms', *Symbolae Osloenses* 59: 29-36.

Swain, S. (1996), *Hellenism and Empire: Language, Classicism, and Power in the Greek World AD 50-250* (Clarendon Press).

Theocharidis, G. (1940), *Beiträge zur Geschichte des byzantinischen Profantheaters im IV. und V. Jahrhundert* (Triantaphyllou).

Too, Y.L. (2000), 'The Walking Library: The Performance of Cultural Memories', in Braund and Wilkins (eds), 111-123.

—— (ed.) (2001), *Education in Greek and Roman Antiquity* (Brill).

Trapp, M.B. (1997), *Maximus of Tyre: the Philosophical Orations* (translated with an introduction and notes) (Clarendon Press).

Valakas, K. (2002), 'The Use of the Body by Actors in Tragedy and Satyr-play', in Easterling and Hall (eds), 69-92.

Versini, L. (1996), *Diderot: Oeuvres*, vol. 4: *Ésthétique – Théâtre* (Robert Laffont).

Vesterinen, M. (2003), 'Reading Lucian's *Peri Orchêseôs* – Attitudes and Approaches to Pantomime', in L. Pietilä-Gastrén and M. Vesterinen (eds), *Grapta Poikila I: Papers and Monographs of the Finnish Institute at Athens* 8: 35-52.

—— (2005), 'Some Notes on the Greek Terminology for Pantomime Dancers and on Athenaeus 1, 20d-e', *Arctos* 39: 199-206.

van Nijf, O.M. (1997), *The Civic World of Professional Associations in the Roman East* (Gieben).

—— (1999), 'Athletics, Festivals and Greek Identity in the Roman East', *PCPS* 45: 176-200.

—— (2001), 'Local Heroes: Athletics, Festivals and Elite Self-fashioning in the Roman East', in Goldhill (ed.), 306-334.

—— (2003), 'Athletics, *Andreia* and the *Askêsis*-Culture in the Roman East', in Rosen and Sluiter (eds), 263-86.

—— (2004), 'Athletics and *Paideia*: Festivals and Physical Education in the World of the Second Sophistic', in Borg (ed.), 203-25.

Vigée-LeBrun, E. (1989), *The Memoirs of Elisabeth Vigée-Le Brun* (trans. from the French by S. Evans; first published 1869) (Camden Press).

Vince, S.W.E. (1957), 'Marie Sallé, 1707-56', *Theatre Notebook* 12.1: 7-14.

Vossius, I. (1673), *De Poematum Cantu et Viribus Rythmi* (Oxford; no publisher data).

Washabaugh, W. (1996), *Flamenco: Passion, Politics and Popular Culture* (Berg).

Webb, R. (1997), 'Salome's Sisters: The Rhetoric and Realities of Dance in Late Antiquity and Byzantium', in L. James (ed.), *Women, Men and Eunuchs: Gender in Byzantium* (Routledge) 119-48.

—— (2001), 'The *Progymnasmata* as Practice', in Too (ed.), 289-316.

—— (2002a), 'Female Entertainers in Late Antiquity', in Easterling and Hall (eds), 282-303.

—— (2002b), Review of I. Rutherford, *Canons of Style in the Antonine Age*, in *CPh* 97.2: 194-9.

Weinreich, O. (1948), *Epigrammstudien I: Epigram und Pantomimus, Sitzungsberichte der Heidelberger Akademie der Wissenschaften* (Philosophisch-Historische Klasse) (Carl Winter).

West, S. (1991), *The Image of the Actor: Verbal and Visual Representation in the Age of Garrick and Kemble* (Pinter Publishers).

Westermann, W.L. (1924), 'The Castanet Dancers of Arsinoe', *Journal of Egyptian Archaeology* 10: 134-44.

—— (1932), 'Entertainment in the Villages of Graeco-Roman Egypt', *Journal of Egyptian Archaeology* 18: 16-27.

Whitmarsh, T. (1998), 'Reading Power in Roman Greece: the *Paideia* of Dio Chrysostom', in Y.L. Too and D. Livingstone (eds) *Pedagogy and Power: Rhetorics of Classical Learning* (Cambridge University Press) 192-213.

—— (2001), *Greek Literature and the Roman Empire: The Politics of Imitation* (Oxford University Press).

—— (2004), *Ancient Greek Literature* (Polity Press).

—— (2005), *The Second Sophistic* (*Greece and Rome: New Surveys in the Classics*, no. 35) (Oxford University Press).

Wiles, D. (1997), *Tragedy in Athens: Performance Space and Theatrical Meaning* (Cambridge University Press).

Williams, R. (1977), *Marxism and Literature* (Oxford University Press).

Winter, M.H. (1974), *The Pre-Romantic Ballet* (Pitman Publishing).

Wiseman, T.P. (1985a), *Catullus and his World: A Reappraisal* (Cambridge University Press).

—— (1985b), 'Who Was Crassicius Pansa?', *TAPA* 115: 187-96.

—— (1988), 'Satyrs in Rome? The Background to Horace's *Ars Poetica*', *JRS* 78: 1-13.

—— (2000), 'Liber: Myth, Drama and Ideology in Republican Rome', in C. Bruun (ed.), *The Roman Middle Republic: Politics, Religion, and Historiography c. 400-133 BC* (Institutum Romanum Finlandiae) 265-99.

Wohl, V. (2004), 'Dirty Dancing: Xenophon's *Symposium*', in Murray and Wilson (eds), 337-63.

Woolf, G. (1994), 'Becoming Roman, Staying Greek: Culture, Identity and the Civilizing Process in the Roman East', *PCPS* 40: 116-43.

Wörrle, M. (1988), *Stadt und Fest im Kaiserzeitlichen Kleinasien: Studien zu einer agonistischen Stiftung aus Oenoanda* (Beck).

Wright, W. (1882), *The Chronicle of Joshua the Stylite*, Composed in Syriac, AD 507, with a translation into English and notes (Cambridge University Press).

Wüst, E. (1949), 'Pantomimus', in *RE*, vol. 18. 3: cols 833-69.

Yegül, F.K. (2000), 'Memory, Metaphor, and Meaning in the Cities of Asia Minor', in E. Fentress (ed.), *Romanization and the City: Creation, Transformations, and Failures* (*Journal of Roman Archaeology,* Suppl. Series, n. 38) 133-54.

Zarrilli, P. (1990), 'What Does it Mean to "Become the Character": Power, Presence, and Transcendence in Asian in-body Disciplines of Practice', in Schechner and Appel (eds), 131-48.

Zeitlin, F.I. (1996), *Playing the Other: Gender and Society in Classical Greek Literature* (Princeton University Press).

—— (1996a), 'The Body's Revenge: Dionysos and Tragic Action in Euripides' *Hekabe*', in Zeitlin, 172-216.

—— (1996b), 'Playing the Other: Theater, Theatricality, and the Feminine in Greek Drama', in Zeitlin, 341-74.

—— (2001), 'Visions and Revisions of Homer', in Goldhill (ed.), 195-266.

Index Locorum

This index is limited to passages directly relevant to either pantomime or Lucian. References to the pages and notes of this book are in bold type.

General Index

239